Subterranean
Cities

SUBTERRANEAN CITIES

The World beneath
Paris and London,
1800–1945

DAVID L. PIKE

CORNELL UNIVERSITY PRESS
ITHACA & LONDON

First published 2005 by Cornell University Press

First printing, Cornell Paperbacks, 2005

Printed in the United States of America

Library of Congress Cataloging-in-Publication Data

Pike, David L. (David Lawrence), 1963–
    Subterranean cities : the world beneath Paris and London, 1800–1945 /
David L. Pike.
        p. cm.
    Includes bibliographical references and index.
    ISBN-13: 978-0-8014-4277-3 (cloth : alk. paper)
    ISBN-10: 0-8014-4277-X (cloth : alk. paper)
    ISBN-13: 978-0-8014-7256-5 (pbk. : alk. paper)
    ISBN-10: 0-8014-7256-3 (pbk. : alk. paper)
        1. Underground areas—England—London—History. 2. Underground
areas—France—Paris—History. 3. Underground areas in literature. 4. City
and town life—England—London—History. 5. City and town life—
France—Paris—History. I. Title.
DA689.U5P54 2005
942.1′00944—dc22
                                                          2005012280

Cornell University Press strives to use environmentally responsible suppliers and materials to the fullest extent possible in the publishing of its books. Such materials include vegetable-based, low-VOC inks and acid-free papers that are recycled, totally chlorine-free, or partly composed of nonwood fibers. For further information, visit our website at www.cornellpress.cornell.edu.

Cloth printing   10 9 8 7 6 5 4 3 2 1
Paperback printing   10 9 8 7 6 5 4 3 2 1

Ché non è impresa da pigliare a gabbo
discriver fondo a tutto l'universo

(For it is not an enterprise to take in jest,
to describe the bottom of all the universe)

DANTE ALIGHIERI, *Inferno* 32.7–8

Contents

Illustrations

Preface and Acknowledgments

The official title of this book is *Subterranean Cities,* but in the real world it has always gone by the name of *A Tale of Two Cities.* It became a routine: each time I was newly arrived on a research visit, the taxi driver, baffled by the weight of the books in my bags, would ask me what I was doing there. Upon hearing that I was writing a book about London and Paris, the invariable response would be, "Oh, yes, *A Tale of Two Cities,*" the title in English no matter what country I was in. Such is the power of a received idea, a vaguely recalled reading from high school, a title floating up from the vestiges of old movie seen on TV. My hope is that the space of this book manages to bridge the images of its real and its shadow title, addressing at once the cold and abstract yet rigorous ideal and the familiar and evocative yet reductive commonplace.

Although the finished book is dedicated to the kitsch-like identification that allowed the project currency in the everyday life of the great cities as well as in the corridors of academe, it is equally dedicated to another threshold between them, one of the many spaces I did not have an opportunity to address in the main text: the unique space of the grand research library, and to its shared population of underground men and women—persons who look as if they could not possibly exist beyond the peculiar air of these reading rooms, corridors, bathrooms, cloakrooms, and cafeterias. But each library also possesses a distinct subterranean identity, although an identity that has been complicated by the existence, in London and in Paris, of a vanished, nostalgically remembered institution alongside the brand-new, high-tech, and high-risk creation haunted by it, a real space and its shadow. The old Bibliothèque nationale was always metaphorically subterranean, epitomized by its *enfer* of restricted books, reserved for the initiated; by its forbidding guardians; and by its location among the central *passages* (covered arcades) of the Right Bank. In the old Library of the British Museum, it was the demons who delivered the books and who possessed a thousand ways to inflict punishment on the sorry scholar who asked the wrong question, looked the wrong look, or was simply in the wrong place at the wrong time. Both of these old spaces were redolent with the shades of their past researchers and adepts, Karl Marx and Virginia Woolf, Walter Benjamin and Georges Bataille, among many others. The new national libraries, by contrast, are literally utopian undergrounds, bright and open, rational and regulated. Nevertheless, they can still remind us of the continuity of their identity with centuries past. In Paris the long, slowly descending moving walkways into the lower level of the Grande bib-liothèque are reserved once again only for initiates, and the space is ruled by a computer system that no one, least of all the hapless librarians, has yet been able to master, a system whose automated gates, once crossed, will hold you in the depths at their pleasure. The faulty ventilation of the otherwise idyllic new British Library—reminding me of those past summer days in what felt like the seventh circle of hell in the sweltering reading room of the old British Museum Library—belied the open-air feel, and soon drove the permanent inhabitants to the extreme of a strike. And, finally, I must not neglect the American cousins. The New York Public Library's uniquely open-armed admissions policy attracts an extraordinary cross-section of the city's population, so mixed as to constitute perhaps the premier threshold space of Manhattan. The Library of Congress, with its marvelous, air-conditioned labyrinth of underground passageways, is the only one of these libraries that has truly inspired me with the fear that I might never again emerge, joining the ranks of underground scholars, workers, and congressional clerks, forever wandering the tunnels beneath Capitol Hill under the deluded impression that this, too, is research for my book.

I would be remiss if, intent on the grand design, I were to neglect to express my gratitude to the smaller, less mythic spaces that contributed equally to my re-search; to the many individuals whose suggestions, ideas, and criticisms helped me along the way; and to those who provided the financial support I have re-ceived over the years of researching and writing. Published and unpublished texts and images were made readily available to me in New York by the Billy Rose Theater Collection. In Paris they were made available by the Bibliothèque du film, the Bibliothèque historique de la ville de Paris, the Bibliothèque de l'Arse-nal, the Bibliothèque nationale de France, the Inspection générale des carrières, and the Photothèque des musées de la ville de Paris. In London they were pro-vided by the Bancroft Library, the Bermondsey Local Studies Library, BFI Films' Stills, Pictures and Designs Library, the Guildhall Library, the Imperial War Mu-seum, the Institute for Historical Research, London's Transport Museum, the Mander and Mitchenson Theatre Collection, the Minet Library, the Museum of London, the Theatre Museum Picture Library, and the Westminster Archives Centre; and elsewhere in England by the Henry Moore Foundation, the Lee Miller Archive, and the Bodleian Library, University of Oxford. Whenever able, the Interlibrary Loan Office at American University's Bender Library made read-ily available to me a wealth of essential materials. And, finally, let me acknowl-edge the gloriously musty and (hopefully still) neglected stacks at Columbia Uni-versity's Butler Library, within the depths of which this book had its origins.

While it was from time to time annoying that everyone I met knew more about the underground than I did, I nevertheless managed, when I got over my annoyance, to stumble in this way upon all manner of invaluable sources. Al-though I cannot hope to name all of those who assisted me with their passing comments and hints, I do want especially to thank the following people whose help went much further, with the inevitable apology for whatever I may have done to distort their suggestions and advice: Michelle Allen, Antoinette Burton, William Cohen, Antoine Compagnon, David Damrosch, Rachel Falconer, Pamela Gilbert, Christina Glengary, David Green, Heidi Holder, Andreas Huyssen, Derek Keene, Michael Levenson, Jonathan Loesberg, Steven Marcus, Joseph McLaughlin, Angda Mittal, Carol Jones Neuman, Karen Newman, Deborah Nord, Stephanie O'Hara, Nicole Pohl, Fred Radford, Michael Riffaterre, Vanessa Schwartz, Myra Sklarew, Scott Manning Stevens, Michael Taussig, David Trotter, Graham Willcox. My students at Columbia and at American University contributed much to the planning and writing of this book, and I am grateful to them. For the space of a year, Mark Stein seemed as much a collaborator on chapter 3 as a research assistant. I want to thank Bernhard Kendler at Cornell University Press for his generous support of my work, manuscript editor Karen M. Laun and copyeditor John Raymond for their efficient and incisive editing, production designer Lou Robinson for untangling and illuminating the book's illustrations, the manuscript's anonymous reader, and everyone else at Cornell Press who helped along the way. Mary Allen de Acosta supported the writing of the book in many ways; I am especially grateful for her generosity in providing me with an ideal place for research in London, and another for writing in Suba. The book is dedicated to Ana, who inspired it and saw it through from start to finish, and to Philip, who came in at the end.

Many of my textual debts should be apparent in the notes, and I have tried to be as clear about theoretical influences as possible; however, due to my combination of broad scope and idiosyncratic focus, I have tended to pillage historical sources, phrases, and images from wherever I could find them. I have in general documented such pillaging; however, especially with older sources, I have not always done so if the reference or quote had nothing whatsoever to do with the source's argument or general subject. I do want to single out my particular debt to Rosalind Williams's extraordinary book, *Notes on the Underground,* which (as will be evident to anyone who has had the pleasure of reading it) I have argued with, rifled through, and revisited time and again since the earliest stages of the project.

I was able to begin the book thanks to a Mellon postdoctoral fellowship at the Society of Fellows in the Humanities at Columbia University. The shape of the work gained enormously from my participation in Michael Levenson's National Endowment for the Humanities Seminar in London, 1995; my thanks to all involved, especially Michael. Further research was made possible by generous grants from American University, the National Endowment for the Humanities, the American Council of Learned Societies, and the Folger Library. A Mellon Foundation Grant from the College of Arts and Sciences of American University helped defray the cost of illustrations. I have benefited from the presentation of work in progress at American University, Columbia University, the British Comparative Literature Association (1995), the American Comparative Literature Association (1997), the Mid-Atlantic British Studies Association (1998), the Modern Language Association (1996, 1999, 2002), the New Modernisms Conference at Pennsylvania State University (1999), the Centre for Metropolitan Studies at the University of London (2000), the Society for Utopian Studies (2001), the Folger Seminar on Early Modern Paris (2002), and the annual Monuments and Dust Conference. Portions of chapter 1 have been adapted from "Modernist Space and the Transformation of Underground London," in *Londons Imagined,* ed. Pamela Gilbert (State University of New York Press, 2002), of chapter 3 from "Sewage Treatments: Vertical Space and the Discourse of Waste in 19th-Century Paris and London," in *Filth,* ed. William Cohen and Ryan Thompson (University of Minnesota Press, 2004), and of chapter 4 from "Urban Nightmares and Future Visions," *Wide Angle* 20, no. 4 (October 1998).

Unless otherwise noted, all translations are my own, rendered as literally as possible within the bounds of English. All emphases are the original author's unless otherwise noted.

Subterranean
Cities

Contemporary Western culture seems obsessed by all things underground. The sewers and catacombs are among the most visited attractions in Paris. London's biggest draw is the disused railway arches that house the shopping arcades of the counterculture-themed Camden Town; close behind on the list are the Tower and the London Dungeon. Even at Disney World, hardcore fans consider a tour of the "Utilidors," the underground utility network serving the immense holiday complex above, to be the ne plus ultra of the Orlando experience. No action movie is complete without a sensational climax in a metropolitan subway, utility tunnel, or sewer, or a showdown in the arch-villain's subterranean stronghold. The image of the late twentieth and early twenty-first-century city is dominated by underworld beings: prostitutes and pimps, dealers and addicts, sexual deviants, mafiosos, terrorists, illegal aliens, slum dwellers. Homeless children live in sewers, men sleep in stacks of rented cages, wild animals roam the streets. Meanwhile, just around the corner, another underground locks its doors to these fears, creating sealed-off, climate-controlled downtown cities beneath the open streets. Other fortresses rule the suburbs: vast windowless malls inaccessible to public transport and carefully policed by private security teams.[1] The countryside is seamed with hidden missile depots, buried toxic waste dumps, secret command centers, and state-of-the-art fallout shelters for the powers-that-be when the surface becomes too dangerous. Desperate to escape from poverty and oppression, refugees attempt to ride a new underground railway of cargo containers, tanker holds, and drainage pipes into the promised land of the West. How did so many disparate phenomena and diverse experiences become so closely identified with the same space?

It all began with the nineteenth century. True enough, man-made spaces such as tunnels, sewers, catacombs, and mines were being excavated beneath the earth by convicts or slaves as far back as the twenty-sixth century B.C.E.[2] The Western city has long been associated with the underworld in moral terms as the center of iniquity and dissolution.[3] But it was only with the development of the nineteenth-century city, with its complex drainage systems, underground railways, utility tunnels, and storage vaults, that the urban landscape superseded the countryside of caverns and mines as the primary location of actual subterranean spaces. This convergence gave rise to a new way of experiencing and conceptualizing the city as a vertical space that is still with us today. The technologies of construction and heavy industry were at the center of urban life, as were the new experiences, fashions, and types of behavior that emerged from them. Bridges and tunnels were visited as tourist attractions and eulogized as heroic enterprises; millions flocked to world exhibitions and the new subways to admire the wondrous inventions of industrial technology, in much the same way that they are currently enthralled by the computer-generated wonders of visual technology (figures 1 and 2). The nineteenth-century capitals of technological novelty were London and Paris. As powerhouse of the industrial revolution and the most populous city in the West, London provided images of modernity as a literally subterranean phenomenon. Paris, by contrast, provided images of a more fantastic and ambivalent modernity: on the one hand, an otherworldly cornucopia of commodities; on the other, an infernal stronghold of revolution, the desire to appropriate that technology in unforeseen ways. Although usually presented in opposition to one another, these two images in fact constituted complementary expressions of a single, highly contradictory attitude toward the experience of the modern city.

The shift from Victorian industrialization to the full-fledged modernity of the twentieth century placed enormous pressure on traditional individual and social attitudes toward everyday life. While the nineteenth century was dominated by the representation of aboveground space as if it were subterranean, and the increasingly predominant experience of underground space in the everyday life of the lower classes, the twentieth century was characterized by the representation of subterranean space as aboveground, and the increasing predominance of underground space in the everyday life of the middle classes. The technological boom of the nineteenth century introduced a novel category of space that has continued to expand in scope while its challenge to the traditionally vertical con-

Intro 1. Celebrating heroic engineering: the opening procession through the Thames Tunnel in 1843, with arches separating the two passages. Illustration from "Thames Tunnel, opened 25 March 1843," *Illustrated London News* (25 March 1843): 227.

Intro 2. Underground spectacle: visitors view the aquarium on the Trocadero at the Exposition Universelle in Paris, 1867. Illustration from "The Paris Exhibition," *The Graphic* (June 1, 1878): 549.

ception has remained unremarked. The new underground is covered, windowless, or otherwise able to give the impression of being subterranean no matter where it may actually be located: the iron-and-glass arcade, the mausoleum, the factory, the prison cell, the interrogation room, the bunker, and the artificial environment of the office block, shopping mall, or climate-controlled apartment. *Subterranean Cities* documents the emergence of this new space out of the underground obsessions of the nineteenth-century metropolis. At the same time, it details the consequences of the continued recourse to those past obsessions to make sense of a contemporary experience of urban space that, in fact, has little in common with the cities in which they first appeared.

The first three chapters trace the effects on urban experience of the development of three types of subterranean space during the nineteenth century: the underground railway, the modern catacomb and necropolis, and the sewer. Each space attracted a specific form of underground reverie and fear. Chapter 1, "The New Life Underground," analyzes the emergence of a wholly modern conception of subterranean space: an underground that would be bright, clean, and dry, the polar opposite of traditional images of the world below. It begins with divergent responses to the first of such spaces, the underground railway in London and Paris, from early plans in the 1840s to the completion of both networks in the first decades of the twentieth century. It develops the key components of this inorganic underground as it appeared in various guides to subterranean Paris and London in the early twentieth century and documents a similar conception of the underground at work in a series of subterranean utopias written in the latter half of the nineteenth and the early twentieth century, from Edward Bulwer-Lytton and Gabriel Tarde to H. G. Wells and E. M. Forster, and in the architectural modernism of Le Corbusier and others, which imagined a city completely rationalized from top to bottom.

Chapter 2, "The Modern Necropolis," describes the flip-side of the rationalized underground through an examination of the nineteenth and early twentieth-century fascination with cities of the dead: the revived interest in the buried past through the invention of archaeology and paleontology, the incorporation of the design of the Roman catacombs and ancient Egyptian iconography into cemetery and urban design in Paris and London. The modernizing impulse to sanitize the ancient burial grounds of Paris and London went hand in hand with an archaizing fascination with the mythic resonances of subterranean space. Two key representations of the city are analyzed in terms of the necropolis: the coal mine (neotroglodytes in an underground cave city) and the subterranean pastoral (the simple life underground as escape from the modern city). "The Modern Necropolis" concludes with a look at instances of the positive fascination with an inhabited underground during the twentieth century, from Tolkien's hobbit-holes to London Tube shelters to Parisian *cataphiles,* contemporary explorers of the city's underground quarries.

Chapter 3, "Charon's Bark," examines the consequences of another sanitizing impulse: the construction and renovation of the sewage systems of Paris and London in response to the urban pathologies both physiological and psychological that haunted the modern city. Urban sanitation became the privileged discourse with which to address the perceived blights of deviance and perversion, but it did so by recourse to the most atavistic space of the modern city, home to its most extravagant legends and mythical beasts. Alien urban categories, such as prostitution, homosexuality, and crime, were likewise metaphorically assimilated to the space of the sewers, with a combination of fascination and repulsion that was mirrored by the growing popularity of the sewer tour and of the sewer tunnel as a setting in popular literature and theater. Descents to this alien underworld took both positive and negative forms, just as rationalizing narratives of sewer construction and touring were manifested differently in London and in Paris. The discourses of prostitution in London and in Paris were likewise complementary but superficially opposed, and they reworked old underworld tropes of fear and desire to polarize the city in terms of gendered spaces.

The conclusion of the book, "Urban Apocalypse," recounts the persistence of visions (some of them realized) of the destruction of London and Paris from the nineteenth century through the end of World War II. It relates this phenomenon to the overturning of the vertical imagination of the city. It then evaluates the applicability of this model for understanding a similar flurry of visions at the end of the twentieth century in some of the cities that took over from London and Paris as centers for the production of underground space after 1945, in particular New York, Tokyo, and Los Angeles. The dominant reactions toward urban decay and poverty continue to invoke the underground imagery of nineteenth-century Paris and London. The raw facts of exploitation may not have changed since then, but they are occurring under the radically different spatial conditions of the globalized urban experience of the contemporary world at large. I conclude with the paradox of the underground at the turn of the twenty-first century: a set of images that has lost none of its power to dominate the imagination of an urban landscape in which those same images have lost any relation to everyday life.

Before turning to this material, I want to introduce several basic concepts that I rely on to decipher the complex simplicity of the underground.

The Vertical City

The underground is a slippery term. On the one hand, it is as straightforward as can be: the opposite of whatever the viewer from the world above considers as belonging to his or her own space. On the other hand, it is rife with the contradictions that emerge from that gesture at definition.

We can begin with anthropologist Mary Douglas's formulation in terms of cultural taboos, "Uncleanness or dirt is that which must not be included if a pattern is to be maintained."[4] In practice, this has made the underground the physical and conceptual trash heap of the modern world above, the place to which everyone and everything posing a problem or no longer useful to it is relegated. It is coherent in that whatever is in it at some point must have posed a threat to social order, but incoherent insomuch as this definition at some time or other has included pretty much everything under the sun—and while garbage may decompose, we are acutely aware these days that it never actually disappears. For example, a primary set of associations persists from the medieval and early modern imagination of the underground in terms of the vertical cosmos of Christianity. Many conflicting images made their way into hell, but there is no doubt that the relationship was rigidly fixed and predominately metaphysical: good was above, evil below, and the earthly city existed in between, with a strongly downward inclination (figure 3). Infernal imagery was easily adaptable to an industrial revolution that saw wage laborers at work in mines and tunnels, or in factories that were underground in all but name: no light, no air—just dirt, grime, and the constant risk of injury or death. Such associations were far less welcomed by those promoting the new feats of engineering aimed at the middle- and upper-class citizens needed to fill the trains, shop in the exhibitions, arcades, and department stores, and blithely ignore the conditions that had produced the goods they were consuming.

Moreover, somewhere between the nightmare visions of hell and the antiseptic promises of a perfectly controlled new underground was a third set of ancient

Intro 3. The medieval legacy to the modern urban underground is the vertical cosmos. In this vision of the Last Judgment the blessed souls march to the heavenly city, and the damned are dragged down into Hell. Drawing by Michael Wolgemut, *Ultima etas mundi*, in Hartmann Schedel, *Liber Chronicarum*, 1493.

associations related to fundamental notions of peace and security. After all, the earliest use of underground space was as shelter from inclement weather, the dark night, and the threat of wild beasts and hostile outsiders. The underground has continued to function as a repository for these and other simple, but nevertheless utopian, desires not met by the strictly regulated society above it. As most of these desires run contrary to the self-denying and materialistic ideology of modern capitalism, they can take concrete form in the world above only as romantic clichés, dangerous urges, or daydreams so anodyne as barely to satisfy for an instant before leaving behind a thirst for more.

There are many different forms taken by the vertical segmentation of society; what concerns me at this point is the framework itself and its function. The world above—the world of law, order, economy, conformity—is given structure and order by what it excludes beneath it as unfit. Needless to say, this is a symbolic gesture, reinforced by myriad linguistic pairings and tropes: high and low, up and down, upper and lower, light and dark, north and south. Most importantly, it was reinforced during the nineteenth century by a realization that the city itself was beginning to reflect the timeworn metaphysics: the poor lived in dark, airless, and disease-ridden tenements and rookeries; the homeless slept rough under bridges, arches, and tunnels; desperate men (and a few women) scavenged the sewers for dropped coins and lost valuables. A whole system of representation emerged that fixed these images as the single unchanging face of the newly dubbed "lower" classes (figure 4). Very gradually, throughout the nineteenth century, the great cities were in fact becoming more and more segregated by class; however, according to images of those cities, that segregation was hard and fast from the beginning. This was the vertical city: a messy blend of half-truths and bygone myths that took over the representation of urban life.

Intro 4. The misery of Paris under siege in 1871 is emblematized by the forced habitation of underground space. The depiction draws on stock iconography of urban poverty. Engraving by E. B., *A Colony in a Cellar*, in "Paris under Bombardment," *The Graphic* (25 February 1871): 185.

For nineteenth-century writers of various political and class outlooks, the underground seemed to hold the key to unlocking the secrets of the modern world (figure 5). Imagery of the underground and its relation to the world above tended to fall into two distinct categories: that of segregation and elimination, and that of incorporation and recycling. The first was conventionally identified with London, the second with Paris. There are certain historical and material reasons for this—the more centralized political structure of Paris; the tidal nature of the Thames and the London port facilities; the earlier industrialization and greater population of London; the greater population density of Paris. Such identifications tended to polarize these qualities, finding in one city whatever was wanting in the other. As we follow these two discourses, it will become evident that neither can fully account for the space of either city, nor can the two models be fully understood separately from one another.[5] Unlike representations of the city in terms of the world above, those of the world below never appeared without manifestly displaying at least some of the underlying contradictions of modern society. No matter how clear-cut the divisions are made in theory, in the actual city the supposedly above and supposedly below are in constant contact. Although there were limit-cases—the mansions and clubs of the rich were more inaccessible than the cribs and hovels of the poor—both extremes were well-represented in fantasy. The promiscuous mixing attributed to Paris infected London, and the spatial segregation attributed to London infected Paris. In both cities, the poor crowded into railway stations, demonstrated in public places, and fomented revolution; in both, prostitutes plied the streets, walking alongside proper ladies.

The View from Above and the View from Below

In a city divided between aboveground and underground, there were two customary vantage points from which to describe its spaces. One could take a bird's-eye view—favored sites were the dome of St. Paul's in London and the towers of Notre-Dame de Paris—that encompassed the entire cityscape at the expense of individual detail.[6] The view from above was epitomized by the "Asmodeus flight," derived from an eighteenth-century Spanish novel where the titular devil on crutches flies above Madrid, unroofing the houses below. This mildly satirical conceit was enormously popular, imitated and adapted to cities everywhere; by the first decades of the nineteenth century, the "Asmodeus flight" had become a commonplace of urban literature in general (figure 6).[7] The view from above figures the modern city in the most general and abstract sense as hell, and in its various versions it runs the gamut from metaphysical speculation to biting moral satire to humorous verbal anecdote and visual tableaux.

Rather than the metonymic abstraction of the city as a whole through its rooftops characteristic of the view from above, the view from below was emblematized by the literal descent into the *bas-fonds*, the lower depths of the city. As a

Intro 5. The world is described in terms of its underground phenomena on the spine of this thousand-page compendium on life underground. From Thomas Wallace Knox, *Underground; or, Life below the Surface* (London: Sampson, Low & Co., 1873).

bona fide underworld journey, the view from below promises a face-to-face meeting with Satan himself, not just the unimposing Asmodeus leaning on his crutches. Like the moral overview, the material descent has premodern antecedents. The underground lore of Paris, for example, contains the story of a "charlatan," known only as César, said to have been strangled by the devil on the eleventh of March, 1615, in a cell in the Bastille, where he had been incarcerated

PROLOGUE

(La scène se passe dans l'autre monde.)

COMMENT IL SE FIT QU'UN DIABLE VINT A PARIS

ET COMMENT CE LIVRE S'ENSUIVIT.

Facilis descensus Averni.
« Il n'est que trop aisé de descendre aux enfers. »
— VIRGILE. —

I

De quoi ne se lasse-t-on pas? — Il arriva qu'un jour, las sans doute de siéger, une fourche en main, sur son trône d'ébène, Satan s'ennuya si fort, qu'il voulut à tout prix se désennuyer. La chose n'est since 1611 because of the "magic tours" he would give to view the devil in the *carrières,* the subterranean quarries in the southern suburbs of Paris near the aptly named rue d'Enfer.[8] Characteristic of the view from below, César's tours brought together the urban thrill seeker and the mythology of the otherworld in a convincingly material form. The view from below involves descent rather than ascent, it proffers knowledge and power at the cost of danger and ordeal, and, rather than reducing the variety of the world to a play of appearances, it deals in contrasts, for this realm below is always predicated upon its opposition to the world above. While the view from above maintains what it regards as underground at a safe distance far below, hierarchized and conceptualized, the view from below revels in the sensations of its proximity to chaos. Like César's tour, it is a trip into the devil's own realm, and it leaves no doubt that the primary allure of the underground in the modern city is the cluster of illicit activities that traditionally were or have been at one time or another associated with various departments of Satan's realm.

As the city changed, and the second industrial revolution in the later nineteenth century introduced an ever more complex and varied underground infrastructure, alongside the more mythic or metaphorically underground spaces of poverty and crime, the two emblems became less predictable and more confused. The actual spaces of sewers, tunnels, underground railways, arches and viaducts, storage vaults, subterranean parking, and covered passageways become intertwined, sometimes materially and often imaginatively. While not always explicitly diabolical, the frequency with which the language of supernatural power found its way into the view from above and the rhetoric of evil into the view from below is symptomatic of the stakes involved in mapping the modern city and separating its constituent spaces. What remains consistently diabolical, whatever the discourse of evil, is the note of excess that haunts the view from below just as a superhuman power continues to mark the view from above. As Salman Rushdie's narrator Rai put it in that great novel of late twentieth-century underworlds, *The Ground beneath Her Feet,* "Our libraries, our palaces of entertainment tell the truth. The tramp, the assassin, the rebel, the thief, the mutant, the outcast, the delinquent, the devil, the sinner, the traveller, the gangster, the runner, the mask: if we did not recognize in them our least-fulfilled needs, we

Facing page

Intro 6. In "How It Happened That a Devil Came to Paris," the prologue to *Le Diable à Paris* (1844), the bored monarch of the underworld sends his courtier Flammèche to report on what is happening in the center of the world. The drawing's vertical layout rehearses visually the view from above that the urban panorama will proceed to describe textually. Vignette by Bertall [Albert d'Arnoux], engraved by F. Leblanc. From *Le Diable à Paris*, ed. J. Hetzel (Paris: Hetzel, 1845–46), 1.

would not invent them over and over again, in every place, in every language, in every time."⁹ The impulses of the night are dangerous to the order of the world because there is no place for them in it. The most persuasive of the modernist theorists of the underground called this force the id, and spoke of the return of the repressed. But it became ever clearer during the second half of the twentieth century that this was a resolutely social and spatial phenomenon, rather than the individual one that Freud theorized; and the devil has continued to embody that excess, demonstrating a persistence long outliving his putative role in Christian theology.

The vertical framework thus serves two distinct functions: it allows those it places underground to give expression to their own unfulfilled desires, and it allows persons placed aboveground by its framework to make some manner of sense out of those desires. Yet it is important to keep in mind that the devil and his underground demesne are not privileged concepts residing outside of capitalism and modern culture; they are figures for the most available and identifiable of the unfulfilled desires that are seamed through every aspect of a society that, for the most part, has not succeeded in keeping its waste safely buried. The vertical conception of space implies that there is a region to which such desires and vices can be restricted, and in which they take a limited and predictable range of forms. Despite its often eerie correlation to actual conditions, this conception remains merely a representation.

The Dialectic of Antiquity and Novelty

The twin modes of representation personified by the devil constituted a potent force in giving form to the dizzying experience of modernity.¹⁰ The combination of mythic endurance with a liberally employed and constantly shifting corpus of underground imagery was uniquely suited for expressing the contradictions inherent to the ever more refined and ever more baldly exposed mechanisms of capitalist—which is to say modern—society. Capitalism invents, uses, and discards; in order to succeed, each new technology, each new invention must present itself as both familiar enough not to frighten and new enough not to be familiar. The underground presents the opposite combination: it is familiar enough to be recognized and unfamiliar enough to be frightening, or at least enticing. To produce, capital needs new lands to exploit and ever new labor with which to exploit it, ever new markets in which to expand and ever new products to be consumed by those markets. Expansion is not a uniform and continuous process; it takes time to find the most efficient form for each technology, and time to find the most attractive wrapper for each commodity. Nor is it an enduring process; the constant movement of capital outmodes technologies and products as quickly as it invents and packages new ones. The advancement of capitalism leaves behind a trail of obsolescence: overexploited land, superfluous labor, and outmoded commodities. These ruins of things, places, people, techniques, and ideas end up both figuratively and literally underground, in the garbage dumps and landfills of the world.

Now, it is not axiomatic that what is no longer useful for capital is no longer useful for anything else; the underground is equally the repository for possibilities of invention, innovation, and labor that were not exhausted in the production of surplus value. Because the underground has been frequently, although not exclusively, popular in origin and has been closely associated with traditional stereotypes, folklore, and the armature of popular culture, such possibilities are more often than not expressed in whatever bigoted forms have been repressed in the process of creating a respectable and cohesive discourse aboveground. As the historian Piero Camporesi has written about the "culture of the poor" in early modern Italy:

> The beautiful, harmonic, symmetric and geometric do not correspond to the popular vision of the deformed, unmeasured, hyperbolical (or miniaturized), monstrous, overflowing and formless. The image of the world, seen from below, appears uncertain, flawed, ambiguous, unbalanced and inhomogeneous, as in the visions of the drugged and possessed. The images can be overturned, the figures turned upside down, the relations of time and space altered, the edifice of the world itself becomes illusory and shady. The natural and divine order is broken up and altered: chaos takes priority over a rational design that presupposes a centre towards which the whole immense periphery converges in unity.[11]

It is important to recall that the underground is not the actual form of a popular *mentalité* but the spatial representation of its interaction with the dominant discourse that figures itself by contrast as existing above that *mentalité*. There are two ways in which this underground representation distorts experience: in the terms of the view from above, which portrays the margins of society as alien but virtuous (the worthy poor); and in terms of the view from below, which portrays the margins of society as alien but undesirable (the undeserving poor and the criminal classes). As Camporesi phrases the clash, in what I have termed the view from below, "the structural ambiguity of folk culture—with its two-dimensional view and its double-edged mental machinery—invaded, with its demonic animism, the spaces where 'superior' culture was attempting to devise different systems of knowledge."[12] Because only the negative extremes of the underground can be made directly visible to the world above, the contradictions they express manifest themselves instead as simple negation. Even at its most demonic and apocalyptic extremes of "two-dimensionality," however, the view from below expresses critical truths about modern life unavailable as such through any other mode of representation.

As Marx maintained, contradiction, not aporia or paradox, is the fundamental characteristic of capitalism, which tends simultaneously toward an ever greater homogenization and an ever greater fragmentation: any one quality, be it time, labor, space, or land must be rendered equivalent to any other in order to be exchanged; each quality, as commodity, must be distinguished from every other in order to be bought and sold. Contradictions appear most forcefully wherever capitalism is newly arrived and in whatever technology it has newly developed, or wherever it has freshly departed from and in whatever technology it has made obsolete. In the nineteenth century, contradictions appeared most readily in the city, and manifested themselves most frequently in some form of the demonic, whether in the general observation that the entire world under capitalism was rife with contradiction (that is, evil), or in the assertion that the urban underground was a vicious space of difference and resistance to the world above. The mildest form of contradiction manifests itself as novelty, and it is intrinsic to the dialectic of consumption; when that novelty is rejected as excessive, frightening, magical, or subversive, we can assume that the contradiction was too strong for the order of capitalism, and so it was handed over to the devil, "the principle of vague *Excitement* in which Satiety always seeks for relief."[13] The devil persisted in nineteenth-century Europe because it was perhaps the only figure powerful enough to contain the fears and express the hopes invoked by the rapidity and magnitude of social change there, in particular the astonishing transformations being wrought by industrial technology on the urban space and those who dwelt within it.

Lefebvre's Spatial Triad

For all its resemblance to conditions in the modernizing city, not even during the nineteenth century could the vertical framework account for the contradictions of actual experience without severe distortion. The architectural historian Siegfried Giedion's analysis of nineteenth-century technology added an important spatial component to the axiom of the *Communist Manifesto* that "within the old society, the elements of a new one have been created."[14] That component was given its most sustained treatment by the French sociologist Henri Lefebvre, who believed that the category of space provided a means to theorize everyday life as simultaneously abstract and material in the same way as Marx had analyzed the commodity. In his 1974 book, *The Production of Space,* Lefebvre wrote, "The social relations of production have a social existence to the extent that they have a spatial existence; they project themselves into a space, becoming inscribed there, and in the process producing the space itself."[15] For Lefebvre, this meant first of all that space, rather than an inert category in which people lived, things existed, and events took place, had always been an integral part of any social process. Most simply, as Edward Soja has summarized it, "There is no unspatialized social reality."[16]

Lefebvre identified three types of space produced through social existence: perceived, conceived, and lived. The earliest spatial practice, he argued, was identical to the "intelligence of the body," the gestures, traces, and marks by which the body in action distinguishes between right and left, high and low, central and peripheral, or by which a spider orientates itself in a web that is produced by and part of its body, while simultaneously marking its place in the space around it. Long before space was considered abstractly, "lived experience already possessed its internal rationality; this experience was *producing* long before *thought* space, and spatial thought, began *reproducing* the projection, explosion, image and orientation of the body."[17]

While perceived space is first and foremost a product of the individual body, representations of space arise out of the "order" imposed by social relations, including knowledge, signs, codes, and, especially, language.[18] This is a visible, ideal, and abstract space; it is represented in topographical terms primarily as aboveground space, in contradistinction to lived, or "representational spaces, embodying complex symbolisms, sometimes coded, sometimes not, linked to the clandestine or underground side of social life, as also to art."[19]

While conceived space is subordinated to the logic and ideology of the dominant social order, lived space need obey no rules of consistency or cohesiveness; rather, it is characterized by the confused traces of the ongoing conflict between childhood and society out of which it has been produced, "a conflict between an inevitable, if long and difficult maturation process and a failure to mature that leaves particular original resources and reserves untouched."[20] Rather than a coherent space of otherness or opposition, representational space and the underground qualities with which it has been associated for several centuries describe the embattled emergence of the "clandestine" as an uneasy compromise between dominant codes of representation and behavior and the exigencies and desires forbidden or distorted by them.

The originality of Lefebvre's spatial triad lies not so much in its individual components, the contours of which are indebted explicitly to Marx and implicitly to Freud, but in the way in which he showed them to be dialectically intertwined within a space itself produced by that dialectic. Once grasped as something that is produced rather than static, space becomes a rigorous category through which to incorporate into critical analysis those aspects of social life traditionally conceptualized only in such ghettoized, romanticized, and reductive Western categories of otherness as myth, folklore, popular culture, Oriental, primitive, childhood, feminine. Our current critical idioms allow us to analyze the dominant discourse of a field or culture and its conception of space; they allow us to analyze categories of otherness in terms of the same conceptions, or as primary evidence of individual experience. They do not allow us to analyze the interrelationship between these categories except in terms of a dominant discourse, or to grasp what we conceive as otherness in anything approaching its complex and contradictory combinations of individual experience and fragmentary past or alien representations of space.

For this reason, I have been less concerned here in reading my material directly through such key rubrics of contemporary critical discourse as race, ethnicity, class, gender, or queerness than in showing how the complex individual experiences invoked, but only partially encompassed, by those rubrics have participated in the dynamics of urban space. My hope is that this spatial analysis will open up different perspectives within the many other critical discourses with which its concerns intersect. The spatial triad does not give the direct access to the margins to which so much of contemporary theory and art aspires, but it does promise a dynamic space for those margins that does not immediately either contain or repress them all over again.

Underground Truth

Because it is a spatial metaphor as well as a material space of difference, the underground is used in both conceptual space and representational space to represent ways in which the everyday is inscribed in social space. "The film lover travels by Underground" promises a utopian London Transport poster of the 1930s (figure 7); "Métro boulot métro dodo" and its London counterpart "Tube work tube bed" run the postwar mantras of urban anomie. Whether selling a dreamworld spectacle or epitomizing a dreary existence, the trope of being hidden underground actually bestows conceptual visibility onto what would otherwise be obscured in the uniformity of the aboveground world. We represent the everyday as underground in order to be able to recognize it; what we recognize is a differently coded version of its relation to the world above. In the vertical framework that continues to dominate the conception of modern space, the key component is the threshold, which figures the moments that link aboveground and underground, where what is hidden emerges into visibility, where all three types of space are figured simultaneously; it is the closest we find in representation to an image of the spatial triad.

In the nineteenth century, the underground was the locus of modernity because it was the material sector most being developed at the time by capitalism. In the twentieth century, it remained the locus of modernity because of its traditional link to everyday life, the sector currently under development, and because, as opposed to the previous century, so much of contemporary everyday life was in fact being conducted in underground conditions. Through much of the twentieth century, rather than being closely tied to the spatial practices of a particular city such as London or Paris, the underground was deployed as an abstract conception of modernity and the modern city.

The proliferation of inorganic space—the subways, subterranean downtowns, and sealed-off interiors of the modern workplace—thus transformed the perceived space of the underground without thereby eliminating the traditional representational associations with the organic underground, rooted in ancient

Intro 7. The utopian promise of the 1930s underground: from the subway to the dream palace underworld. Advertising poster for London Transport by Charles Pears, *The Film Lover* [1930]. Reproduced by permission from London's Transport Museum.

spaces such as caves and burrows. There was simply no cognitive recognition that there was any overlap between these spaces, or any contradiction between, on the one hand, conducting a respectable everyday life underground, and, on the other, writing off whole sectors of the modern city as ghetto underworlds inhabited by neotroglodytes. One could joke about Dante and Virgil on the subway one minute and rant or lament about the infernos of degradation or poverty the next.

Each of the clichés does contain a kernel of insight about urban experience, but far too often that kernel has either been taken as the truth itself or has been discarded as being too hackneyed to be of any use. The underground is a spatial heuristic: it locates truths that cannot otherwise be said, truths unpalatable to the representations of space proper to the world above, but it cannot thereby grant them the depth or breadth of expression required of rational discourse. There are two reasons for this. First, the view from above allows for expression only in the broad platitudes of mainstream ideology, while the view from below allows for expression only in the raw brutality of material existence. Second, the truths that convention places belowground can only be fleshed out and realized by synthesis with the world above, where control, power, and constructive ability are held to exist. The vertical framework makes the existence of truth visible, but it cannot make it concrete; it can manifest crises but cannot link up actual cause and effect; it can posit mysteries but can resolve them only in underground commonplaces of plot, never in aboveground apportionment of responsibility.

The modern underground has undergone a remarkable variety of inflections of what is in fact a quite limited set of narrative and spatial choices, a set of choices governed by the definition of its threshold spaces and divided between variations on a view from above and a view from below. While this book surveys a diverse range of materials in order to assemble its argument, the primary distinction it draws is between those representations that reflect in a fairly straightforward way the dominant representation of space in the milieu from which they arose and those that, for a wide variety of reasons, provide a critique of the representation of space they employ. In the mode of its division, this approach resembles the traditional distinction between high art and popular culture; the essential difference is that unreflective representations of subterranean space appear in everything from architectural plans to playbills to canonical works of literature, just as cracks in those representations can be imaginatively mobilized in everything from penny dreadfuls to high modernism.

Still—and here I part company with the more thoroughgoing practitioners of cultural studies—there is no question that the most sophisticated confrontations with the complexities of urban space arise from literary and artistic sources, and from those theoretical writers most influenced by those sources, rather than from popular culture or the social sciences. Such works are a small minority, however, and their insights emerge from an engagement with rather than a separation from the competing discourses around them—nor are they by any means free of their own distortions and contradictions. Just as a comprehensive description of subterranean space will emerge only from an analysis of the full spectrum of its representations, so I have drawn on a range of media. Rather than taxonomizing my argument in terms of those media, however, I have preferred to let their similarities and differences play off one another through their juxtaposition in my argument. This does not mean I have been inattentive to the important differences between, for example, visual and linguistic modes of representation, journalistic and essayistic discourses of writing, or literary genres; rather, I have attended to differences insomuch as they helped to draw out the different ways in which their particular conventions and discursive strategies impact the spatial representation of the city.

An analysis of these spaces and modes of representation should neither lose sight of the strict limitations of the vertical model nor ignore the creative ways in which they have nevertheless been appropriated and the brief glimpses of alternate modes of experience that periodically have emerged from them. In the pages that follow, I keep one eye fixed on this pair of caveats, but with the other eye I remain concerned with a description of the vertical city itself, as it was manifested in the subway, the cemetery, and the sewer. For only through a proper appreciation of its range and function will the limitations and also the untapped potentialities of the underground city take comprehensible form.

I

THE NEW LIFE UNDERGROUND

"Ah! Paris," he offers in an encouraging tone, "what a beautiful city. See if it isn't beautiful."

"I don't give a shit," says Zazie, "what I wanted to do was ride the Métro."

RAYMOND QUENEAU, *Zazie dans le métro* (1959)

In 1899, a few years after he had immortalized the vertical city in his first novel, *The Time Machine*, H. G. Wells returned to speculative urbanism. This time, however, the simple division between troglodyte Morlocks and effete Eloi had given way to an architectural labyrinth that could change in the drop of a hat from a perfectly ordered future to a subterranean nightmare. The London of *When the Sleeper Wakes* is an intricate network of ramps and squares, walkways, stairways, high-rises, lower depths. The confusion of its architecture mirrors the confusion of its narrator, who never quite wakes from his sleep until the very end of the novel. It is a surprisingly undefined metropolis, nearly everything in it conceivable as a threshold of one sort or another rather than a fixed space. In one sequence, during the first of several revolts that rock the city, the narrator experiences a sensation that reads like a forecast of the disorientations of modernism, dark spaces from which the material world has not yet properly been eliminated: perhaps the eerie stillness of the trench before an explosion, or the nightmare image of a 1920s movie palace:

> In actual fact he had made such a leap in time as romantics have imagined again and again. And that fact realised, he had been prepared, his mind had, as it were, seated itself for a spectacle. And no spectacle, but a great vague danger, unsympathetic shadows and veils of darkness. Somewhere through the labyrinthine obscurity his death sought him. Would he, after all, be killed before he saw? It might be that even at the next shadowy corner his destruction ambushed. A great desire to see, a great longing to know, arose in him.[1]

The sense of "vague danger" that the modern city drives its inhabitants both to fear and to desire to see was materialized by the dark corners and mixed-used spaces that the new urbanism would in its turn attempt to replace.

The London of *The Sleeper Wakes* can be conceived either as a space without an underground or as a wholly utopian underground space. Wells's novel charts the gradual disintegration of the façade of perfection and order with which the Sleeper is first presented. The idealized city, bereft of all the features that traditionally have defined underground space, is revealed finally to include every one of them within its scope. Such an idealization was a common feature of the series of literary visions of underground utopia and of the rationalist guides to underground space that appeared around the turn of the nineteenth century; the return of the mythic and organic underground was not always so intentional. It is a commonplace that every utopia reveals itself equally as a dystopia; recast in terms of space, the commonplace takes on the new meaning that the devil will out: every underground space eventually reverts to its properly subterranean identity; the everyday will insinuate itself into every space, no matter how abstractly conceived. It is a dictum that should be increasingly kept in mind; for, if the nineteenth century had been characterized by a complex interaction between the archaic underground of natural excavation and otherworld myth and the technological underground of the modern city, the twentieth century saw a steady increase in the dominance of the abstract space of representation over the literal underground. This dominance was matched only by a steadily increasing nostalgia for the representational underground. "The New Life Underground" studies the emergence of the technological underground from the development of the underground railway in London and Paris through the utopian subterranean societies of late nineteenth-century literature and underground guides of the same period, and through the architectural fantasy of the split-level, divided-use metropolis to the underground city and shopping mall of late-twentieth century capitalism.

Beck's Map and Guimard's Thresholds

> Great was our joy, Ronald Hughes Wright's and mine,
> To travel by the Underground all day
> Between the rush hours, so that very soon
> There was no station, north to Finsbury Park,
> To Barking eastwards, Clapham Common south,
> No temporary platform in the west
> Among the Actons and the Ealings, where
> We had not once alighted. . . .
> We knew the different railways by their smells.
>
> JOHN BETJEMAN, *Summoned by Bells* (1960)

The most triumphant and enduring example of an abstract representation of underground space has been Harry Beck's map of the London Underground (figure 1.1). Beck's schematic diagram was recently singled out by historian Eric Hobsbawm—accurately, if somewhat polemically—as the single successful example of modern British art between the wars.[2] It certainly represents a perfect marriage of abstract design and practical utility. By simplifying the complex network of urban railway lines into a visually pleasing and easily legible map bearing little or no relation to either the experiential or the physical metropolis of London, Beck's ubiquitous map fulfilled all the requirements of the segmentation of space dreamed of by modernists between the wars. First, he suppressed almost completely the Victorian character of the technology of the original, shallow railway lines—the Metropolitan, District, and Circle. Moreover, he imposed a single vision of the Underground that dominates the system to this day. Unchanged in its basic design since first sketched out in 1931, the Tube map is arguably today the predominant summary image of London worldwide. Not only does the map govern perception of the Tube in the world above through its reproduction on everything from maps and postcards to umbrellas, mugs, T-shirts, and playing cards, and in the ways in which it has been copied, especially in its color scheme, on underground diagrams around the globe; it even governs the perception of the Tube for the rider underground, its pleasing symbolization assuaging the eye and the mind, the sole distraction from the fact that the system, true to its Victorian roots, is overcrowded, overburdened with trains, and underfunded.

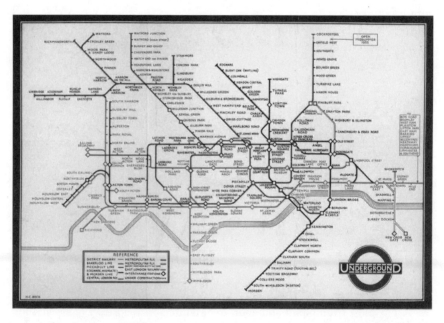

1.1. Modernist space: Beck's schematic map of the London Underground. Harry Beck, first topological Underground map, 1933. Reproduced by permission from London's Transport Museum.

The London Underground map represents within a tidy rectangle an urban sprawl extending some twenty miles from Charing Cross in every direction. In this, it is faithful to the character of the metropolis, for no one has ever known the boundaries of "London," unless they are the restricted legal spaces of the City or Westminster, or the broad expanse designated by the formation of the Greater London Council in 1965. As Ford Madox Ford asserted in 1905, at the height of London's growth: "One may easily sail round England, or circumnavigate the globe. But not the most enthusiastic geographer—one must of course qualify these generalisations with 'as a rule'—ever memorised a map of London. Certainly no one ever walks round it. For England is a small island, the world is infinitesimal amongst the planets. But London is illimitable."[3] The "Modern Spirit" that Ford saw London as epitomizing was uniquely encapsulated by the Tube map, which has indeed been memorized by many Londoners—train-spotters, commuters, and tourists alike. Even the Thames, the only major topographical landmark to survive Beck's abstraction, has been schematized, with 45- and 90-degree angles instead of its natural curves. Furthermore, just as it makes no distinction between center, suburb, and countryside beyond the sideways-lying-bottle shape delineating the Inner Circle, the Underground map makes no actual distinction between surface and underground railway. Many of the suburban tracks run aboveground; the entire system, however, is conceived as if existing in a subterranean space all its own.

While the Metropolitan and District lines were designed primarily to connect the large railroad termini with the center of the city, and eventually to link up with each other via the Circle line, the suburban extension had been a dream from early on. Edward Watkin, the Metropolitan Railway's chairman from 1872 to 1894, envisioned his railway as a main line, extending to Northampton and Birmingham, and, eventually, "from Lancashire and Yorkshire through London to the South Eastern Railway, and thence to Dover and by means of a Channel tunnel to the continent of Europe."[4] In this conception, the reach of the urban sprawl of London was theoretically boundless, but however broadly it would reach, the map would be able to include it. In 1938, Frank Pick's proposal that the Tube should set the limits of what could be considered London was accepted by the Royal Commission on the Geographical Distribution of the Industrial Population.[5] The twelve-to-fifteen-mile limit defined by Pick has been pushed somewhat, but the general rule has held.

Another effect of the Underground map was the social map of the city it engraved on its readers. While the diagram made no overt distinctions based on social class, it eliminated South London almost entirely, while the east and northeast took on equal weight only with the recent commercial development of the Docklands and the inclusion of suburban and light-rail lines such as the North London railway (although these are still shown in empty rather than colored-in lines, as if to signify their insubstantiality by comparison with the Tube). The result is that, on the newest maps, the east looks messy but undeniably present, while the south continues scarcely to exist, although the new Jubilee extension has opened up Bankside for redevelopment, a sure ticket for conceptual visibility (figure 1.2). The London of the Underground map continues to be dominated by the center and the middle-class suburbs, especially those to the northwest served by the Metropolitan. This is certainly not accidental—the Metropolitan was extended in close conjunction with the speculative development of the suburbs known and advertised as "Metro-land"—while the less wealthy south was left on its own. One reason for the failure to include South London within the Underground system, with the sole exception of the Northern line to Morden, was that railway competition between Watkin and J. S. Forbes, respective chairmen of the South Eastern and East Kent companies as well of the Metropolitan and District, had "quartered South London with such a network of lines that when these were electrified they kept the tubes out."[6] The south was left off the map both literally and figuratively, and whatever transport service it did receive was conceived as unrelated to the new identity of the metropolis. As late as the 1930s, guidebooks continued to place all of the railways together over a physical map of the county of London, the "Underground" barely distinguished from the others (figure 1.3). Designed between the wars, and dominant by the 1950s, Beck's map changed all

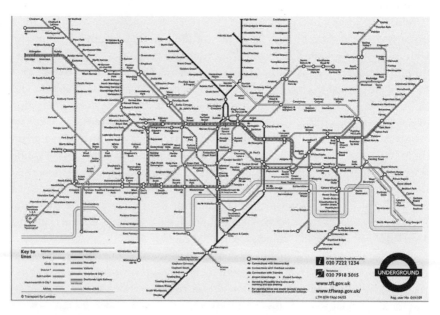

1.2. Beck's legacy: the representation of Underground London circa 2003. April 2003 diary map of the London Underground with colored lines adapted for black and white reproduction. Reproduced by permission from Transport for London.

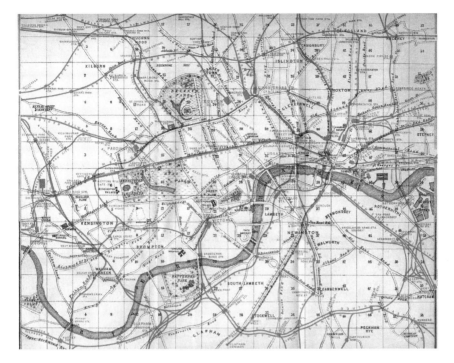

1.3. Transport representation before Beck: surface and underground, urban, suburban, and long distance superimposed on a standard map of the city. Railway plan of London and its suburbs, from Karl Baedeker, *London and Its Environs* (Leipzig: Karl Baedeker, 1905), n.p.

that. He reconceived the traditional division between West London and East London, and threw out the metaphorical verticalization of the city between above and below that had governed this division; his underground was more ordered, more systematic, more comprehensible, and more stable than the city above it.

By contrast, the Paris Métro map, like the Métro itself, has always occupied a more strictly subordinate relationship to Paris as a whole. Because the system was not built until the start of the twentieth century, it partook less of the technological dreams of the heroic age of engineering. The Paris Métro figures a more organic and traditional relationship between above and underground, epitomized by its physical design rather than its cartographic representation. The celebrated *édicules* (or entranceways) by Hector Guimard, which resulted in art nouveau being known as *le style métro,* highlighted the otherworldly character of the descent into the station; far from the utilitarian modernity aspired to by the Underground design of the same years, Guimard's *édicules* were willfully atavistic, alien enough to be criticized for their resemblance to the "'spines of ichthyosaurs' or the waving tentacles of 'creatures from the deep'"[7] (figure 1.4). The word itself was ambiguous, referring simultaneously to the neutral kiosk or roadside shelter, the sacred "little house" built over ancient Christian tombs, and the profane public conveniences that dotted the city of Paris. These meanings played on the thrill of the subterranean location of the railway rather than attempting to negate it.

Both in London and in Paris there had been skepticism about the technical feasibility and the social plausibility of normal people traveling underground. There were questions of ventilation and lighting, as well as doubts as to the desirability of what many saw as a step backward in progress. Only two years before the Metropolitan was opened in 1863, an article in the *Times* had summed up these questions in the negative language of the organic underground:

> A subterranean railway under London was awfully suggestive of dark noisome tunnels, buried many fathoms deep beyond the reach of light or life; passages inhabited by rats, soaked with sewer drippings, and poisoned by the escape of gas mains. It seemed an insult to common sense to suppose that people who could travel as cheaply to the city on the outside of a Paddington 'bus would ever prefer, as a merely quicker medium, to be driven amid palpable darkness through the foul subsoil of London.[8]

1.4. *Le style métro*: one of Hector Guimard's celebrated édicules (métro entrances) at place Victor Hugo. Photograph in Jules Hervieu, *Le Chemin de fer métropolitain de France*, 2 vols. (Paris: C. Béranger, 1903–8), 1:44, fig. 9.

Perhaps because the Parisian Métro was built almost exclusively just below the surface, whereas the London Underground was best known for the deep-level tube tunnels it was building in the 1890s and early 1900s, there was less eventual concern over the descent itself, something the Londoners had never really talked about, having become so accustomed to the cut-and-cover early lines that by the time of the Tube they did not mind the elevators. At the same time, the Paris Métro was celebrated primarily in its aboveground manifestations in Guimard's édicules and the elevated sections or *métro aérien* in the northeast and southwest, praised for their design and the vistas they provided (figure 1.5).

Rather than the abstract space of Beck's London modernism, the map of modern Paris resembles what Walter Benjamin's modernism saw as the mythic spaces of ancient Greece on which entrances to the underworld would be marked. "Our waking existence," he continued with 1930s Paris in mind, "likewise is a land which, at certain hidden points, leads down into the underworld—a land full of inconspicuous places from which dreams arise."[9] The paradigmatic map of Paris pictures the city above ground, schematized by the winding network of its streets, with the famous monuments clearly indicated, among them the entrances to the catacombs and the various métro stations (figure 1.6). The

1.5. Building the soon-to-be iconographic *métro aérien* on the "North Circular," now line no. 2, near La Chapelle station. Photograph in Jules Hervieu, *Le Chemin de fer métropolitain municipal de France* (Paris: C. Béranger, 1903–8), 1:222, fig. 70.

modern Métro map, although it now employs the color scheme and angular lines pioneered by Beck, is still inconceivable without superimposition onto the mental map of the city above (figure 1.7). Unlike London, Paris has a fixed geographical identity: the early nineteenth-century fortifications, the largest in a long sequence of concentric fortifications, or *enceintes,* have not ceased to represent the city (figure 1.8). Still, there does exist a Parisian predecessor of Beck's abstraction in the colored lines used by Napoleon III to prioritize the cuts he wanted the prefect of Paris, Baron Georges-Eugène Haussmann, to make through the city. In his memoirs, Haussmann recalled that "the Emperor was anxious to show me a map of Paris, on which one saw traced by himself, in blue, in red, in yellow and in green, according to their degree of urgency, the different new routes he proposed to have undertaken."[10] The difference is that Beck's map remains wholly unrelated to the actual growth of the Underground, while the conceived city of Paris is as centralized as the administrations that have governed it and developed it over the centuries. The emperor's map would be physically superimposed by his prefect onto the aboveground cityscape. It did not alter the basic identity of the city's *enceintes,* but it radically changed the relationships within and outside

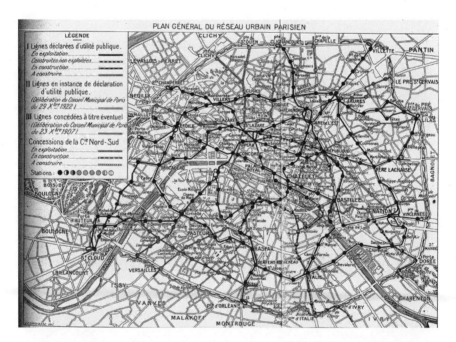

1.6. The Paris Métro as mapped in 1928, with some of the outer segments still to be constructed. The designer has outlined monuments and major buildings as well as streets and boulevards. Back cover of Louis Biette's *Les Chemins de fer urbains parisiens; historique— modalités de la concession, construction de l'infrastructure* (Paris: J-B. Baillière et fils, 1928).

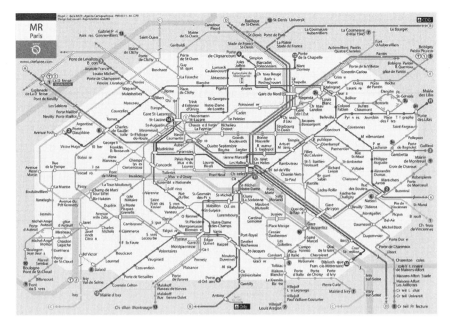

1.7. The Paris Métro as depicted today. Map of the Paris Métro, 2004. Reproduced by permission from RATP (Régie Autonome des Transports Parisiens).

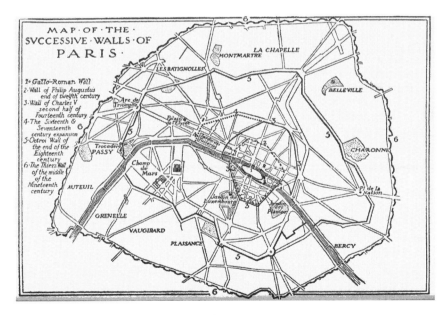

1.8. The outward-radiating fortifications of Paris from the Middle Ages through the nineteenth century. Map of the successive walls of Paris, from T. Okey, *Paris and Its Story* (London: J. M. Dent & Co., 1904).

of those bounds. Rather than alter this ideological map to keep up with the changes in the *banlieue* (suburbs) over the last century, until recently the Paris authorities simply put arrows around the borders of the oval in all directions, and added another map entirely, "Ile-de-France," to which most of the Métro lines have now been extended, and which is also served by the Reseau Express Régional (RER), a second and wholly distinct under- and aboveground suburban railway network. The Ile-de-France map retained the oval in the center and filled in the detail around it, leaving no doubt that the banlieue, where most of the city's poor and immigrant populations are housed in purpose-built *cités* (high-rise housing projects), constitutes a different space altogether, a periphery that revolves around and is subordinated to the eternal center. Current practice mimics London, mitigating the segregationist effect somewhat, reflecting perhaps a new self-consciousness and fretting about the center-periphery relationship: the métro map distinguishes the center with a white background; the RER map shrinks it to a white central ellipse, the inner-fare zone.

The centrality of the urban space of Paris is deeply rooted in its spatial practices. The very design of the nineteenth-century railway enclosed the city: the "chemin de fer de Ceinture," constructed by decrees of 1851 and 1861, encircled Paris, following the contours of the fortifications except in the east, where it curved somewhat further inward (figure 1.9). The *petite ceinture* (little ring), as it became known, was run through a deep cutting, covered over when passing under public thoroughfares, and incorporating two tunnels, a kilometer each in length. Long since discontinued, the petite ceinture has devolved into a natural underground, overgrown, and the haunt of homeless persons, graffiti artists, cataphiles, and other twentieth-century underworld dwellers and visitors. Its beltway conception survives, however, in the petite ceinture bus line, which circles the city on the outermost ring of boulevards, stopping at each of the traditional *portes* (gates) of Paris in turn.

Following Lewis Mumford, Benson Bobrick has argued that the railway was the primary "agent of transformation" that made it "possible for people to reconcile themselves to living in the Underworld."[11] This is correct insofar as the railroad, and especially underground urban transportation, constituted the first occasion that the majority of the population, and especially the middle class, spent any significant amount of time below the earth. It is inaccurate insofar as the underground railway both conceived of and created a new sort of subterranean space in which this transformation could occur. The form and identity of this new underground space were happened upon quite slowly; throughout the nineteenth century, representations of the underground railway envisioned it primarily as a threshold space, an underground masquerading as a world above. What Bobrick deems a reconciliation with living in the underworld would eventually become, in fact, the embrace of an emotionally invested space quite at odds with official representations of the new underground. Ford found the epitome of the

1.9. The inner curve of the *petite ceinture* as it enters the Belleville tunnel under the Buttes-Chaumont. Photograph by Emile Gérards, from his book *Paris Souterrain* (Paris: Garnier-Frères, 1908), 558.

irrational attachment of the Londoner to his or her city in affection for the Underground: "I have known a man, dying a long way from London, sigh queerly for a sight of the gush of smoke that, on a platform of the Underground, one may see, escaping in great woolly clots up a circular opening, by a grimy, rusty iron shield, into the dim upper light. He wanted to see it again as others have wished to see once more the Bay of Naples, the olive groves of Catania."[12] When the exiled jewel thief Pépé le Moko, eponymous hero of Julien Duvivier's highly successful 1936 film, wishes to pay a compliment to the elegant *parisienne* he is wooing in the casbah of Algiers, he tells her that she smells of the Métro. The underground railway was at first opposed because of fears of its subterranean nature; it was eventually embraced by virtue of the same. It is the "gush of smoke," the odors, its qualities as a lived space that caused the underground railway to stand in for the urban experience in the memory of the nostalgic exile. The sensory experience comprises the Métro's essence as a public space as well: Pépé

(Jean Gabin) and Gaby (Mireille Balin) seduce each other through an incantation of the names of métro stations, charting the different social spaces with which they identify—she lives in the west, he in the east—until their reveries meet at place Blanche, in the heart of Pigalle nightlife (figure 1.10). In the tradition of subterranean Paris, the Métro brings them together in a torrid, if tragic, fantasy: Gabin and Balin were the quintessential movie couple of the fatalistic 1930s genre of urban populist melodrama known as "poetic realism."[13]

Surprisingly, the Métro had seen only a few books devoted to it, primarily memoirs of its construction, until quite recently. By contrast, each line of the London Underground has had at least one volume devoted to it; monographs currently available range from technical manuals on the rolling stock to coffee table collections of Underground poster art; there are anthologies of Underground writing arranged by station, there are modern travelogues, novels, and even monthly periodicals such as *Underground News,* published by the London Underground Railway Society, which assembles clippings from the daily press, crime reports, and the minute details of London Transport activity; all of this has

1.10. Romance, Paris style: Pépé dreams of the Métro, Gaby smells of it—and their hearts meet under place Blanche. Frame enlargement from *Pépé le Moko,* directed by Julien Duvivier (Paris-Films Productions, 1936). BiFi: Bibliothèque du film.

now been supplemented by countless Web pages. Some date the Underground boom to the role of the Tube shelters during the Battle of Britain; I would push the date back at least as far as Beck's map of the '30s. One could easily push it further, all the way to the nineteenth-century fascination with railways and a civic pride in the British origin of so much of train technology and culture. Certainly, the nineteenth-century origin of the Underground is essential to the curious place it occupies in the space of London. Beck's map gave it the ideological form it needed to survive into the twenty-first century, but the initial attachment had developed long before. Very little that was built in either London or Paris during the twentieth century has yet taken on the symbolic role attached to nineteenth-century achievements such as the Underground, the monumental train stations, the Eiffel Tower, and the Paris boulevards. We are clearly at a time when the works of the nineteenth century have a special historical resonance; the underground is an integral feature of this resonance. The Tube, in the fortuitous combination of the interwar modernism of its representation and the Victorian condition of its infrastructure, epitomizes the current turn-of-the-century attitude toward the underground in general. Aboveground, its colors and lines exude utopian modernism; below, its cramped conditions and tiny tunnels recall not the utopian underground but the subterranean space it strives so strenuously to avoid—the same space that has made the disused stations a cultish tourist attraction and a popular setting for thrillers, music videos, and performance pieces.

Talk of the Tube

Hearthstone Ned opened his mouth like an underground railway, and yelled.

The Wild Boys of London (a serial novel of the mid-1860s)

When the first urban underground railway, inspired by the opening of Brunel's Thames Tunnel, was proposed by Charles Pearson for London in 1843 it was roundly ridiculed.[14] Among other possibilities, Pearson proposed "a majestic eight-track 'covered way'—which he imagined as a cheerful arcade—running the length of the Fleet Valley from King's Cross to Holborn-Cheapside."[15] Traffic congestion and insalubrious slums were to be eliminated in the same gesture of progress. Opposition mobilized mythic, social, and material versions of underground space. Doctor Cumming took the theological approach: "Why not build an overhead Railway? . . . It's better to wait for the Devil than to make roads down into Hell"[16] (figure 1.11). *Punch* dubbed the proposal "the Sewer Railway" and imagined the tunnels running past the cellars of respectable houses, delivering coal, much too close for comfort (figure 1.12).[17] As Henry Mayhew later put

1.11. An elevated competitor to Pearson's Underground proposal: a pneumatic railway all too cozily passing by curtained apartment windows, creating a sheltered arcade beneath for strolling. Illustration by G. E. Madeley, *Perspective View of the London Union Railway*, for proposal by James Clephan, ca. 1845. Reproduced by permission from the Guildhall Library. © Corporation of London.

it, "Learned engineers were not wanting to foretell how the projected tunnel must necessarily fall in from the mere weight of the traffic in the streets above, and how the adjacent houses would be not only shaken to their foundations by the vibrations of the engines, but the families residing in them would be one and all poisoned by the sumptuous exhalations from the fuel with which the boilers were heated."[18] The need for new urban transport was acknowledged, but the representational forms did not yet exist to make any significant portion of the public comfortable with it. As Sir Joseph Paxton, architect of the Crystal Palace, commented in his proposal for a ground-level alternative to the Underground, "People, I find, will never go much above the ground, and they will never go under ground; they always like to keep as much as possible in the ordinary course in which they have been going."[19]

The Thames Tunnel (opened in 1843) had proved that Paxton was partially wrong: the middle-class Londoner was quite willing to go underground in the capacity of a tourist in search of a novel sight. Early depictions of the Metropolitan Railway look very similar to those of the Thames Tunnel; borrowing the conventional iconography, they promised stations "open, or covered with a glass roof" or "commodious, airy, and well-lighted with gas," as in this illustration of the Baker Street station, which shortened the platforms to the length of a draw-

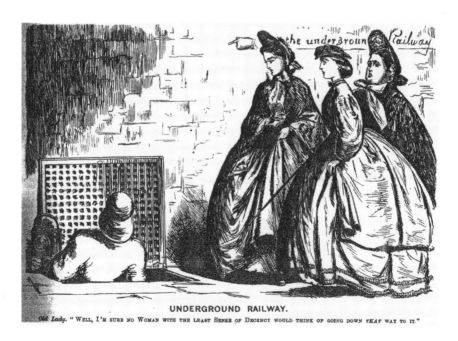

UNDERGROUND RAILWAY.

Old Lady. "Well, I'm sure no woman with the least Sense of Decency would think of going down that way to it."

1.12. The negative class and gender associations of the Underground in Victorian London, as satirized in *Punch*. "Underground Railway," *Punch* (28 May 1864): 227.

ing room, inhabited them with well-dressed men and women decorously arranged in scattered groups, showed a bright exit light at the end of the tunnel, and sketched in the locomotive on the scale of a model train (figures 1.13 and 1.14). As with the Thames Tunnel, however, the cutaway view also did stress the subterranean character of this space, although here it is only a short and civilized staircase that separates the station from the street above. The respectable Londoner, it was thought, would never venture underground unless persuaded that it was a safe, familiar space. Paxton was correct about everyday behavior; the middle-class Londoner still considered the underground in general as the province either of a separate population of persons habitually suited to it, whether workers or criminals, or as an infrastructure not suitable for any persons at all.

A comic "ballade" in *Punch* in 1885 testifies to the endurance of this representation of the new Underground. Treating a ride on the Metropolitan as a spelunking expedition, the "intrepid" balladeer betakes himself "Underground" with a lamp, "Some sal volatile, a fan, / A stick, of potted shrimps a can, / A brandy-flask, of weeds a pound," and a pistol.[20] Once below, the train gets stuck for several hours between stations, an ordeal ended only by the explosion of a Fenian bomb. Mistaken for an Irish nationalist anarchist, the traveler concludes his tale in court. In addition to the ballad's associations with natural subterranea and with the principal underground political movement of the time, a cartoon printed beside it suggested that for the staff of *Punch* at least, the Metropolitan had been assimilated as a space of urban nuisance (figure 1.15). Entitled "Metropolitan Improvements. No. 3," the cartoon by Harry Furniss depicted a quartet of peddlers, their barking mouths wide open, surrounding a customer. They are relegated to a low-ceilinged archway; a policeman is just visible on a stairway leading up in the background. According to the caption, this is, "A Cheapside Arcade for the Penny Hawkers. Let anyone wanting their Noise and Rubbish go Underground for it."[21] It is likely that these twin satires accurately portray the popular perception of the new underground railway: rather than the new space as it would eventually appear to be in the next century, it was seen as simply another threshold in the vertical space of the city, another repository for dirt, disorder, and, in the unstable political climate of the 1880s, danger.

What is truly striking about this revolutionary new space is the degree to which it was assimilated into daily life once it had been built. Although the nearly ten million persons carried during the first year of its opening in 1863 could be attributed to the same technological novelty that led so many visitors to Brunel's tunnel, the numbers (pace *Punch*) steadily increased, and the system was rapidly expanded. The early railways cloaked their novelty in classical garb, remaining firmly nineteenth century in their public presentation of industrial technology. The new locomotives were given mythological names: "Jupiter, Mars, Juno, Mercury, Apollo, Medusa, Orion, Pluto, Minerva, Cerberus, Latona, Cyclops, Daphne, Dido, Aurora, Achilles, Ixion, and Hercules."[22] The ne-

1.13. Domesticating subterranean space: the pioneering iconography of Thames Tunnel publicity. Engraving by W. Lacey, from an original color study by T. H. Jones (fl. 1836–55), *Thames Tunnel, Wapping Entrance.* Reproduced by permission from Southwark Local Studies Library.

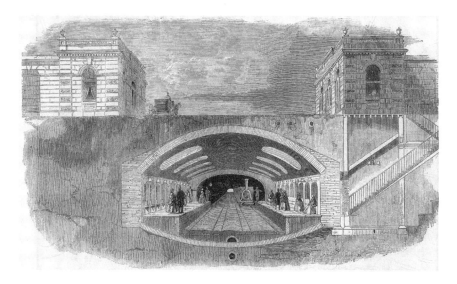

1.14. Packaging the new Metropolitan: the Baker Street railway station as underground drawing room. *Proposed Station at Baker Street*, in "The Metropolitan Railway," *Illustrated London News* supplement (7 April 1860): 337.

METROPOLITAN IMPROVEMENTS. No. 3.

A CHEAPSIDE ARCADE FOR THE PENNY HAWKERS. LET ANYONE WANTING THEIR NOISE AND RUBBISH GO UNDERGROUND FOR IT.

1.15. The late-century Metropolitan Railway: accepted and controlled, noisy and dirty. Harry Furniss. *Metropolitan Improvements. No. 3. Punch* (17 January 1885): 34.

cessity of using steam locomotion until electrification at the turn of the century made the experience smoky, noisy, suffocating, and malodorous. Control was not wholly taken over the environment until the 1920s and '30s, when filtered, ozonized air was injected into the system.[23] As the poet John Betjeman described it in retrospect, the Central line "was . . . regarded as a sort of health resort, because it was ventilated by the Ozonair system, which was meant to smell like the sea, and certainly did smell of something."[24] In the fifty years before that movement to a sanitized underground, the discomfort was tolerated belowground just as it was in the streets above.

The discomforts were readily admitted, but they made no difference to the trains' popularity; as we are informed about 1887 London by an aside in John Galsworthy's novel *The Man of Property,* "(. . . everyone today went Underground)."[25] An entry in American journalist R. D. Blumenfeld's *Diary* from 23 June 1887 stressed the atmospheric nightmare of the underground journey:

I had my first experience of Hades to-day, and if the real thing is to be like that I shall never again do anything wrong. I got into the Underground railway at Baker Street . . . I wanted to go to Moorgate Street in the City. . . . The compartment in which I sat was filled with passengers who were smoking pipes, as is the British habit, and as the smoke and sulphur from the engine filled the tunnel, all the windows have to be closed. The atmosphere was a mixture of sulphur, coal dust and foul fumes from the oil lamp above; so that by the time we reached Moorgate Street I was near dead of asphyxiation and heat. I should think these Underground railways must soon be discontinued, for they are a menace to health.[26]

While probably an accurate depiction of the physical state of the Underground, Blumenfeld's language equally adapted the new space to the familiar trope of the infernal industrial city. The same trope could also be applied humorously, as in the 1891 burlesque, *Orpheus and Eurydice,* in which the poet, now a suburban jingle-writer, makes the trip by Underground into "Little Hades," changing lines at "Baking Street."[27] The pun compressed the infernal comparison and the literal reality of Blumenfeld's account into the name of the station.

The view from above gave a different range of representations. For essayist Alice Meynell, writing during the same period, the exhalations of the railroad were simply one more aspect to incorporate into a picturesque image of nocturnal London:

London at night has begun, of late, so to multiply her lights that they make all her scenery. A search-light suddenly draws the eye up to the chimney-pots (sweetly touched, they too, on the westernmost of their squalid sides) and to the unbroken sky; and then at once the eye travels down its shaft, revealing clouded air; and here a puff of steam from some machine at work on the new underground railway takes colour on its curves.[28]

The American columnist and biographer Elizabeth Robins Pennell similarly concluded that "in picturesqueness, the underground makes rich atonement for vile atmosphere."[29] The stations aboveground did little for her, but she found the play of light below suitable for Rembrandt's vision. "The marvel is," she concluded, "that the artist has but just discovered the underground." Viewed by a practiced eye, subterranean discomfort could still be transformed into aesthetic vision; novelists in the main saw something else. For Galsworthy's omniscient narrator, the same experience resembled the detour through a derelict arcade. Soames Forsyte embarks at Sloane Square, with his fellow passengers, "bolting like rabbits to their burrows. . . . And these shadowy figures, wrapped each in his own little shroud of fog, took no notice of each other. In the great warren, each rabbit for himself, especially those clothed in the more expensive fur, who, afraid of carriages on foggy days, are driven underground."[30] In another well-worn trope, fog describes both exterior and psychological space; the underground may provide shelter from the one but not from the other.

Such perspectives from above incorporated the Underground into the meta-phorical framework of the otherworldly city, either enchanted or infernal; other voices employed the same trope to protest from below against the ramifications of the increasing exploitation of the space beneath the city. Mayhew commented that the Metropolitan had been so successful that Parliament was swamped with bills for new lines, "until it was found that nearly one-half of the City itself would have to be demolished if the majority of proposals were carried out."[31] A less sanguine critic complained of the new "Railway Mania" that "London is to be burrowed through and through like a rabbit-warren, and its main thorough-fares and rivers bridged over in every direction. . . . If London is to be cut up in such style, London will have to move elsewhere."[32] Unlike Galsworthy's inclusive use of the natural image of the rabbit warren, this critic saw the network of ani-mal tunnels as a nuisance threatening the stability of the human-occupied ground above. Modernization meant a stratified city; the backward-looking thinker could conceive of London only in horizontal fashion.

Describing the Underground as a contemporary source for the old urban mysteries of which modern London, like its Victorian predecessor, continued to be full, the journalist, playwright, and novelist George Sims imagined a vivid ex-ample of the novel experience of this new space:

> The series of diabolical crimes in the East End which appalled the world were com-mitted by a horrible maniac who led the ordinary life of a free citizen. He rode in tramcars and omnibusses. He travelled to Whitechapel by the underground railway, often late at night. Probably on several occasions he had but one fellow-passenger in the compartment with him, and that may have been a woman. Imagine what the feel-ings of those travellers would have been had they known that they were alone in the dark tunnels of the Underground with Jack the Ripper![33]

The modern devil rides the Underground, but he is now disguised as a com-muter, leading "the ordinary life of a free citizen." He is neither high, singled out by his carriage, nor low, distinguished by his disreputable appearance. If the Un-derground sanitized the underworld, colonizing it for the world above, it equally gave birth to a new underworld, all the more pernicious for being unrecognizable as such. No longer as clearly marked as the traditional urban underground—sewers, arches, rookeries, dens—the Tube was instead, like its newly adapted denizens, a potentially duplicitous space. In order to render it as a sinister space, Sims had recourse to a contemporary strategy, that quintessential trope of turn-of-the-century urban mysteries, the emptied city. The underground railway liter-alizes the image of the emptied city; the innocuous passenger beside one is cast in the image of one of the thrillers that were to dominate the screen during the teens and the twenties, like one of the Vampire gang out of Louis Feuillade's blockbuster serial movie of 1915–16, ready to strike at any moment out of the most harmless of appearances.

The underground railway is the only thing that is new in Sims's rather tired collection of tropes of urban mysteries; it provides a framework for his rational, documentary approach to the turn-of-the-century city, "the romance of reality." In a passage soon to be echoed by German sociologist Georg Simmel, Sims observed that "in the 'buses and the trams and the trains the silent passengers sit side by side, and no man troubles about his neighbour. But the mysteries of modern London are represented in the crowded vehicle and in the packed compartment."[34] Such encounters are threatening only by night; by day they provide the thrill of brushing directly against the scandalous headlines of the day's papers. Sims reports leaving the Old Bailey, getting into a third-class carriage at Farringdon Street, and recognizing the two women sitting nearby:

> No one took any notice of them. But what objects of interest they would have been to the other passengers had the identity of one of them been known!
>
> She was the affianced wife of a young man who had that day been condemned to death for the barbarous murder of the woman to whom he was already married. The girl who was sitting with her mother in the crowded compartment of the Metropolitan Railway had just parted with the man who had murdered another woman to make her his wife, and had that day been sent to the gallows.[35]

This could just as easily have been a crowded city square or omnibus in the Victorian city, but it is significant that Sims chose the Metropolitan as setting for both of his anecdotes. Until the inclusion of advertising and subway maps, there was nothing else to look at in the Underground except the other passengers. The first electric tube train, the Central & South London Railway, which opened in 1890, did not even include a pretence of windows; hence the coaches' nickname of "padded cells" (figure 1.16). The underground continued to be defined as what one could see, but instead of the hidden spaces of the metropolis, it was the hidden interiors of the apparently blank and empty faces around one that either frightened, intrigued, or went wholly unnoticed.

The fantasy of the empty city reflects the emptying out of both its literal and its metaphorical undergrounds, its sources of disease as well as of difference. The Underground replaced one type of underground space—the space of poverty, slums, crime—with another—a space increasingly sanitized and middle-class. As the novelist and travel writer W. J. Passingham put it in the 1930s, the underground railway destroyed "Dickens' London" and replaced it with the garden cities in the suburbs.[36] It was the most effective instrument of metropolitan improvement thus far. The likely demographic effects of the construction of the underground railway had been remarked from the beginning. The Rev. William Denton, vicar of St. Bartholomew's in Cripplegate, published a pamphlet during the construction of the first Underground entitled *Observations on the Displacement of the Poor by Metropolitan Railways and Other Public Improvements* (1861), where he argued that investors were particularly enamored of the project because

1.16. A Central & South London Railway "padded cell": nothing to watch but your fellow passengers (unless you are a child with a vivid imagination). "A 'padded cell' car built for the world's first deep level electric tube railway, the City & South London, opened in 1890." LTM 172 (1R). Reproduced by permission from London's Transport Museum.

"the line will pass only through inferior property, that is through a densely peopled district, and will destroy the abode of the powerless and the poor, whilst it will avoid the properties of those whose opposition is to be dreaded—the great employers of labour."[37] The Underground displaced the lower depths from representational space just as it did from the physical space they occupied in the city. Where they did remain in force, it was in ever more exposed positions, as in the multitude that crowded the benches of the newly completed Embankment Gardens each night.

Whereas the earlier mystery may have required a slight movement in space, Sims's version necessitated only the purchase of a third-class ticket. As there was less and less of any real distinction between one sort of space and another, the underground railway asserted its character as an aboveground space by equating itself with the main lines, separating its passengers into various classes. This was not enough, however, in that the Underground was urban and short-range, and hence theoretically open to all manner of people. Special third-class, "workers'" trains were run early in the morning and late at night.[38] Gustave Doré included an engraving of such a scene, sketched at Wapping station at the entrance to the converted Thames Tunnel, in *London: A Pilgrimage,* as part of his and William Blanchard Jerrold's thesis on the separation of London into two cities (figure 1.17). The workers appear hunched and anonymous, and while the lights and indication signs denote a normal space, the omnipresent round hats and uniform character connote a factory train or, more likely, a giant mining train. But physical separation was in fact more difficult than Doré portrayed it to be, as workers tended to accumulate in the station in anticipation of the late night return train, "in such large numbers and were such a constant source of annoyance by expectorating all over the station and smoking very much with short black pipes," as one contemporary complained, "that we felt we had far better let them go home."[39] It became progressively more difficult to maintain that there was anything but a superficial difference between Doré's automata-miners and Galsworthy's rabbits in their warren; only the price of the ticket and the wrapping of a "more expensive fur" allowed one space to be distinguished from the other. The numbingly inclusive postwar phrases of middle-class monotony, "Métro boulot métro dodo" and "Tube work tube bed," were already present many decades earlier in all but name.

The Tube railways, emerging into the turn-of-the-century city and wholly underground in specialized carriages, took a different representational strategy than the earlier Underground lines. As Eric Banton gushed in the article, "Underground Travelling London," in the prolific Sims's three-volume compendium, *Living London,* the "tube railways have revolutionized the Londoner's idea of rail-

1.17. *The Workmen's Train*: Doré's vision of subterranean drudgery. Illustration by Gustave Doré, in *London: A Pilgrimage*, by Doré and Blanchard Jerrold (London: Grant & Co., 1872), 116.

way travelling."[40] Banton put a positive spin on the leveling effect of the Tube. Rather than a negative experience for the "retiring man, looking for an empty carriage," as on a standard train, the roomy, forty or fifty-person carriages had taught him "to tolerate the presence of his fellow creatures."[41] The City magnate, rather than being upset by the single-class Tube trains, had learned to mingle with the hoi polloi, assuaged by "the cheapness of the fares"; the early nickname of the Central line—"Twopenny Tube"—registered approval of the uniform fare. Conversely, "the office boy, finding that these trains have no third-class carriages, has sat down in great content beside the City magnate, and still the heavens do not fall!"[42] Rather than stress their resemblance to nineteenth-century surface transport and customs, the Tube trains were presented here as something desirable—cheap, safe, efficient—and their underground nature stressed as utopian instead of threatening—the image of a future in which social distinctions would no longer exist. It was a mild and sanitized utopia, bereft of any threat of real change. The vision of toleration went no further than the ability of the different classes to sit beside one another without the heavens falling; by contrast, the old-fashioned underground had always been predicated on apocalypse, the fact that the fall of the heavens was either imminent or had already occurred.

The same space that regimented the daily routine—the City magnate, the office boy—did continue to offer the traditionally liberating space of the underground to those not subject to that routine. Just as Sims could find himself next to the lover of a condemned man or even Jack the Ripper himself, the same carriages that shuttled commuters endlessly back and forth could contain in their seats passengers on a different itinerary. The poet John Betjeman, for example, devoted his school holidays between 1916 and 1921 (ages ten to fifteen) to the goal of memorizing the entire system.[43] Rose Macaulay's novel, *Told by an Idiot* (1923), describes the possibility of endless amusement offered by the perpetual motion of the Circle line. While most passengers would probably view such a possibility as nothing short of infernal, for Imogen and Tony, Macaulay's pair of young teenagers, it constitutes a liberation of the imagination:

> They knew what they meant to do. They were going to have their money's worth, and far more than their money's worth, of underground travelling. Round and round and round and all for a penny fare. . . . This was a favourite occupation of theirs, a secret, morbid vice. They indulged it at least twice every holidays. The whole family had used to do it, but all but these two had outgrown it. . . . Sloane Square. Two penny fares. Down the stairs into the delicious, romantic, cool valley. The train thundered in. Inner Circle its style. A half empty compartment; there was small run on the underground this lovely August Sunday. . . .
>
> And so on, past King's Cross and Farringdon Street, towards the wild, romantic stations of the east: Liverpool Street, Aldgate, and so round the bend, sweeping west like the sun. Blackfriars, Temple, Charing Cross, Westminster, St James's Park, Victoria, SLOANE SQUARE. O joy! Sing for the circle completed, the new circle begun.

"Where great whales come sailing by,
Sail and sail with unshut eye,
Round the world for ever and aye.
ROUND THE WORLD FOR EVER AND AYE. . . ."

Round the merry world again. Put a girdle round the earth in forty minutes. Round and round and round. What a pennyworth! You can't buy much on an English Sunday, but if you can buy eternal travel, Sunday is justified.[44]

The shared experience transforms the underground railway into a microcosm of the world. The idiosyncrasy of the "secret, morbid vice," the slight thrill of illicitness, the necessity to change cars when the conductor begins eyeing them after they have exceeded the limit allowed by their ticket, remind us that the traditionally utopian underground space is always represented as contrary to the norms of the world above. Although the world above was extending itself rapidly into the world below in the 1920s, it remained susceptible to the imaginative practice of *détournement*.

One would expect the excursion on the Circle line to have been difficult to enjoy to this degree before the electrification of the Underground in 1905, but Macaulay sets this journey in 1901, and implies that in earlier years, when the Inner Circle was more novel (it was completed in 1884), the circuit had appealed to the entire family, and not just its youngest representatives. By 1901, the now mature Phyllis, for example, prefers the Central line: "It's cleaner. . . . It takes you where you want to get to; that's the object of a train."[45] Pennell fondly recalled the "fine glamour of adventure" of the Underground as a stranger to the city in 1884, contriving to spend several hours in a "skilful evasion of so simple a journey's commonplace."[46] The representation of women in fiction similarly suggests the heady combination of accessibility, adventure, and romance offered by the Underground to respectable London women, whatever Phyllis may have asserted about "the object of a train." In novels of society, the Underground figures as a slightly risqué—and consequently alluring—space for the woman with a reputation to uphold. In Anthony Trollope's words in *The Way We Live Now* (1874–75), "that afternoon Hetta trusted herself all alone to the mysteries of the Marylebone underground railway, and emerged with accuracy at King's Cross."[47] The Underground inaugurates a rare descent into subterranean space in Henry James's oeuvre in his short novel, *A London Life* (1889). The visiting American, Laura Wing, agrees to allow an English acquaintance to take her on a tour of London:

Mr. Wendover called for his *cicerone* and they agreed to go in a romantic, Bohemian manner (the young man was very docile and appreciative about this), walking the short distance to the Victoria Station and taking the mysterious underground railway. In the carriage she anticipated the inquiry that she figured to herself he presently would make and said, laughing, "No, no, this is very exceptional; if we were both English—and both what we are, otherwise—we wouldn't do this."[48]

The ironic tone should not distract the reader from the fact that the Underground journey in fact initiates Laura into a new perspective on life, including the discovery that her sister is conducting an illicit affair. It was a properly genteel way, in other words, to introduce another stratum of London life into the propriety of the society novel.

A similar scene in H. G. Wells's 1909 novel of a milieu at the lower end of the middle classes, *Tono-Bungay*, paints a most likely more realistic portrait of the more personal uses to which the space was put:

> One night I was privileged to meet her [Marion] and bring her home from an entertainment at the Birkbeck Institute. We came back on the underground railway and we travelled first-class—that being the highest class available. We were alone in the carriage, and for the first time I ventured to put my arm about her.
>
> "You mustn't," she said feebly.
>
> "I love you," I whispered suddenly with my heart beating wildly, drew her to me, drew all her beauty to me and kissed her cool and unresisting lips.
>
> "Love me?" she said, struggling away from me, "Don't!" and then, as the train ran into a station, "You must tell no one. . . . I don't know. . . . You shouldn't have done that. . . ."
>
> Then two other people got in with us and terminated my wooing for a time.[49]

The first-class Underground could be simultaneously a space of propriety and one of transgression, by turn private and public. There is, however, nothing particularly subterranean about the scene Wells gives here; it could as easily have occurred in a deserted street, a drawing room, or an empty restaurant. As did James's characters, this couple is struggling not with a threshold encounter with something alien, but with their own middle-class values.

Unlike the earlier spaces of subterranean London, the underground railway found a ready place in high and middle-brow literature from the outset, from Trollope and James to Ford, Galsworthy, Wells, and Shaw. In later years, it found its artist in Henry Moore with his Tube-shelter sketches and its poet in Betjeman. As perhaps the most celebrated public works project in a city notorious for its laissez-faire urban development, the Underground was an important symbolic representation for what was then the world's most populous metropolis. Moreover, as opposed to the sewers, it was completed long before the Parisian competition, the first proposals for which also date from 1843, but for which no agreement could be mustered until the last years of the century. The construction of the Underground within the rapidly changing space of the 1860s was partly responsible for the easy entry of the system into the symbolic vocabulary of London culture. Like the Thames Tunnel in London, and like the arcades in both London and Paris, the Underground mixed old and new architectural forms and technologies in such a way that the Metropolitan and District lines impressed themselves immediately into the experience of the inhabitants as simultaneously necessary and novel. By the end of the century the novelty had worn off, and, as the reactions of Macaulay's family suggest, it is quite possible that, if they had not been electrified in 1905, the two lines, along with the Inner Circle formed by them, would have disappeared when faced with the competition from the efficient new, electrified, and deep-tunneling tube-trains.[50]

The Plebeian Métro

As bordellos go
I prefer the métro
It's gayer
And it's also warmer
LOUIS ARAGON, "Modern" (1929)

The Paris Métro was built at just the right moment to incorporate the new technology from the ground up into a now-familiar design, learning from the examples not only of London but of urban rail transport in Berlin (the Ringbahn, 1871–77, and Stadtbahn, 1882), New York (the Elevated Railroad in 1872–74; the Subway in 1904; figure 1.18), Budapest (1896, the first underground on the Continent), and Vienna (the Metropolitan, 1898). Indeed, one motive for the Municipal Council's repeated blocking of the state's proposals was "the wait for a less polluting mode of locomotion . . . the wait for a technical solution."[51] The Métro was thus introduced as an integrated and state-run system into a new century where novelty played much less of an overt role in development than did rationalization and streamlining. Moreover, it was introduced to a city in which the problems of urban housing and segregation it addressed had already been enunciated fully; in London, by contrast, the public had grown accustomed to the Underground during decades of slowly accumulating dissatisfaction that finally came to a head in the urban crises of the 1880s and '90s. Within four years of opening, the Paris Métro was carrying ten million more passengers a year than the London Underground.[52]

In its gestation, however, the Métro stimulated many more anxieties than the London Underground, if running the same gamut of underground fears. M. Madrer de Montjau summarized his opposition to the underground before the Chamber of Deputies quite succinctly: "The Métro is antinational, antimunicipal, antipatriotic and a threat to the glory of Paris."[53] *Punch* had argued that the construction in London would undermine "the nation's monuments"; engineers in Paris warned the authorities that "driving through a tunnel may cause the collapse of houses 50 meters from its axis."[54] The architect Louis Heuzé worried about disturbing the spiritual and physical past of the city buried in the "deep

1.18. Subway construction at Union Square and Fourth Avenue in 1912. Photograph in Gilbert Haskell Gilbert, Lucius I. Wightman, and W. L. Saunders, *The Subways and Tunnels of New York* (New York: J. Wiley & sons, 1912), 20.

parts of the Parisian subsoil, receptacle of secular refuse, fetid heritage of past generations. . . . What mephitic exhalations may be released from this earth. . . . Shouldn't we worry that epidemics might break out in Paris following so much exposure of putrid ground?"[55] Critics in both cities had refused to believe that travelers would consent to be "buried beyond the reach of light or life; in passages inhabited by rats, soaked with sewer drippings, and poisoned by the escape of gas mains," to descend "by a slippery stairway, between walls which would always be damp and dirty, arriving on a wet platform between a wall and pillars you would have to avoid approaching too closely, being dripped on from the vaulted ceiling, unable to sit down on the benches which are damp in spite of the maintenance, boarding the sodden carriages."[56] The fear that the entire city would be transformed into an underground space of the most organic and atavistically conceived sort was eventually assuaged by creating a new form of subterranean space, divorced as much as possible from the powerful traditional connotations of underground Paris.

The battle over the Métro was of much longer duration and more fiercely contested than that over the Underground. Official visits were made to London in 1876 to view the Metropolitan, and in 1889 to study the progress of Tube construction. Both were deemed unsuitable for the geology and the way of life of the *ville-lumière.* The engineer Jules Garnier asserted in 1884 regarding the success of the Metropolitan that "indeed, what difference does it make to an inhabitant of London to be underground surrounded by vapor, smoke, and darkness; he is in the same condition aboveground. But take the Parisian who loves the day, the sun, gaiety and color around him, and propose that he alter his route to seek, in darkness, a means of transport which will be a foretaste of the tomb, and he will refuse, preferring the *impériale* [upper deck] of an omnibus."[57] Heuzé echoed the image of underground London, arguing that Parisians would never put up with "descending by long staircases into veritable catacombs," and coining the word "Nécropolitain" to describe the proposed Métro.

Heuzé and Garnier were at least partly motivated in their opposition by the fact that each had submitted a proposal for an elevated railway: Heuzé's, a glorified system of *passages,* or covered arcades, sheltered by the seven-meter-high tracks, Garnier's an elevated trestle running down the center of the Seine, with stations doubling as bridges.[58] Other proposals included Paul Haag's elevated railway, cut like Heuzé's through the Right Bank and including, among other fantasies, an open-air café under the viaduct (figure 1.19); Charles Tellier's "Le Véritable Métropolitain" (1891), also running down the middle of the Seine[59]; Edouard Mazet's plan to run a squadron of gondola-like carriages from streetlight to streetlight;[60] and Jean Chrétien's proposal for an electrified elevated railway run on a single viaduct down the middle of the main inner boulevards.[61] The projects shared two primary characteristics: the desire to integrate the transport system into the aboveground, illuminated space of Paris, and a nineteenth-century representation of space based on the *passage,* the viaduct, and what Le Corbusier would later dub the "corridor-street." Even Heuzé's scheme, which cut the *passage*-viaducts through the existing street plan, envisioned a space that would be incorporated into the cityscape, "destined to make up for the boulevards that we still lack."[62]

The various elevated plans were eventually rejected, primarily because of the prohibitive cost of obtaining the necessary rights of way in central Paris. Instead, during the same years that the Northern, Central, and Piccadilly lines were being bored deep beneath London, Paris began work on a cut-and-cover network similar in design to the older Metropolitan, District, and Circle lines in London, work that would continue over the next thirty years. The municipal council had nearly granted a concession to Jean-Baptiste Berlier for a tube-train run from the Bois de Boulogne to the Bois de Vincennes, but it was revoked at the last moment. As Louis Biette, chief engineer of bridges and roads, rather snidely commented, echoing the earlier images of underground London, such difficult construction in separate tunnels was logical for digging under rivers but not par-

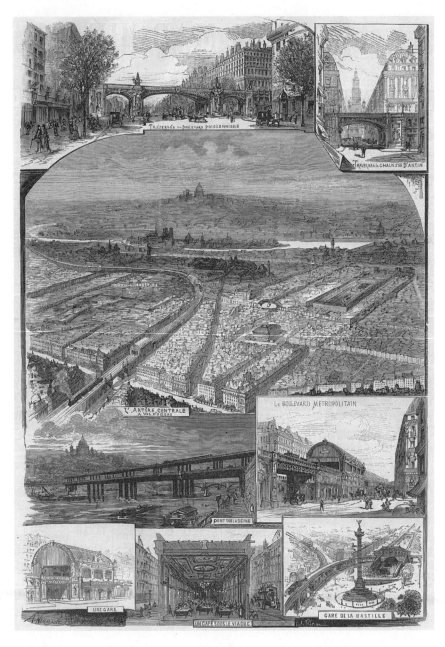

1.19. Paul Haag's proposal for an elevated Métropolitain cut through the Right Bank of Paris. Illustration by Paul Haag in *L'Illustration* 87, no. 2249 (3 April 1886): 225.

ticularly justifiable for the rest of the system.[63] The English, in other words, were going to great expense and trouble when they could simply have continued using the techniques they had used for the Metropolitan, the ones the Parisians had wisely adopted for their entire system. Shield tunneling was used only to drive the no. 4 line under the Seine at the île de la Cité, the deepest part of the network. While perhaps not geologically necessary, tube-tunneling did avoid the problem of right-of-way as well as of surface disruption, and, significantly, permitted the London lines for the most part to ignore the path of the streets above, creating for the first time an underground urban network with no morphological relation to the space above it. As a piece in 1901 put it, "To the engineer of the tube railway, as to the passengers who travel through it, the buildings overhead are a matter of supreme indifference."[64]

The Métro did almost wholly follow the existing lines of the city streets. Although there was less literal displacement of housing stock than there had been in the construction of the Metropolitan in London, Paris still underwent the same physical inconvenience and psychic trauma of streets being torn open all over the heart of the city (figure 1.20). The degree to which this trauma was felt is evidenced by Jules Romains' choice to open his mammoth roman-fleuve, *Les Hommes de bonne volonté,* with a description of the construction site of the no. 4 line in 1908, a portrait of chaos and disaster:

> The scaffoldings of the subway, which rose up all over the place like fortresses of clay and planks, armed with batteries of cranes, had ended up strangling the streets, blocking all the intersections. Not to speak of the fact that this driving of tunnels was undermining the ground in all directions and threatening Paris with collapse. (That very October 3rd, part of the parade-ground of the Cité barracks had fallen into the Châtelet–Porte d'Orléans subway under construction, and a mounted policeman's horse had suddenly been swallowed up by the abyss.)[65]

Particular monuments were cause for special concern; Léon Bailby described the "Opéra hole" as "an enormous pit, a mouth which is going to stay wide open, quite ready on gala days or during strikes or popular fairs to devour the crowds which have the misfortune of approaching its orifices."[66] Marcel Allain and Pierre Souvestre took advantage of the ongoing construction around the Opéra to make it the escape route (with disastrous effect) from a robbery of the vaults of the Banque de France in the third volume of their best-selling crime series *Fantômas,* first serialized in April 1911.[67] Unlike the flooding of the Metropolitan Railway works in London by the sewage-laden river Fleet, however, the accidents that befell the Métro construction were easily assimilated within the long tradition of Paris cave-ins, which had previously been caused by badly reinforced quarry tunnels, most memorably only two decades earlier, in 1880, when a seventeen-meter section of the Boulevard Saint-Michel had suddenly fallen into the *carrières* beneath it.[68]

1.20. The heart of the city opened up: work on line no. 1 of the Métro, Champs-Elysées station. Photograph in Jules Hervieu, *Le Chemin de fer métropolitain municipal de France*, 2 vols. (Paris: C. Béranger, 1903–8) 1:138, fig. 49.

The Métro was quite successful in preserving an easily assimilated relationship with the world above. Indeed, this can be regarded as its primary concession to tradition. As the underinspector of Paris Works, Emile Gérards, observed, even the design of the tunnels preserved the height of eight meters shared by "nearly all the subterranean works in Paris: sewers, pipes for electricity and compressed air, etc."[69] Unlike the gala opening of the Metropolitan in London, the inauguration of the first line of the Métro on 19 July 1900 was little remarked. The primary attention was given to Guimard's édicules and the otherworldly connection they gently announced. Boosted no doubt by the presence of the Exposition Universelle, over seventeen million persons used the new line by the end of the year. But the early fame of the Métro derived mostly from accidents, especially the tragedy of 10 August 1903 that left eighty-four persons dead from smoke inhalation, all but three of them commuters from the working-class northeast quarter of the city. The explosion of a disabled train near the station of Ménilmontant had sent a heated cloud of smoke and poisonous gas back through the tunnel where it reached the following train at the Couronnes station. Before the passengers could be evacuated, the power was cut, leaving them in pitch darkness. Only those passengers familiar with the station knew that the exit stairs were located at the southern end of the platform, the same end from which the smoke was issuing; the majority died in a massive pile trying to escape in the other direction (figure 1.21). Not surprisingly, the otherworldly aesthetic of the entrances was immediately translated into angry visions of hell, particularly in a special issue of the satirical illustrated newspaper, *L'Assiette au beurre,* guest-edited by the celebrated illustrator, Théophile Steinlen. Dimitrios Galanis reworked Guimard's lampposts as the portals of a mausoleum inscribed with Heuzé's old taunt, "Nécropolitain" (figure 1.22), while Steinlen's drawing "Le Métro-Nécro" depicted Death installed behind a counter, issuing tickets to hell (figure 1.23).

1.21. "The Métropolitain Catastrophe, August 10. Finding the bodies at 'Couronnes' station. In the background, the wall against which the victims piled up searching for an exit." Caption to the cover of *L'Illustration* 122, no. 3155 (15 August 1903).

1.22. Nécropolitain: the *édicule* identifies the otherworld as necropolis. The caption: "*L'Assiette au beurre*'s design for future Métro stations." Illustration by Dimitrios Galanis for "Le Métro-Nécro," special issue of *L'Assiette au beurre* 125 (22 August 1903): 2114.

1.23. Le Métro-Nécro: Death as a ticket agent. Front cover illustration by Théophile Steinlen, for *L'Assiette au beurre* 125 (22 August 1903).

The fear of fire continued to loom large in the iconography of the Métro, although since the Metropolitan Railway Company (Compagnie du chemin de fer métropolitain) soon replaced the wooden carriages with steel, the main practical complaint was of overcrowding. A drawing by Guillaume from around 1905 showed the figures of Dante and Virgil beside a mad crush at the doors of a carriage. Dante waves his hand in disgust, as if to say that they will wait until the next train to continue their journey. The glowing illumination of the top of the carriage reinforces the Dantesque recollection of infernal flames. A second métro issue of *L'Assiette au beurre* (4 March 1911), devoted this time to overcrowding, took a more mundane approach to fire in its theme of the passengers as green peas. Most of the illustrations, by Jules Grandjouan, were devoted in one way or another to the theme of food; two directly invoked accidents. In the first, a conductor is running along a platform in front of a carriage in flames, cursing, "Darn, I've lost the key for opening the tin" (figure 1.24). The last word is given by the

1.24. The caption: "The Employee—Darn, I've lost the key for opening the tin." Illustration by Jules Grandjouan, in "Les petits pois au métro," *L'Assiette au beurre* 518 (4 March 1911): 791.

1.25. In *After an Accident,* the firemen comment that the passengers were "cooked in their own juice, the sweet peas . . . and braised." Back cover illustration by Jules Grandjouan, in "Les petits pois au métro," *L'Assiette au beurre* 518 (4 March 1911).

back cover illustration, "After an Accident," which pictures two enormous helmeted heads of firemen peering like gods (or chefs) through a jagged hole in the roof of a train carriage extended in perspective far into the distance (figure 1.25). The first one remarks, "Cooked in their own juice, the sweet peas." "And braised," the second adds, punning on the verb *étouffer,* which can also mean "to suffocate." For *L'Assiette au beurre,* the new steel carriages only provided a more tightly sealed pot for the peas. The overall thrust of the satire was that if the passengers continued to allow themselves to be treated like vegetables, then the Metropolitan Railway Company would continue, quite literally, to treat them that way.

The reporting of the *L'Assiette au beurre* emphasized the populist thrust of the representational Métro, portraying the official inauguration of one of the lines as an affair of "Grosses légumes," showing the Shareholders in another cartoon transforming green peas into "cent mille balles"—that is, one hundred thousand francs—and caricaturing the employees as being so reduced in weight by company policies as to float away into the air. Even with the separation of carriages by class, this populist perception seems to have persisted. The biweekly women's magazine *femina,* which was devoted to fashionable living, dedicated a two-page layout to "La Parisienne et le métropolitain" and "La Parisienne en électrique," with the underlying message that the Métro was quick, inexpensive, and "à la mode," but not particularly genteel. The message was understated; one photo noted that the smile of the Parisienne opens every barrier, even if then she might have to run to catch the departing train (figure 1.26). An overheard conversation demonstrated that "the Métro reduces distances" by recording a conversation between a "pretty society woman muffled up in her furs" and a "worthy woman in a bonnet": asked if she lives far away, the *mondaine* answers no, she lives on the avenue de Villiers (in the chic northwest of Paris behind the parc Monceau); the *brave femme* returns that she lives only "a few minutes away," in the avenue Gambetta (all the way at the other end of line no. 3 in working-class Ménilmontant). The punch line combines a poke at the naïveté of the brave femme with a further hint at the inherent leveling effect of the Métro: "Didn't I tell you that the Métro reduces distances?"[70] The companion article made the undesirability of such an effect quite clear. The Métro was "a foreign import" (recall the London examples of the same trope), while the electric automobile was quintessentially Parisian, "a traveling boudoir"; banned from the Métro, Tricksie the lap dog rides quite contentedly in the *électrique;* the chauffeur shares with the Métro conductors only his cap, and for the rest, he possesses "the sober elegance suitable to the conductor of an électrique"[71] (figure 1.27). The Métro was a fad to be indulged in or a necessary economy to be suffered, but its popular character was seen to be intrinsically alien to the mondaine.

Unlike the London Underground, the Paris Métro remained primarily within the popular imagination rather than becoming also the province (whether positive or negative) of middle-brow and high culture. In a reversal of the nineteenth century, where "Paris *souterrain*" played a central role in major works of literature and art, it was the Tube that made underground London a culturally respectable subject in the twentieth. Métro lore recorded not middle-class thrills but the faits divers: the mysterious coat-slashers of 1929–30; the woman in black who pricked her victims with a needle; the woman who would appear at six in the evening to speckle passengers with drops of blood; the young woman in a green dress, who in 1937 was stabbed through the neck somewhere between the porte de Charen-

1.26. "The Parisian Woman and the Métropolitain: The fashion of the Métropolitain.—A long journey in three minutes.—Economy and speed." Henri Duvernois, "La Parisienne et le métropolitain," *femina* 5, no. 99 (1 March 1905): 120.

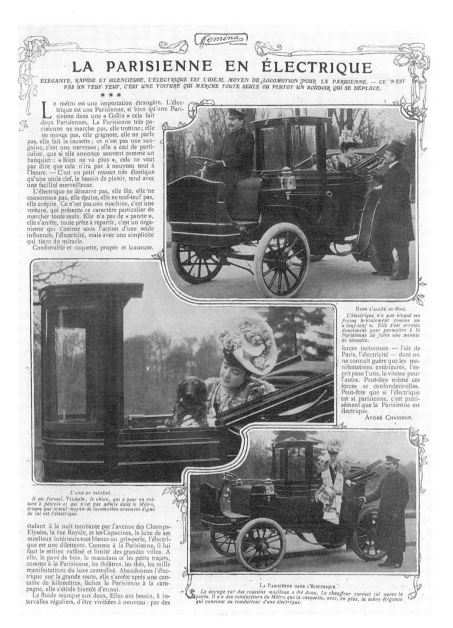

femina

LA PARISIENNE EN ÉLECTRIQUE

ÉLÉGANTE, RAPIDE ET SILENCIEUSE, L'ÉLECTRIQUE EST L'IDÉAL MOYEN DE LOCOMOTION POUR LA PARISIENNE. — CE N'EST PAS UN TEUF-TEUF, C'EST UNE VOITURE QUI MARCHE TOUTE SEULE OU PLUTOT UN BOUDOIR QUI SE DÉPLACE.

* * *

LE métro est une importation étrangère. L'électrique est une Parisienne, si bien qu'une Parisienne dans une « Gallia » cela fait deux Parisiennes. La Parisienne très parisienne ne marche pas, elle trottine ; elle ne mange pas, elle grignote, elle ne parle pas, elle fait la causette ; ce n'est pas une sanguine, c'est une nerveuse ; elle a ceci de particulier, que si elle annonce souvent comme un banquier : « Rien ne va plus », cela ne veut pas dire que cela n'ira pas à nouveau tout à l'heure. — C'est un petit ressort très élastique qu'une seule clef, le besoin de plaisir, tend avec une facilité merveilleuse.

L'électrique ne démarre pas, elle file, elle ne consomme pas, elle épuise, elle ne teuf-teuf pas, elle crépite. Ce n'est pas une machine, c'est une voiture, qui présente ce caractère particulier de marcher toute seule. Elle n'a pas de « panne », elle s'arrête, toute prête à repartir, c'est un organisme qui s'anime sous l'action d'une seule influence, l'électricité, mais avec une simplicité qui tient du miracle.

Confortable et coquette, propre et luxueuse,

DANS L'ALLÉE DU BOIS.
L'électrique n'a pas bloqué ses freins brutalement comme un « teuf-teuf ». Elle s'est arrêtée doucement pour permettre à la Parisienne de faire une minute de causette.

forces inconnues — l'air de Paris, l'électricité — dont on ne connaît guère que les manifestations extérieures, l'esprit pour l'une, la vitesse pour l'autre. Peut-être même ces forces se confondent-elles. Peut-être que si l'électrique est si parisienne, c'est précisément que la Parisienne est électrique.

ANDRÉ CHAIGNON.

L'AVIS DU PRÉFÉRÉ.
Il est formel. Tricksie, le chien, qui a peur en voiture à pétrole et qui n'est pas admis dans le Métro, trouve que le seul moyen de locomotion vraiment digne de lui est l'électrique.

étalant à la nuit tombante par l'avenue des Champs-Elysées, la rue Royale, et les Capucines, le luxe de ses moelleux intérieurs tout blancs ou gris-perle, l'électrique est une dilettante. Comme à la Parisienne, il lui faut le milieu raffiné et limité des grandes villes. A elle, le pavé de bois, le macadam et les petits trajets, comme à la Parisienne, les théâtres, les thés, les mille manifestations du luxe centralisé. Abandonnez l'électrique sur la grande route, elle s'arrête après une centaine de kilomètres, lâchez la Parisienne à la campagne, elle s'étiole bientôt d'ennui.

Le fluide manque aux deux. Elles ont besoin, à intervalles réguliers, d'être vivifiées à nouveau : par des

LA PARISIENNE DANS L'ÉLECTRIQUE.
Le voyage sur des coussins moelleux a été doux. Le chauffeur correct lui ouvre la porte. Il n'a des conducteurs du Métro que la casquette, avec, en plus, la sobre élégance qui convient au conducteur d'une électrique.

1.27. "The Parisian Woman in an Electric Automobile: Elegant, quick and silent, the electric automobile is the ideal means of locomotion for the Parisian woman.—It's not a putt-putt, but a car that runs on its own, or, better, a moving boudoir." André Chaignon, "La Parisienne en électrique," *femina* 5, no. 99 (1 March 1905): 121.

ton and the porte Dorée.[72] Léon Daudet, editor of the right-wing daily *Action Française,* viewed this last murder as the long overdue manifestation of a crime uniquely suited to the Métro: "The decor, the hour, the scene of the crime create a disconcerting atmosphere of irreality, exacting in the criminal's favor a seldom-seen string of coincidences."[73] The dual themes of crime and eroticism delineate an emotive, representational, traditionally subterranean space dominated by a masculine imagination. As Louis Aragon proclaimed the surrealist creed in *Paris Peasant,* "Let pebbles be served on caresses and assassinations in Métro carriages!"[74] The probably apocryphal story that Marcel Allain and Pierre Souvestre coined the title of their influential and wildly successful serial *Fantômas* while riding on the Métro to meet their editor for the first time suggests the power of this space in the popular imagination.[75]

Two volumes of Allain and Souvestre's best-seller involved the Métro as a central setting, their titles evoking the sensational identity of métro culture: *Le Mort qui tue* (*The Lethal Corpse,* 1911) and *Fantômas rencontre l'amour* (*Fantômas Encounters Love,* 1947). *Le Mort qui tue* included not only the master criminal's demolition of the construction site of the Métro at the place de l'Opéra in order to rob a bank car in broad daylight, but also a smuggling operation in the sewers of the île de la Cité broken up by the police inspector Juve in low-life disguise; it was faithfully adapted by Louis Feuillade to the screen in 1913 (see figure 3.25).[76] One of the last volumes, written by Allain after Souvestre's death, *Fantômas rencontre l'amour* played on the Montmartre associations of the Métro and crime. Having robbed the day's receipts from the Anvers station, Fantômas escapes through a private line he has added to the system running through the old tunnels of the Montmartre quarries, robbing the train's passengers in the bargain. Allain recounted that he had later overheard the station chief at Anvers maintaining that there did in fact exist a utility tunnel in the location indicated in the book, which had been used during the construction (Anvers is one of the deepest stations in the system), and that it communicated with the quarries.[77] *Fantômas* was firmly rooted in the popular mythology of subterranean Paris.

Although the First World War increased usage of the Métro because omnibus traffic was forbidden in the evenings,[78] it did not transform it as a representational space, as the next war achieved for London. Proust's depiction of the Métro as a space of shelter in *Le Temps retrouvé,* for example, is dominated by the role it played as a sexual underworld, consistent with the popular perception. The descent into the Métro to shelter from a 1916 air raid comes at the climax of an extended nocturnal wandering in which Paris has taken on by turns the identities of Sodom and of Pompeii: "Others were tempted not so much by the thought of recovering their moral liberty as by the darkness which had suddenly settled upon the streets. Some of these, like the Pompeians upon whom the fire from heaven was already raining, descended into the passages of the Métro, black as catacombs."[79] The liminal space of the darkened Métro issues out to cloak the entire city in another, underworld level of meaning: the homosexual Jupien affects nervousness only "so as to have a pretext, as soon as the sirens sounded, to rush into the shelters in the Métro, where he hoped for pleasure from brief contact with unseen figures."[80]

The Métro turned out to resemble an apocalyptic city not only in terms of biblical morality: several bombs hit stations, causing high fatalities, again in the east of the city, where sixty-six suffocated in the Bolivar station during a stampede down the stairway to find shelter. During the Allied bombing of Paris in the next war, over four hundred persons were killed when a bomb broke through the vaulting at the porte de Saint-Cloud station. For most of the Second World War, however, the Métro was simply the sole means of transport in an occupied city. The Germans fortified much of subterranean Paris but focused their attention on the carrières; unlike the tunnels of the London Tube, those of the Métro, with few exceptions, were too shallow to be of much use either as storage or as shelter.

The popular identity of the Métro thus remained, until quite recently, associated less with the other literally subterranean spaces of Paris than with its metaphorical underground, as part of the working-class, the bas-fonds, the underworld. While the London Underground was a cinematic setting for middle-class melodramas, such as Anthony Asquith's *Underground* (1928), and thrillers, such as Alfred Hitchcock's *Blackmail* (1929—the director made his signature cameo appearance aboard the Tube), Walter Forde's *Bulldog Jack* (1935) and Fritz Lang's *Man Hunt* (1941), it was the métro aérien in the southwest, at Pasteur station, then on line no. 5, that featured in the principal prewar Parisian counterpart, Maurice Cam's *Métropolitain* (1938), and the northern elevated line no. 2 that continued to dominate popular representation in the immediate postwar years (figures 1.28–30). For the literal spaces of underground mysteries, it was the carrières, the *catacombes,* and the *égouts* (sewers) that continued to dominate. Consistent with their artistic slumming, the surrealists were interested in the Métro, but, like Proust, more as part of a figuratively subterranean city, a city that they wanted to excavate from the oppression of everyday reality rather than explore as a space in its own right. One working title of Luis Buñuel and Salvador Dali's classic surrealist film *Un Chien andalou* (1929) was "'Forbidden to Lean Inside' . . . the reverse of the sign on Paris subway trains warning riders not to stick their heads or arms out the window."[81]

The sites that became mythified owed their status less to their place in the métro system than to their association with the Parisian working class and the nightlife and underworld of Montmartre. In addition to Pépé le Moko's nostalgia for Place Blanche and the romantic odor of the trains, we find Yves Montand's nitroglycerine-carrying truck driver in Henri-Georges Clouzot's thriller, *Le Salaire de la peur* (1953), preserving a talismanic métro ticket for Pigalle in his pocket in South American exile. First seen framed on his wall, the ticket is the only personal item he takes with him on his fatal journey. When the novelist

1.28. Melodrama in the Waterloo Tube station: the camera singles out shopkeeper Nell (Elissa Landi) from the crowd. Frame enlargement from *Underground*, directed by Anthony Asquith (British Instructional Films, 1928). BFI Films: Stills, Posters and Designs.

Facing page, top.

1.29. In the 1935 film *Bulldog Jack*, an investigation by Jack Pennington (Jack Hulbert) and Algy Longworth (Claude Hulbert) in "Bloomsbury station" leads via a secret tunnel to the Egyptian room at the British Museum. The scene was based on the disused British Museum station (closed in 1933), which was rumored to be haunted by an Egyptian ghost. Frame enlargement from *Bulldog Jack*, directed by Walter Forde (Gaumont—British Picture Corporation, 1935). BFI Films: Stills, Posters and Designs.

Facing page, bottom.

1.30. In the 1938 film *Métropolitain* Pierre (Albert Préjean) is enmeshed in the steel web of the *métro aérien* at Pasteur station after witnessing, from his métro carriage, an apparent crime of passion in a hotel. Frame enlargement from *Métropolitain*, directed by Maurice Cam (S.B. Films Paris, 1938). BiFi: Bibliothèque du film.

Louis-Ferdinand Céline chose the Métro as metaphor for his postwar style to compete with the cinema and modern culture, it was Pigalle and the Nord-Sud line that embodied it:

> No "nonsense!" . . . I won't put up with your "nonsense" Colonel! . . . I'm giving you the truth, pure and simple . . . take advantage of what I'm telling you! . . . be fore-warned: I'm leaving nothing to the movies! I've made off with all its effects! . . . all its fancy melodrama! . . . all its fake sensitivity! . . . all its effects! . . . decanted, refined, the whole bit! . . . right into the nervous system on my magic train [*rame magique*]! con-centrated! . . . I stuff it all in! . . . my métro with "three dot ties" carries it all away! . . . my magic métro! . . . traitors, suspect beauties, foggy wharves, autos, puppies, brand-new buildings, romantic chalets, plagiarists, dissenters, everything! . . . . I've grabbed all the emotive stuff! . . . have I explained it, Colonel? . . . "Pigalle station to Issy" in the wink of an eye! . . . even the biggest sops feel moved![82]

The subterranean location of the Métro is indeed important here, but only, as for the surrealists, as a convenient means for appropriating it as a figurative space of popular culture. When the Nord-Sud line opened up in November 1910 to link Montmartre and Montparnasse, it became indelibly associated with the two Parisian centers of art, intellectual activity, and nightlife, its name even borrowed by the cubist poet Pierre Reverdy for the avant-garde review he published from 1917–18, the pages of which included such friends and acquaintances as Guil-laume Apollinaire, Louis Aragon, André Breton, Max Jacob, Philippe Soupault, and Tristan Tzara.[83] The Métro's modernity went hand in hand with the advanced art of cubism, Dada, surrealism, and even Italian futurism, for which Paris was a key site in its activity to eliminate the past. The futurist painter Gino Severini, for example, in *The Nord-Sud (Speed and Sound)* (1912), attempted to capture, the "complex of dynamic elements" through the energy of the lines, colors, and direc-tional signs of the new line, "carriages in the Métro + stations + posters + light + crowd."[84] The Nord-Sud had nothing in common with "the earth's deepest bow-els" in which the futurists vowed to bury the dead, and into which they would sweep the "mummies" off "the threshold of the future." For them it was a conduit to the future, one of the "tangible miracles of contemporary life—the iron net-work of speedy communications which envelops the earth."[85]

Along with the Nord-Sud and the Pigalle stations, the métro aérien running from Barbès-Rochechouart to Jaurès on line no. 2 was another topos of métro lore. The northern elevated line was a frequent motif in the celebrated film dia-logue of the poet Jacques Prévert. Prévert's contribution to Jean Renoir's film, *Le Crime de Monsieur Lange* (1936), included the lyrics to "Au jour le jour, A la nuit la nuit," in which the laundress Valentine (played by the popular chanteuse Flo-relle) describes her younger days as a prostitute under the rails: "On the Boule-vard de la Chapelle, where the elevated métro passes, there are a few beautiful girls, and a lot who aren't worth much."[86] The celebrated music-hall singer and film star Arletty's incarnation of the good-hearted tough-talking Paris prostitute in the iconographic film of late 1930s populist poetic realism, Marcel Carné and Prévert's *Hôtel du Nord* (1938), plies her trade under the elevated tracks, counting the trains between customers; even though hers is a good station, she recounts, she once had to wait "fifty trains" for a client. When the first postwar collaboration by the same tandem, *Les Portes de la nuit,* was being filmed in 1945, press invitations were issued in the form of métro tickets to view the full-scale reconstruction of the Barbès-Rochechouart station by the celebrated German set designer, Alexander Trauner, who had also been responsible for *Hôtel du Nord* (figure 1.31). One side of the invitation read, "Inauguration of the new Barbès-Rochechouart station on the Pathé-Cinéma–Portes de la Nuit line"; the other contained a métro map relabeled with station names such as "Marcel-Carné," "Jacques-Prévert," and "Pierre-Brasseur," one of the stars.[87] Like the canal Saint-Martin along which *Hôtel du Nord* had been set, the elevated section of the porte Dauphine-Nation line entered Paris lore thanks to its geographical location in the north of the city, between Montmartre and République, and its symbolic identification with a particular myth of the Parisian working class and *la pègre,* its underworld counterpart.[88]

1.31. In the 1946 film *Les Portes de la nuit* the doomed lovers Diego (Yves Montand) and Malou (Nathalie Nattier) meet at night beneath the *métro aérien.* Frame enlargement from *Les Portes de la nuit,* directed by Marcel Carné (Pathé Cinéma, 1946). BFI Films: Stills, Posters and Designs.

Because of its metonymic association with this myth, the Métro never entered the lore of the city with a specific technological or spatial identity. Raymond Queneau played on this paradox by making it the single goal of young Zazie's weekend in Paris, a goal that he then frustrates by means of a transit workers' strike. The self-assured and savvy Zazie has no doubt about the difference between the underground and the elevated parts of the system; when her uncle Gabriel tries to assuage her disappointment by pointing out "something in the air":

> "The Métro?" she repeats. "The Métro," she adds contemptuously, "the Métro is underground, the Métro. That's that."
> "That one," says Gabriel, "is the el."
> "Then it's not the Métro."[89]

Zazie's stubborn refusal to recognize the Métro in the aérien exemplifies her refusal to subordinate her idiosyncratic vision to the more traditional Montmartre folklore of her bohemian uncle and his friends the taxi driver and the staff of the local café. Her obscene and anarchic language and behavior and the chaos that follows in her wake suggest that Queneau was seeking in the underground a more disruptive symbol of submerged forces than the by-then-domesticated topoi of "*vieux* Paris" and the aérien. Just as the sudden and violent death of the widow Mouaque in the absurdist denouement hearkens back to early surrealism, so does the subsequent escape from the cellar of Aux Nyctalopes (At the Sign of the Nightseers) through the sewers and into the tunnel of the no. 1 line recall the underground settings of *Fantômas* and Gaston Leroux's novel, *La Vie double de Théophraste Longuet* (1903). Apparently activated by this descent, the Métro is finally running again, but Zazie, unconscious throughout this part of the novel, remembers nothing. Asked by her mother if she saw the Métro, she replies, flatly, "No." Like the mythic Métro of her imaginings, Zazie is apparently incompatible with the Paris everyone knows, and it is equally incompatible with her.

When the Métro did begin appearing in film as a properly subterranean space, it was in the context of the world-wide interest in the subway as a setting for cinematic spectacle. Although the trend began in the 1950s, subway chase scenes became de rigueur the world over during the 1970s. The intimate knowledge of the Métro system allows Alain Delon's hit man, Jef Costello, to elude the police beneath the streets of Belleville in Jean-Pierre Melville's iconic *Le Samouraï* (1967), further establishing his reputation as the perfect assassin, but the extended location shooting of the scene derives more from the urban aesthetic of American film noir than the studio work of earlier French filmmakers such as Carné (figure 1.32). Although Melville did consciously highlight the characteristic features of métro architecture—the low, ovoid, double-railed tunnels, the labyrinthine stairways and corridors connecting the platforms of different lines, the gates to the platform that used to snap shut when the train doors were closing—his inspiration was meta-cinematic rather than specific to the Parisian underground.

1.32. In *Le Samouraï* (1967) Jef Costello (Alain Delon) eludes the police in the Place des Fêtes station. Frame enlargement from *Le Samouraï*, directed by Jean-Pierre Melville (Filmel/Compagnie Industrielle et Commerciale Cinématographique/Fido Cinematografica, 1967). BFI Films: Stills, Posters and Designs.

More intrinsically Parisian was Luc Besson's cult film *Subway* (1984), except that what is most Parisian about it is that it is concerned less with the Métro itself than with the countercultural life it portrays in the deep tunnels and corridors beneath and surrounding the vast new Châtelet–Les Halles complex, where ten years earlier a multilevel subterranean mall had been opened above a new station linking the suburban RER system with the Métro proper (figure 1.33). The English of the film's original title warned the French viewer that the underground railway itself was international and Americanized, an anonymous, mechanized space that mirrored the alienated world above. In contrast, the real underground, designed once again by the seemingly ageless Trauner, is home to an alternative community of squatting musicians, dropouts, and eccentrics with monikers ranging from Drummer to Florist and epitomized by The Roller (Jean-Hughes Anglade), a petty thief who spends his life roaming the endless corridors of the station on roller skates. The hero Fred (Christopher Lambert) arrives in this space in flight from gangsters; he finds meaning, companionship, and love with Helena (Isabelle Adjani), herself in flight from a loveless marriage. The subway space remains alien and threatening, part of the world above, but at night, after the Métro closes, Roller, Fred, and Helena emerge to repossess the space, raiding its shops for food and wine, and throwing a party. Besson's film adapted and gave a broad iconographic appeal to the traditionally countercultural and romantic elements of Paris souterrain, contrasting them with the multinational capitalism of the subterranean mall and the modern rationalism of the Métro itself.[90]

Guides to the Underworld

"What's it like, working down there?"

He sits back, requiring himself to be patient. "Like anywhere. No." He is thinking, so that when he talks his English will be clear, precise as his thinking. "The Underground starts out perfect. At first it isn't like the city above it because it is perfect. Everything must be created, heat and the passage of air. For the engineers and architects it begins as a perfect technical form. Then years go by—decades. Cross-tunnels are found to be unnecessary, so they are bricked up. Deeper tunnels are added by the government, then closed down. Limestone comes through the concrete as if it were muslin. Up above, communities die out. Stations are abandoned. . . . The Underground becomes a reflection of the city above—organic, not perfect. Full of small animals and weak plants. Good hiding places, and places that are dangerous."

TOBIAS HILL, *Underground* (1999)

Besson's subterranean division between a nurturing, emotive space and a rationalized, anonymous one rehearsed a split first made by the London Underground in the nineteenth century. Whether feared or desired, loathed or praised, the underground had traditionally been conceived and represented as a dirty, damp, unstable, labyrinthine space. There had long been techniques of channeling and controlling this epitome of wild nature through sewers, and exploiting it through quarries and mines, but the means and the idea of wholly replacing it with an improved vision of aboveground space began with the underground railway. As a physical space, the earth has always been associated with female archetypes in Western myth; the male-controlled realm of the afterlife was always a world apart, only metaphorically underground. The close spatial relation to seasonal cycles of birth and death may have contributed to the connection with the female, but it is a connection that has become ever more arbitrary, while remaining extraordinarily persistent. The equation between activities and persons imagined as subterranean invokes the physical qualities of traditional underground activity and adds to them associations with the feminine that have become a fundamental metaphorical division in modern society—fluid, unruly mobs; diseased and immoral slum dwellers; and, at the center, the figure of the urban pros-

1.33. In *Subway* (1984) Fred (Christopher Lambert) discovers the Force in the utility tunnels deep beneath the Châtelet–Les Halles complex. Frame enlargement from *Subway*, directed by Luc Besson (Les Films du Loup/T.S.F. Productions/Gaumont/T.F. 1 Films Productions, 1984). BFI Films: Stills, Posters and Designs.

titute.[91] I will explore such metaphorics further in chapter 3 in the context of urban pathology; for the moment, I want to examine how the new underground space represented itself to be in every way in contradistinction to the old: not just clean, bright, safe, and well-ordered, but masculine as well. It is not accidental that Lefebvre could characterize the abstract space of modernity in terms of its "phallic verticality," the representation of a visible, masculine space in contradistinction to a dominated, hidden, cryptic, feminine space.[92] Whether it purports to abolish the feminine completely, or to consign it to its highly controlled depths, the vertical city defines itself in opposition to the traditional underground in every way.

The article "Underground" in Charles Knight's six-volume encyclopedia, *London* (1841–44), provides a good introduction to the ways in which rationalizing language and the scientific approach were incorporated into the depiction of the subterranean city. Rather than the sensational aspect of the mysteries of the underground in mid-century popular culture, the article's authors, J. C. Platt and J. Saunders, employed a new trope: the ignorance of the world above regarding its technological achievements below the ground. Retaining the familiar nineteenth-century image of the city in ruins, Platt and Saunders imagined the future excavation of a London of which only its subterranean infrastructure had survived:

> One could not but almost envy the delight with which the antiquaries of the future time would hear of some discovery of a *London below the soil* still remaining. We can fancy we see the progress of the excavators from one part to another of the mighty, but for a while inexplicable, labyrinth, till the whole was cleared open to the daylight, and the vast system lay bare before them, revealing in the clearest language the magnitude and splendour of the place to which it had belonged, the skill and enterprise of the people.[93]

The writers project forward in time the rhetorical effect of their article: what was widely perceived as the labyrinthine, mysterious, and dangerous underground would be revealed "in the clearest language" as a "vast" and perfectly rational system that accomplishes automatically everything that used to be a daily concern:

> Do we want water in our houses?—we turn a small instrument, and the limpid stream from the springs of Hertfordshire, or of Hampstead Heath, or from the river Thames, comes flowing, as it were by magic, into our vessels. Do we wish to get rid of it when no longer serviceable?—the trouble is no greater; in an instant it is on its way through the silent depths. Do we wish for an artificial day?—through that same mysterious channel comes streaming up into every corner of our chambers, counting-houses, or shops, the subtle air which waits but our bidding to become—light! The tales which amuse our childhood have no greater marvels than these.[94]

This is not yet the subterranean city—the article stresses the rural origin of the water; the relationship remains one of the world above—home, business, shop— to the world below; however, we can already glimpse the core new values wrapped up in the trappings of familiarity, "the tales which amuse our childhood."

What is noteworthy here is that the world below is reimagined as an empty infrastructure rather than an infested, stinking, unhealthy warren of poverty and vice. The article is ideological in the extreme, as the reference to the filthy water of the Thames as "limpid" indicates, and replete with endless debates over how to solve exactly those problems that this vision writes out of existence (see figure 3.5). It is the typical rhetoric of the popular encyclopedia and the boy's own paper, of man-made wonders explained in the brightest possible light, a rhetoric that would peak in popularity at the turn of the century, although it returned periodically, especially in the 1950s. As Rosalind Williams has argued about images of the industrial sublime in the early nineteenth century, "The aesthetic fantasy is closely related to the social fantasy of eliminating class conflict, of exploiting nature without exploiting people."[95] Platt and Saunders's "Underground" follows a similar pattern, visible in the observation that "we seldom think of it, except when some such picturesque scenes . . . call our attention to these gloomy regions, or when we hear of people wandering into them from the Thames till they find Cheapside or Temple Bar above their heads."[96] What was needed, the authors implied, was a new approach to underground space that would represent it as it ought to be—an abstract system of automatic service—rather than as it was—a mixed-use, haphazardly developed, and conflicted space. The water and drainage systems that the article featured were the first focus of this approach to the underground, but it was the underground railway that provided a far more concrete image of a space from which all difference could be eliminated, into which no unforeseen or undesired element could intrude, and which would be safe and comfortable for all.

The turn of the century saw many versions of journalistic and encyclopedic writing about underground London and Paris, with prefixes such as "The Romance of . . ." and "The Mysteries of . . ." signaling by their titles the replacement of the sensationalistic attitude of the past century with scientific wonder, just as the contemporaneous flood of books on "Mysteries of the Underworld" rationalized the mythic metaphor to treat the conquest of crime by the new police detective. The positive and the negative subterranean spaces were separated taxonomically from one another, if not yet perhaps in the representational world of the popular imagination. The back pages of Sims's *Mysteries of Modern London,* where the Underground provided entry to a new, interior form of mysteries, advertised "The 'Romance' Series" by Archibald Williams, including topics such as *The Romance of Modern Invention, . . . Modern Engineering, . . . Mining,* and *. . . The Mighty Deep.* Passingham's 1932 history, *The Romance of London's Underground,* came at the end of the construction of the Tube, in the same years as Beck's schematic diagram, and was thus able comprehensively to celebrate the "Wonders of the Modern Underground." The separate companies having been fully amalgamated in 1914 by the American transport tycoon Charles Tyson Yerkes, the Underground was now to be discussed in terms of proper functioning: safety, ticketing, training of employees, rolling stock. The "Spirit" of this modern Underground was no longer mythic in any traditional sense but embodied by the wholly tamed force of "the Power-House."[97]

Similar language occurs in earlier versions, such as Banton's enthusiasm over the Bank station, "one of the most remarkable railway stations in the world," with its "high-level subways—well-lighted thoroughfares lined with white glazed bricks, through which circulates continuously a kaleidoscopic procession of pedestrians avoiding the crowded streets above," from which the platforms can be reached by "a number of commodious and smoothly working lifts" (figure 1.34).[98] Already by the end of the 1920s, the similarly complex Piccadilly Circus station was able to embody not only the principle of progress but "the appearance of some intestinal anatomical drawing," as Frederick Etchells characterized it in the introduction to his translation of Le Corbusier's manifesto of architectural modernism, *Urbanisme:* "Perhaps the complications of the scheme, and the consequent waste of time for the passenger, are due to lack of foresight when the Tubes were first constructed."[99] When Banton was writing, however, the system was still under construction, and he was able to extrapolate its ongoing perfection; such praise during the 1930s surveys and in Beck's map found it necessary to eliminate any sense of everyday activity from its purview. By contrast, Banton's article was constrained to incorporate the activity of the navvies into its model space. Hence the hybrid metaphor that recalls earlier visions of the Thames Tunnel under construction: nearly a century later, underground labor remains "an eerie sight in the dimly lighted tunnel," while "the iron shield slowly, relentlessly forces its way, like a great scientific mole, through the bowels of the earth, and the slowly lengthening tube of iron approaches daily, in obedience to calculations of the most marvellous precision and accuracy, nearer to its unseen goal."[100] Although Banton's image of the "great scientific mole" retains traces of the nineteenth-century ambivalence between the organic and inorganic undergrounds and an uneasiness over the everyday human cost of the daily advancement, the "unseen goal" toward which the construction unerringly aims is the modernist fantasy of total mechanization, an underground from which the contingencies of humanity would completely disappear. F. L. Stevens, in his 1939 volume *Under London,* for example, was fascinated by the ability of the Underground workers to shift the platforms and lower the tracks at the Aldgate East station, "to extend the junction and save a few seconds of time for the passengers" without interrupting train service "until the very last moment, and then for little more than twenty-four hours."[101] Stevens stressed the "careful synchronization" of the labor, the meticulous planning in advance, even a full-scale rehearsal; he then moved on to the even more intriguing matter of how an escalator functions, and how rats had been entirely eliminated from the system.

A very different sort of scientific underground is evident in the magnum opus of rational subterranean volumes, the 650-page study *Paris souterrain* (1908) by Emile Gérards. Unlike the London surveys of the time, which tended to separate the traditional underground from the modern one, Gérards subsumed the former within the scientific framework of the latter. He began his study of the city with the beginning of the world; rather than anthropological speculation, however, Gérards stuck to what he saw as the facts, although he did preserve the epic framework of a *descensus ad inferos*. It would be a brave and tenacious reader, he asserted, who would be able to follow him all the way through the study of the ground of his city:

> We are going to attempt to make this history come alive very rapidly and in as precise a fashion as possible by reviewing in succession for the courageous reader willing to follow us, all the great facts of a material nature that have been produced since the beginning of time, and which are recorded in the rocky archives of Paris with an impeccable fidelity.[102]

1.34. The turn-of-the-century London Underground: a suitable place for women and policemen. Photograph in Eric Banton's essay, "Underground Travelling London," in *Living London: Its work and its play. Its humour and its pathos. Its sights and its scenes*, ed. George R. Sims, 3 vols. (London: Cassell & Co., 1901–3), 3:62.

In an imaginative expansion of the subterranean laboratory of the National Museum of Natural History established in the carrières beneath the Jardin des Plantes in Paris in 1896, Gérards rendered all of the city beneath the soil as a combination of laboratory and library.[103]

The survey that Gérards made included not only the predictable histories of the construction of the sewers, the completed works on the carrières and the Catacombes, and the work-in-progress of the Métropolitain, but 150 pages on the "formation and composition of the soil of Paris" and chapters on the "subterranean waters" and on "the subterranean fauna and flora of Paris." Even the legends are there—a comprehensive account of César's seventeenth-century tours of the carrières to see the Devil, for example—but only insofar as of "archival interest"; hence, Elie Berthet's popular nineteenth-century thriller, *Les Catacombes de Paris,* is mentioned twice, only to be immediately dismissed: "but . . . the less said about it the better."[104] The new London Underground survey would erase contemporary traces of the older underground; as Sims asserted, an "Avernus" of poverty and vice might exist hidden in the midst of Kensington, but "wall off Hoxton, and nine-tenths of the criminals of London would be walled-off."[105] Similarly, Gérards, himself an underground official, incorporated the underworld past as he did the prehistoric fossils, but whatever may have remained in the present was pushed firmly beyond the bounds of the city, out to "the Zone" that was filling up with shantytowns during the same decades in which Gérards was writing (see figure 3.27). The only metaphorical underground in the new underground literature, English or French, was that of transparency. In the comprehensiveness of its ambition, the obvious pleasure it took in its "87 maps, cross-sections and ink drawings," its "more than 500 illustrations," and its refusal to hierarchize within the totality of underground Paris it imagined, Gérards's book remained in the nineteenth-century tradition of Mayhew, the mysteries, and the panoramic literature. In that he replaced the prior century's material view from below with the literal material of the soil, in that the human dropped out along with the sordid, Gérards looked resolutely forward to the paradigmatic twentieth-century separation of the human from the technological, of man from machine, of the feminine from the masculine underground.

Rosalind Williams has drawn an important distinction between two types of sublimity related to the experience of subterranean space: "those featuring the nocturnal fire of hell and volcanoes," which became important in the response to technology of the first industrial revolution, and "those of 'artificial infinity'," which "slowly moved from architecture to art to literature, from realistic constructions to fantastic illuminated enclosures." By the 1870s, she argues, "pleasing images of technological magic" had mostly displaced "the more frightening ones of diabolic sublimity."[106] This superb study is motivated by fear of the "less tangible losses" that follow in the wake of the "loss of natural surrounding" as a consequence of the changed attitude toward "artificial infinity," toward what I have termed the masculine underground.[107] What Williams underestimates, I think, is the degree to which the sublimity of hellfire was itself also always susceptible to appropriation in other forms; insofar as it expressed the power of nature, the power of the underground, the power of the Devil, it could also be experienced as a force for positive change, even if it could not easily be represented as such. Moreover, the key moment in the shift toward "pleasing images of technological magic," I would argue, was motivated by changing conceptions of space. Rather than representations of the new underground as a novel version of familiar aboveground space—as in the case of the *passage,* the Thames Tunnel, and even the original underground railway—we begin to find representations of the new underground as an unfamiliar version of subterranean space made familiar by its resemblance to traditional images of utopia.

Underground Speculation

The houses were never high enough to satisfy the people. They kept on making them still higher. They built them of thirty or forty storeys, with offices, shops, banks, societies, one above another. They dug cellars and tunnels ever downwards. Fifteen million men laboured in a giant town.

ANATOLE FRANCE, *Penguin Island* (1908)

The modernist dream of the vertical city analogous to the conception of Beck's subway map emerged out of several decades of fervid literary speculation on the nature of this new underground. From a time-honored way of dividing up the actual city both physically and metaphorically, subterranean space became a means of conceptualizing the ideal city. The nineteenth-century obsession with the subterranean was appropriated to envision the city of the next century; the results of such a combination were, not surprisingly, both eccentric and informative. Novels such as Bulwer-Lytton's *The Coming Race* (1871), William Delisle Hay's *Three Hundred Years Hence* (1881), Auguste Villiers de l'Isle-Adam's *L'Eve future* (1886), Gabriel Tarde's *Fragment d'histoire future* (written 1884, published 1896), Wells's *The Time Machine* (1895) and *When the Sleeper Wakes* (1899), and E. M. Forster's story "The Machine Stops" (1909) took the rationalization of underground space implicit in the Metropolitan Railway and extended it into an organizational principle. If, as Michel Ragon has observed, the term "urbanism" was employed for the first time only in 1910,[108] then its enunciation as a field of discourse occurred in the midst of literary speculation over the new forms being taken by underground space within the urban environment. In a process shared by the technology on which it was based, the discourse of urbanism was enunciated not in a modern, empty space but in a representational underground, the traces of which stubbornly persisted into the future. The key to the mysteries of the new subterranean cities turns out to be located in the hidden recesses upon which they were built.

The most straightforward depiction of the coming underground was *Three Hundred Years Hence*, which projected not only a subterranean landscape rendered regular, light, and inorganic, but a population equally homogenized by a genocidal "Epoch of Final Wars," which has eliminated all class and racial conflict by eliminating all unwanted classes and races. Their traces remain, however, in the pastiche of architectural styles of the underground cities: "Chinese pagodas, Muslim mosques, Grecian temples, and Swiss chalets all hang from the cliffs and rocky platforms."[109] The new underground space, Hay's narrative implied, was to be achieved by the elimination of every aspect of difference traditionally represented by underground space. That such a fantasy needed to be imagined in the bunkerlike space of the subterranean city suggests the uncomfortable awareness that there was something unnatural about it, something only to be achieved in a delimited, carefully controlled area. The ten underground states with 21 billion people represent only a fraction of Hay's total future population of 130 billion. One cannot but find a new stratification in the implantation of this perfect society fifty miles below the surface of the earth.

In its elimination of every element of the feminine underworld, Hay's conceptual extremism matched that of his social Darwinist politics, and, except in what Williams has accurately termed the "world's fair" aesthetics of its architecture, predicts the extremist stance of much of architectural modernism. The other underground utopias instead imagined in different ways a space composed out of the conflicts of the two types of underground space. *The Coming Race*, for example, envisioned a subterranean race, the "vril-ya," made aristocratic and refined by their control of the magical technology of "vril," a sort of all-purpose electricity. As Williams has noted, the vril-ya's city "perfectly blend[s] comfort, gadgetry, and beauty";[110] nevertheless, the final thrust of the novel is negative, expressing Bulwer-Lytton's fear of the progressive social ideas of his time. The result of such utopias, he wrote to his son, would be "a race . . . fatal to ourselves . . . which we would find extremely dull."[111] Williams explains this hostility partly by Bulwer-Lytton's political conservatism and, more particularly, his unhappy personal life. What I find more revealing, however, is that the vril-ya and their utopia from which the narrator is so relieved to escape constitute a collection in rebus of the primary motifs of the traditional feminine underground that the inorganic utopia appears to deny. Bulwer-Lytton does not imagine a utopian underground freed of the infernal sublime; his technological world is replete with the archaic.

The hyper-evolved vril-ya are constituted out of an undercurrent of ancient myths of the underworld city. They are descended from the inhabitants of "a band of the ill-fated race . . . invaded by the Flood," which Bulwer-Lytton dates to long before the "historical and sacred Deluge" but to which he assimilates it nonetheless.[112] Scions of a new race of Cain consigned to the center of the earth, the vril-ya have developed into a society dominated by the taller and more technologically adept females. Their buildings first remind the narrator of alien, Eastern cultures, "symbolical images of Genius or Demon that are seen on Etruscan vases or limned on the walls of Eastern sepulchres—images that borrow the outlines of man, and are yet of another race."[113] Yet they equally recall an infernal London. His first vision of the underworld duplicates descriptions of the Thames Tunnel, "a broad level road at the bottom of the abyss, illumined as far as the eye could reach by what seemed artificial gas-lamps placed at regular intervals, as in the thoroughfare of a great city" (figure 1.35); he later adds that the public edifices remind him of "the architectural pictures of [John] Martin," whose visions of the

1.35. The Thames Tunnel and its trademark receding gaslit corridor-tunnel. Illustration in "The Thames Tunnel," *London*, ed. Charles Knight, 6 vols. in 3 (London, 1841–44): 3:49.

industrial sublime were influenced equally by modern London and by an infernally urban apocalypticism.[114] Raymond Williams observed of the world of *The Coming Race* that "its desire is tinged with awe and indeed with fear."[115] The desire for this underground is very clearly depicted in the symbolism of light: vril is pure light; the vril-ya have "a great horror of perfect darkness, and their lights are never wholly extinguished."[116] The cost of that desire—awe and fear—is pictured through the vehicle of traditional antitheses to the symbolism of enlightenment—Cain, female, Oriental, infernal, urban—antitheses that traditionally were relegated to the world below, a space now occupied by a different underground.

The desire for light is interwoven with the desire for the hidden riches of the earth. The descent to this underground realm occurs as the result of a week spent with a Liverpool engineer exploring the "gloomy wonders" of a mine, "the vaults and galleries hollowed by nature and art beneath the surface of the earth."[117] The wish to possess "far richer deposits of mineral wealth than had yet been detected" leads to the discovery of a dangerous and alien vision of a utopia where the narrator must regard himself as an underground man in the eyes of the now ascendant underground race in whose power he finds himself.[118] "In short," confesses the superwoman Zee, unknowingly condemning the man for whom she has inexplicably developed an unconquerable passion, "the people I speak of are savages groping their way in the dark towards some gleam of light, and would demand our commiseration for their infirmities, if, like all savages, they did not provoke their own destruction by their arrogance and cruelty."[119] The narrator's shock of recognition at this statement reeks less of the social guilt that underlay late nineteenth-century descents into the world of poverty than of the horror of being forced to conceive of himself in the position of miners or of the degenerate urban poor, of realizing that he was witnessing not just a different race but a "coming race" that would paradoxically embody the principles of revolution: what was below would now be on top, and what was on top would now be below.

A similar shock of recognition runs through *The Time Machine,* again based on a series of social identifications naturalized as species differences. Where Bulwer-Lytton had projected the city into the future, the socialist Wells used the future directly to critique 1895 London. Consequently, his underground is darker and more physically threatening, in the urban mysteries tradition rather than that of the view from above. The Time Traveller begins his theorization about the structure of the world of 802701 AD by presupposing the horizontal model of the traditional social utopia: what he sees on the surface—the childlike Eloi living a version of the golden age, feeding on nuts and berries—is all there is. He apologizes to the reader for his failure to have discovered more of the nuts and bolts, the sanitary arrangements, the question of sepulture, and the problem of production; his apology functions as a critique of traditional utopias, which, by analogy, would view only the surface of the matter, and never go into the depths, the real problems of society.

The first shock to the Time Traveller's assumptions occurs when he becomes aware of the existence of a complex underground infrastructure, a division between Capital and Labor naturalized through evolution over the millennia. The model for the second theory is less the objective study of where he is than the new technological space of underground London in 1895, which Wells explicitly relates to the older metaphorical underground of the East End:

> There is a tendency to utilize underground space for the less ornamental purposes of civilization; there is the Metropolitan Railway in London, for instance, there are new electric railways, there are subways, there are underground workrooms and restaurants, and they increase and multiply. Evidently, I thought, this tendency had increased till Industry had gradually lost its birthright to the sky. I mean that it had gone deeper and deeper into larger and ever larger underground factories, spending a still-increasing amount of its time therein, till, in the end—! Even now, does not an East-end worker live in such artificial conditions as practically to be cut off from the natural surface of the earth?[120]

The Time Traveller's identification with the "refined beauty and etiolated pallor" of the Eloi leads him to trace them back to the ruling class of the late nineteenth century; the same identification leads him to confuse the class-divided space of the worker with the utilitarian use of the underground by all city dwellers.

His first misinterpretation derived from overreliance on the horizontalist assumptions of traditional utopias, which cannot account for the problems of the modern city: production and disposal. His second misinterpretation lies in his ignorance of the actual space beneath his feet; he induces from prejudice rather than direct experience. His third interpretation is reached only after a material descent into the realm of the Morlocks, the underworld of the future, driven by the need for knowledge and for the technology to return to his own world: "I felt assured that the Time Machine was only to be recovered by boldly penetrating these underground mysteries."[121] Similar to *The Coming Race,* fantastic technology is paired with an atavistic nightmare: for Bulwer-Lytton, vril was wielded by the empowered subterraneans of his own society; for the Time Traveller, the mastery of technology leads to the breaking of, for him, a fundamental social taboo. His response is to deny any relationship to either race: "Why should I trouble myself? These Eloi were mere fatted cattle, which the ant-like Morlocks preserved and preyed upon—probably saw to the breeding of."[122] The subtlety of Wells's novel, and a point overlooked in most readings of it, is that the Time Traveller rationalizes away his necessary evolutionary relationship with *both* new species. While he initially identified with the Eloi through a desire to belong to the aristocracy, however simple and passive it might have become, he cannot at all acknowledge his much stronger resemblance to the Morlocks, on whom he projects all his fantasies of a technology gone haywire. The strong but never-proven suspicion of cannibalism is the only way he can distance himself from the evidence of resemblance: his technological mind, his obsession with action, and a constant craving for the meat denied him by the vegetarian diet of the Eloi.

While the second interpretation makes in passing a conventional socialist argument against class divisions, the third interpretation makes a less self-evident argument against the division of space. There is no longer any clear evolution between the vertical space of the future and that of 1895; it is not apparent whether the Morlocks are descended from underground workers, from a technocratic elite, or simply from a random group of survivors who sheltered underground. Consequently, it is the physical division of space rather than any comprehensible chain of events that leads to the new social division; time has changed everything except the essentially vertical division of space. In this reading, the greatest fault in the Time Traveller's personality would be his failure, from beginning to end, ever to examine any aspect of this space in depth. For all his pioneering spirit, he proves unable to draw any knowledge from his journey to the future, treating it instead as any tourist would. This failure is clearest, perhaps, in Wells's apocalyptic vision of the future's end, where the final stage of evolution has been reached in a flopping, limbless, shapeless monster on a radioactive beach. Only the person able to grasp the mystery of the steps whereby the world of 1895 reached first the Morlocks and Eloi, and then the creature at the end of time, Wells implies, would be able to grasp what it might be necessary to do in order to prevent this vision from occurring.

An instructive comparison can be made with *When The Sleeper Wakes,* published four years later, where the entire structure of the London of the future is predicated on its immediate relationship with the present. The solution to the mystery is money; for Graham, the deathless Sleeper in suspended animation, turns out to be the living but disempowered heir to the fortune of centuries of compound interest accumulated as he has lain senseless. Awakened by subversives within the complex society of another vertical city, Graham, like the Time Traveller, is forced to interpret the world around him with little help from its inhabitants. Graham's first descent is very nearly a fall. Escaping pursuit, he finds himself in the dark, letting himself down over ledges into the unknown: "[He] had a horrible sensation of sliding over the edge into the unfathomable, splashed, and felt himself in a slushy gutter, impenetrably dark."[123] Descent in this unfathomable "latter-day London" is not a simple matter of above and below, light and dark; he finally lands inexplicably in the middle of a great theater, the center attraction of "The people! His people! A proscenium, a stage rushed up towards him" (67). The social truths of the nineteenth century—capitalism unbound, rampant exploitation, segregation and division, uninformed but enthusiastic crowds, half-baked revolutions—remain, but are enacted within a new cityscape lacking any apparent rhyme or reason. It is as if the space of the city had finally caught up with the irrationality and contradictions of its economic system.

The representation of space no longer overlaps the representational space of the city. Graham is able to take "a bird's eye view of the city from the crow's nest of the wind-vane keeper," a thousand feet above the roofs, above the pollution, amidst the wind and the sun, looking down on the "dazzling expanse of London" (114). The suburban landscape survives intact in the distance, Highgate and Muswell Hill, except covered by innumerable wind-vanes that send power "incessantly through all the arteries of the city" (114). As opposed to the distant future of *The Time Machine,* where southeast England could be identified only by the fact that the Time Traveller is sure he has not journeyed in space but only in time, here the topographical situation of the metropolis remains the same, another point of continuity with 1899. But within the city itself, everything recognizable has been buried under the domes: "St Paul's he knew survived, and many of the old buildings in Westminster, embedded out of sight, arched over and covered in among the giant growths of the great age" (115). In the future, the view from above cannot provide even the most general truths about the world below.

> So vast was its serenity in comparison with the areas of disturbance that presently Graham, looking beyond them, could almost forget the thousands of men lying out of sight in the artificial glare within the quasi-subterranean labyrinth . . . forget, indeed, all the wonder, consternation and novelty under the electric lights. Down there in the hidden ways of the anthill he knew that the revolution triumphed, that black everywhere carried the day, black favours, black banners, black festoons across the streets. (115)

Even within the hierarchized society organized by the "Labour Company," development has been uneven; the underground retains its traditional features in the midst of the technology of the future.

The past resides underground as well. In one of the most striking images, Graham begins his descent to the "real" underground of the workers when his guide takes him to the now-buried dome of Saint Paul's. The traditional vantage point for the view from above is itself now physically part of the underground:

> "I want to see the workers. I have seen enough of these." . . .
> He led the way along a closed passage that presently became cold. The reverberating of their feet told them that this passage was a bridge. They came into a circular gallery that was glazed in from the outer weather, and so reached a circular chamber which seemed familiar, though Graham could not recall distinctly when he had entered it before. In this was a ladder—the first ladder he had seen since his awakening—up which they went, and came into a high dark, cold place in which there was another almost vertical ladder. This they ascended, Graham still perplexed.
> But at the top he understood, and recognized the metallic bars to which he clung. He was in the cage under the ball of St Paul's. The dome rose but a little way above the general contour of the city, into the still twilight, and sloped away, shining greasily under a few distant lights, into a circumambient ditch of darkness. . . . "This," he said at last, smiling in the shadow, "seems the strangest thing of all. To stand in the dome of St Paul's and look once more upon these familiar, silent stars!" (184–85)

Unlike the Time Traveller, for whom the underground conceals only truths he does not want to accept, Graham finds in it the nostalgia of the familiar place. For both characters, their pasts survive in the ground of the future, but only Graham is able to recognize this fact, for his character is predicated on his inhabiting simultaneously the past and the future. *The Time Machine* poses the problem of recognizing oneself in a social nightmare; *When the Sleeper Wakes* asks how to find one's place in a world to which one knows one belongs but in which one can no longer find one's way.

As they descend into the actual factory quarter, the futuristic underground slips away, and Graham finds himself in a more familiar subterranean space:

> Even the pretence of architectural ornamentation disappeared, the lights diminished in number and size, the architecture became more and more massive in proportion to the spaces. . . . Many of these great and dusty galleries were·silent avenues of machinery, endless raked out ashen furnaces testified to the revolutionary dislocation, but wherever there was work it was being done by slow-moving workers in blue canvas. . . . That walk left on Graham's mind a maze of memories, fluctuating pictures of swathed halls, and crowded vaults seen through clouds of dust, of intricate machines, the racing threads of looms, the heavy beat of stamping machinery, the roar and rattle of belt and armature, of ill-lit subterranean aisles of sleeping places, illimitable vistas of pin-point lights. And here the smell of tanning, and here the reek of a brewery and here, unprecedented reeks. And everywhere were pillars and cross archings of such massiveness as Graham had never before seen, thick Titans of greasy, shining brickwork crushed beneath the vast weight of that complex city world, even as these anaemic millions were crushed by its complexity. And everywhere were pale features, lean limbs, disfigurement and degradation. (190–91)

Wells's narrator comments that the only change is the poor physical condition of the workers, but he is tendentious; such complaints were already commonplace in late nineteenth-century writing on urban degeneration. The truth with which Graham returns from his descent prompts him to take the leadership of the premature revolt; he flies off to certain death in one of Wells's beloved visions of flight, the "aeropile."

Williams is correct in seeing images of "social sublimity" and echoes of "Piranesi's prisons" in this subterranean city; it is certainly an overwhelming vision.[124] But what is most striking is the structural role played by sublimity in the novel, for it signifies not the unimaginable, the frightening, and the majestic, but the familiar, the remembered. This is the space of truth, of memory, of what Graham calls "reality," what he most desires. It is not an "artificial infinity" so much as a tangible and existent one, the ruin of an artificial infinity that has long since been incorporated into the natural cityscape. For all its enormous scale and technological complexity, it is strikingly organic, greasy, and shining, full of dust, the "smell of tanning," and "the reek of a brewery." It is perversely comforting to Graham to discover the familiar imagery of Victorian hell buried beneath the fu-

turistic domes of latter-day London, just as he had found the forgotten stars
from atop the hidden dome of Saint Paul's. This is a space of degradation, to be
sure, but also one of revolution and empowerment; unlike the alien labyrinth
above, this walk leaves "a maze of memory," a maze of which the meaning is graspable, a labyrinth whose passages Graham can follow back to the world he
knows. *The Time Machine* gave the same message, but negatively, in that the
Time Traveller refused ever to identify the world in which he found himself as
being of his own making or as still including him within its space.

One can observe the same historical blindness in a tract such as C. F. G. Masterman's *Condition of England* (1909), which described the "two differentiated
classes which the modern industrial life is daily creating": those who enjoy "all
branches of eager and sometimes morbid amusements" in the "Pleasure Cities,"
and "the new race which will be evolved out of these strenuous gnomes who
labour in the heart of the city congestions."[125] Masterman continued his commentary on the latter group with an urban vision that reeks of the dystopian future of the Morlocks, but without even the grudging admission of technical and
physical accomplishment Wells had grafted onto the racial evolution of the latter.
Masterman's creatures are born of subterranean technology rather than the passage of time: "You may discern in places the very pavements torn apart, and tunnels burrowed in the bowels of the earth, so that the astonished visitor from afar
beholds a perpetual stream of people emerging from the middle of the street,
seemingly manufactured in some laboratory below."[126] There was a large dollop
of irony in Masterman's vertical separation of classes, but no sense of the utopian
potential that the distance of speculative fiction allowed to be intertwined (consciously or unconsciously) with its dystopian realism.

The hallmark of the abstract space desired by so much of modernist architecture is to be placeless, severed from any past whatsoever. The turn-of-the-century
subterranean utopias anticipated this new placelessness in their determination
that the only space in which a perfectly ordered society could still be imagined
was an inorganic future underground. By contrast with the practical considera-
tions of urbanism and the ideological unity required of abstract space, speculative fiction readily exposed the commodity character of space as simultaneously
abstract and concrete: "abstract inasmuch as it has no existence except by virtue
of the exchangeability of all its component parts, and concrete inasmuch as it is
socially real and as such localized."[127] The analysis is especially pointed in Wells's
fiction. After his initial impulse to take for granted the space in which he finds
himself, the Time Traveller cannot avoid concretely localizing the Eloi and Morlocks in terms of their temporal relation with the social space of 1895 London,
just as Graham recognizes his own memories in the underground factories of latter-day London. What the Time Traveller is unable to do, as opposed to Graham,
is to recognize the social contradictions displaced temporally from their reality in
the present.

This thesis was programmatically illustrated by E. M. Forster ten years later in his short story "The Machine Stops," where the underground London of the future is not the topographical materialization of a vertical society but an allegorical representation of capitalism. The Machine, which has enabled the creation of a perfectly masculinist subterranean space, is described in the language of progressive alienation: "No one confessed the Machine was out of hand. Year by year it was served with increased efficiency and decreased intelligence. The better a man knew his own duties upon it, the less he understood the duties of his neighbour, and in all the world there was not one who understood the monster as a whole. . . . Progress had come to mean the progress of the Machine."[128] The way to freedom from the Machine passes through the discovery of a dark, organic underworld, a space replete with meaning and history that eventually leads Kuno, the story's youthful protagonist, to the surface and to a vision of the rolling hills of Wessex.

The first step is to "recover" the "lost . . . sense of space," the meaning of "near" and "far."[129] He knows that the "vomitories," the official links to the surface through which airships connect to other subterranean cities, will not allow him to reach the real surface; instead, he decides to look for the ventilation shafts that must have been made for the workers when the city was built. In other words, he recovers the material history of the site, its everyday character as a lived space.

> One thing was certain. If I came upon them anywhere, it would be in the railway-tunnels of the topmost story. Everywhere else, all space was accounted for. . . . The tunnels, of course, were lighted. Everything is light, artificial light; darkness is the exception. So when I saw a black gap in the tiles, I knew that it was an exception, and rejoiced. . . . I loosened another tile, and put in my head, and shouted into the darkness: "I am coming, I shall do it yet," and my voice reverberated down endless passages. I seemed to hear the spirits of those dead workmen who had returned each evening to the starlight and to their wives, and all the generations who had lived in the open air called back to me, "You will do it yet, you are coming."[130]

Kanu leaves behind the white light of the tunnels as he leaves behind their white noise, the omnipresent hum of the Machine.

Once he has emerged, the tone of the narrative veers sharply into horror. It is as if, now that the veil of alienation has been lifted, the ideology of the Machine can be made visible, revealing the "Mending Apparatus" as a swarm of giant, white worms, maggots eating away at the rotting body of the Machine: "A worm, a long white worm, had crawled out of the shaft and was gliding over the moonlit grass. . . . The worm let me run all over the dell, but edged up my leg as I ran. . . . Oh, the whole dell was full of the things. They were searching it in all directions, they were denuding it, and the white snouts of others peeped out of the hole, ready if needed . . . and down we all went intertwined into hell."[131] The de-

nouement of the story is also classically Marxist: the Machine, simply and inevitably, stops. What follows is not, however, revolution, but death and destruction for Kanu and for Vashti, his mother, epitomized in an apocalyptic crash of
the underground railway:

> For the tunnel was full of people—she was almost the last in the city to have taken
> alarm. People at any time repelled her, and these were nightmares from her worst
> dreams. People were crawling about, people were screaming, whimpering, gasping for
> breath, touching each other, vanishing in the dark, and ever and anon being pushed
> off the platform on to the live rail.[132]

The analysis of the space of monopoly capitalism is astonishingly prescient,
down to the repression of the traditional underground space that Forster, along
with other modernist writers such as Lawrence and Woolf, valued so highly.

Because Forster's conception of space within the story remains wholly
metaphorical (except, perhaps, for the final vision of the train crash), his story
cannot offer any possible solution to the problem it presents. Apart from the underground apocalypse and the brief earlier glimpse of aboveground survivors living a precapitalist life hiding in the Wessex hills, it is a hopeless vision, received
at the time it was published primarily as a parodic critique of Wells's projects for
a socialist future.[133] This is typical of the modernist response to changes in the
representation of urban space. Unlike late nineteenth-century underground visions, which retained a strong sense that the world was moving forward and that
what was needed was a correct understanding of the direction in which it was
moving, modernist undergrounds were static—either highly mythic or wholly
displaced from the urban space they continued to depend on; either a space of
capitalism, as with Forster, or a precapitalist but unreal space, as we will see in
chapter 2. When materially urban, on the other hand, they lacked any underground, any apparent sense of the vertical space of the city.

In William Morris's 1890 socialist utopia, *News from Nowhere,* by contrast, the
vision of an attainable future could still be prompted by a routinely nightmarish
ride on the District line not dissimilar to Vashti's experience: "As he sat in that
vapour-bath of hurried and discontented humanity, a carriage of the underground railway, he, like others, stewed discontentedly."[134] Morris imagined a future society—achieved, like Forster's, following war, destruction, and suffering—
in which the vertical space of capitalism would have been leveled out without
eliminating historical memory. The antinomies of modern society projected onto
the vertical space of capitalism—labor vs. leisure, drudgery vs. pleasure, childhood vs. adulthood, working class vs. leisure class—are resolved by reconfiguring
the cityscape. Monumental and mythic London remains—the houses of Parliament, Trafalgar Square, the British Museum, the East End—but bereft of their
traumatic connotations: the museum is inhabited by an old man who yearns for

the "bad old days"; the houses of Parliament are used as a dung heap, simultaneously solving the primary Victorian problem of waste disposal and taking a cheap shot at the political topography of London. The journey taken by the narrator is neither below ground nor to the surface but out of the city and up the river to a pastoral vision of loss and longing. Unlike the later modernists, Morris was able to excavate a positive image from the traditional underground buried beneath the present-day cityscape.

While the London-based utopias of Hay, Bulwer-Lytton, Wells, and Forster all constituted their future cities in varying degrees on the coming space of the inorganic underground, the utopias of Paris-based writers Auguste Villiers de l'Isle-Adam and Gabriel Tarde duplicated Morris in their attempt to envision a pastoral utopia, although they rooted that utopia firmly in the tradition of the organic underground. Notwithstanding that the central figure of *L'Eve future* was the American inventor Thomas Alva Edison, Villiers took the familiar appellation "the Wizard of Menlo Park" quite literally, depicting an Edison longing to have invented his phonograph in an earlier age, when he could have recorded the voice of God, or the Sibyl's chants. Edison's "underground Eden" is composed of two huge caves where the Algonquin tribe once buried their dead. His is not an ideal community so much as an ideal space concealing an ideal invention, the "artificial, electromagnetic woman," the future Eve. Villiers imagines a technological underground reunited with the feminine underworld of magic and desire: "—You have here a sort of scientific materialism that puts to shame the imaginary world of the Arabian Nights! cried Lord Ewald.—But you must also realize, Edison replied, what a marvelous Scheherazade I have here in Electricity. ELECTRICITY, my lord!"[135] Edison imprints the features of Ewald's recalcitrant beloved onto the body of the artificial woman, and Ewald departs with his perfect companion for his English castle; but the new Eve is destroyed during a shipwreck and fire. According to Rosalind Williams, Villiers was a deeply religious writer who was warning his materialistic society against the dangers of technological paradise. If so, he did it with recourse to the entire paraphernalia of the traditional underground. Whether the potentials of electricity are a further temptation of the Devil or another lost paradise, the subterranean metaphors of Villiers do not evidence the slightest break with the tradition before him; the technological underground is incorporated into the vast and holistic subterranean armature of the cultured Parisian of the late nineteenth century.

The case is somewhat different with the physicist and philosopher Tarde, who produced, like Hay, a bona fide subterranean utopia; unlike Hay, it was predicated on the repudiation of the technological underground as it was being conceived at the turn of the century. Williams's account of Tarde is uncharacteristically confused. She first introduces Tarde's "neo-Troglodytes" in the context of the technological utopias of Hay and Bulwer-Lytton; later on, however, she admits that "this utopia has nothing to do with technological invention."[136] Her explanation is that Tarde uniquely depicts "what might happen if an authentic social revolution were to direct technological change."[137] This is accurate in that Tarde, like Morris, was concerned with projecting social revolution into a viable urban future. It is inaccurate in that the formation of the underground society occurs only following an aboveground conflagration and ice age put down to the decadent abuse of new technology by the global state. Tarde's satirical target may have been Platonic idealism, but the causality of the narrative clearly predicates the dying of the sun on the misplaced energies of the "grand Asiatico-Americano-European federation," its perfect domination of nature, and its new tower of Babylon.[138] The choice of the neotroglodytes to return to the caves is, quite literally, a retreat from technology and a return to nature. Led by the eccentric Miltiades, a throwback to the great explorers of the past, the few thousand survivors burrow into the earth, where they create an inorganic wonderland bereft of all living things except people. For food, they scavenge the deep-frozen stores of meat that had been stockpiled for the billions who had inhabited the surface; they tap the energy of the earth's core for machines to pipe down and melt great blocks of ice for water. There are some restrictions on their lifestyle, most particularly the prohibition of sexual intercourse to avoid overpopulating the fragile ecosystem. Nor is the new world trouble free; the leader himself is killed near the end of a savage war between the "workers' cities" and the "artists' cities," followed by a violent schism in the latter between those favoring unrestrained love and those legislating "wisely regulated love."[139] Broadly speaking, however, Tarde's future vision simply imagined a space in which a hunting-and-gathering society could enjoy the same quality of life as the modern Parisian.

The central principle of Miltiades's doctrine of "neotroglodytism" is a natural metaphor of "interiorization": to turn away from the cold external gaze of the dying sun and into the "warm heart" of the earth: "There, down there, far down, is the promised Eden, the place of deliverance and beatitude."[140] This inorganic but natural world offers the key elements sought by later subterranean urbanism and bunker architecture: electric light and good ventilation (along with artificially preserved food). As René Schérer observes, Tarde's utopia is an anti-Platonic philosophical tale, espousing a radical and materialist monadism in place of the external and unreliable ideals of Platonic forms.[141] It is typical for his time that Tarde chose to couch his philosophy in a subterranean landscape, whereas later philosophies of interiority would bypass the macrocosm for the less concrete and more narrative metaphor of descent into the self. The two navel points of Tarde's text indicate the past and future of the philosophical underground. The theme of neotroglodytism is purification (and it is thus significant that no mention is ever made of the sanitary measures necessary to deal with the inevitable organic waste); its endpoint is described in the sociological speculation of one of the eminent scholars of the future, who with "Dantesque precision" predicts a concentric concentration of social types as the neotroglodytes move progressively closer to the cooling core of the earth, down to "the last man, sole survivor and sole heir to a hundred successive civilizations, reduced to himself and self-sufficient amid the immense provisions of science and art, happy as a God because he understands everything, because he is capable of anything, because he has just discovered the last word of the great enigma."[142] Rather than propel humanity forward, the pinnacles of technology and aesthetics seem rather to enable a paradoxical devolution all the way back to God in the garden of Eden before he has even created Adam, and long before evil has entered the world from somewhere outside. Somehow, Tarde could not resist incorporating the mirror-image of devolution and neotroglodytism as well. One day, exploratory excavations discover the society's negation inhabiting the same utopian space: a group of Chinese who had gone below with none of Miltiades's precautions and who had soon been reduced not only to cannibalism but to the cultivation of vegetables, having lost all memory of their life above: "In what promiscuity, in what filthy rapacity, lies, and theft did these unfortunates live!"[143] Faced with the choice of civilizing or exterminating these barbarians, the neotroglodytes instead simply seal up the opening and move on. Even the repressed image of the other underground past, "those ancient servants of men," cannot sidetrack for long Tarde's vision of a world reduced to its essence, honed like a diamond with all organic untidiness left behind. It is testimony to the difficulty of representing that vision in an urban society, however, that Tarde must still poach from the organic tradition the philosophical and material victuals of his future.

Only in the representational space of the Paris underground, however, could such a sublation of the organic by the inorganic underground have occurred; for Tarde left no doubt that even the extreme end of his vision occupied a city, if a city subsumed within a single body. Morris, by contrast, was able to imagine reconciliation only by the elimination of the city as he knew it. His medievalist London is charming and compelling, but predicated on a disastrous war. The underground cities of his contemporary utopians were equally separated from the present by some sort of man-made cataclysm, but their spatial imagination remained contemporary. The underground city was constituted out of nineteenth-century iconography. The London underground was especially potent as the dystopian imagination of the city and the forthcoming masculine space; underground Paris foresaw technology banished from the underground altogether or wedded to it in unforeseen and eccentric ways. The ferment for change contained in the oppositional underground could be situated within the new space; the new space in London could exist only in opposition to it.

Subterranean Order

This book deals strictly with *urban* conditions, and its main thesis is that such a vast and complicated machine as the modern great city can only be made adequately to function on a basis of strict order. We are to forgo, or to relegate to a minor place, pleasures arising out of picturesqueness or of what is merely pretty or wilful, and to confine ourselves to the sterner delights which severe and pure forms can give us.

FREDERICK ETCHELLS (introduction to the English translation
of Le Corbusier, *The City of To-morrow and Its Planning,* 1929)

Just as the majority of plans for the London Underground and the Paris Métro began at the same time in the 1840s, and resembled each other closely, so were architectural plans for reordering the metropolitan centers quite similar. The representation of space varied far less than the representational space that resulted from, first, the long process from plans to realization, and, second, the everyday use of the place. The two dominant ideas of the twentieth-century city, "spatial urbanism" and "subterranean urbanism," writes Ragon, were sketched out in the nineteenth century.[144] Both were predicated on the underground: the first, derived from the view from above, became the vertical city; the second, derived from the view from below, became the new underground. They are two approaches to the same fundamental urban problem: to order the "quintessentially disordered" space of the city.[145] As Peter Hall argues, this disorder was both physical—the problems of food, water, waste, and transport—and social and moral —the problems of crime and of penury.[146] The connection between the two was explicitly drawn throughout the nineteenth century; it remained operational through the twentieth, but far less openly. In this section, I address the strategic approach to physical disorder; chapter 3 specifically addresses the social and moral aspects that were enunciated as underground pathology.

The *passage* was a major influence on the nineteenth-century urban utopianists: the covered "gallery-streets" of Fourier's phalanstery; the sidewalks and street-crossings of Etienne Cabet's "Icarius," covered with glass in the winter and retractable canvas in the summer; the elevated and covered arcades encircling the city in William Mosely's Crystal Way and Sir Joseph Paxton's Great Victorian Way; even Ebenezer Howard's Garden Cities were conceived with covered commercial galleries. Unlike the *passage* itself, however, these plans were all self-contained pedestrian networks; rather than a threshold through which to pass or in which to linger, they envisaged a complete separation of the pedestrian both from vehicular traffic and from nature. Joseph Paxton's 1855 scheme, banking on the enormous cultural capital he had accumulated from the success of his Crystal Palace design for the Great Exhibition of 1851, projected a circuit of the city on the basic model later followed by the Circle line. The Great Victorian Way, however, was to be built aboveground, seventy-two-feet wide, with four tracks, incorporating shops and private houses, the entire ten-mile "girdle" to be lined with Staffordshire tile. Nevertheless, the scheme was regarded as commercially viable, and the drawings were exhibited in the House of Lords and shown to Queen Victoria and Prince Albert, who approved of the project.[147] In his monograph on Paxton, George Chadwick argues that the importance of the project lay not in the large-scale use of glass, iron, and vitreous tile but in the principle of a workable combination of street and railway.[148] The distinction is instructive: what drops out of the scheme for the twentieth-century architect is precisely what was utopian about it, for the only way to realize the combination of street and railway in this manner without the transparency of iron and glass was to build it underground. In practice, it is difficult to imagine what Paxton's Great Victorian Way would have done to the cityscape around it; what is undeniable is that it combined what was seen as positive in underground London—shelter from weather, noise, and traffic—with an avoidance of what was seen as negative in it—the disorder, darkness, and stuffiness of the world below.

The same image is evident in Fourier's *rues-galéries,* which made the covered arcade a general architectural principle, stressing the primary concerns of shelter and control over space that would characterize later subterranean urbanism:

> The Phalanx has no outside streets or open roadways exposed to the elements. All portions of the central edifice can be traversed by means of a wide gallery which runs along the second floor of the whole building. At each extremity of this spacious corridor there are elevated passages, supported by columns, and also attractive underground passages which connect all the parts of the Phalanx and the adjoining buildings. Thus, everything is linked by a series of passageways which are sheltered, elegant, and comfortable in winter thanks to the help of heaters and ventilators.[149]

The degree to which Fourier's project was more progressive than Paxton's can be measured by the degree to which it remained purely speculative. In its systematic application, it applied the same principle to the entire social space, rich or poor, high or low; Paxton's would clearly have served an exclusively middle-class clientele, and would inevitably have created a physical space below its elevated tracks that would have been reserved for the rest of the population. Mosely's Crystal Way, similar in scheme to Paxton's except that it divided the railway level from the pedestrian and was relatively less ambitious in scope, envisioned an entrance fee for "the privilege of climbing up and using it"[150] (figure 1.36). Whereas verticalized space cannot help but remain a hierarchized space, the global scope of subterranean urbanism levels out spatial hierarchy, and consequently it remains socialistic in potential, although seldom in practice.

What happened in the twentieth century was that the utopian aspects of subterranean urbanism, expressed in the nineteenth century first through the potential of iron-and-glass architecture and then through electricity, were wholly sub-ordinated to the principle of urban order. As Ragon has observed, it was the embrace of industry by socialism that paradoxically made available the "new ideology . . . of production and technology" to the bourgeoisie.[151] To express the matter differently: the capacity for a holistic view of the underground proper to the space of Paris was applied to the vertical segregation endemic to the space of London to create the landscape of modernism. The first three decades of the twentieth century saw not only the emergence of a new awareness of space and its production but also the development of a global conception of space, of the idea that "things can not be created independently of each other in space."[152] From Bauhaus in Berlin to the futurists in Turin and Paris to Le Corbusier in Paris, the global conception of space put forth by the avant-garde of art and architecture led in practice to a positive embrace of the technological extreme of the modern metropolis, an urge to eliminate all traces of the past, of the disordered, of the domestic. Although spanning the spectrum of political (and apolitical) stances, nearly every one of these movements declared itself to be a progressive social and aesthetic force. Nevertheless, as Lefebvre noted in retrospect, their practical effect was to eulogize a space perfectly characteristic of and suited to the abstract space of capitalism: the vertical city.

For Le Corbusier, the matter came down to a choice between an organic but diseased past and an inorganic but healthy future in a machine for living. "Our world, like a charnel-house, is strewn with the detritus of dead epochs," he proclaimed. "The great task incumbent on us is that of making a proper environment for our existence, and clearing away from our cities the dead bones that putrefy in them. We must construct cities for to-day" (figure 1.37).[153] Presented in the Pavilion of the New Spirit at the 1925 Exposition of Decorative Arts in Paris, Le Corbusier's scheme called for the demolition of the historic center of Paris from the Marais in the east to the Champs-Élysées in the west, and from the Seine in the south to the grands boulevards in the north.[154] In its place would be erected a grid system of sixty high-rise office buildings, low-rise apartments, divided highways, subways, and green spaces. Like the street-cuttings of the Second Empire before it, Le Corbusier's plan responded to a real crisis in housing and a widespread concern over the living conditions of the urban poor by eliminating the entire site of the problem.

Characteristic of Le Corbusier's modernism was the insistence on revolutionary change; to his mind, nothing was more futile than the current practice of small-scale demolition and reconstruction, work undertaken primarily with profit in mind anyway.[155] Instead, he proposed eliminating the traditional conception of the "corridor-street" altogether as entirely unsuitable for the problems of modern circulation. Where his predecessor Eugène Hénard had proposed a rationalized plan of striated underpasses to allow space for automobiles, pedestrians, and the Métro to circulate independently of one another, Le Corbusier was

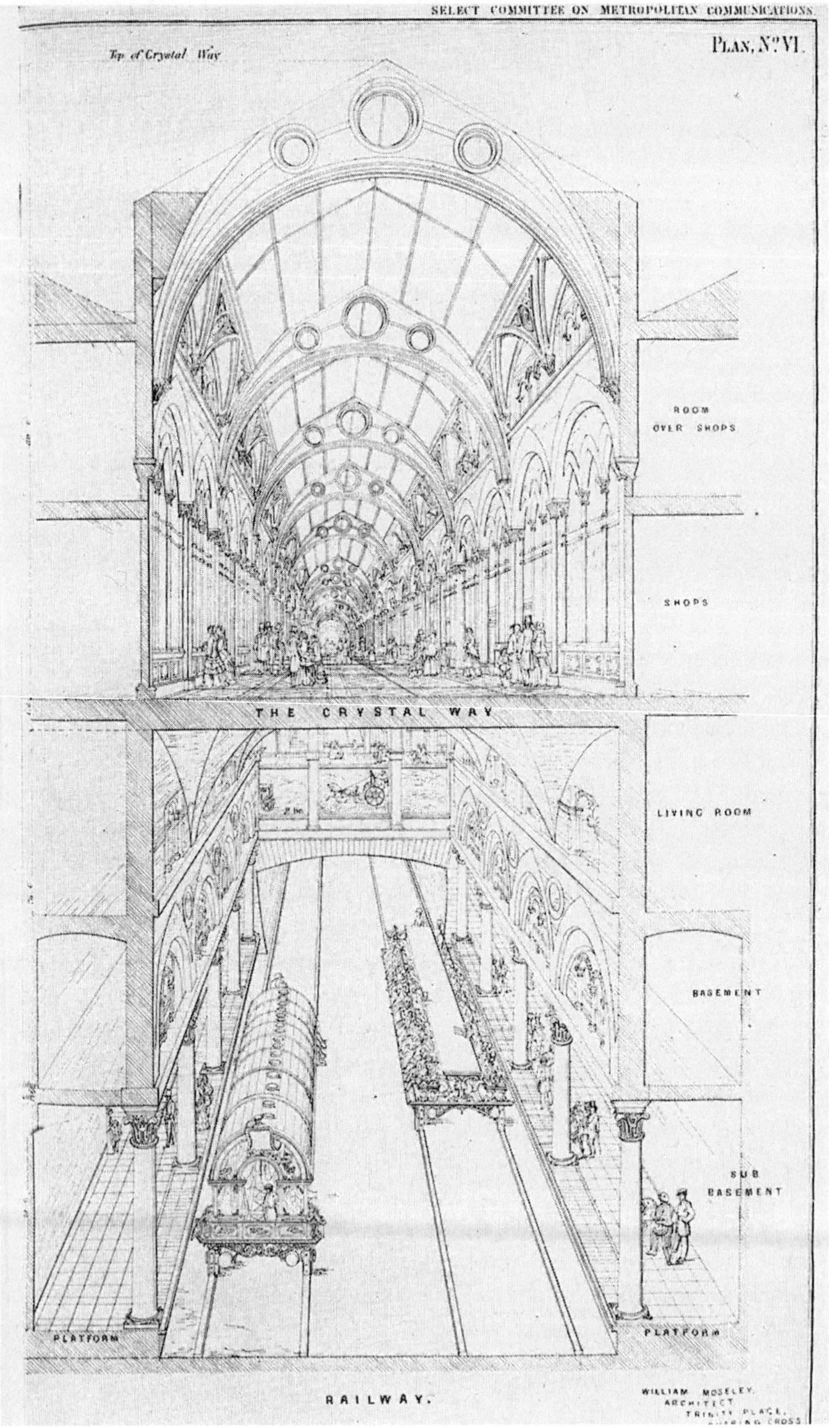

Top of Crystal Way

ROOM OVER SHOPS

SHOPS

THE CRYSTAL WAY

LIVING ROOM

BASEMENT

SUB BASEMENT

PLATFORM

PLATFORM

RAILWAY.

WILLIAM MOSELEY,
ARCHITECT,
TRINITY PLACE,
CHARING CROSS.

Facing page

1.36. Subterranean urbanism in Victorian London: William Mosely's Crystal Way. Illustration by William Mosely, *The Crystal Way*, in "Report from the Select Committee on Metropolitan Communications," *Parliamentary Papers* (1854–55), vol. 10, plan no. 6. Reproduced by permission from the Institute for Historical Research, London.

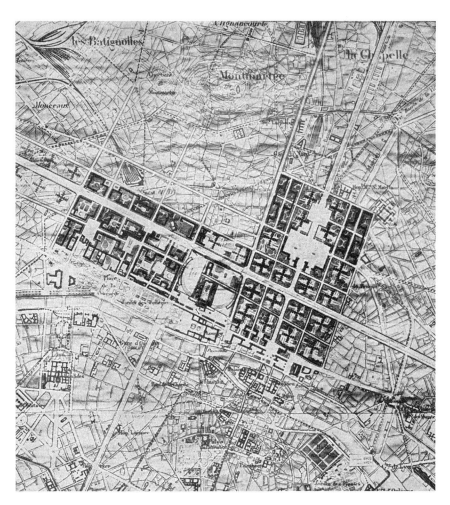

1.37. Le Corbusier's Voisin Plan: a modernist solution to a nineteenth-century problem. From Le Corbusier, *Urbanisme* (Paris: Crès, 1925): 272–73.

persuaded that the entire city should be remade, thus "creating a *vertical* city, a city which will pile up the cells which have for so long been crushed on the ground, and set them high above the earth, bathed in light and air."[156] The "most diseased quarters of the city" would disappear, narrow and congested streets would be replaced by wide highways and swaths of green space in a "gridiron" organized around the new high-rise city made possible by technological advances in reinforced concrete. In the center would be the business city, around it the residential city, and linking them would be subterranean railways and roads, with the central underground station located beneath what had been the Palais-Royal.

To make his argument, Le Corbusier made ample use of the nineteenth-century rhetoric of urban hell. "Is this a picture of the seventh circle of Dante's Inferno?" he queried rhetorically in the caption to an aerial photograph of a central Paris the height of which had long been legally limited to seven stories (figure 1.38). "Alas, no! It shows the terrible conditions under which hundreds of thousands of people have to live. . . . In our walks through this maze of streets we are enraptured by their picturesqueness, so redolent of the past. But tuberculosis, demoralization, misery and shame are doing the devil's work among them [*triomphent sataniquement*]."[157] The "bird's-eye view" was necessary to forestall the sentimental attachment to the past that was anathema to the "spirit of to-day."[158] Although clearly born of the debates over the shape of Paris and that city's tradition of top-down public works, the Swiss-born Le Corbusier's template was designed to be applied to any city, anywhere; that is the essence of the view from above, the abstract conception of urban space. The "international style" reflected a new detachment of representations of space from national concerns. Le Corbusier did make the concession in his Voisin Plan of preserving some of the central Parisian monuments amid the new business city; like the Disneyfied downtowns at the end of his century, they would become isolated relics of the past. The most influential aspect of his and the other modernists' plans were the generic office blocks and the inhospitable and alienating low-income housing projects that sprang up all over the developed world in the 1950s and '60s. As the nostalgic Parisian Jacques Tati wryly pointed out in his 1967 film comedy, *Play Time,* the modern tourist felt at home everywhere because everywhere boasted the same international style architecture. Detached from such fundamental questions as "how to make a human architecture in an age of machines,"[159] architectural modernism's appropriation of the utopian aspects of inorganic space eschewed the egalitarian potentialities of the new underground—everyone living and riding together in an identical space. It also ignored the potential for spatial reorganization; the underground public transport networks and open public spaces might have allowed the social networks eliminated by the forced relocation of traditional public space to reemerge in new forms. Tati gamely predicated his film on the possibility of rediscovering the stubbornly playful vieux Paris within the anonymous and mechanized spaces of the new, and on the inevitable crumbling of the modernist ideal of order. Where such myths of representational space were less deeply rooted, however, the contradictions of abstract space were much more likely to register as a negative underground of crumbling infrastructure, poor quality of building material, and high levels of crime than as a positive space of utopian potentiality and freedom.

1.38. A bird's eye view of central Paris in 1925: Le Corbusier's "seventh circle of Hell." From Le Corbusier, *Urbanisme* (Paris: Crès, 1925): 267.

Why did this occur? Just as many of the urbanists between the wars were pro-gressive if not radical, proponents not only of the Le Corbusian vertical city but of the horizontal, decongested satellite cities genuinely expected to eliminate so-cial and spatial hierarchies rather than to solidify them.[160] Rejecting the vertical stratification and negative underground space of London, the Garden City movement in England, influenced by Morris, sought to eliminate the traditional city entirely in favor of smaller-scale, semirural, pastoral agglomerations, scat-tered horizontally in linked constellations (figure 1.39). The development and marketing of these developments around London were closely tied to the expan-sion of the underground railway far into the suburbs. "Underground" became a slogan for the novel combination of pastoral living and high-tech transportation infrastructure, with "Metro-land" as its specific tag (figure 1.40). The *cités indus-trielles* of the Lyon-based urbanist Tony Garnier also eliminated problems of housing and traffic by spreading out horizontally in self-contained cities of thirty-five thousand inhabitants each. Space was to be divided and zoned, but on horizontal rather than vertical principles.[161] In his admiration at Garnier's ability to synthesize the nineteenth century's predictions into an "international style" before the fact, however, Ragon underestimates the problems created by horizon-tal expansion and segregation of this sort (even Le Corbusian high-rises were usually constructed on cheap land away from expensive central real estate): the loss of community, the dependence on long-distance and usually private trans-port, the creation of dead rather than green space, and the apparently inevitable social segregation. The success of Garnier's cité industrielle, like that of Morris's utopia, depended a priori on a radical change in social structure; without that change the rational divisions inevitably became hierarchical barriers as well, adapted to the exigencies of twentieth-century capitalism, that resulted in gated suburban communities for the wealthy and high-rise concrete housing projects for the poor.

Although aspects of modernist urbanism predated the First World War, 1914 marked a cutoff point for many of the progressive alternatives to the vertical, technologized city and sprawling suburbs that would come to dominate. Trench architecture and technology and the experience of trench warfare both at the front and at home had a formative effect on attitudes toward underground space, and, consequently, toward the modern cityscape; and it was London rather than Paris that offered the closest resemblance to that space. A new level of order had been obtained in the use of underground space, and a new level of tolerance reached for its most negative material aspects. At the same time, any positive or utopian aspect of the underground had been negated to its most diabolical ex-treme. The period between the two wars was marked, on the surface at least, by a hardened division between the rational and the irrational, the literal and the mythic, the aboveground and the underground. What most distinguished the projects of the interwar period from those of the nineteenth century was the dis-

1.39. Horizontal urbanism: the Garden City movement in England. Diagram by Ebenezer Howard in *Garden Cities of To-morrow* (London: S. Sonnenschein, 1902): 143.

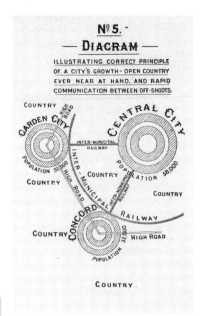

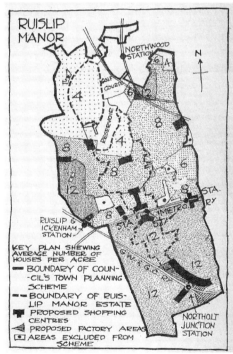

1.40. The Ruislip Manor Estate (development began in 1912) is shown within the larger region encompassed by the Ruislip-Norwood Town Planning Scheme. The area is served by both Underground and interurban railway lines. Diagram in Ewart G. Culpin, *London, The Garden City Movement up-to-date* (London: Garden Cities and Town Planning Association, [1913]): 42.

appearance of what now appear to us to have been the quaintness and naïveté of the material forms in which utopian dreams had previously been expressed.

Rather than projecting ambivalence, the Italian architect Antonio Sant'Elia, in *The Futurist Manifesto of Architecture 1914,* embraced the negative essence of modernity to a degree unthinkable to even the most enthusiastic nineteenth-century urbanite:

> We must invent and rebuild the Futurist city like an immense and tumultuous ship-yard, agile, mobile and dynamic in every detail; and the Futurist house must be like a gigantic machine. . . . The house of concrete, glass and steel, stripped of paintings and sculpture . . . must soar up on the brink of a tumultuous abyss: the street will no longer lie like a doormat at ground level, but plunge many storeys down into the earth, embracing the metropolitan traffic, and will be linked up for necessary inter-connections to metal gangways and swift-moving pavements.[162]

Instead of conceiving the future in terms of the past, Sant'Elia and the futurists tried to conceive of a concrete urban space that would have nothing of the past in it: "It will be for each generation to build its own city." The technology was no longer speculative; only the conception of space was. Although the desire of so much of modernism was an understandable impulse to reject nineteenth-century ornamentation of any sort, whether plastic, linguistic, or political, it is difficult to imagine the accompanying nihilism without reference to the abyss about to be realized in the trenches.

To continue to incorporate the urban underground it became necessary to embrace it completely or to eliminate it completely: hence the Dada and surreal-ist desire to demolish conceived space altogether into a chaos of representational space, the expressionist distortion of the surface appearance of the city into a riot of color and contorted lines, or the Brechtian alienation effect; hence architec-tural modernism's embrace of a new conception of the underground based on the elimination of the existing cityscape. Conversely, the affective underground could be found only outside the city: hence the conservative, especially German, recourse to rural myths of blood, soil, and home so influentially formulated by Spengler and Heidegger; hence the high modernist retreat into a mythic under-world ostensibly divorced from the realities of urban life. The utopian could be expressed only in terms of a complete break with the past; the past could be con-ceived only in terms of pure ideology. And yet, paradoxically, it was during these same decades that the first comprehensive theories of nineteenth-century urban culture began to be formulated: Walter Benjamin, Humphrey Jennings, Lewis Mumford, Mikhail Bakhtin, Henri Lefebvre, Siegfried Giedion, Siegfried Kra-cauer, and Dolf Sternberger all wrote or began writing their crucial formulations of the past hundred years during this period. Our ability to read the bas-fonds together with the infernal city in the imagery of the nineteenth-century under-ground depends on the interwar insights of these writers; a similar recourse to current urban theory can uncover similar connections between the above collection of cultural phenomena and movements of the entre-deux-guerres, which are usually treated in isolation one from another.

Over the last several decades, conventions of representation have shifted back toward a combination of the everyday with the abstract, and the latest underground volumes have tended to search for the quirky, the unexpected, and the folkloric as much as, if not more than, the technological. As Peter Jukes has persuasively argued, "Not so long ago people used to look at the city to get a glimpse of the future. In the first half of the [twentieth] century, projections of what the metropolis *would become* were as much a pastime as what it *has been* is today."[163] Jukes is interested in the "trick" played by history on such visions of change as a continuous, seamless process; instead, he writes, we get "the law of uneven development," the future metropolis cheek to jowl with traces of the old, and—indelible token of the current turn of the century—the imminent disappearance of the past. The underground is at the peak of the current wave of what Jukes sees as nostalgia for the past, the "buying and selling of the rubble" that remains from the constant redevelopment of, to borrow his example, Thamesside London.[164] And certainly one can argue that the underground is omnipresent in late twentieth-century and early twenty-first-century visions of the city because it is rapidly disappearing in its traditional form from the late twentieth-century and early twenty-first-century Western city. The hallmark of critical urbanism of the past few decades has been the conviction that the traditional representational space of the city is vanishing, wholly colonized by what Lefebvre termed the "abstract space of capitalism." Viewed from this perspective, the fascination with the feminine, organic underground negatively expresses unfulfilled desires displaced by the masculine, inorganic underground.

It is perhaps difficult to be enthusiastic over the fin-de-siècle obsession with commodifying the past, not only the much decried Disneyfication of city centers such as Time Square, but also the erstwhile bohemian neighborhoods just outside the inner fare zone in London—Camden Town, Islington, Shoreditch, Hoxton, and the newly redeveloped south shore of the Thames from Rotherhithe to Battersea—and the Paris swathe stretching from Les Halles and the Centre Pompidou through a sanitized Marais, a hipster's Bastille, and up into Belleville in the east. These retro underworlds offer subterranean shopping not only as the modern mall but as alternative culture: cheap fashion knockoffs, artifacts from the third-world, drug paraphernalia, thrift shops, underground music, dirt, grime, youth, noise. But lack of enthusiasm should not blind us to the fact that these spaces are quite similar to underground urban culture of the nineteenth century, down to the cacophony, squalor, and vitality, just as dismissals of them as pointless consumerism or nostalgia for the purer forms that existed before them can be found already in writers such as Mayhew. Development may move unevenly, and it may repeat itself, but it never literally moves backward. As Siegfried Giedion wrote back in 1928 about the nineteenth century, "Industry . . . had produced (unconsciously sometimes) forms of building that had taken architects a century or more to absorb into their formal armory"; in partnership with Walter Gropius, Giedion foresaw a new kind of architecture that would "help to heal the breach between industry and society," just as Le Corbusier during the same decade tried to answer the problem of "how to make a human architecture in the age of machines."[165] The failure of modernism to find a lasting synthesis of the antinomy of industry or machines and society or humanity is less a call to a new solution than to a recognition that the antinomy was in fact irreconcilable, at least within the economic system within which industry, machines, and people have been confined over the last few centuries. And as long as representations of underground space continue to emerge from the cracks that have formed in these concrete edifices, we will know that no resolution has been reached.

What we need to do instead of decrying change is to apply Giedion's insight to the analysis of the twentieth-century forms of building that architects have not yet or only just begun to absorb. We must inquire of the current forms of the urban underground the same things that we must learn to recognize in the nineteenth-century ones: what is being opposed, what is being displaced, what is being desired. If the simple answer is always capital, the sites of power, and happiness, respectively, it still remains to be seen which specific forms are taken by them. Like the traditional spaces of the village and the country that were overly eulogized by Lefebvre in the 1960s and '70s, the traditional space of the city offers both a glimpse of a utopian space and a reminder that that space was always also hellish. Despair over the apparently inexorable progress of global warming, the rapid diminishment of biodiversity, and the rampant destruction of the environment by those of us privileged enough to be able to notice them should not cause us to forget that life always has been well-nigh unendurable for most of the inhabitants of the planet. What is done to make the unendurable endurable may alter with the passage of time, but the fact that the task is usually managed does not. That it continues to be made bearable, that alternative spaces always appear, that the underground never disappears, is equally a given, for the simple reason that the human species is not distinct from but part of nature, however alienated from and destructive of nature that species may be. In the next two chapters, I explore this dialectic through two of the most dominant and most conflicted spatial representations of the nineteenth-century underground: the necropolis and the sewer.

2

THE MODERN NECROPOLIS

> We need not go to Herculaneum or Pompeii to find buried cities, for they occur beneath our own feet. And although they be cities or communities of *insects,* instead of *men,* the interest created by these underground habitations increases the more we study them.
>
> J. E. TAYLOR, *Natural History Rambles: Underground* (1879)

When Baudelaire asserted in *Les Fleurs du mal* that his brain was "A pyramid, an immense vault, / which contains more bodies than the common pit. / . . . a cemetery abhorred by the moon," he was reminding his readers of the existence of another city in the midst of Paris, its inhabitants far outnumbering the living beings of the metropolis above.[1] This subterranean city, too, had undergone massive change during the first half of the nineteenth century: evicted, dug up, and transplanted to the even more crowded but modernized confines of the Catacombes. Yet while it constituted a material Parisian link to the "otherworld"—of the past and of the afterlife—the necropolis remained subject to the fashions and fads of the nineteenth century. Baudelaire alluded to two of these in the lines above: the mania for things Egyptian inaugurated by Napoleon Bonaparte's North African campaign of 1798, with its particular fascination for the mysteries of the pyramids, the sphinxes, and the obelisks; and the vogue for the early Christian catacomb, the "cemetery abhorred by the moon," which began at the end of the eighteenth century and dominated the practical design and the popular conception of the nineteenth-century cemetery (figure 2.1). The paradox of Baudelaire's image—the city of the dead as a place teeming with life—was grounded in the religious beliefs underlying both ancient forms of burial. Those beliefs took on new meaning when revived in the western European metropolis, where more and more, both in metaphor and in reality, there arose separate, underground cities, teeming with life and bursting with misery, disease, and suffering: the mine, the modern cave dwelling, the slum. I wish to explore the relationship between these two cities as it was played out in two physically distinct spheres linked by their ties to an organic underworld of caves, tombs, and soil: the recourse to ancient forms of burial architecture to design the new cemeteries, and to ancient modes of subterranean habitation to make sense of new forms of underground living.

2.1. 5 October 1866: last entry of the year to the Paris Catacombes. Visits were allowed twice monthly to persons obtaining authorization from the prefect of the Seine. Illustration by Jules-Descartes Férat, *Interior of the Catacombs*, based on photograph by Félix Nadar (see fig. 2.4), in A. Hermant, "Les Catacombes de Paris," *Le Journal illustré* 3, no. 141 (21–28 October 1866): 1.

Later developments would seek to eliminate any sense of the organic from the process of modernization: the underground railway would introduce a new, technological space to the underground city; the drainage works of Bazalgette in London and Belgrand in Paris would bring a new order to the threshold spaces linking inhabitants above to dangerous waste below. The earlier necropolis, by contrast, appropriated the oldest spaces of the city precisely for their associations with antiquity. The fascination was rooted in the Roman ruins that were being excavated at this time out of the soil of both cities; in the man-made tunnels and caverns that had been dug in the Middle Ages under Paris as well as in suburban London villages such as Chislehurst and Blackheath, and which were now considered part of the natural landscape; in the cemeteries, charnel houses, and crypts scattered throughout both cities; in the plague-pits half-remembered in

London; in the Paris Morgue on the bank of the Seine. The necropolis provided, as is evident in Baudelaire's "Spleen II" above, a way of viewing the city from below, of concretizing its contradictions as a dialectic of antiquity and modernity; for much of the most technologically advanced work in the city was being undertaken within the most ancient of its spaces.

As I argued in chapter 1, the new underground would be conceived as a technological space emptied of social relations, distinct in space and outside of time, existing only in an abstract realm of instrumentality and efficiency. The twentieth-century cemetery would mirror the rationalized, segregated forms of other aspects of the modern city, such as transportation and dwellings; however, its nineteenth-century origins characteristically blended ancient and modern, familiar and novel, in the search for a form able to contain the contradictions that emerged from the application of the new conception of space to the underground. The most enduring image of equality—as well as one of the most ancient uses of underground space—, death and the rites accompanying it remains a place where the contradictions of modern society forcibly emerge. In contrast to the Devil, who features in thresholds to the underground and always figures conflict in the world above, the new underground and the necropolis both feature the underground qua underground, figuring conflict with the world above only when their ideal functioning is seen to have been disturbed.

Because its primary association was with death, the necropolis provided a naturalized image of a timeless and well-ordered space. The ancient sepulchral rites it evoked were spatial practices of reconciliation with mortality: the Egyptians built their pyramids as second palaces for the pharaohs; the early Christians sheltered in their catacombs alongside the remains of the martyred companions whom they would soon join in heaven. Whereas the new underground found security in imagining the complexities of the modern world perfectly ordered, controlled, and sealed off beneath the ground, the necropolis wedded those imaginings uneasily with traces of mythic reconciliation with disorder. Far more than the artificial environment characteristic of the inorganic, masculine underground, the security offered by the necropolis played on the attributes of an organic underground steeped in the feminine. These attributes range from the metaphysical to the practical: the rest and quiet of death; escape from the superficies of earthly concerns; safety from the authorities and the persecutions of the world above; the physical shelter that caves have provided from time immemorial. Such desires were straightforwardly expressed in ancient religions but not in the modern city, where the underground took on a far more contradictory symbolic function. In the discourse of Paris, that function could still be expressed as a social totality, incorporating both positive and negative attributes of the underground within a unified space. It emerged nevertheless as a cataclysmic image, fraught with conflict: his brain teems with the vitality of urban life, Baudelaire tells us, but the only fitting image for that totality is the necropolis, a city of the dead. So, while the necropolis provided an important vehicle for envisioning the primordial desires of autonomy, security, peace, and tranquility, that vision was invariably distorted by a hardened urban materialism that saw life underground as inhuman and debased, and death as a physical assault of rotting flesh and diseased corpses.

The Parisian necropolis retained the association between the utopian promise of security and the reality of urban hell as natural phenomena, but only bound up in imagery of violence and death. London presented a different relationship: the city of the dead could be depicted in all its pathology, but even the modest reconciliation of the modern cemetery could be found only in the suburbs. So, we do find imagery of an organic underground of a utopian purity unimaginable in France, but only in a pastoral setting explicitly inimical to the uninhabitably subterranean metropolis of London. Witness the following description in Kenneth Grahame's 1908 celebration of rural England, *The Wind in the Willows* (figure 2.2):

> The Mole found himself placed next to Mr. Badger, and . . . he took the opportunity to tell Badger, how comfortable and home-like it all felt to him. "Once well underground," he said, "you know exactly where you are. Nothing can happen to you, and nothing can get at you. You're entirely your own master, and you don't have to consult anybody or mind what they say. Things go on all the same overhead, and you let 'em, and don't bother about 'em. When you want to go up, up you go, and there the things are, waiting for you."
> The Badger simply beamed on him. "That's exactly what I say," he replied. "There's no security, or peace and tranquillity, except underground. And then, if your ideas get larger and you wanted to expand—why, a dig and a scrape and there you are! If you feel your house is a bit too big, you stop up a hole or two, and there you are again! No builders, no tradesmen, no remarks passed on you by fellows looking over your wall, and above all, no weather."[2]

It is central to the ideology of Grahame's novel that the "solid vaultings . . . the pillars, the arches, the pavements," the so-called "domestic architecture" of Badger's magnificent dwelling, a center of stability and shelter in the midst of the threatening Wild Wood, have been appropriated out of the ruins of a great city, presumably some refracted image of London. But by "clean[ing] out the passages and chambers," Badger has merely repossessed as natural space what had been there originally: "There were badgers here, I've been told, long before that same city ever came to be."[3] The modernist pastoralism of *Wind in the Willows* made explicit an unspoken rule of nineteenth-century representation: a natural urban underground—an urban space capable of giving positive expression to fundamental desires—can exist only in the past, dead, antique, in ruins.

It is instructive to compare Grahame's pastoralism with Gaston Leroux's roughly contemporary fantasy of a utopian community living in an unknown section of the Left Bank quarries under Paris. Entitled *Promenade de M. le com-*

2.2. Subterranean comfort: Mole and Rat relaxing in Badger's drawing room beneath the Wild Wood. Reprinted by permission of Atheneum Books for Young Readers, an imprint of Simon & Schuster Children's Publishing Division, from *The Wind in the Willows*, by Kenneth Grahame, illustrated by Ernest H. Shepard. Copyright 1933 Charles Scribner's Sons; copyright renewed © 1961 Ernest H. Shepard; and by permission of Curtis Brown Ltd., London, ©.

missaire de police Mifroid et de l'âme réincarnée de Cartouche A L'ENVERS DE PARIS, ou, Trois semaines chez LES TALPA, the episode occupies the final fifth of Leroux's early novel, *La Vie double de Théophraste Longuet* (1903).[4] It begins with the police commissioner and his quarry, Longuet, lost together in the Catacombes after a freak accident involving a drunken street worker. Following two days of subterranean wandering, they happen upon the lost city of the Talpa (Latin for "mole"), which has apparently been sealed off from the world above since the fourteenth century; its inhabitants still speak the medieval French *langue d'oïl.* Rather than the standard displacement into the future we saw in chapter 1, the Talpa are a lost enclave from the past, some twenty thousand–strong, living in individual cells of four hundred each. Like the anthropomorphized creatures of *The Wind in the Willows,* they are a benevolent cross between man and beast. After just half a millennium of isolation, they have evolved to suit their surroundings: their eyes have vanished, their noses and ears have grown enormous, and they possess ten highly sensitive fingers on each hand. The Talpa live on fish from an underground lake and migratory hordes of rats, from the remains of which they make clothing as well. Their architecture is tactile and ornate, and their society knows neither laws nor private property nor morality nor crime. Unable to exercise his quintessentially urban and modern profession, Mifroid loses patience after a fortnight; by contrast, his accidental companion Longuet loses himself in dissipation to the degree that he ceases temporarily to be homicidally possessed by the spirit of Cartouche. Unlike the later community in *Les Gaspards* (1973, discussed below), the Talpa are feminized and childlike, pre-Edenic noble savages, neither threatening nor pliable, content to inhabit a forgotten corner of subterranean Paris. The representational space of early twentieth-century Paris could thus still contain a pastoral utopia, but only severed from the modernized city above—the episode preceding that of the Talpa concerns a missing métro train and a highly technical discussion of routes and signals. Nor can it any longer be reconciled with the negative and transgressive power of the legendary criminal Cartouche, who, we are told, also sheltered underground in his day, and whose spirit retakes possession of Longuet once Mifroid has coaxed his new friend back to the surface of the present-day city.

To make sense of the enduring power of these pastoral images and their relation to urban change, we begin with the construction of the necropolis in late eighteenth-century Paris and the discourse surrounding it, then shift to related developments in London and the very different form taken by them there. The nineteenth-century fascination with relics, antiquities, archaeology, Egypt, Troy, Nineveh, Babylon, and Rome was in part a way of getting around the difficulty of expressing underground desires within the constraints of the modern metropolis. The constraints arose from the mobilization of subterranean imagery in its most negative form to represent conditions in the slums of the cities and the mines they so much resembled. As the newspaper columnist Delphine de Girardin wrote in 1838, "How one stifles in these dark, damp, narrow corridors which you are pleased to call the streets of Paris! One would think one was in an underground city, so heavy is the air, so profound the obscurity. Yes! One breathes more freely in the grotto of Posilippo. . . . And thousands of people live, bustle, and press together in the liquid darkness, like reptiles in a marsh."[5] There were two available identities through which to imagine oneself at home in such an environment: as a wild beast or as a corpse. Possessing far less actual subterranea and far less of a revolutionary past to be identified with them, the London discourse generally projected these qualities directly onto its poor. In Paris, by contrast, the Catacombes and carrières provided a location both real and mythical in which to play out the real and mythical consequences of the Revolution. Evoked as such in the present, this location was generally threatening, criminal, and atavistic, occupied by beasts, or, at best, urban savages. Unlike equivalent (mostly fictional) spaces in London, it never appeared without a sense of intrinsic connection with the world above and a promise of change, in however threatening a form.

For any of this material to be distanced enough to be contemplated intellectually required a further displacement in time, either in a historical fiction or in a novel re-creation of the past as a commodity in the present. As a tourist attraction, the Parisian Catacombes took on the trappings of a journey into the past of Christianity and a meditation on death, whether serious or comical in tone. In London, the catacomb became an integral and popular feature of the new, suburban cemeteries built to resolve overcrowding and disease in the urban center. For nineteenth-century writers, the catacomb, in specific, and antiquity, in general, possessed an epistemological function based on the simultaneously mythic and contemporary qualities of their role in nineteenth-century urban space.

We then move from the catacomb as a privileged space of knowledge to its counterpart as a nineteenth-century necropolis: the representation of the mine as an underground city inhabited by neotroglodytes, and the modern city as an expansion of the same representation, especially as formulated in the late nineteenth century by Emile Zola in his savage depiction of mining in *Germinal* and Jules Verne in his utopian paean to it in *Les Indes noires*. Where Zola mobilized the discourse of Paris to paint a social totality of suffering and rebellion, Verne set his novel in the countryside of Scotland, using the London discourse to imagine a subterranean pastoral. Following these French approaches to underground living near the end of the nineteenth century, I conclude with changing attitudes in London: first, English modernist appropriations of the nonurban necropolis and the subterranean dwelling to enunciate alternatives to a London increasingly regarded as an abyss of alienation in which nothing of value has survived; second, reactions to the experience of an entire city living underground during the Battle of Britain; and third, late twentieth-century mutations of these attitudes in countercultural movements in both London and Paris.

Revolution Underground

From the beginning, the history of the Revolution is . . . attached to that of the Catacombes.

EMILE GÉRARDS, *Paris souterrain* (1908)

Even more than the sewers, the carrières and the Catacombes lie at the base of the French equation between underground space and revolution. We see it, for example, in Victor Hugo's metaphor of the "mines" of religion, philosophy, economy, and revolution that undercut "the social edifice [*la construction sociale*]" and "call to each other . . . from one catacomb to the other"; we see it as well in the topographical symbolism of the space itself.[6] Philippe Muray has argued that the nineteenth century—or what he terms the concept of "*dixneuvièmeté*"—began not with the Revolution in 1789 but three years earlier, with the removal of the bones of the dead in the Cemetery of the Innocents to the newly established Catacombes.[7] The creation of the Ossuaire municipal in the carrières beneath the Montsouris Plain at La Tombe Issoire closely paralleled the chronology of the Revolution: ordained in 1785 by the Conseil d'Etat and consecrated the following year, the Catacombes were prompted by the need to suppress the Cemetery of the Innocents following the death by asphyxiation of several persons in the basements of nearby houses on the rue de la Lingerie near what is now Les Halles (figure 2.3). Parallel to the excesses of the Revolution, as Gérards ironically noted, equality reigned in the Catacombes "in an absolute manner."[8] Or, in the words of Félix Nadar, celebrated photographer of the Catacombes and the sewers:

> In this confused equality that is death, the Merovingian kings maintain an eternal silence side by side with the victims of the massacre of September '92; Valois, Bourbons, Orléans, and Stuarts haphazardly conclude their decomposition, lost among malingerers from the Cour des Miracles and the two thousand "of the Religion" put to death on Saint-Bartholomew's Day.[9] (figure 2.4)

As opposed to traditional church and churchyard burial, where status was marked by the location, size, and durability of the funerary monument, the only order of classification for the Catacombes was a record for each district of the cemetery from which the remains had been removed. The first cadavers to be interred directly into this egalitarian resting place were some of the earliest victims of the Revolution: workers, burghers, and soldiers who had been killed in the un-

2.3. *Le Charnier des Innocents, 1588*: a long tradition of the dead crowded in with the living. Illustration by Edwarmay, in the Musée Carnavalet, Paris. © Photothèque des musées de la ville de Paris.

2.4. The photographer Félix Nadar restages the transport of bones from the Catacombes. Photograph by Félix Nadar, "Mannequin pulling a cartload of bones," 1861. Cliché Félix Nadar. Archives photographiques. Coll. MAP © CMN, Paris.

rest following the dismissal of Louis XVI's finance minister, Jacques Necker. The quick-limed bones of casualties of later fighting and victims of prison lynchings all passed likewise straight into the passages of the Catacombes, which by the late nineteenth century would contain the remains of some eleven million Parisians.

The Catacombes gave material form to the principle of fundamental equality, although they did so in the brutal manner of millions of bones stacked upon and interlaced with one another. The literal pathology of the pre-Revolutionary city was seen to mirror its political unrest. In the words of Louis-Sébastien Mercier in 1783:

> The stench of cadavers makes itself felt in nearly every church; that is why many people are turning away from them and refuse to set foot in them. . . . And when one remembers that there have been burials in the Cemetery of the Innocents for over a thousand years, without waiting for the earth to finish consuming those deplorable remains—the imagination recoils in revolt at the pictures that assail it.[10]

The new Ossuaire not only cleared the air in the world above, it also reordered the world below, making it newly available for bourgeois visitors and less amenable to the criminal purposes of which it had traditionally been the province; the name and the new representation of space embodied in it soon referred by extension to the entire Left Bank network of carrières. As Elie Berthet explained his decision to set his 1854 novel, *Les Catacombes de Paris*, in the previous century, before the Revolution:

> But the *Catacombes*, with the admirable order that reigns today in their somber passages, would not have offered any great resources to the novel. I have thus carefully studied the period when the galleries were, so to speak, discovered, the time when their dilapidated state was compromising the solidity of a part of Paris and every day, at every hour, new cave-ins occurred to the consternation of the neighborhoods of the Left Bank.[11]

The ambivalence that reigns over this passage is characteristic of Parisian attitudes to the depths of their city: Berthet is quite convinced that the current order, both political and physical, is superior to that of previous centuries (his opening scene portrays an execution at the Place de Grève, "full of memories, but bloody memories"[12]); at the same time, he is clearly uneasy about the powerful forces contained within that space—among other threads, his novel concerns a plot to undermine the entirety of southern Paris through a series of subterranean explosions.

The very name coined for the Municipal Ossuary introduced the Roman lexicon by which the revolutionary Republic would soon identify itself; as Muray has observed, that allusive identity equally incorporated a new relationship between secular government and repressed church.[13] The Catacombes and carrières were a metonymy for the Revolution, whether the writer was Republican or Royalist, whether he or she supported the Restoration, the July Revolution of 1830, the July Monarchy of Louis-Philippe, the insurrection of 1848, the Second Empire, the Commune, or the Third Republic (figure 2.5). In a letter of 1798 to the Council of the Five Hundred pleading for the restoration of funds for consolidating the carrières, the commissioner of the Seine compared the ancien régime's ignorance that it "was dancing with its chains on top of a precipice" and the Revolution's overturning of natural order:

> On the one hand, the Revolution sometimes delayed, often suspended the works consolidating the ground we live on; on the other, the Conflict of Despotism and Liberty, the political ordeals, the *cannons of free men resounded through these vast subterranean passages, and shook the natural pillars supporting the Theater of our memorable battles.*[14]

What is clear even in this letter's somewhat incoherent set of analogies is that the author framed his argument not in favor of common sense but in terms of contrasting attitudes toward the bas-fonds of Paris. The Revolution had abolished all tradition and precedence; what could be counted on was its knowledge of and sympathy with the world below.

The physical instability, the concealed nature, and the unknown extent of the Catacombes, as well as of the carrières du Diable or de Montmartre in the north and the carrières d'Amérique in the northeastern Buttes-Chaumont, provided during each successive moment of unrest both legends and facts: a vivid metaphor for the city above and a concrete example of its hidden spaces. According to Gérards, many reports appeared during the revolutionary period that the Left Bank carrières were being used by conspirators.[15] In the north, the still active quarries whose gaping entrances dominated the base of the Butte Montmartre were the focus of similar lore: the site became known as Mont-Marat after the fugitive leader had taken refuge in its carrières in December 1789; rumors circulated following the flight of Louis XVI in 1791 that the king had also hidden himself there.[16] In the 1855 melodrama *Les Carrières de Montmartre,* set during the war of 1814, the local quarriers, joined by engineers from the Ecole Polytechnique and members of the National Guard, successfully repel the advancing enemy, despite the attempted sabotage of the tunnels in the hills on which their guns are placed.[17] During the June insurrection of 1848, some hundred insurgents had hidden themselves in the same quarries, where they were massacred by Cavaignac's troops and buried on the spot (figure 2.6).[18] Those taken prisoner were transferred from fort to fort by means of subterranean passages and quarries. According to one chronicler of the time, "The prisoners gave all the tunnels [*passages*] names of Paris streets, and whenever they met one another, they exchanged addresses."[19] In *L'Education sentimentale* (1869), Flaubert's novel of Paris around 1848, rumors of less controlled and more explosive activity in the Left Bank quarries are used to mock drawing-room speculation: "Many bourgeois had the same fantasy; people believed that men in the Catacombes were going to blow up the faubourg Saint-Germain; rumors issued from the cellars; suspect things could be

2.5. The underground metonymy made real: Versaillais forces hunting communards in the Catacombes in June 1871. Engraving by Smeeton Tilly, *La chasse à l'homme 17 juin 1871 dans les Catacombes*, in *L'Illustration* (17 June 1871). Musée Carnavalet, Paris. © Photo-thèque des musées de la ville de Paris.

seen through the windows."[20] In the practice of revolution and conspiracy, sub-terranean spaces functioned no differently than barricaded districts above or other secret meeting places. In the common fantasy of an apocalyptic blast from below, however, as with legends of Marat and Louis XVI sheltering under-ground, the fragmented space would be unified to express the power of opposi-tion through a single, determinant figure or event capable of overturning a social order projected onto the vertical topography of the city.

The vivid image of the physical disinterment of the centuries-old burial places of vieux Paris, the quickliming of the remains, and their removal pell-mell and in the dead of night into anonymous equality, fittingly reproduced the upheaval of the times. It was a directly ideological move; one of the first initiatives of the Convention related to sepulture was to transfer control over all aspects of it from the Church to the communal authorities.[21] Just as the guillotine was conceived as a means of eliminating inequity in modes of execution, burial was to be stripped of any trappings of hierarchy. In 1793, the remains of the rulers of France buried at Saint-Denis were dug up, the skeletons interred in two common pits, and the lead of the tombs and seals melted down to make bullets.[22] Louis XVIII later commissioned a botched restoration of the royal chapel; Napoleon III, wishing

2.6. "The pursuit of insurgents into the carrières of Montmartre, June 1848." From a lith-ograph by Eugène Cicero, in Emile Gérards, *Paris souterrain* (Paris: Garnier-Frères, 1908): 383.

to make Saint-Denis the resting place of his family as well, had the work done over by the Gothic revivalist, Eugène-Emmanuel Viollet-le-Duc. The tombs were restored, but only as cenotaphs; even if the symbolism could be reinstated, the material remains could not be recovered.

As Thomas Carlyle's language in *The French Revolution* suggests, the metonymy suited the depths of the Terror as well as the heights of its idealism: "The harvest of long centuries was ripening and whitening so rapidly of late; and now it is grown *white,* and is reaped rapidly, as it were, in one day. Reaped, in this Reign of Terror; and carried home, to Hades and the Pit!"[23] The bonelike whiteness of the harvest, the compressed time scheme, the echo of the London plague pits: Carlyle's "abyss" of terror equally invokes the Catacombes. The remains of celebrated figures ranging from Scarron, Couperin, Rameau, and Colbert to Danton, Robespierre, and Saint-Just all eventually found their way to the anonymity of the Catacombes, either as the remains from the cemeteries in which they were buried were transported there or directly from the guillotine at the Madeleine.

The religious tenor of Carlyle's language recalls the Christian tradition behind both the Catacombes and the equalizing effect of death. Just as the Revolutionary Tribunal revived Roman dress, so the Catacombes revived the tradition of Christian martyrdom in late pagan Rome. While the symmetrical arrangement of exposed bones echoed the practices of early modern Catholicism, the stone inscriptions scattered through the corridors and the book in which visitors were encouraged to contribute their thoughts recalled the sepulchral inscriptions of the Roman catacombs (figures 2.7 and 2.8). The rediscovery of the Roman catacombs themselves was a phenomenon of early modern Europe. Once the relics had been removed during the eighth and ninth centuries to protect them from invaders, the catacombs had been almost wholly forgotten. They were happened upon by accident by workmen in 1578, revealing, as one report had it, "the existence of other cities concealed beneath their own suburbs."[24] The pioneering explorations of Antonio Bosio were published in a massive folio volume, *Roma sotterranea,* in 1632, three years after his death. Séroux d'Agincourt began his own thorough but destructive research at the end of the eighteenth century, and the first half of the nineteenth saw a general revival of interest in early Christian art spurred by work in the Roman catacombs.[25]

Evidence of the endurance of this revival through the century, and of its syncopation with the mythology of the Revolution, is provided by *Les Catacombes de Rome,* a midcentury historical novel by "le bibliophile Jacob," nom de plume of the prolific antiquarian Paul Lacroix (1806–84). While Lacroix's eighteenth-century Rome, especially its catacombs, is carefully and ostentatiously documented, its Parisian echoes beg the reader to receive the central Catholic-Jewish conflict as the struggle between the upper and lower classes during the Second Empire. There are two subterranea in this Rome: those of the ancient Christians, deserted and dangerously labyrinthine, not yet opened up for the tourist trade; and the

2.7. Nineteenth-century *vanitas*: one of the five rooms in the crypt of the Capuchin convent of Santa Maria della concezione, Piazza Barberini, Rome. The crypt was dedicated in 1797. Photograph in Padre Domenico da Isnello, *Il Convento della Santissima Concezione de' Padri Cappuccini in Piazza Barberini di Roma* (Viterba: Coop. Tipografica "Unione," 1923): 126.

2.8. Inscription of Pope Damasus in the papal vault, catacomb of St. Callixtus. Illustration in Albert Kuhn, *Roma: Ancient, Subterranean, and Modern Rome, in Word and Picture* (New York: Benziger Brothers, 1913–[16]): 241, fig. 291.

metaphorically underground space of the Jewish ghetto, legacy of the ancient Roman cloacae or sewers, as the catacombs are of their burial practices. While the necropolis contains the buried secrets of the past and of martyred truth, the Jewish ghetto is another underworld, a separate city of poverty and vice redolent with the language of nineteenth-century social reform:

> The ghetto last century was as it remains today: a labyrinth of twisted lanes and pestilent cul-de-sacs; a pile of houses made of wood, pebbles, and pozzuolana, low, dark, hideous, and no less fetid than the streets they overhang. . . . In Rome, then as now, the Jewish quarter was the muddiest, foulest-smelling, darkest, and most horrible of the city's neighborhoods. . . . Among the sounds filling the air could be heard the muffled grumbling of the water draining into and flowing through the subterranean sewers bequeathed by ancient to modern Rome.[26]

The spatial displacement onto a different city permits the visualization of distinctions that in Paris were supposed to exist more invisibly. Lacroix's Rome is divided between a paranoid Jewish minority and a tyrannical inquisition; its common people are superstitious and easily manipulated. In between are to be found the resident Frenchmen—artists and archaeologists—and a noble Roman priest whose body, concealed in the catacombs, is the requisite object to resolve the complications of the plot.

Lacroix uses historical figures—the painters Hubert Robert (1733–1808) and Jean-Honoré Fragonard (1732–1806)—as principal characters, as if to certify the displacement of French concerns onto Roman soil.[27] Similarly, the plot relies on the temporal coincidence of Easter weekend and Passover, the confusion of lamb's blood with that of a priest, and accusations of cannibalism suitable for the mythical customs of an underground race. While presenting a detailed description of the catacombs and their rediscovery for the delectation of his readers, Lacroix eschews the utility of material knowledge of the world below for the resolution of the novel's plot. The hero listens with impatience to a "long archaeological digression . . . on the catacombs of Rome, on their origin, their history, their tombs."[28] Nevertheless, the local rituals of Easter Week in Rome—the conversion of a Jew, the "elevation" of the body of a saint from its niche in the catacombs—provide the necessary coincidences for a happy resolution. Meanwhile, the catacombs, although outside the city proper, turn out to issue, through an aqueduct, at the Piazza di Spagna, allowing Robert to emerge with the corpus delecti in time to prevent an unjust execution: "What whim led him into the subterranean aqueduct? But no, he was in the catacombs!"[29]

In the displacement to Rome, Lacroix divides the revolutionary image into two underground spaces. Confusion over the central crime revolves around whether it occurred within the confines of the ghetto or beyond the city walls, whether Father Alexander was butchered and eaten by the Jews in a variation of the traditional blood libel or whether his body was thrown into the catacombs.

The Jewish ghetto remains an ambivalent source of otherness, whether good, evil, or indifferent; by contrast, the catacombs present a mysterious power of justice superior to the equally occulted space of the inquisition: they swallow up the villainous inquisitor Badolfo; they release the body of Father Alexander, elevated as a modern saint, inspiring a chapel "still visible today"[30] to be erected at the place where Robert emerged with his body.

The familiarity of Lacroix's readers with the city of Rome, and the increase of tourism between the time of the novel and the time of writing is a recurring theme. Before making his descent into the catacombs (where he will become lost nevertheless), Robert studies Bosio and the other classics on the subject: "By comparing the map of *Roma sotterranea* with the one of the Roman countryside he had brought with him, he was able to limit the space he had to cover."[31] The plot describes the prerevolutionary irreconcilability of beliefs between the corrupt aristocracy of the Inquisition and the maligned and mysterious but basically mercantile Jews; the space partakes both of the distant resonance of early Christianity and the contemporary thrill of underground tourism. Rome is the "capital of the ancient and the modern world"; it was a combination that Parisian readers were equally invited to appreciate in the city around them.[32]

Although visited by the likes of the future king Charles X near the time of their first establishment in 1787, the Parisian Catacombes were not opened to the public until the beginning of the First Empire. Evidence for the popularity of visits at that time, especially among foreigners, can be found in an 1822 broadsheet, "Green in France; or Tom and Jerry's Rambles through Paris," one of many sequels to Pierce Egan's popular 1821 volume, *Life in London*. The illustration, one of twelve Parisian scenes, depicts a wall of skulls as background for the comic action described in a short verse:

> They went to view the Catacombs, and the place being dull and dark,
> Tom (as his usual custom was) resolved to have a *lark*.
> So he flipp'd into a corner, and as the company came on,
> He held a skull in Jerry's face, and gave a most tremendous groan.
> Jerry, started back amazed, and roared in a fright,
> And all the ladies shrieked in horror at the dreadful sight;
> Tom laugh'd at his adventure, to think how he had Jerry gull'd,
> And fear'd a living sportsman by a dead Dandy's skull.[33]

Just as their Regency rambles took them through high and low life in London, Tom and Jerry treat the morals of the Catacombes with equal aplomb, joking at the Dandy's skull, the *vanitas* of the dissolute life of the swell Londoner and his Continental counterpart.

The verses and reflections recorded in the register of the Catacombes, extracted by L. Héricault de Thury, Napoleon's inspector general of Subterranean Works, in his *Description des Catacombes de Paris* (1815), give a sense of the range of pious Catholic sentiment, platitudes, and bad jokes one would expect from such a site, neither wholly a church cemetery nor wholly a tourist destination. A short poem signed Causson plays on the ambivalence between order and disorder in the afterlife, the uneasy marriage between the symmetrical arrangements and the dissociation of particular bodies:

> Je suis un grand partisan de l'ordre,
> Mais je n'aime pas celui-ci.
> Il peint un éternel désordre,
> Et, quand il vous consigne ici,
> Dieu jamais n'en révoque l'ordre.[34]

> [I am a great partisan of order,
> But I do not like the one here.
> It depicts an eternal disorder,
> And, when he consigns you here,
> God never revokes the order.]

The order of the Catacombes reveals an underlying disorder that is compared by the concluding wordplay to the order of God, which is eternal and irrevocable. An echo of the revolutionary metonymy remains, as its new order is regarded as having caused an immense disruption of the divinely sanctioned ancien régime.

The Catacombes have seldom been associated with piety. Berthet, like Alexandre Dumas in *Les Mohicans de Paris,* set meetings of secret societies there; Dumas also staged the Charbonnerie from their depths. Travel writers such as Thomas Wallace Knox combined the tourist antics of Tom and Jerry with the indispensable crisis of separation from the group, and the loss of one's source of light and experience of absolute darkness. According to Dumas, young lovers of the quartier Saint-Jacques would use the Catacombes for their trysts; one midnight in the spring of 1897, a group of aesthetes staged a clandestine concert there, performing such predictably morbid pieces of music as Chopin's *Funeral March* and Saint-Saëns's *Danse Macabre.*[35] And, since at least the 1960s, loosely affiliated groups of cataphiles have explored, assembled and thrown parties in the carrières, the physical manifestation for them of the network of underground culture throughout Paris and France.

Public visits were forbidden between 1830 and 1859, on putative grounds of the degradation being suffered from the vandalism of visitors. In 1832, the mayor of Montrouge wrote to the prefect of the Seine, Count Rambuteau, requesting that the Catacombes be reopened in deference to the commercial interests of the area. The prefect's response suggests that the space was considered dangerously uncontrollable. Following the stock complaints about the need for structural work and the cost of guides and guards, the prefect entered into the heart of the matter: "Dangers that in spite of the guards' best efforts of surveillance could serve as a refuge to criminals" and the "profanation of thus exposing to view these masses of bones laid out with a quite unsuitable symmetry."[36] The combination of an attribution of impiety to the entire conception of such an ossuary with a fear of underground crime leads clearly back to the revolutionary associations of both. One could respond that the Capuchin crypt in Rome contains skeletal designs far more shocking than the symmetries of Paris—including chandeliers, picture-frames, and moldings of human bones—and that the corridors beneath the Capuchin convent in Palermo are lined with the mummified remains of five hundred years of patricians, dressed and propped upright. But in 1832, with the July Revolution still echoing, atheism and atavism were nevertheless the prefect's touchstones.

A popular novel such as Lilian Herbert Andrews's *Marie: A Story of the Morgue and Catacombs of Paris,* written in 1893 for Collier's "Once a Week Library," demonstrates the durability and the widespread dissemination of this underground mythology. The everyday world is so ordered, so well controlled by the likes of Henri, an undercover agent at the Palais de Justice, that the underground has separated off into a dreamworld, evident from above only in the ancient houses of the Latin Quarter: "so old that the only thing in the world toward which they can feel any reverence is the catacombs that whisper to them, through their cellars, ghostly tales of prehistoric ages."[37] The morgue and its exhibit of fresh cadavers and wax models is the focal point of the novel's pulp fantasies: women cut into bits, suicides bloated by the water of the Seine. Near the waterside entrance to the morgue is a hidden stairway into the Catacombes, an infinite maze under the city, the counterimage of its rational organization as the morgue is the counterimage of its assertion of law and order.[38]

The wild nature represented by the Catacombes is evident in the narrator's reverie on the origins of its tunnels:

> Who dug all the miles of them through the solid rock, and why? Quarries? Men do not dig miles of passages six feet high and three feet wide for quarries. It may be that thousands of ages before Adam some race akin to the cave-dwellers lived here in darkness. Some mole-like race of humanity, blind as the eyeless fish that live in the lakes of Mammoth Cave. For many centuries they burrowed further and further away, living like wild beasts upon each other, burying their dead that died of sickness in the pits that still yawn beside the long passages. At last, those who had been spared by disease had eaten the others until there was no one left to eat. Then these, too, crawled away into some of the recesses that have never been exposed since the days of Paradise, and there died.[39]

Several years before *The Time Machine,* we find another set of Morlocks, here imagined inhabiting the distant past. But whereas Wells used the underground race of the future to allegorize class stratification, Andrews crystallized a set of sepulchral fantasies into a cannibalistic race of mole people who either devoured their dead or cast them into plague pits in a vicious cycle ending in their own extinction. The connection with the unclaimed dead of the morgue and the stock urban mystery plot of heirs kidnapped by gypsies suggests an underlying class fantasy to the reverie. More fruitful for interpretation, and perhaps related to the American origin of the novel, is the utter lack of insight to be found in this underground. There is no residue of the revolutionary origins of the specific terror of this underground space, just as there is no structural purpose for the hero's wandering within it. The residual power of the underground is not merely atavistic here, it is severed from the present by the absolute divisions of an extinct evolutionary tree. And yet, even so, an echoing horror remains, "whispering through the cellars" about something unknown and unknowable lurking below.

The two primary nineteenth-century literary exploitations of the Paris Catacombes, Berthet's *Catacombes de Paris* and Dumas' *Mohicans de Paris,* gave a far more coherent and properly Parisian form to those fears, and expressed that form through a cohesive network of above- and underground space. Berthet's novel was serialized in 1854, Dumas' far longer work between 1854 and 1859. Both were centrally concerned with revolution, and both used the Catacombes as a central metonymy for it. Berthet's underworld, as befits its pre-1789 setting, is chaotic and disorganized. It includes within its expanse an illegal printing press; an underground "factory" in which half-a-dozen workers are imprisoned, counterfeiting money for their usurious employer; a "subterranean temple" in the Roman ruins of the Palace of Thermes, where several hundred Knights Templar hold their secret meetings; and the surviving family—wife and son—of a former quarrier and leader of a criminal band of thieves and smugglers, executed at the place de Grève four years before. It is this son who has grown up into the Petit-Diable des Carrières and who is plotting to blow up the Left Bank. Berthet exhibits ambivalent sympathy to every aspect of this underground population, even the Petit-Diable, who replays Quasimodo's relationship to Notre-Dame within the space of the carrières.

The central thesis is enunciated by the anti-royalist hero Philippe during his initial exploration of the underworld:

> The first Christians took refuge in the Catacombs of Rome while waiting until God permitted them to change the surface of the world. We others, free-thinking writers charged with spreading the doctrines of emancipation, are persecuted just like the Christians of the early Church; we must wait as they did, hidden in the depths of the earth, until our hour of triumph or of martyrdom has come.[40]

The historical setting allows Berthet to place the collection of underground opposition comfortably on the other side of the Revolution, and thereby to render wholly rhetorical any positive resonance in a speech such as Philippe's. Whatever good came of the Revolution is now safely ensconced aboveground, he assures his readers; whatever was bad has since been eliminated.

There are various ways in which Berthet signals this shift. He includes, for ex-

ample, a digression on demographics, suggesting that now the upper classes prefer the wide and airy quarters, whereas last century, in even the narrowest and
muddiest alleys, "the mansion and the hovel were fraternally intertwined."[41] The
nineteenth century has brought equality in general and spatial segregation in specific. Just as Berthet clearly favored Haussmann's expansion and opening up of
the city, so he asserted the stability of the Second Empire through analogy to the
carrières of the past. During their subterranean wanderings, Philippe and his
companion, the bon vivant abbé Chavigny, imagine themselves beneath the Luxembourg Palace on the evening during which a great fête is scheduled. Philippe
fantasizes overturning the palace; Berthet immediately reassures his readers with
a footnote: "The voids that existed in the past beneath the Luxembourg Palace
have been *bourrés,* that is to say filled in by masonry supports in such a way that
today there is no longer anything to compromise the stability of this magnificent
edifice."[42] Berthet's information was accurate: consolidation of the former carrières began at the same time as the Municipal Ossuary was conceived, in 1776,
and continued through the nineteenth century. Nevertheless, he attributes to
these facts a metonymical weight that leaves no doubt that the space of the Second Empire is altogether more ordered and regulated than that of pre-Revolutionary Paris.

The narrative vehicle of this order is already in evidence in the novel's version
of 1774, in the figure of the police lieutenant Sartines. The plot of Petit-Diable is
foiled by Philippe and Chavigny; Sartines assists them, obtaining in the process
the invaluable map of the Catacombes made by the smugglers, "a trifle worth its
weight in banknotes!"[43] Thus even the criminal activity of the smugglers' gang,
like all underground dreck in Berthet's Parisian scheme, can be turned to good;
by virtue of the map, the nether regions can be properly ordered and kept under
surveillance: "The following day an army of workmen and skilled engineers took
possession of these formidable carrières, which were from that point onward
bereft of mystery and which were to become the *Catacombes.*"[44] The fact of the
mapping and consolidation of the carrières is extended into a common mid-
nineteenth-century trope by virtue of Sartine's authority: what is irrevocably
dangerous and unusable will be filled up; what can be appropriated within a new
order was domesticated as, in the words interpolated by the later English transla-
tor, "one of the many interesting sights of Paris."[45] What began as a study in pre-
revolutionary mysteries concludes as a paean to Second Empire solutions of
them.

A quite different attitude was taken by Dumas in *Les Mohicans de Paris,* as be-
fitting its setting in the far more immediate past of the three years between 1827
and 1830. Rather than placing his enigmas literally underground, as in the urban
mystery genre used by Berthet, Dumas located them in the entirety of society,
"its stairways that climb to the highest level of society, its ladders that descend
into the deepest abysses."[46] His Mohicans are those relegated to the lower end by

birth or by misfortune; but while the ragpickers and cat-killers live in conditions the nineteenth century generally figured as underground, Dumas reserves the actual subterranean space for the historical and thematic heart of the novel, the July Revolution. As if in response to the prefect's fear of the power of the space of the Catacombes, Dumas makes the uprising literally explode from beneath the city, from under the weight of inequality and injustice: "It is true that one swallowed up oneself in swallowing up Paris, but isn't that the way Samson died?" (1568) The unusually high degree of moral probity attributed by Dumas to his underground conspirators is sealed by the reference to Old Testament martyrdom in the ruins of the Philistine temple in Gaza.

The fusion of the representational space of the actual carrières with the representational space of underground labor is established through the character of the black-faced *charbonnier* (coal-man) who guards an entrance to the carrières on the rue d'Enfer, nicknamed Toussaint-Louverture by one of his fellow Mohicans in honor of the leader of the Santo Domingo slave revolt of 1791. It is repeated through the wordplay of the sinister police inspector, Jackal, who has fortuitously found himself eavesdropping on a secret meeting of the Carbonari beneath the quartier Saint-Jacques: "Ah! said M. Jackal . . . now I understand why it is so dark: we are in the middle of the Charbonnerie! I thought that mine had been exhausted since the La Rochelle affair" (1035–36). Jackal's pun draws out the broader meaning Dumas wants to attribute to the Bonapartist conspiracies of the Carbonari: it is both a mine waiting to explode beneath the decadent Restoration society above and a cause legitimated by the darkness imparted by the labor of the workers it represents in the mines of nineteenth-century France: "Bonapartists, Orléanists, Republicans were all thus mixed together, and, if M. Jackal had had the hundred eyes of Argus, he would doubtless have seen, shining in the bottom of the catacombes, in a corner opposite the Bonapartists, the torches of the Orléanists and the Republicans" (1041). The comparison of Jackal with Argus is not fortuitous, for the lieutenant is a prototype of the omniscient, modern detective, an all-seeing guardian with agents scattered throughout the city, watching and reporting: "Be assured, gentlemen," speaks the king's prosecutor at the show trial of a detained revolutionary, "the judiciary police has the hundred eyes of Argus; it was vigilant, it was going to seek out the modern-day Cacuses in their most hidden retreats, in their deepest caves; for nothing is impenetrable to it" (1482). Jackal enacts this vision of surveillance: nothing escapes his gaze, except the notion of difference within the underground space of rebellion. The only time he finds himself disoriented, the only time he is in a Parisian space that "he had never seen," is when he is led, blindfolded, by the Carbonari through the carrières to their secret meeting place in the "virgin forest of the rue d'Enfer" (2222). The hell of the Mohicans of Paris is the blind spot of surveillance from above.

As opposed to Berthet's historicism, Dumas could use the consolidated carrières for his setting because he intended his novel to be continuous with the present day: he begins the serialization by invoking the historical period as that of his own youth, "ascending half the course of [his] life," just as he expects to return from his "pilgrimage" with a meaning for the present (9). Rather than the absolute break of the Revolution posited by Berthet, Dumas insisted on the continuity of history, both his own and that of the city. He introduces the second extended episode belowground, another secret meeting, with a lengthy digression concerning his own visit—back when he was twenty years old, kept a mistress on the rue d'Enfer, and was given to the "habits of the touristic nightwalker"—to the overgrown garden, the "virgin forest," of a deserted, possibly haunted house on the same rue d'Enfer, guided by one of his own characters, the charbonnier Toussaint-Louverture (1553). His readers are even encouraged to verify the legendary sites below Paris: "Consult, for example, a worthy café man named Giverny on the rue Saint-Jacques, nearly across from Val-de-Grâce; ask him to give you a tour of his cellar and he will recount its legend to you: he will walk ahead of you and will tell you that this tunnel once was part of the garden of the Carmelites" (1569). Just as the Mohicans are portrayed as an integral part of the social fabric of Paris, so the novel's reader and the city are represented in it as united, at least rhetorically, within a single space, both lived and conceived.[47]

Both books were extremely popular, and it seems likely that the reopening of the Catacombes to the public was motivated by their consequent literary celebrity. Thanks to Haussmann and Belgrand, attention had already been focused on all aspects of the Parisian infrastructure. But while the Catacombes presented a space that could be controlled as tourism, it was not physically malleable in the way Haussmann attempted with the sewers, and in the way he succeeded in the outlying arrondissements, the annexations that could be built from scratch in the image of a new, ordered, rational city. Two of the most symbolically significant of the latter spaces were the Père-Lachaise Cemetery and the parc aux Buttes-Chaumont. The latter, created out of the former carrières d'Amérique and the legendary site of the gibbet at Montfaucon, will be examined in the next chapter. Père-Lachaise, the first modern cemetery to be created independently of a church, was a suburban prototype for the sort of hierarchized city desired by Haussmann and his emperor. Established in 1803 and opened in 1807 to house the newly deceased as the Municipal Ossuary was to house the old remains of the closed urban cemeteries, Père-Lachaise is the counterpart of the Catacombes, an image of things to come to complement the repository of Paris past.

We find the link between the two retained, but the associations inverted as a sign that all is not well in the future, in Jules Verne's early novel, *Paris au XXe siècle*.[48] In the form of the Catacombes, the Parisian underground continues to be represented as the essential motivating force of the city; in the future, however, that force has been materialized and rendered economically viable. Under the auspices of the "Société des Catacombes de Paris et de la force motrice à domicile," the Left Bank carrières, "those immense tunnels for so long unused," have been adapted as chambers for the manufacture of compressed air, the driving force of the machinery of the city and of its boulevard railways.[49] In a technologized variation on the old smuggling routes, the air is forced underground by nearly two thousand windmills atop the Montrouge Plain before being disseminated through the city. The subterranean potency of the city has been wholly domesticated, made practical, a gesture symptomatic of the novel's ambivalent view of the future and typical of the Paris discourse of subterranean space. Verne's fascination with imagined future technology and his ambition for rendering useful what appears to have become obsolete are paired with a vision of a soulless future, haunted by the twin "demons" of wealth and electricity.

This critical vision emerges in the protagonist's despairing walk through the snow-covered paths of Père-Lachaise, now become the repository of the past as the Catacombes have become the dynamo of the future. Young Michel Dufrénoy comes to the cemetery from the terrifying sight of a scaffold erected on the nearby rue de la Roquette: the final token of Paris's possession by the "demon of electricity," of mechanization, is a proto–electric chair, a man-made simulation of Jove's divine lightning bolt. The cemetery, an archaic mixture of "Greek, Roman, Etruscan, Byzantine, Lombard, Gothic, Renaissance, Twentieth Century," is for Michel the last remaining space for a different sort of leveling, the equality of death, "these bodies, all reverted to dust."[50] Rather than the salutary message of the Catacombes beneath the nineteenth-century city, Père-Lachaise appears to Michel as the death knell of Paris, the dissolution of the differences of art and literature that gave meaning to his life. In good Romantic fashion, he can do nothing but sink into the snow and fantasize about bringing electric ruin to the entire metropolis over which he is gazing from the height of the cemetery: "Let the city collapse under a deluge of fire!"[51] Bereft of its subterranean wastefulness and its suburban monuments, Paris has no identity, no reason to exist.

A look at two grand but failed sepulchral projects, one at the Catacombes and the other at Père-Lachaise, suggests the same complementary symbolic meaning. As part of his renovation of the Catacombes, Héricart de Thury planned a "monumental entrance" through the exposed quarry known as the Fosse-aux-Lions, long-time haunt of the local ragpickers, on the boulevard Saint-Jacques between the rues de la Santé and Dareau (figure 2.9).[52] Conceived as a slowly descending avenue of trees, Héricart de Thury's plan would have established a visible threshold between Paris above and the Catacombes below, a leisurely, contemplative passage between one and the other. Later projects, a chapel at the entrance, proposed around 1860, and a "commemorative monument" at the place d'Enfer entrance (1870), were less ambitious but equally directed toward endowing the place of descent with a symbolic meaning. It is not surprising that none were funded; not that there was any shortage of unnecessary construction undertaken at the time, but the relationship between above- and underground Paris has always been unobtrusive and on the scale of the inhabitants, the lived space of the manhole cover, doorway, or kiosk rather than the conceived space of a monument. There was nothing to commemorate in the Catacombes that could be expressed through such a design.

As opposed to the subterranean Catacombes, a bald symbol of the Janus-faced Revolution, Père-Lachaise was conceived, as Ragon has suggested, as "a museum of death. Moreover, it was necessary, after the indifference of the revolutionary period to sepulture, for the consulate to reinvent a mortuary ceremony that would owe nothing to the religious ceremonies of the ancien régime."[53] The Catacombes echoed through the century as an emblem of the demand for and cost of absolute equality; Père-Lachaise charted the emergence of the bourgeoisie and of a middle-class space in reaction to those demands. Although an apparent image of equality in death in an open space above the city, Père-Lachaise in fact expressed the spatial segregation that would emerge from the metropolitan clearances of the nineteenth century. For the first time, individual tombs were designated. Personalization, which began as an exception, was the rule by 1814.[54] The first family tomb, a bourgeois version of the tradition of nobility, was erected by the Greffuhle family in 1815. Writing in *Le Livre des cent-et-un* twenty years later, Nestor de Lamarque compared "the inequal cemetery of Père-Lachaise, dominated by the aristocracy of tombs" with "the total loss of names" that separated the Catacombes from all other modes of burial.[55] The funerary chapel, as Ragon notes, functioned as a miniature church in the miniature city that was the modern cemetery.[56]

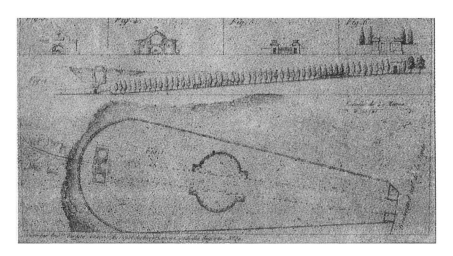

2.9. Héricart de Thury's monumental threshold entrance to the Catacombes in the Fosse-aux-Lions. Illustration in Emile Gérards, *Paris souterrain* (Paris: Garnier-Frères, 1908): 481.

It equally functioned as a miniature, individualized dwelling. The funeral chapel introduced at Père-Lachaise took the form of a "standard house-tomb . . . which included a subterranean vault with a small chapel above"; this single-family unit became "*the* exemplar . . . for those who wished to form public cemeteries laid out on spacious, rational, hygienic lines."[57] A microcosm of the city as a whole, Père-Lachaise provided a graspable image of the ungraspable metropolis. Rather than the bleak message of the Catacombes, answerable in middle-class discourse only by piety or mockery, the new necropolis produced a different meaning for death within the cityscape: the parklike space, the cultured art of its tombs, and the implicit order of its grounds. While most Parisians continued to live in apartment buildings, the new necropolis proposed an English-style cityscape of separate houses, combining a suburban ideal with the classicism of the Egyptian-derived mausoleum design.

Shifted aboveground, the negative power of death, like that of the Devil, was vitiated as a reproduction of the absolute space of the city's growing divisions, a faithful mirror of ideology rather than a distorting reflection:

> For the most part, one keeps to one's own quartier, since the demographic distribution of the cemetery is, on a smaller scale, exactly that of Paris. . . . You descend to the west toward a monotonous Monceau plain of small mansions in grey stone, and the southwest recalls the 16th [arrondissement] with its streets *comme il faut* brightened up with *modern'style* vaults. The central sections evoke the grands boulevards, they receive the largest number of visitors while the silence of the faubourg Saint-Germain reigns over the picturesque paths of the oldest part. . . . The east is the left of the cemetery, the west its right.[58]

We find a similar, if less self-conscious, demographical microcosm in *Paris au XXe siècle,* where the hero wanders the deserted cemetery from "a village of tombs neat and tidy like Dutch houses" through "the wealthy quarter" to the quarter of the artists and writers. True to Verne's vision of the city, there is no quarter for the poor, no bas-fond. Ragon writes of the necropolis that it is "the reverse of the metropolis. Its reverse or its site, it depends. For the cemetery, idealized double of the city, appears at the same time as the perfect reproduction of the socioeconomic order of the living."[59] Père-Lachaise is both the reverse of the metropolis, in that it is designated as a space of death rather than life, and a location within it, in that it encapsulates the spatial dynamics and ideology around it.

Ragon oversimplifies this principle of reflection, however, by underestimating the distortions that occur even in an abstract space as it is appropriated through everyday life. Its location in an outskirt on the popular, radical side of Paris foreshadowed the opening up of the entire city to speculation and the shifting of the working classes beyond the traditional banlieues of the metropolis. At the same time, the events of 1871 demonstrated that Père-Lachaise remained for the moment at least part of the terrain of the people. During the last week of May, the surviving communards were cornered by the invading Versaillais in the spaces beneath the funerary chapels. In a physical and metaphorical assertion of control over the entire space of the city, they were shot against the eastern wall of the cemetery and then buried at its foot. It would henceforth be known as the Mur des Fédérés; a memorial to the opposition dead was erected at the opposite, west extreme of the cemetery (figure 2.10). Whatever symbolic divisions the microcosmic layout of the cemetery retained of the city around it, the walls enclosing it physically delineated the control of the state over the entirety. Viewed from below or viewed from above: as repository of the past, the Catacombes could be allowed to assert their revolutionary message in the distinctness of their underground space; as aboveground space of the present, Père-Lachaise posited an interlocking area controlled by an encircling wall of capital and property.

There was still an underground impulsion in this space, however; the people of Paris clung to it tenaciously when Haussmann proposed closing Père-Lachaise along with the Montparnasse and Montmartre cemeteries and shifting all sepulture to a vast site twenty-two kilometers outside of Paris. Still, this was not a radical impulsion, but rather an adherence to the traditionally representational

2.10. Symbolic topography: Atget's photograph of the Mur des Fédérés, at the "working-class" east end of Père-Lachaise. Eugène Atget, *Père-Lachaise: Mur historique des Fédérés*, No. Atget: 3832, 1900. Reproduced by permission from Bibliothèque nationale de France.

space of the urban, church-based cemetery that had characterized Parisian life from the Middle Ages through to the eighteenth century. Although suburban and parklike, Père-Lachaise did resemble the central urban spaces in its potential as a public space. Rather than a specialized site for special visits and quiet promenades, however, the traditional churchyard and charnel house, without monuments or trees, had been the principal open space in the medieval city:

> The cemetery was the noisiest, the busiest, the most commercial area of the rural or the urban agglomeration. The church was the common house, the cemetery the open space, equally common, at a time when there were no other public spaces except the street, no other meeting-places, for the houses in general were too small and overcrowded.[60]

In a characteristic movement toward specialization, uses and associations were split up. To the Catacombes went the proximity to the matter of death, although the stench and decay of the overcrowded churchyards had been replaced by the symmetrical stacking and ordering of the quick-limed remains. To Père-Lachaise went the open space, but separated from visible evidence of death; the only signs were the artistic monuments and the carved tombstones. Neither space retained a connection to commerce and market activity, which were consigned to another form of nineteenth-century architecture: the covered iron-and-glass structures of the Halles Centrales, part of which were erected over the space once occupied by the Cemetery of the Innocents (see figure 2.3). By 1844, its horrors already forgotten, the latter was once again available for reveries on a vanished society:

> A cemetery gave way to a market; however, the cemetery was gayer than the market. In effect, the Cemetery of the Innocents was the Palais-Royal of our ancestors. . . . The dead were sheltered by the living; on every tomb a seller of ribbons, of lace, of trinkets, or of frills daily spread out his merchandise while smiling at the regulars. Never had one been so familiar with death.[61]

The separation of the functions of life and death served here as a metaphor for the division of space and of time in the modern city. The author's concluding irony underlined the changed attitude toward death: "In Paris, life and death still meet; for is there not a great market at the entrance to the morgue?"[62] Rather than the agglomeration of the necropolis, this famous Paris attraction served up death in individualized portions, each body telling its own (highly ritualized) story before giving way to the next tableau.[63]

The abstract as well as the representational meanings of Père-Lachaise and the Catacombes were distinct. Just as the monumental entrances to the latter were never built, so were two plans in the 1850s for a set of catacombs under the former rejected. In 1850, new land had been acquired to expand the cemetery, and there were two separate proposals for excavating the minerals under the soil through carrières that would then be transformed into catacombs with the funds raised by selling the minerals.[64] In 1859, the inspector general of carrières presented the plans of one Lamé-Fleury, mining engineer, for what would be a four hundred thousand–cubic-meter annex to the southern Catacombes, representing the potential inhumation of the remains of some four hundred million individuals. Five years earlier, a different plan had been presented by another mining engineer, a M. de Fourcy, on the model of the Roman catacombs: eight thousand funerary niches to be built within the galleries left behind by the exploitation of gypsum. The niches would be sold as concessions in perpetuity as per the conventional tombs above; the corridors would be gaslit and ventilation assured by eighteen vertical pits (figure 2.11).[65] Both plans were scuttled by Haussmann's annexation of the villages surrounding the metropolis; regulations forbade any new subterranean quarrying within the city limits. Nevertheless, dispensations could probably have been obtained, as they were for other putatively forbidden developments. Père-Lachaise retained its aboveground character, although it did receive a columbarium for cremated remains on the Roman model during the Third Republic in 1887; the Catacombes retained their singularity, as they accumulated human remains throughout the nineteenth century and even into the twentieth when excavations for the Métro uncovered further bones requiring relocation. The suitable space for the Roman-style catacomb turned out to be not Paris but the suburban cemeteries of London, from the design of which de Fourcy's rejected plan had been most likely borrowed.

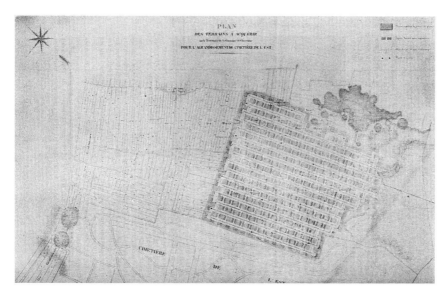

2.11. De Fourcy's proposal for new catacombs under the Cemetery of the East (Père-Lachaise). Illustration by E. de Fourcy in Emile Gérards, *Paris souterrain* (Paris: Garnier-Frères, 1908): 479.

The Catacombs of London

It was a solemn consideration what enormous hosts of dead belong to one old great city, and how, if they were raised while the living slept, there would not be the space of a pin's point in all the streets and ways for the living to come out into. Not only that, but the vast armies of dead would overflow the hills and valleys beyond the city, and would stretch away all round it, God knows how far.

CHARLES DICKENS, "Night Walks" (1860)

Because of their close association with issues of death and religious beliefs, funereal monuments could not so easily partake of the utilitarian ideology of other modern building forms. Consequently, when nineteenth-century concerns over disease and decay shifted burial from the overflowing churchyards to the suburban cemetery, the new spaces were decorated instead with the forms of antiquity and the neo-Gothic. There were two primary sources for these forms: the constructed ruins characteristic of both the picturesque eighteenth-century English garden and the sublime terror of the gothic novel, and the material ruins popularized by Napoleon's Egyptian campaign, the archaeological excavation of the pyramids and other antique sites, and the renewed study of the Roman catacombs, as well as Roman ruins discovered at this time during underground exploitation and construction within both Paris and London. A 1901 article, "Burying London," described the changing modes of funereal practices during the previous century:

> Note, too, how the cemetery companies are affected by fashion. When the subterranean tombs at Brompton, Kensal Green, and Highgate were made catacombs were in great favour. Now they have as completely 'gone out' as crinolines. At present the public taste is veering in the direction of cremation—a change for which some provision was long since made in the great cemeteries.[66]

Altogether, ten cemeteries were constructed with catacombs in mid-nineteenth-century London, the majority around 1840: Kensal Green (1832), Norwood or South Metropolitan (1837), Highgate (1839), Abney Park, Brompton, Nunhead (all 1840), Tower Hamlets (1841), City of London (1856; figure 2.12), Saint Mary's Roman Catholic (1858), and Great Northern or New Southgate (1861; planned, but not completed). They give an important indication of London attitudes not just toward underground space and death but toward the changing cityscape as a whole.

By contrast to sepulture in Paris, the new London cemeteries were opened by private enterprise, the majority of them before the Burial Act of 1855 had abolished interment within the limits of cities and towns. The Roman catacombs

2.12. The catacombs at the City of London Cemetery, opened in 1856. Like those in Highgate (see fig. 2.16), although less elaborately, they can be approached from ground level or from above. Color lithograph by William Haywood, engraved by R. M. Bryson, *Catacombs, City of London Cemetery, Ilford, Essex*, 1856. Reproduced by permission from the Guildhall Library, © Corporation of London.

made a prominent entry in the article, "London Burials," in Knight's *London,* as the origin of the traditional contiguity of church and burial ground. Once no longer necessary for security, the author relates, "we learn from St. Jerome in what affectionate reverence the place was still held, in spite of its natural horrors. . . . The churches being thus at first erected over the place of the dead, the next step was to reverse the process, and to bury the dead where convenience and growing prosperity caused the erection of churches."[67] "Natural horrors" may refer explicitly to the subterranean location of the catacombs, but the ambivalence of the phrase extends to the general role of sepulture in the modern West. The catacomb was revived not only as novelty but also as a powerful new image of that ambivalence to replace the no longer viable multiple-use and communal space of the churchyard.

The same article began with a reference to that outmoded space and an allusion to the social problems associated with its existence in the midst of the cityscape:

> We hear complaints sometimes made of the indiscriminate character of the burials in them; we hear regrets expressed that men of erring, or violent, or criminal lives, should

at their last enjoy the shelter of the neighbourhood, the communion they have done so little previously to deserve. Are we wrong in thinking this very circumstance one of their most touching features?[68]

In this view, the virtue of the churchyard—its ecumenical acceptance that every person was equal in death and unto God—was equally what had outmoded it. Not only had it literally been filled to overflowing through its generous acceptance of all and sundry, but it had also represented a mixing of activities and classes now seen as overly promiscuous. The oft-rehearsed nightmare scenes of half-decomposed bodies being dug up, cut to shreds, and discarded to make room for more—gruesomely detailed even in the genteel pages of Knight's "cyclopaedia"—joined with the bodysnatching scandals of the 1830s and sensational reports of sudden death due to the "mephitic exhalations" of graves to propel the larger discourse of urban pathology into a call for the "divorce of places of worship and of burial from each other."[69] Rather than be incorporated into the fabric of the church and the social totality it had represented (in theory, if not in practice), the horror was to be left behind in the city, while the "affectionate reverence" would be established in the private, strictly controlled, segregated, and individualized precincts of the picturesque cemetery-parks.

Dickens evocatively linked the demographic shifts, the changes in burial practice, and the haunted memories of the condensed life of the past in "The City of the Absent," an essay collected in *The Uncommercial Traveller*.[70] Although the conceit of the piece was a simple one, it shaded easily into later, more psychological imagery of urban alienation: "Where are all those people who on busy working-days pervaded these scenes?"[71] He begins with the old churchyards as an emblem for the City of London on a weekend or after hours. As often with Dickens, a veneer of playful irony appears to conceal an undertone of the sinister and macabre: "A contagion of slow ruin overhangs the place."[72] The City without business is a city in ruins; the City without permanent inhabitants is equally a dead city. Dickens finally discovers the "absent" inhabitants of this emptied city in the most morbid space of the essay, one of his "best beloved churchyards," which he calls "the churchyard of Saint Ghastly Grim." Rather than its actual name, he identifies it by its symbolic location,

> at the heart of the City, and the Blackwall Railway shrieks at it daily. It is a small small churchyard, with a ferocious strong spiked iron gate, like a jail. This gate is ornamented with skulls and crossbones, larger than the life, wrought in stone; but it likewise came into the mind of Saint Ghastly Grim, that to stick iron spikes a-top of the stone skulls, as though they were impaled, would be a pleasant device. Therefore the skulls grin aloft horribly, thrust through and through with iron spears. Hence, there is attraction of repulsion for me in Saint Ghastly Grim.[73]

The "attraction of repulsion" is the spatial memory of this remnant of old London hidden at the heart of the modern City, the heads of executed criminals on the bridges, the popular history of the church that attributed the skulls to a commemoration of the plague victims buried within it, the sublime imagery that leads the narrator to hail a hackney cab on a stormy night to witness Saint Ghastly Grim "by light of lightning."[74]

The empty city must consciously be reanimated through the imagination and memory of the lone stroller. While Saint Ghastly Grim provides a mnemonic for the past, the rest of the essay's images are in the present, mediated through their location in the underground spaces of the City. First, Dickens reinhabits the City through the mindset of the criminal classes who have been successfully excluded from it: "About College-hill, Mark-lane, and so on towards the Tower, and Dockward, the deserted wine-merchants' cellars are fine subjects for consideration; but the deserted money-cellars of the Bankers, and their plate-cellars, and their jewel-cellars, what subterranean regions of the Wonderful Lamp are these!"[75]

Bereft of inhabitants, bereft of lived space, the City is emptied of mysteries; Dickens would clearly have welcomed the return of Paul Féval's Great Family and the tunnel it hired Saunders the Giant to dig under the Bank of England in *Les Mystères de Londres* (1844).

The final reverie centers on Garraway's Coffee House, on Exchange Alley, Cornhill, one of the City's chief auction houses, and a recurring locale in Dickens' novels. Its imagery of the clerks' specters haunting the precincts brings out the underlying tone of dispossession at the emotive core of the essay. Dickens apparently cannot decide if these ghosts are trying to break into the house out of which they have been expelled or if they have been unwillingly confined to its crypts:

> When they are forcibly put out of Garraway's on Saturday night—which they must be, for they never would go out of their own accord—where do they vanish until Monday morning? On the first Sunday that I ever strayed here, I expected to find them hovering about these lanes, like restless ghosts, and trying to peep into Garraway's through chinks in the shutters, if not endeavouring to turn the lock of the door with false keys, picks, and screw-drivers. But the wonder is, they go clean away! And now I think of it, the wonder is, that every working-day pervader of these scenes goes clean away. . . . There is an old monastery-crypt under Garraway's (I have been in it among the port wine), and perhaps Garraway's taking pity on the mouldy men who wait in its public-room all their lives, gives them cool house-room down there over Sundays; but the catacombs of Paris would not be large enough to hold the rest of the missing. This characteristic of London City greatly helps its being the quaint place it is in the weekly pause of business, and greatly helps my Sunday sensation in it of being the Last Man.[76]

Where else should the central mystery reside but in a trading post of empire? Dickens's clerks are, by turns, faithful workers who would not dream of ever leaving their posts (or, reversing the irony, bureaucratic drudges to such a degree that they cannot conceive of leaving); cunning thieves, breaking into their employers' premises after hours just like the robbers Dickens previously imagined; suburban commuters; or simply anonymous skeletons locked away in the catacombs and reanimated each working day by the magic of capitalism.

The concluding turn of the essay reveals the perversity of the author who, instead of taking his Sunday stroll in the newly opened, picturesque parklands of the suburban cemeteries along with the rest of the hordes, journeys to the true necropolis of the workplace to view a different order of picturesque. Or perhaps he is suggesting that it is only the bodies that commute to and from the suburbs where they are buried nights and weekends and the souls that remain wholly captive to the source of money and power, the underground chambers beneath the visible city. It was not lost on Dickens that Garraway's, like many other London establishments, was built over the ancient underground space of a monastery crypt. Secrets of exploitation, secrets of crime, secrets of money, but also secrets of imagination, of happiness, of truths, were wrought into this twofold space. The working week, Dickens implies, divided life and death just as much as the churchyard and the coffeehouse divided them. To visit the City by night, by weekend, was to transgress the modern divisions between life and death, above- and underground, work and leisure, present and past. Invisible in the rush of the weekday just as they would be in the suburban gatherings of the evening and weekend, the specters emerged only after hours.

In "The London Sunday," her late-century update and riposte to Dickens's morbid, backward-looking vision of the City as a graveyard, Alice Meynell put forth an image of the city as a natural rather than an economic space, preferring to gloss over its underground aspects and stress its ability still to release color and pleasure, the traditional picturesque. The brightest moments of this picture are female: "It may be noted that the great majority of the London Sunday women are fresh to see"; and it clings to the past rather than nostalgically seeking it: "The tradition—a Dickens tradition, it seems—of the desolate City church is still true as to the numbers of the congregations; in this open church there are but three people, exceedingly devout; but the old woman, the beadle, the gloom are gone."77 What Meynell finds is the lived space of the City, where even on a Sunday can be found a few stubborn worshippers and a multitude of smartly dressed pedestrians, not lingering, surely, but passing through from their East End homes to the West End parks: "Even in the centre of the City it cannot be said that the main streets are deserted; for they evidently are all thoroughfares towards the unknown places to which these thousands and thousands of crossing feet are bent."78 Still, it takes a willful viewer to pick out the pleasing bits of color from among the frightening hordes of young men, who "go in great straggling gangs, and though they do nothing—not even that much talking—they give a false air of lawlessness to the streaming street."79 The color of their clothing tinges their social identity as well, for "in this light-grey London, colourless but clear, you re-alise how much man darkens and blackens the earth in these latitudes by his mere presence"—a color tinged with foreignness that contradicts the white, "natural surface of the world." As Meynell concludes, "It is a pity that mere black, brown, and grey dyes should so change the colour of the race—squalid dyes, in which are steeped the unchanged and the unwashed garments of these quite innumerable young men."[80] The dark forces of the city are read into the very layout of its streets and patterns of movement—the light, sunny main thoroughfares cannot quite lay to rest the more threatening and unsavory darkness of the winding old side streets where Dickens had been so at home: "We all know that there are alleys and corners where the women look otherwise, but those who take their part in this Sunday, so famous in allusions, who join in the day-long movement on foot and load the tramcars, are clean and cleanly clad."[81] Dickens saw fit to recast the City in the image of his own obsessions; Meynell prefers to chart the forces and counterforces that she saw pushing the life of the city out to the suburbs, while the unwanted specters of prostitution and foreigners loitered in the alleys and corners of the old center.

Similar traces of what had been left behind in the city remained in ciphered form in the suburban catacombs, although cloaked in several layers of denial. That traces were left behind, however, is apparent in the mixed reaction toward the popular embrace of what was considered an excessive morbidity. The most famous and influential attack, by the Gothic revivalist architect Augustus Pugin, argued that the popular allure of the word "catacombs" and the archaeological finds in Egypt were being cheaply exploited by commercial interests (figure 2.13). The style, he wrote, was "generally Egyptian, probably from some associations between the word catacombs, which occurs in the prospectus of the company, and the discoveries of Belzoni on the banks of the Nile."[82] The architectural travesty of classical forms was equated in the attack to the commercial travesty of sacred space. Although exaggerated, Pugin's illustration pinpointed the characteristically Victorian adaptation of the classical and the mythological to the exigencies of capital, including practices that would become wholly acceptable by the end of the century, as, for example, a tearoom within the grounds of the cemetery. Particularly suggestive of the midcentury confusion are other foreground sketches, such as "Shillibeer's Funeral Omnibus" on the right, and advertisements on the left for Vauxhall Gardens and "Magic Cave, Strand." Pugin was correct in seeing in Highgate not so much a burial ground as a new form of popular entertainment and amusement park, the Egyptianizing motifs being a central aspect of its novel attraction.

A similar, if less highbrow, order of complaint was raised by other writers. In 1869, for example, the Reverend Thomas Barker described the catacomb beneath the chapel of the Abney Park Cemetery in Stoke Newington as a "cold and stony death place. . . . The chilliness is awful and repulsive."[83] Or, as Mrs. Basil Holmes put it in 1896, "Kensal Green is truly awful, with its catacombs, its huge mausoleums, family vaults, statues, broken pillars, weeping images, and oceans of tombstones, good, bad, and indifferent."[84] In this litany of woes, the catacombs

2.13. The commercialization of antiquity: Pugin's satirical rendering of Highgate Cemetery. Illustration by Augustus Welby Northmore Pugin, in his *An Apology for the Revival
of Christian Architecture in England* (London: J. Weale, 1843; rpt., Edinburgh: J. Grant,
1895): 12–13, plate 4.

took pride of place as emblem of the vastness, impersonality, and bad taste of
what was then the largest cemetery in the metropolis. When made in retrospect,
such an evaluation was usually joined by a commentary on the "grisly" habits of
a past generation, far less civilized than one's own. Nevertheless, the catacombs at
Kensal Green, for example, remain in active use today, with three-quarters of
their four-thousand-place capacity filled. Just as the cemetery space would later
prove amenable for black magic, pagan rituals, criminal activity, vandalism, and
even vampirism, so does the eeriness of which a cemetery is never totally lacking
serve as a reminder that its space can never wholly be rationalized.

The catacombs of the London cemeteries varied in form, but all were based to
some degree on the Roman model of deep corridors lined on both sides with
burial niches, or *loculi,* usually stacked four or five high. The space was rationalized in several ways for Victorian use. Rather than the labyrinthine layout of the
Roman catacombs, due both to their haphazard excavation over a long period of
time and to the later Christian desire for security from Roman authorities, the
London catacombs were designed on a grid, usually a central cross surrounded
by smaller passages. The galleries are in arched brick, the standard architectural
form of underground Victorian London, divided into arched insets, with deep
cuts at their ends to let light in from above. They were usually installed underneath the cemetery's chapel, echoing the traditional church crypt. Within the in-

dividual arches, various arrangements occur. Most frequent is a division into separate loculi, one for each coffin, inserted lengthwise to conserve space, but one also encounters arches reserved for a single family, or arches never readied for use (figure 2.14).

2.14. A typical family *loculus* in the West Norwood Cemetery catacombs: the iron grill protects an arch containing several rows and columns of individual coffins. Photo by author, West Norwood Cemetery, Lambeth, London, 1998.

The message of the catacomb paradoxically combined preservation and denial with decomposition and morbidity. A key feature in several of the chapels was a hydraulic lift whereby the catafalque would be mechanically lowered at the opportune moment from the chapel into the catacombs below.[85] The mechanism would be obscured by the trappings of the coffin; hence the conceit, if not the actual illusion, of a miraculous descent into the underworld. Consonant with Pugin's criticism of the commercialization inherent to Egyptianizing funereal architecture, there was something eminently theatrical about the London catacombs in particular, a characteristic combination of contemporary technology and ancient myth made into popular spectacle. Rather than the preindustrial practice of digging a hole, lowering a wooden coffin into it by means of a rope, and filling in the hole with a shovel, the catacomb gave the appearance of automation within an inorganic, man-made environment of brick, lead, iron, and, sometimes, glass. The lead-lined coffins gave the illusion both of being inorganic and machinelike, and of bestowing an incorruptible body on the deceased, like those of the first Christians, saints, and martyrs. This did not in fact prevent decomposition, however, and visitors to the catacomb would have witnessed the same gruesome details visible today in imperfectly sealed or warped coffins, where the liquid ichor has seeped out of the coffin ends to form viscous pools on the ground below.

The visit is the other key paradox. Rather than returning to gaze at a tomb from above, or ground level, the visitor to the catacomb, whether family member or curiosity seeker, could have the illusion of descending into the otherworld itself. There was no plaque over the entrance as in Paris, reading "Arrête, c'est ici l'Empire de la Mort!" but the possibility of physically entering the tomb alludes spatially to the same crossing of a threshold into another world (figure 2.15). The domestication of such a space demonstrates the change in attitude toward the underground since the period of the Gothic several decades earlier. The catacomb retained a welcome frisson of the organic underground, but a thrill that had been well contained within a modern paradigm of rational space. Such a journey would always have been possible to the possessors of a hereditary mausoleum, or to visitors of a church crypt. What was different about the catacomb was that, even more than the house-tomb, it was truly middle class. The wealthy continued to erect mausoleums, tombs, and monuments on the model of Père-Lachaise in the aboveground landscape of the fashionable new cemeteries. But few Londoners could afford to purchase a plot of land in perpetuity. The catacomb niche was a compromise, analogous to owning a flat or a semidetached rather than a genuine house. At the same time, it was a modern space, as opposed to the classicist traditionalism of the mausoleum; its cousin was the columbarium for the cremated, and both could be regarded as progressive, enlightened, and democratic. Hence also the mythic resonance with the early Christians, judged by their piety rather than their status, all equal under God and underground.

2.15. West Norwood Cemetery: the business-like entrance to a London catacomb. Photo by author, West Norwood Cemetery, Lambeth, London, 1998.

Although the majority of the London cemetery catacombs followed the Christian model and were situated under chapels, those at Highgate are of a more mixed provenance, an exemplary blend of Egyptian, Roman, Christian, and contemporary Victorian images of the necropolis. The centerpiece of the cemetery, chosen as representative in the majority of the contemporary illustrations, is the Egyptian Avenue, or Catacombs, and the Lebanon Circle to which it leads (figure 2.16). Rather than a verticalized relationship between chapel and sepulcher centered on descent from one world to the next, Highgate grants the visitor a double viewpoint on an otherworldly space inserted into a naturalized landscape as into an English garden. Excavated into a steep hillside, the Egyptian Avenue provides a ground-level entrance to its natural underworld. Rather than the modest brick staircases leading to the catacombs of other cemeteries as if into a cellar, the avenue has a monumental entrance flanked by a pair of obelisks. The entryway leads into the Valley of the Kings, flanked on either side by metal doors covering vaults built into the twelve-foot-deep hillside cutting. The shadowing of the steep hillsides and the narrow walk is heightened by the overgrowth of vegetation planted along it to give an effect midway between a shady avenue and an underground gallery. At its other end, the avenue opens up into the Lebanon Circle, similarly cut into the ground, and lined on its inner and outer circumferences with a further twenty vaults. Over each vault is an Egyptian-style pediment. A single, giant cypress tree is planted in the isolated ground in the center of the circle, lending its symbolism of longevity, of death, and of Old Testament authority to the space. Two staircases lead out of the sides of the circle flanking the Valley of the Kings, allowing the visitor the second option of ascending from or descending into the space, and viewing it from above as well as from below. Although constructed with contemporary technology—metal doors, brick-lined

2.16. The view from above into the catacombs of the Lebanon Circle at the center of Highgate Cemetery, two years after it opened. Illustration in "London Burials," in *London*, ed. Charles Knight, 6 vols. in 3 (London, 1841–44), 4:164.

vaults—Highgate proposed a reconciliation between the spaces of life and death, as it did between nature and the city.

The reconciliation was made possible, of course, by the exclusivity of these catacombs, consonant with the predominantly pharaonic (and Napoleonic) iconography. A vault in the Valley of the Kings would have cost 130 guineas in 1878, and one in the Lebanon Circle an even 200: they were apparently in great demand nonetheless.[86] The Terrace Catacombs, above and behind the Lebanon Circle, provided a less expensive, if less exclusive and less spectacular alternative. Built below the eighty-yard-long terrace that lines one of the outer walls, niches in these catacombs sold for around ten pounds each. According to Felix Barker, however, they were primarily for temporary use, while a family decided on a permanent plot.[87] Here, too, as in the loculi that line the sides of other pathways sunk into hillsides around the cemetery, there remains both an image of reconciliation and a note of exclusivity. Like the other early London cemeteries, Highgate was private, and, more than the others, it exuded that aura of privacy in its reconciliation of death with the combined reassurance of picturesque nature and ancient grandeur.

A similar effect is evident in the planned ruin into which the architect Sir John Soane transformed his terrace house at 13 Lincoln's Inn Fields.[88] In its studied disorder, its apparently haphazard collection of arts, curiosities, and antiquities, and the incorporation of underground space into its exhibition, Soane's house, later bequeathed as a museum, duplicates much of the spatial symbolism of Highgate. In his 1865 guide to London, for example, Élisée Reclus complained of the difficulty of access and the chaos of the collection, while pausing to savor the names of the different spaces: "All these recesses are decorated with fantastic names: the Monk's Parlor, the Catacombs, the sepulchral Chamber, the Crypt, Shakespeare's Refuge, etc."[89] "The most interesting object in the whole collection," counseled Baedeker at the turn of the century, "is an Egyptian sarcophagus, found in 1817 by Belzoni in a tomb in the valley of Bîbân el-Muluk, near the ancient Thebes."[90] What relates Soane's collection to Highgate is not so much the omnipresent Egyptomania of the age as the new context in which both sites placed the meaning of Egypt.

Soane's use of the sarcophagus was less directly related to the sepulchral symbolism employed by Highgate's architect, Stephen Geary; nevertheless, it was equally concerned with finding a contemporary form for making sense of what was dead and what was past. Robert Harbison's recent description of the space gives a good sense of the effect achieved by the crypt in which Soane placed the sarcophagus and other underground artifacts he had collected:

> At the heart of it is the Dome, a continuous space cut through these three floors, made of discontinuities, of which the model is ruin not building, and where the figmental underlying structure is drastically obscured by corruscating fragments of many sizes

and sorts, chunks of huge cornice, roof ornaments, colossal heads or feet, urns, and chaotic syllables of vegetable scroll-work.

All these objects (ancient marble, modern plaster, Gothic wood tumbled randomly together) float as if in some phantasmagoric dream, as if all the ghosts from nearby graves (the lower reaches of this house contain Egyptian, monkish, and classical tombs) have been summoned at once and come together in strange conglomerate life.
. . .

This architect knew what he was doing of course; it was a calculated transport, a picturesque effect which conflated mausoleum and museum, individual and cultural memorial, to make a lavish monument or house for Memory. Which is also the lesson of his more purely architectural conceptions, where the lightly traced classical forms, like inscriptions which fade when the viewer comes near (an effect archaeologists in the field have commented on), signifies a tenuous hold on one's historical models or ancestral memories.[91]

Harbison is accurate in viewing Soane's museum-house as a twisted form of memory walk, but his overly postmodernist stance chooses to revel in rather than also to interpret the "phantasmagoric dream." While the accepted categories of quality, of chronology, and of taxonomy have indeed been thrown into question here, the phantasmagoric quality is channeled through a highly ordered, vertical structure. The effect of the overriding image of the ruin is to expose the underground structure and spaces of a building to the open air, giving a different meaning to the aboveground world around it. The subterranean, necrological material in the catacombs of the museum casts new light on the library and paintings above.

It is in this sense of the ruin that Henry James appears to have chosen Sir John Soane's Museum as the setting for the turning point of his short novel, *A London Life* (1889). I described in chapter 1 how James employed the novelty of the "mysterious underground railway" to bestow the character of an unforeseen, slightly transgressive journey onto the sightseeing tour on which the young Englishman, Mr. Wendover, escorts the visiting American debutante, Laura Wing. That train ride also inaugurates a destabilizing space of which the Soane museum is the ultimate destination. Shortly after she has finished recriminating with herself over unjust suspicions about the relations between her married sister Selina and one Captain Crispin, Laura finds herself temporarily trapped in the museum by a thunderstorm, and lured into the depths of its crypt:

One of the keepers told them that there were other rooms to see—that there were very interesting things in the basement. They made their way down—it grew much darker and they heard a great deal of thunder—and entered a part of the house which presented itself to Laura as a series of dim, irregular vaults—passages and little narrow avenues—encumbered with strange vague things, obscured for the time but some of which had a wicked, startling look, so that she wondered how the keepers could stay there. "It's very fearful—it looks like a cave of idols!" she said to her companion; and then she added—"Just look there—is that a person or a thing?" As she spoke they drew nearer to the object of her reference—a figure in the middle of a small vista of curiosities, a figure which answered her question by uttering a short shriek as they approached. The immediate cause of this cry was apparently a vivid flash of lightning, which penetrated into the room and illuminated both Laura's face and that of the mysterious person. Our young lady recognised her sister, as Mrs. Berrington had evidently recognised her. "Why, Selina!" broke from her lips before she had time to check the words. At the same moment the figure turned quickly away, and then Laura saw that it was accompanied by another, that of a tall gentleman with a light beard which shone in the dusk. The two persons retreated together—dodged out of sight, as it were, disappeared in the gloom or in the labyrinth of the objects exhibited. The whole encounter was but the business of an instant. . . . She was glad her companion could not see her face, and yet she wanted to get out, to rush up the stairs, where he would see it again, to escape from the place. She wished not to be there with *them*—she was overwhelmed with a sudden horror . . . so astonishing that in the immensity of London so infinitesimally small a chance should have got itself enacted. What a queer place to come to—for people like them![92]

The labyrinthine, catacomblike character of Soane's subterranean architecture finds its social purpose in peeling away its visitors' veneer of respectability.

The descent into the underworld—spatially through the underground railway and the museum's structure, atmospherically through the darkening of the thunderstorm, temporally through the antiquities contained in the catacombs, and anthropologically through the commentary on the "cave of idols"—leads to a confusion between person and thing followed by a flash of recognition itself both material (lightning) and mental. It is not so much a restoration of memory, for the underground contains nothing that does not actually also exist (or did not once exist) in the world above, as it is a vindication of memory: "She has lied—she has lied again—she has lied!"[93] The journey underground prepares Laura to be educated in an unmediated, "primitive" fashion on the interpretation of her perceptions. Her immediate thoughts remain formulated in the language of the world above, to which the realm below appears an incoherent assemblage, "so astonishing that in the immensity of London so infinitesimally small a chance should have got itself enacted." The principle of fiction is equally the assertion of the Soane museum: through a web of coincidence, an unforeseen if perhaps also all-too-familiar development emerges out of an apparently haphazard collection of facts.

The conclusion of the episode throws back onto Laura not so much the guilt of her sister as the distorted reflection of the suspicious appearance of her own conduct. When she and Wendover emerge from the museum, they find that Mrs. Berrington and Captain Crispin have taken the carriage in which the former pair had come from their apparently uneventful (because undescribed) visit to St. Paul's. Wondering why her sister and her sister's lover had risked traveling in the open, without cab or carriage, Laura concludes, "The pair had snatched a walk together (in the course of a day of many edifying episodes) for the 'lark' of it, and for the sake of the walk had taken the risk, which in that part of London, so detached from all gentility, had appeared to them so small."[94] Given that her own excursion had begun similarly with the "Romantic, bohemian manner" of the Underground, it is evident that the descent has also revealed to Laura the ambiguity of her own behavior.[95] Her reaction to the museum is no less ambivalent than her reaction to this insight: "There were uncanny, unexpected objects that Laura edged away from, that she would have preferred not to be in the room with."[96] The Victorian ambivalence toward the underground is commonplace; James's rooting of it within the now somewhat disreputable but characteristically Victorian space of Soane's Museum illuminates the mechanism of the ambivalence as it is deployed within the structure of the plot. It is the same ambivalence diagnosed by Dickens in his visit to the churchyard on a stormy night, and the same ambivalence deployed, in diluted form, as a selling point for the new London cemeteries.

Coal City

Has anybody considered what a clamor in the world this astonishing news would cause: "they have discovered a coal mine beneath Paris"?

LOUIS SIMONIN, *La Vie souterraine* (1867)

We have seen how the catacomb was the form most adequate for expressing the contradictions between ancient and modern, organic and inorganic, above- and belowground, within the space of the contemporary metropolis. But there was another city of the dead in the nineteenth-century imagination, a city that embodied the same contradictions, although with a generally much less happy resolution. This was the coal mine: its inhabitants may still have been putatively alive, but they were portrayed as a race apart, as good as dead in their subterranean metropolis. The closest material reality to the fantasies of Lilian Herbert Andrews's prehistoric mole people or H. G. Wells's Morlocks was the authentically neotroglodytic lifestyle of the coal miner. If, as Lewis Mumford argued in the 1930s, the coal mine had bequeathed to the modern city the wonders of industrial technology, the space of the mine itself was consistently represented as an underground city in return.[97] In the words of Thomas Wallace Knox, "A great city, in its moral or immoral life, is cut and seamed with subterranean excavations more extensive than those of the richest coal-fields of England or Belgium."[98] Knox was referring primarily to financial speculation, but like the majority of such comparisons, he played on the mine's likeness to the slums and lower depths of the contemporary metropolis. There were other comparisons, however, that stressed the technological connection, proposing the mining city as a model for the subterranean life of the future, a dream of reconciliation similar to that offered by the modern catacombs.

Even a rationalistic writer such as Louis Simonin could not resist the urban metonymy in his comprehensive and influential celebration of mining, *La Vie souterraine* (1867), evoking the traffic and activity of the metropolitan street for the armchair tourist through the shared feature of horse and railway transport: "Let us visit these different quarters of the mine, let us enter the subterranean labyrinth. In the blasting sites, where you hear the noise, where you smell the odor of powder, here are the hewers. In the galleries, the rollers. And the horses hurry along, the trains come and go."[99] For Simonin, the horse was the only true inhabitant of the subterranean city; its senses and reflexes adjusted to the exigencies of its space, it lived and died in the world below. In his study, the horse stood in for the miner himself; for Simonin flatly rejects the "fables, the tissue of errors," that would claim that the same adaptation might apply equally to the workers. In his model, the mine was simply a factory: "The inhabitants stay there only a part of the day or night, only in order to carry out their tasks . . . There are thus neither promenades there, nor shops, nor houses, as one might imagine, and still less are there live-in miners who never again see the light of day once having descended into the works." The city-mine was a powerful image, he implied, but one suitable only for "the romantic, dramatic side of things."[100]

Nevertheless, Simonin's inclusion of the city suggests a spatial experience not to be encompassed by that of the single-use factory. In its enormity, in its darkness, in its combination of the natural and the man-made, the mine did resemble the factory, but surpassed it as well. To map it as a modern city remained the only way Simonin could find in which fully to express his thesis, the wonder of the achievements of mining:

> The galleries crisscross in every direction like city streets with a thousand twists and turns [figure 2.17]. . . . There are intersections and squares. Each path has its own name and destination, but there are no signposts; the first days, you get lost, but then you find your way around through habit. Some of the galleries—long, wide, well-ventilated—form the main arteries, the main streets: this is the mine's good neighborhood. The others are sometimes low, narrow, winding, almost without air, maintained and worked for less time: these are like the old neighborhoods, soon to disappear. This subterranean city is inhabited night and day; it is illuminated, but by smoking lamps. It has railroads drawn by horses, by locomotives. It has streams, canals, and fountains, sources of running water that, it is true, one could do without. It even has certain indigenous plants and creatures, and life, as we have said, seems to take on special forms in it. It is the black and deep city, the city of coal, an animated center of work.[101]

The model for Simonin's city was the rationalizing metropolis of the Second Empire: just as Haussmann's improvements had replaced the tortuous, dark slums

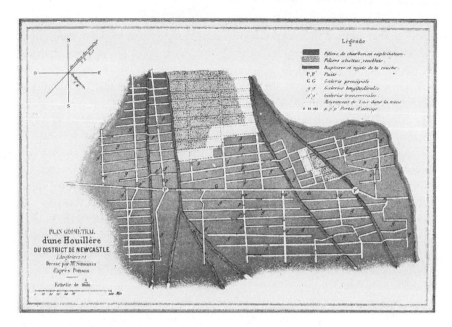

2.17. "The galleries crisscross in all directions like city streets." *Geometrical map of a Coal mine in the Newcastle district (England).* Adapted by M. Simonin from Ponson, in Louis Simonin, *La Vie souterraine; ou Les mines et les mineurs* (Paris: Hachette, 1867): 268, map 15.

with wide, airy boulevards, so new technology and improving conditions had made the modern mine a space of order and control.

Still, there is a paradoxical reversal in the terms of the comparison. In this model, the order of the city above comes from its signposts, its new house numbering; Simonin imagined it as a conceived, controlled space. The order of the mine is lived, representational, it comes from "habit"; like its horses, the description implies, its workers come to inhabit it as second nature, even if they just work there. The only thing that follows the same rules in the subterranean city as in the metropolis above is the layout of the streets and the infrastructure of transportation. Water, by contrast, is as unwelcome and dangerous below as it is both ornamental and useful above. The ways of life below take on "special forms." Those special forms, however, never appear outside of their subordination to the city above. There are cracks in Simonin's *ville souterraine,* but not to a degree to shake the conceptual framework of technological progress and urban improvement.

Such a combination of similitude and difference is even more apparent in a popularizing work addressed to the "young reader" such as *Half Hours Underground,* in which both city above and city below function seamlessly, with the sole exception that one is wholly exclusive of the other, once a "black hole" like that of Calcutta, now an improved "black city" full of "black citizens."[102] The mine is a city much like London, its limits defined by the thoroughfares of business (figure 2.18):

> There are two shafts or ways into the town, one at each end. So let us conceive the height of St. Paul's and of the Monument of London to represent the two shafts, and ourselves and the streets we traverse the workmen and the interior of the pit. St. Paul's Churchyard and the Monument-yard shall be the busy spaces at the bottom of the shafts; Cheapside, Cannon Street and Thames Street, shall be the main streets of the pit; the numerous streets branching off right and left from it, and Bread Street, Queen Street, &c., may be the side streets. The streets crossing these again give us an idea of the narrow continuous courts and smaller passages. The blocks of warehouses on every side of the streets would be the coal walls in the pit; and could we but suddenly let down a thick covering over our heads just a few feet above them to exclude light and air, we should have the counterpart of a northern coal-pit.[103]

Most Victorian writers would have concluded with the predictable flourish likening the "thick covering" to the London fog; its omission by the author of *Half Hours Underground* underlines the conceptual rather than natural grounds of the comparison.

The subsequent paragraph corrects the comparison by asserting that the dimensions of a coal town are far too vast to be conveyed adequately by imagining

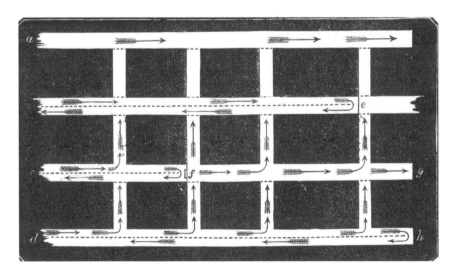

2.18. *Coal-Town Streets*: a simplified version of the urban metonymy as befits a simpler representation of the space of the mine. Illustration in *Half Hours Underground: Volcanoes, Mines, and Caves*, The Half Hour Library of Travel, Nature and Science for Young Readers, 1878 (London: James Nisbet & Co., 1900): 191.

the distance between St. Paul's and the Monument. Why not, then, have summoned up the entirety of sprawling London, as Simonin did the expanse of Haussmann's Paris? The City presented itself as the fitting comparison because it represents the coal town as an abstract, ordered, and controlled space. As opposed to the urban mysteries, which depicted underground space as threatening and destructive, the juvenile popular science genre of this volume or the more technologically mature version in Simonin strives to incorporate the underground within the framework of man-made space. Hence the mapping of the coal town onto the City of London, not merely through the horizontal street network, but through the verticalized space of the view from above. The representation of the mine begins from the traditional vantage points of St. Paul's and the Monument; the city below is put into perspective, abstracted before the act of descent proper. For both Simonin and the author of *Half Hours Underground,* the controlled city controls the mine.

The commonest point of intersection between city and mine metonymized the mine on this verticalized model: a city of the poor, of workers, beneath the city of the wealthy. This verticalized space was already current enough to be satirized by John Leech in his 1843 cartoon in *Punch,* "Capital and Labour" (figure 2.19). The artist imagined an underground society of exactly the sort denied by Simonin. Mining tunnels in the background, slowly rising to but never intersecting with the drawing rooms of the wealthy above, characterize a subterranean space inhabited by hunched old beggars, scrawny children, and despairing parents. There are two intruders on the scene: a fat foreman sits scowling upon a rock to the left next to some bags of gold, and two young children, still plump and presumably rosy-cheeked, embrace each other in fear in the center of the image, standing in the basket by which they have apparently just been lowered down into this infernal space. Down to the abandoned babes, "Capital and Labour" graphically projected the social topography of the London melodrama onto the space of the mine.

The accompanying text sarcastically outlined the principal tenets of the vertical world:

It's gratifying to know that though there is much misery in the coal mines, where the "labourers are obliged to go on all-fours like dogs," there is a great deal of luxury results from it. The public mind has been a great deal shocked by very offensive representations of certain underground operations, carried on by an inferior race of human beings, employed in working the mines, but *Punch's* artist has endeavoured to do away with the disagreeable impression, by showing the very refined and elegant result that happily arises from the labours of those inferior creatures. The works being performed wholly under ground, ought never to have been obtruded on the notice of the public. They are not intended for the light of day, and it is therefore unfair to make them the subject of illustration. When taken in conjunction with the very pleasing pictures of aristocratic ease to which they give rise, the labours in the mines must have a very dif-

2.19. Verticalized space: the argument for social hierarchy graphically rendered. Illustration by John Leech, *Capital and Labour, Punch* 5 (May 1843): 48.

ferent aspect from that which some injudicious writers have endeavoured to attach to them.[104]

The view from above places underground space in proper perspective, asserting its ever-improving conditions even while maintaining a strict separation. *Punch,* by contrast, played on the view from below, the sensationalistic portrayal of underground life in all of its horrors. The satire takes in shocked reactions by newspapers such as the *London Times* to popular representations of crime and poverty as well as political assertions of the necessity of such labor, emphasizing by the combination the double desire to look the other way.

The verticalized argument has been an enduring one. It is perhaps nowhere more distastefully expressed than in an 1853 serial entitled *Jane Rutherford; or, the Miner's Strike,* by "A Friend of 'The People.'" *Jane Rutherford* was serialized in the first two volumes of a penny weekly entitled *The True Briton,* which aimed to be "Christian and moral . . . without being decidedly religious," and which presented ways both spiritual and practical in which members of its working- and lower-middle-class readership could improve themselves. Its first serial was *Uncle Tom's Cabin.* simultaneously to *Jane Rutherford* ran something entitled *Confes-*

sions d'un ouvrier, printed in French, accompanied by an interlinear "scholar's translation" into English, and followed each week by a chapter of "French in easy lessons." The reader of *The True Briton* could thus better him or herself culturally while ingesting important lessons about the importance of industry and the destructiveness of radical politics. The plot of the serial is forgettable beyond its naturalization of a vertical society in which both the capitalist and the worker are inherently virtuous and the strike harmful to all concerned, disrupting the natural trickle-down effect of wealth. True to the characterization of *Punch* ten years earlier, the author asserted that he or she would never have written this book if not for the chance of having "descended one fine summer day into a coal-pit" to view "the mysterious occupations of those who labour therein."[105] A similar process of naturalization occurs with the horses, which are purported to be blind, assimilated by evolution to their environment just as, by extension, the miners will have been.

Consequently, the operation of mines is also an unfortunate but inevitable iniquity of nature. The narrator begins with the familiar injunction that we should be "ashamed . . . when we remember that thousands, yea, tens of thousands of our fellow creatures get their living from day to day, and from year to year, in these miserable holes."[106] From here, the analysis passes to a general principle of a vertical society, with the coal mine as metonymy for the workplace:

> It is evidently the lot of one portion of our fellow-creatures to pass their lives in labouring for living or for wealth—not in sight of the warm sun of the heaven, nor enjoying the pure breeze, nor basking in all the glories of the external earth, but in glimmering darkness, in subterranean caverns, in strange and murky mines, where one ray of sun-light never penetrates, where the balmy atmosphere never disperses fragrance, but where danger and death stalk around in fearful proximity.[107]

The rhetorical confusion between a feeling of empathy for the subterranean worker and an aesthetic reaction of wonder ("strange and murky") and terror ("where danger and death stalk around in fearful proximity") suggests that the conscience of a middle-class audience was being palliated more than the resentment of the working-class being quelled.

The way in which the language slips from a discourse of social commentary to one of sensational fiction can remind us of the double effect of the view from above. First, it allows one to distance the underground life by placing it within a holistic perspective accepted as inevitable. Second, it allows an aesthetic pleasure to be gained from the fantastic aspects of that life; for from above the underworld always appears in an alien light, alluring or repellant as the case may be. The conclusion of the passage stresses the propriety of both aspects of this view. No pleasure is possible without the suffering of others: "And yet, how could the world be carried on, but for the product of these labours? The misery and danger of thousands of our fellow-beings, is the source of happiness to millions."[108] A statistical sleight of hand has reversed the numerical balance of labor and capital. Even so, one should not feel any guilt in enjoying both the fruits of the labor and the spectacle of it, for the plight of those underground is primarily of their own making: "Part of the miner's misery is unavoidable, much more is occasioned by his own reckless conduct in the mine, and improvidence out of it."[109] Christian resignation and Christian morality are the final guarantors of separation between the world above and the world below.

Viewed from above, the space of the mine could only ever be a natural space to which one was condemned. Indeed, before the industrialized exploitation of coal began in the eighteenth century, mining, a practice dating back to several millennia BCE, was almost universally conducted as forced labor under appalling conditions. Even less than space in general does subterranean space ever shed any representational character that has once been attributed to it. And yet, the mine, as origin and epitome of industrial space, was as powerful a distillation of the city as hell as the trench would be in the early twentieth century. As conditions within the modern city came more and more to resemble those of the coal mine—polluted, mechanized, dangerous, monotonous—so its inhabitants were ever more easily assimilated to the representational space of the mine.

In the view from below, by contrast, the savagery and sensationalism were exaggerated, with no palliatives, there being no contrasting high point to which to escape. In G. W. M. Reynolds's best-selling *Mysteries of London* (1844–48), for example, the life story of the Rattlesnake, common law wife of an associate of the body-snatching Resurrection Man, mining is depicted not as a daily occupation but as a world unto itself.[110] Although the view from above stressed the possibility of difference, while assuring that no change would ever occur, the view from below exaggerated in the other direction, asserting that there was no difference at all but that change was imperative. The rationalizing texts cited above pretend toward analysis while naturalizing an artificial division of labor; the sensationalism of the urban mystery makes the underground into an artificial infinity, threatening to overturn society by its irredeemable horror.

Born in a "damp cave" during a brief break in her mother's work shift, the Rattlesnake epitomizes the representation of the miner as atavistic. She is reared in "a complete state of mental darkness," and it makes no difference that she may have since then lived part of her life outside of the mining environment; she is a cave dweller through and through. Reynolds's portrait of the mines through the voice of the Rattlesnake, documented with copious footnotes, presents a space of leisure as well as of labor, a lived space, for better or for worse, and a space no different in its physical and moral characteristics than those attributed by him and many others to the rookeries and low lodging houses of London:

> In a few minutes, I saw the *undergoers* (or miners) lying on their sides . . . I perceived that these men were naked—stark naked. . . . The passage abruptly opened in to a

large room,—an immense cave. . . . This cave was lighted by a great number of can-dles; and at a table sat about twenty individuals—men, women, and children—all at breakfast. There they were, as black as negroes—eating, laughing, chattering, and drinking. . . . I saw that the women and young girls were all naked from the waist up-wards, and many of the men completely so. And yet there was no shame—no embar-rassment. . . . At length I grew quite hardened . . . I became familiar with the constant presence of naked men and half-naked women . . . I walked boldly into the great cav-ern, which served as a place of meeting for those who took their meals in the mine.[III]

The prurience of the description is inseparable from the essential detail of every-day life—"eating, laughing, chattering, and drinking"—wholly absent from the dehumanized portrayal of the rationalized mine workers discussed above. And while the Rattlesnake comments that "the entire population that labours in the pits appears to belong to a race that is accursed" and determines to leave the mine, the gypsy world into which she is later assimilated and the urban under-world in which she ends up are inhabited likewise by "a race that is accursed."[112]

As the amplification of the mine into a microcosm of the industrial world, the view from below took two directions in the later nineteenth century. On the one hand, naturalist novelists such as Zola and George Gissing expanded the patho-logical dimension into a principle of nature. Without the material space of the mine to underpin its imagery, and rejecting the theological trappings implicit in its title by voicing the theme of damnation exclusively through the rantings of Mad Jack, Gissing's *The Nether World* (1889) reduced its representation of oppres-sion to the iteration of degeneracy—powerful and seductive in its bleakness, but unredeeming in its dehumanizing portrait of the inhabitants. Although as dehu-manizing a portrait as Gissing's, Zola's *Germinal* at least grounded that process in the atavistic associations of underground living and the economic circumstances of mine labor: consequently, relief can be found in animal comforts as well as in destruction. The mine retained an idealistic aspect unavailable to the discourse of Gissing's London. This aspect can be glimpsed negatively in Reynolds's elabora-tion of the "great cavern" of an Edenic community free of shame; amplified and romanticized, it surfaces also in the mining utopia of Jules Verne's Coal Town in *Les Indes noires,* shorn, of course, of its sex and violence—and hence also of any trace of realism.

The meaning of underground space in *Germinal* hinges on the double sense of the word *mine,* both in English and in French: one can either exploit the un-derground by digging out its valuable ore, or one can undermine it, destroy it through hidden explosives. The two meanings merge uneasily in the everyday practice of mining, for what is of value can usually be extracted only after it has been loosened by explosives; they come together metaphorically only late in the novel, in the image of the city. It is significant to the form and ideology of Zola's novel that this convergence occurs negatively: the mine comes to resemble a city only once it has become a ruin, once it has been destroyed by the sabotage of the Russian anarchist Souvarine. The workers' positive demands for fair conditions are never to be reconciled with the impulse to revolution; the rational underground can be reconciled with the underworld only in annihilation.

City and revolution first occur in the novel in paratactic rather than metaphorical proximity. The former is characterized as a blind, instinctive labor, when the outsider Etienne, like the new mining horse, Bataille, successfully incorporates the space of the mine into his perceptions as second nature: "From then on, he knew the galleries of the mine better than the streets of Montsou, knew that you had to turn here, had to duck further on, had somewhere else to avoid a pool of water. He was so habituated to those two kilometers beneath the earth that he could have done them without a lamp, hands in his pockets."[113] Zola's view from below borrows directly from Simonin's *La Vie souterraine* in its endeavor to reproduce the miner's perception of space and experience of everyday life. At this point, the resemblance to the city derives from the rhythms dictated by a modern space rather than the requirements of symbolism. Unlike Simonin's rationalization, however, Zola's mine is dominated by a conflict between conceived space and lived space, as epitomized in the conflict between miners and management over payment for fortification of the tunnels; for the miners a luxury of safety they cannot afford, for the management a need to rationalize the space in order to reduce breaks in production caused by cave-ins. Moreover, there is another space entirely within the mine, a physical extension of the instinctive knowledge of its passages. This is the abandoned entrance first developed as a hideout by Maheud's son, Zacharie, later used by Etienne as a refuge from the authorities after the strike leads to violence, and finally providing the means of Etienne's rescue from the flooded mine.

The life of Souvarine, too, is introduced as a materially underground experience, even as the metaphorical repercussions of his character remain present:

> For a month, he had lived in a fruit merchant's cellar, digging a mine across the street, charging the bombs, in constant danger of blowing himself up with the house. Disowned by his family, penniless, placed as foreign on the index of the French workshops that saw him as a spy, he was dying of hunger when the Montsou Company had finally taken him on in an hour of pressing need.[114]

Souvarine embodies the underground man, convinced that only out of total destruction of the world above could any new life be formed. Generally, the late nineteenth-century anarchist, as, for example, in Joseph Conrad's *The Secret Agent* or Henry James's *The Princess Cassamassima,* was described as a metaphorical mine in the underworld of the metropolis.[115] In his fin-de-siècle novel, *Paris* (1898), Zola would follow a similar but more literal pattern: the protagonist's elder brother, a mad inventor, attempts to blow up the still unfinished Sacré-

Coeur in a plot punctuated by fictionalized versions of the anarchist attacks that shook Paris in the 1890s.[116] The priest and the scientist battle in the quarries beneath Montmartre before brotherly love defuses political fanaticism. "Let the temple crumble along with its god of lies and servitude!" the scientist Guillaume raves. "And let it crush the faithful under its ruins, so that the catastrophe, like the geological revolutions of ancient times, resonates through the very entrails of humanity, renewing and transforming it!"[117]

In *Germinal*, Zola similarly grounded the metaphor within the cycles of nature, just as he used the mine as a material realization of the general phenomenon of the exploitation of labor. When the metropolis finally enters the picture, it does so emphatically and grandiloquently, as the sabotage of Le Voreux takes on the dimensions of a cataclysm, an underground flood of an accursed city by the uncontrollable forces of nature summoned into being by the ongoing exploitation of man by man. First, the foreman descends to survey the damage, no longer able to recognize the rationalized space of before: "He thought he could make out the streets and intersections of the destroyed city, very far off, in the play of the great moving shadows. No human work was possible any longer."[118] From below, however, the changed space is even more terrifying. In another detail from Simonin's book that Zola bent to his own purpose, the horse stands in for the human cave dweller:

> It was Battle [Bataille]. . . . He seemed to know his way in this subterranean city he had inhabited for eleven years; and his eyes saw clearly into the depths of the eternal night in which he had lived. . . . The roads followed one after the other, the crossings forked off, but he never hesitated. Where was he going? Down there perhaps, toward that vision of his youth, to the windmill where he had been born, to the hazy memory of the sunshine burning in the air like a giant lamp. . . . And a rebellion carried off his old resignation, after having blinded him, this pit was killing him. (476)

The horse's name underlines the allegory of its death, raising the essential question of the novel through the dissolution of the only space in which it could have been raised: how to battle against exploitation without simply destroying the unique space in which one has to live?

Hence the dead city, the necropolis in which is buried the hope for change, the "sewer, the ruins of a city that has collapsed and sunk into the mud" (468). This is the moment when Zola shifts out of the view from below and into a broader conception of space. The flood begun by the underground river broken loose by Souvarine's explosives threatens the very fabric of modernity, whether as a rational consequence of inequality or as a punishment from the heavens: "The mine was drinking up this river, the flood would now submerge the galleries for years. Soon the crater filled up, a lake of muddy water occupied the place where Le Voreux had been, just like those lakes underneath which the damned cities slumber" (459). The image of the thirsty mine drinking up the river preserves a trace of the natural impulse of the uprising of the poor; the form of that uprising, however, remains sterile and deadly, embodied in the virus of Souvarine, making his way from the mine to the city:

> He set off without a look back, into the now black night. . . . He was going down there, into the unknown. He was going, with his calm air, toward extermination, wherever there was dynamite, to blow up cities and men. That would be him, no doubt, when the agonizing bourgeoisie will hear beneath itself, at every step, the pavement of the streets torn apart [*éclaté*]. (459)

Paris, until the climax of the novel evoked only as the seat of the headquarters of the mining company, is drawn directly into the sphere of the novel, the inevitable endpoint of the trajectory of violence.

The view from below results in a powerful image of devastation, with not a little bit of righteous anger mixed in with a conventional distaste for the destruction of property. Zola pushed the constraints of the genre and tried to conceptualize a plausible resolution that would be less apocalyptic. The ray of hope comes, again, through nature, the metaphor of the novel's title, it, too, a play on words. The primary meaning throughout appears to be a reference to the month Germinal in the revolutionary calendar, a fitting image for the running theme of bona fide, radical intentions gone awry in terror. But the concluding sentence returns to the roots of the revolutionary intention to retrieve a natural rhythm out of the underground: "Men were sprouting, a black and vengeful army, which was germinating slowly in the furrows and fissures, growing for the harvests of the future century, and their germination was soon going to tear apart [*faire éclater*] the earth" (502). A natural revolution cannot emerge from the standpoint of naturalism, however; the violence of the final verb *éclater* once again falls back into the perspective of the urban mysteries. The powerful underground can be natural only in a degenerative, atavistic sense; it can lead to survival but not to change, and if it ever succeeds in emerging aboveground its blinded senses will cause nothing but destruction.

In *Les Indes noires,* Jules Verne posed the question of the end of the mine and the changes in mining conditions from the point of view of the rational scientist. Zola's novel concludes with the failure of a strike and the forced closing of a ruined mine; Verne's opens with an equally realistic scene, the shutting down of an exhausted coal mine, "like the body of a mastodon of a fantastic size from which one has removed the various vital organs and left only the ossature," which he conjoins with a fantasy, the amicable parting of ways of the engineer, James Starr, and his loyal workers.[119] The comparison to the skeleton of a beast evokes a sense of waste: everything still usable, the narrator recounts, has been removed; nothing is left but a deserted ruin. To call it a dinosaur's skeleton, however, conjures a different idea as well, of something lost, hidden, and obscure—and able, consequently, to be rediscovered. It is also to recall, as Verne explicitly does later on, that in nature nothing in fact is ever wasted, that coal is the result of a transformation of "vegetable into mineral" no less magical than the survival of the traces of an extinct monster (21). By naturalizing the conditions under which the earth is exploited, Verne creates a space in which he can address the pressing issue of what to do with the apparently desolate spaces left behind by that exploitation; for, he observes most presciently, "One day we will lack coal—this much is certain" (23).

Verne set his mine in Aberfoyle, Scotland—as far from London as the British Isles could take him, and even farther from the mines of northern France and Belgium—for several reasons. First of all, Scotland lends his narrative a certain imperial resonance, suitable to the metaphor of the novel's title, coined, he says, by the British because "these Indies have perhaps contributed more than those of the Orient to increasing the surprising wealth of the United Kingdom" (3). Second, it allows him to contrast the new genre of the scientific romance with the historical romances of Sir Walter Scott. When, ten years after the mine is closed, James Starr receives an invitation from his foreman, Simon Ford, who has been living in the mine with his family at the foot of the shaft, to visit him there, and another mysterious letter telling him to stay away, he rushes through the streets of Edinburgh, oblivious, for the first time in his life, to the memory associations of its landmarks with the events and characters of Scott's novels. Throughout the novel, the romance of the world below Scotland is favorably contrasted with the now outdated legends of the "old Caledonian" landscape above. In a curious way, Verne's strategy makes explicit the link between historical re-creation and current ideology in Scott: the story of coal, too, is a romance with roots in ancient history but with ramifications for the present and the future.

Much of the strength of Verne's book lies in its reversal of certain generic expectations; its primary weakness lies in the predictability with which it fulfills others. On his return to the mine, James Starr crosses the now deserted countryside, no longer covered by "dark vapors," no longer full of chimneys "vomiting smoke," the soil no longer "dirtied by coal dust" (32). Rather than finding pleasure in the return of pastoral nature, he is beset with nostalgia for industry. Removed from the sphere of human influence, the once teeming industrial space has reverted to nature; Verne repeats the skeleton metaphor to stress the role of death in a natural cycle. Just as nature transmuted organic remains into the inorganic mineral coal, so nature has transformed the inorganic machinery of exploitation into gigantic skulls, backbones, and rib cages (35). The reversal of expectations is utopian, for it is conciliatory. Once stripped of its mythic connotations, once removed from the polarizations of aboveground vs. underground, organic vs. inorganic, natural vs. manmade, and labor vs. capital, the world of the mine—and by extension that of the city for which it will come to stand—can be reconceived in wholly unforeseen ways.

The first step is to discover organic nature within the mine, and we find it in the Ford family's "habitation—to which he would willingly grant the name of 'cottage' . . . a subterranean dwelling dug into the schistose massif at the very place where once the powerful machines worked to operate the mechanical traction of the Dochart pit" (48). Verne is careful to distinguish Simon Ford from the run-of-the-mill cave dweller: Ford is comfortably off, and could in fact live wherever he pleases. Still, his choice reinforces the colonial undertone of the novel, for his is a frontier mentality: underground there are no taxes and no censuses; here, he is king of all he surveys. In this implicit update of *Robinson Crusoe* and other fictions of colonial settlement, it is not surprising that there are alien presences: a strange girl, "the child of the cavern," who protects the exploring engineers; a mysterious man who attempts to sabotage their forays; and an enormous owl, pet of the old man but now attached to the girl he had raised. The simple plot involves resolving the mystery of Silfax, an apparently native inhabitant of the underground realm with an inexplicable hostility toward his new neighbors.

The colonial motif remains an undertone, however, because the novel eschews a verticalized structure, making no hard distinction between peripheral colony and imperial center. Verne does make implicit connections to North America, naming the community "New Aberfoyle," and comparing the extensive passages discovered by Ford and Starr to the natural wonders of Mammoth Cave in Kentucky.[120] Nevertheless, these allusions seem more likely to be invoking the possibility of undiscovered resources than a distinctly center-periphery relationship. As "Coal Town" begins to be developed, Verne stresses the proximity to the surface rather than the distance: a rail tunnel is dug leading out, making possible rapid communication with the cities of Scotland. At the same time, hints do appear of the more familiar nineteenth-century underground, as when the narrator speculates on the possibility of using extinct mines "in these temperate zones" as "refuges" "for the impoverished class of the United Kingdom."[121]

As befits his utopianism, Verne is careful to stress the pleasures of his new city rather than its potential hardships. Its enormous chamber, partially filled by an underground lake, is natural, "God-given," and beyond comparison to any "apogee of the Egyptian era" or "catacombs of the Roman era" (87). It lacks only the sun's rays or starlight to be habitable, and, indeed, the lakes would not be "without charm" under some electric light" (88). Such charm is a characteristically French combination of the natural and the man-made, a novel but recognizably picturesque experience. Coal Town, established by Starr and Ford to house the workers exploiting the newly discovered veins, combines nostalgic motifs of a "Flemish village"—cottages and a chapel on the edge of a lake—with the modern technology of the transport revolution, the futuristic technology of rotating electric disks to light the town, and the "fantastic" aspect of the subterranean setting (figure 2.20) (136). Not surprisingly, it quickly appears in the "Murray and Joanne Guides"; with the paired titles, Verne is careful to involve both British and French tourists in the experience.

2.20. Technological utopia, Paris style: Coal Town rivals the Scottish capital as first city, with better weather, electric lights, and dancing to boot. Illustration by Jules-Descartes Férat, engraved by Charles Barbant, *Holiday in Coal Town*, in Jules Verne, *Underground City; or, The Child of the Cavern*, tr. W. H. G. Kingston (Philadelphia: Porter & Coates, [1883]: 140), of *Les Indes noires* (Paris: Hachette, 1877).

The scale is important; for there is an underlying ambivalence between boundless enthusiasm for exploring and invention, and fear of overstepping natural and divine bounds. The explorers almost die when they are trapped by a landslide. It occurs directly after the first discovery of New Aberfoyle, when Ford's son, Harry, carried away with excitement, has speculated on the possibilities of the exploitation of coal: "Let us dig our trenches under the waters of the sea! Let us dig a hole like a skimmer in the bed of the Atlantic! Let us go rejoin our brothers in the United States with shovel-strokes across the Ocean's basement! Let us dig all the way to the center of the earth if necessary in order to root out every last lump of its coal!" (96) The transatlantic fantasy in fact would grow in attraction as the century drew to a close, but Verne seems to prefer to limit such fantasies. Coal Town remains deliberately small-scale, a population "sharing the same interests, the same tastes, all about equally well off . . . a big family" (136). His lesson is that the underground can be kept limited and controllable; the aboveground cannot.

It is a lesson embodied in the character of Nell, rescued by Harry from the bottom of a deep pit into which he could not resist venturing in his relentless exploration of New Aberfoyle. Nell is a test case, for before Harry will be allowed to marry her, she must be shown the world above, so that she can know what she will be choosing to leave behind. The group tours once again "the land of Rob Roy and Fergus Mac Gregor," the capital city and the rugged countryside (189). But Harry's descent into the true depths of the cavern has reintroduced a vertical structure to the space of Coal Town, and conflict into the utopian village, as individual desire always will do in such narratives. The genius of the place has been aroused, and while Nell is touring the world above, the lake she is boating on floods into the world below, nearly drowning the boaters and nearly destroying Coal Town.

The truly underground figure, about whom earlier theories proposed a devil haunting the area or a band of counterfeiters, turns out to be the remnant of the bad old days of mining, a so-called "penitent," whose job, accompanied by his owl, was to seek out firedamp and explode it on a small scale with a torch in order to avoid large-scale disasters. The practice, as Verne explains, had died out with the invention of the Davy safety lamp. Driven insane by the repeated explosions, Silfax had remained underground, nursing the fantasy that the mine belonged to him, and raising his granddaughter, Nell. Silfax is a familiar image of the return of the repressed, scoffed at on the surface of the novel, but, like all such mysteries, obscurely identifying genuine conflicts. Like all underground misfits, Silfax wishes to destroy the order around him; the novel concludes with his failed attempt to blow up Coal Town, finally reversing the terms of his longtime occupation as a penitent.

While Starr and the Ford family propose the model of a nonhierarchical, utopian future imagined in the conciliatory space of Coal Town, the underground trio of Silfax, Nell, and the owl(torn in loyalty between its two masters) are all three remnants of a previous, stubbornly verticalized order. In traditional romance fashion, the underground splits into the positive, redeemable Nell and the negative, irredeemable Silfax. The owl is a less common feature, the token of Verne's investment in the reality of coal mining rather than simply an underground fantasy akin to those of Bulwer-Lytton, Wells, and Tarde. Partially domesticated as part of the apparatus of coal mining, the owl nevertheless remains wild at heart, unlike the horses of *Germinal* and Simonin. Its appearance in the illustrations, drawn by Jules-Descartes Férat and engraved by Charles Barbant, reminds us of its traditional association with Athena, goddess of wisdom, especially in the three plates that frame the volume: the frontispiece, the title page, and the concluding struggle (figures 2.21–23).

2.21. A generic mystery: What lies within? Illustration by Jules-Descartes Férat, engraved by Charles Barbant, frontispiece to Jules Verne, *Les Indes noires* (Paris: Hachette, 1877).

UNDERGROUND CITY;

OR,

THE CHILD OF THE CAVERN.

BY JULES VERNE,

AUTHOR OF "TWENTY THOUSAND LEAGUES UNDER THE SEA," "AROUND THE
WORLD IN EIGHTY DAYS," "AT THE NORTH POLE," ETC., ETC.

TRANSLATED BY

W. H. G. KINGSTON,

AUTHOR OF "SNOW SHOES AND CANOES," "PETER THE WHALER," ETC.

PHILADELPHIA:

PORTER & COATES.

2.22. The emblems of mining: mineshaft, owl, pick-axes, Davy lamp. Illustration by Jules-Descartes Férat, engraved by Charles Barbant, title page of Jules Verne, *Underground City; or, The Child of the Cavern*, tr. W. H. G. Kingston (Philadelphia: Porter & Coates, [1883]).

2.23. The threat of urban apocalypse: reckoning with the dark forces of the underground. Illustration by Jules-Descartes Férat, engraved by Charles Barbant, *The Supreme Moment*, in Jules Verne, *Underground City; or, The Child of the Cavern*, 241.

The frontispiece places the owl over the entrance to a mine shaft, mining tools gripped in its talons and a small lamp dangling from them, guarding a dark threshold. At the base of the opening is a group of well-dressed gawkers, backs to the viewer as they lean over the edge of the shaft, peering into its depths. It is a simple image, although enigmatic in its interpretation: It is promising something, but what? Entry into the dark space? Light in the dark? A view from above? What exactly are they looking for, and why? It is partly the question of a new genre (what Verne called the "scientific romance"): we as readers do not yet know exactly what *we* are looking for. The title page clarifies the situation somewhat, as it shows the same owl, now in flight, the lantern held in its beak, the tools behind it, the shaft now opening horizontally in the background, as if a tunnel, or as if we are now looking out from the bottom of it. The view from above offers nothing but an alluring darkness, the same allure as the initially enigmatic title, *Les Indes noires*. the view from below provides movement, action, and a precarious, unreliable light.

The precarious nature of the owl is emphasized not only when it battles Harry in the pit for the possession of Nell, but in the dénouement, where it holds in its beak not a safety lamp as in the front matter but the exposed, burning fuse torn from the lamp by its master, Silfax, ready to ignite a massive pocket of firedamp. In this illustration, faithful to the text, Silfax appears as an Old Testament prophet of doom in flowing robes and beard, silhouetted by the lamplight, arms upraised, the owl with its wings spread above his head, the machine of his vengeance. Nell wins out over the owl, the town is saved, and Silfax sinks beneath the surface of the lake, to become once again a legend. Although turned aside, the bird is never domesticated either, and is rarely seen, nursing a hatred for Harry and haunting the place for years to come.

Safety plays an important role throughout, as one should expect from a novel about mining, and the sight of a safety lamp is grounds for excitement for Starr; it means the mine could be made active again. Similarly, Ford first suspects the existence of New Aberfoyle when he comes across a patch of firedamp. The owl is in the mine as a sign of danger and never ceases to be associated with it; if Silfax and Nell are the human poles of the traditional underground, then the owl is the mythic natural residue, the double-edged promise of the world below—riches, knowledge, and danger. *Les Indes noires* concludes with Nell recuperated and Silfax and the owl reduced to legend. Unlike the urban mysteries, there are no revelations of fortunes, legacies, or lost heirs, no rises and falls; there is instead a speculation on the possible contribution of the subterranean climate to the longevity of its inhabitants. In addition to wishful thinking, the speculation encodes an epistemological belief in labor and conflict as the bases of human existence that appears in the utopian thinking of conservatives such as Bulwer-Lytton and Verne as well as in that of Fourier, Marx, and other socialists. The underground expresses both the continued need for security and the ongoing desire for danger and novelty at the core of this epistemology; hence its use as a setting in so many nineteenth-century utopias and dystopias, and hence its frequency as a figure of speech in so much related rhetoric.

Such a paradox was at work sixty years later in George Orwell's book-length essay on working-class life in the north of England between the wars, *The Road to Wigan Pier* (1937); by that date, however, it was a supremely self-conscious paradox. On the one hand, the hardship of the mines had of necessity created "the most noble bodies . . . with not an ounce of waste flesh anywhere. . . . It is impossible to watch the 'fillers' at work without feeling a pang of envy for their toughness."[122] On the other hand, the drudgery and monotony of modern, rationalized urban poverty had produced another underground, "the feeling of stagnant, meaningless decay, of having got down into some subterranean place where people go creeping round and round, just like blackbeetles, in an endless muddle of slovened job and mean grievances" (17). The simile Orwell chose to describe this life stressed the shared space of the two aspects of the experience. The difference, for Orwell, was that out of the first, even though "most of the things one imagines in hell are there—heat, noise, confusion, darkness, foul air, and, above all, unbearably cramped space"—there emerges a figure for admiration; out of the second comes only the urban degenerate decried by so much of late nineteenth and early twentieth-century social commentary (21).

It could be argued that the infernal yet impressive vision—"You can never forget that spectacle once you have seen it"—was a remnant of the industrial sublime of the previous century. After all, Orwell compares the fillers to "hammered iron statues" (23). It is a heritage Orwell attempts to downplay by the stress on his participation in the other underground: he lives in the low lodging houses, eats tinned food and butchers' discards, crawls like a black beetle through the endless tunnels. In this context, sublimity emerges as a consolation prize of sorts, as it also is wielded to explain the apparently irrationally spendthrift behavior of the unemployed as a resistance to the dullness of everyday life. Early on, Orwell describes Old Jack, a seventy-eight-year-old former miner who "seemed only to remember his boyhood experiences and to have forgotten all about the modern mining machinery and improvements. He used to tell me tales of fights with savage horses in the narrow galleries underground. . . . It was no use telling him that the 'travelling' was better than it used to be" (9). The safety of the modern-day mines is of no more account than the availability of canned food; while it may lessen the rate of catastrophic accidents, it makes everyday survival all the more meaningless and dull, eliminating the last vestiges of liberty the miners may have had.

Orwell uses so many nineteenth-century concepts partly because he sees modern-day solutions as absolute failures, which had managed only to render the working classes more invisible than ever. Hence the appeal to two quintessentially Victorian conceptions of the mine: the aboveground ignorance of the separate world below, and the comparison with the metropolis. Orwell formulates the former concept in the critical language that runs from *Punch* through Marx to Mumford:

> Our civilisation, *pace* Chesterton, *is* founded on coal, more completely than one realises until one stops to think about it. . . . Their lamp-lit world down there is as necessary to the daylight world above as the root is to the flower. . . . It is only because miners sweat their guts out that superior persons can remain superior. . . . All of us *really* owe the comparative decency of our lives to poor drudges underground, blackened to the eyes, with their throats full of coal dust, driving their shovels forward with arms and belly muscles of steel. (12, 35)

The myth is more exciting than the reality; physical suffering and feats of strength and endurance produce pangs of envy as well as pangs of guilt.

Orwell updates his description in crucial ways, all of them echoing changes in twentieth-century perceptions of and attitudes toward the city. What is terrifying to him in descending into the mine are the aspects he had never considered (because they did not predominate in nineteenth-century images of the mine, however bleak), but which were characteristic of the new metropolis: noise, lack of space, and sprawl. The key to the nineteenth-century mine as a separate world and as a city was its essentially vertical relation to the world above. It was the same, but underground: "When you think of a coal-mine you think of depth, heat, darkness, blackened figures hacking at walls of coal; you don't think, necessarily, of those miles of creeping to and fro" (29). Depth, heat, darkness, dirt: these were primary elements in nineteenth-century representations of the city, especially its slums and its poor. Creeping to and fro, the life of the black beetle: the mindless, drudging animal metaphor is new. Orwell compares it to the turn-of-the-century experience of the underground commute: "I had not realised that before he even gets to his work he may have to creep through passages as long as from London Bridge to Oxford Circus. . . . It is not part of the miner's work at all, it is merely an extra, like the City man's daily ride in the Tube" (25, 29). Just as Orwell finds less and less inspiration in the modern, rational, anonymous city, so he finds the modern mind so full of machine noise—"the frightening, deafening din from the conveyor belt which carries the coal away"—so cramped, so endless, that "the mere effort of getting from place to place makes it difficult to notice anything else" (22, 24). Verne had imagined the revitalization of an exhausted mine by an anticity city and the paradox of a naturally technologized underground; Orwell saw the dulling effect in the actual rationalization of that same space. From scientific socialism to model housing, he argued, the modern underground and the modern city kill the spirit.

The Subterranean Pastoral

They say that every time they go below they find something changed in the lower Eusapia; the dead make innovations in their city. . . . From one year to the next, they say, the Eusapia of the dead becomes unrecognizable. And the living, to keep up with them, also want to do everything that the hooded brothers tell them about the novelties of the dead. So the Eusapia of the living has taken to copying its underground copy.

They say that this has not just now begun to happen: actually it was the dead who built the upper Eusapia, in the image of their city. They say that in the twin cities there is no longer any way of knowing who is alive and who is dead.

ITALO CALVINO, "Cities and the dead. 3," *Invisible Cities* (1972)

Nearly every text emerging out of the Parisian discourse of the underground contains at least a trace of a holistic view of space and a hint of reconciliation with the world above. By contrast, positive underground habitation on the English model, as in *The Wind in the Willows,* occurs only within a pastoral setting, in the ruins of or, better still, the negation of London. As the categories hardened in the early twentieth century, representations of the city became severed from those of the physical underground, at least in the art and literature that has generally been associated with various aspects of modernism. Applied to the city, underground metaphors generally took the form of infernal imagery, as in Eliot's calque of Dante's *Inferno* to describe the passersby on London Bridge in *The Waste Land,* or Louis-Ferdinand Céline's extended comparison of the river Seine to the river Styx, full of the souls of the dead, in *D'un château l'autre.* The mine as referent was replaced by the trench, and the trench was always displaced, a trauma that made the city appear unreal, as it does for the shell-shocked Septimus Smith in Virginia Woolf's *Mrs. Dalloway,* rather than analogous.

Expressed another way, the underworld came to provide only a negative, mythic insight into urban alienation, a new variant of the view from above, with a greatly diminished sense of relation to any particular urban experience, even as modernist artists and writers more than ever flocked to the European capitals. The urban modernist view from below, adopted by various proponents of avant-garde movements, embraced the city as it was, dissolving any distinction between spaces as it dissolved the one between life and art. Finally, any overtly positive and social intuition appears literally underground, but only in the country, disconnected from the urban space to which it had been associated in the previous century. These categories reflect traditional divisions of art and literature of the first half of the twentieth century: respectively, the high modernist, putatively formalist, and experimental work, primarily of European novelists; the successive

manifestoes of radical schools, including Italian futurism, Russian construc-
tivism, vorticism, Dada, and surrealism; and the more-or-less marginal figures
who fit into neither canon. The traditional division is valid insomuch as it repro-
duces a distinctively modernist set of attitudes toward the city and toward underground space; it is deceptive insomuch as it posits any sort of extreme and definitive distinction between one form and another. At this point, I want to look at
the least familiar, least canonical, and least well defined of the trio: the positive
pastoral underground.

As discussed above, the Roman catacombs provided one such space already in
the nineteenth century, as in the transparently displaced Paris of Lacroix's *Les
Catacombes de Rome.* Walter Pater's 1885 novel, *Marius the Epicurean,* suggests a
similarly displaced space, but here, as in *Les Indes noires,* the underground community appears as an alternative to the corrupt, pagan city nearby. Seeking
meaning and fulfillment in a quintessentially modern fashion, Marius finds it in
the proto-Christian community that is centered, like social life in the medieval
city, on the burial ground:

> An old flower-garden in the rear of the house, set here and there with a venerable
> olive-tree—a picture in pensive shade and fiery blossom, as transparent, under that af-
> ternoon light, as the old miniature-painters' work on the walls of the chambers
> within—was bounded towards the west by a low, grass-grown hill. A narrow opening
> cut in its steep side, like a solid blackness there, admitted Marius and his gleaming
> leader into a hollow cavern or crypt, neither more nor less in fact than the family bur-
> ial-place of the Cecilii, to whom this residence belonged. . . . Here, in truth, was the
> centre of the peculiar religious expressiveness, of the sanctity, of the entire scene. That
> "any person may, at his own election, constitute the place which belongs to him a *re-
> ligious* place, by the carrying of his dead into it":—had been a maxim of old Roman
> law, which it was reserved for the early Christian societies . . . to realize in all its con-
> sequences. Yet this was certainly unlike any cemetery Marius had ever before seen;
> most obviously in this, that these people had returned to the older fashion of dispos-
> ing of their dead by burial instead of burning. Originally a family sepulchre, it was
> growing to a vast *necropolis,* a whole township of the deceased, by means of some free
> expansion of the family interest beyond its amplest natural limits.[123]

In Pater's description, the family burial place of the Cecilii resembles far more the
mausoleums and tombs of the nineteenth-century cemeteries than the
labyrinthine and populous expanse of the Roman catacombs on which he was
ostensibly basing himself. For the emphasis here is on intimacy, domesticity, on
bodies that seem "homelike and hopeful" (230).

This is a subjective rather than an objective effect; Marius reacts in such a positive manner to the very "high walls [that] seemed to shut one in into the great
company of the dead," the "row upon row" of loculi, and the passages, "so narrow that only one visitor of a time could move along," because he feels something else rather than seeing it (230). In the same passage, Pater explicitly com-

pares Marius's experience of the catacombs under the influence of the "homelike" atmosphere of nascent Christianity with that of the nineteenth-century Protestant tourist:

> The stern soul of the excellent Jonathan Edwards, applying the faulty theology of John Calvin, afforded him, we know, the vision of infants not a span long, on the floor of hell. Every visitor to the Catacombs must have observed, in a very different theological connection, the numerous children's graves there—beds of infants, but a span long indeed, lowly 'prisoners of hope', on these sacred floors. It was with great curiosity, certainly, that Marius considered them, decked in some instances with the favourite toys of their tiny occupants . . . and when he afterward saw the living children, who sang and were busy above—sang their psalm *Laudite Pueri Dominum!*—their very faces caught for him a sort of quaint unreality from the memory of those others, the children of the Catacombs, but a little way below them. (231)

Pater explicitly compares Marius's return to that of Dante from Hell, "emerging again, like a later mystic traveller through similar dark places 'quieted by hope', into the daylight," as if to emphasize that death and hell have not disappeared, but only been imbued with "the dominant effect of tranquil hope" (232).

Rather than conversion through surviving and making sense of a horrible vision, Marius is converted through experiencing what should be horrible as an "effect of tranquil hope." The key image in this conversion is the "sort of quaint unreality" of the "children of the Catacombs." The reference to modern tourism and modern sermonizing should remind us that no late nineteenth-century reader could read of "infants, not a span long, on the floor of hell" without thinking of the unrelenting stream of reports on the state of children in the slums of London and other British cities. Yet such is the power of Marius's vision, Pater implies, that it succeeds in dissociating the womblike, natural resonances of this underground—after all, the house and its catacombs belong to the Roman widow Cecilia—from the negative associations of the modern city, a cyclical view of death from a clinical one. Pater follows through this cleansing process with reference to the metaphorical register as well, describing the church's "emerge[nce] for awhile from her jealously-guarded subterranean life" and Marius's feeling "for a moment as if he had stumbled upon some great conspiracy" (246). Just as the only language available to describe Marius's experience is tainted by modern urban life, so is the only language accurate for describing the force of early Christianity equally tainted. The resolution, again, comes through the children of the Catacombs, "with features not so much beautiful as heroic . . . they retained certainly no stain or trace of anything subterranean this morning" (247). The fact that Christianity is chosen as the resolution of Marius's despair retains an applicability to the present; the subterranean identity given to that Christianity informs us that it is a Christianity altogether hidden for the past millennium and a half; the cleansing of the meaning of the subterranean informs us of the degree to which the current order is being rejected.

The current order is incarnated by and ensconced within the English metropolis; what remained underground within the metropolis, as Orwell later suggested, had ceased to inspire anything but numbness and disinterest by the turn of the century. The cleansing of meaning and the emptying of space may have been necessary philosophically and aesthetically; in form and in ideology the same processes by necessity proposed a withdrawal socially as well. It is a tenet of modernism that this was a necessary decision; certainly it was a common one. One of the most successful and influential versions was that of D. H. Lawrence, who placed a reevaluation of spatial dynamics at the center of a revaluation of the physical world. Published just before the war, *Sons and Lovers* traced the conflict between the rural organic and the inorganic urban undergrounds in the intense battle between a Nottingham engineer's daughter and a lifetime coal miner for the future of their son, Paul. In her first encounter with her future husband, Gertrude Koppel is intrigued by Walter Morel's peculiar dialect and affinity with the creatures of the earth: "You live like th' mice, an' you pop out at night to see what's going on. . . . Yi, an' there's some chaps as does go round like moudiwarps [moles]." Her reaction echoes nineteenth-century rhetoric but humanizes it with the tint of everyday life: "She realised the life of the miners, hundreds of them toiling below earth and coming up at evening. He seemed to her noble. He risked his life daily, and with gaiety."[124] Paul, whose mother will keep him from the mines, has a similarly anthropomorphic attitude to the pit as "wonderful" and "beautiful": "Look how it heaps together, like something alive, almost—a big creature that you don't know."[125] The Nottingham factory of surgical appliances where he works as a clerk, although described in Victorian terms as a dark, gloomy, and "insanitary ancient place," is also susceptible of human interaction, but not of assimilation to the rhythms and spaces of nature. White-collar work in London wastes his brother to his death; the factory nearly kills Paul. The modernist city, where Paul will head at the end of the novel, offers alienation, art, and a break from the past. The pit offers the sometimes deadly but natural rhythms of the English countryside, the sublime experience of the pastoral underground. When Clara, his urban lover, responds to the sight of the colliery by lamenting the way its "immense heap of slag" contrasts with the land "where it is so pretty," Paul answers that not only is he accustomed to the combination, but that as a boy, "I always thought a pillar of cloud by day and a pillar of fire by night was a pit, with its steam, and its light and the burning bank—and I thought the Lord was always at the pit-top."[126] In *Sons and Lovers,* Lawrence depicted a life-and-death struggle between two compromised ways of life, one a debased but still recognizably natural and beautiful inheritance of the rural past, the other a denatured but artistically and epistemologically enticing urban modernity.

In a travel essay written near the end of his life and published posthumously in 1932, by which point the mine could no longer support the symbolic association with the pastoral or the sublime, Lawrence found a much more distanced expression of the same conflict in the way the Romans had covered over the necropolises of their agrarian predecessors. *Etruscan Places* proposed the Etruscan integration of life and death, above- and underground, as itself a subterranean trace in modern culture, almost wholly written over by the oppressive Roman conceptions of aesthetics and order. For Lawrence, the underground contained all that was left of this authentic lifestyle:

> The Etruscan cities vanished as completely as flowers. Only the tombs, the bulbs, were underground. . . . On the parallel hill opposite they liked to have their city of the dead, the necropolis. So they could stand on their ramparts and look over the hollow where the stream flowed among its bushes, across from the city of life, gay with its painted houses and temples, to the near-at-hand city of their dear dead, pleasant with its smooth walks and stone symbols, and painted fronts.[127]

Although like Pater's catacombs this too is a necropolis, a city of the dead, its effect is that of a home, "a stillness and a soothingness . . . and a feeling that it was good for one's soul to be there" (106). Rather than in its identity as subterranean, this underground is significant in that it retains the traces of a past existence in which there was no vertical separation between life and death, in which "everything was in terms of life, of living" (109).

Lawrence begins his catalog at Cerveteri, which appears for him as the tomb-city best preserving the traces of the life he is seeking. Other visits, to Tarquinia, Vulci, and Volterra, are less easily shaken of the patina of more recent underground space. The Etruscan places function in Lawrence's essay as an ambivalent image of the unconscious. Just as we can only tentatively and subjectively distinguish between what is genuinely Etruscan and authentically underground and what belongs to later Greco-Roman and Christian corruption, so are his descriptions and impressions colored by his own subterranean associations. At Tarquinia, for example, Lawrence finds himself, more atavistically, in "a warren of tombs. . . . We dive down them just like rabbits popping down a hole" (138). While the experience of Cerveteri is available fairly readily, that of Tarquinia requires more of a loss of self and rationality, more of a descent into childhood, into primitivism, into an emotional clarity of "things mentally contradictory fusing together emotionally, so that a lion could be at the same moment also a goat, and not a goat" (167).

Such productive confusion gives way easily to another form of underground: the infernal. Volterra is gloomy and sublime, "a Dantesque, desolate world. . . . The lower depths are dark grey, ashy in colour, and in part wet, and the whole thing looks new, as if it were some enormous quarry all slipping down" (201, 203). The visit at Tarquinia concludes, similarly, in the fourth-century Tomb of Orcus, Roman god of the underworld:

> a great gloomy, clumsy, rambling sort of underworld, damp and horrid, with large but much-damaged pictures on the wall. . . . In the Tomb of Orcus begins that represen-

tation of the grisly underworld, hell and its horrors, which surely was reflected on to the Etruscans from the grisly Romans. The lovely little tombs of just one small chamber, or perhaps two chambers, of the earlier centuries give way to these great sinister caverns underground, and hell is fitly introduced.

The old religion of the profound attempt of man to harmonize himself with nature, and hold his own and come to flower in the great seething of life, changed with the Greeks and Romans into a desire to resist nature, to produce a mental cunning and a mechanical force that would outwit Nature and chain her down completely, completely, till at last there should be nothing free in nature at all, all should be controlled, domesticated, put to man's meaner uses. Curiously enough, with the idea of the triumph over nature arose the idea of a gloomy Hades, a hell and purgatory. To the peoples of the Idea the afterlife is hell, or purgatory, or nothingness, and paradise is an inadequate fiction (172–74).

Lawrence resolutely separates what he sees as the negative, verticalized space of the Greco-Roman cosmos from the ideal traces of an earlier harmony. Like Pater, he distinguishes an unreal, horrible hell from a material underground tomb; even in its vanished, repressed traces, Lawrence suggests, the latter is more real than the former.

While Tarquinia and Volterra elicit mythic resonances of a negative afterlife, Vulci summons a material nineteenth-century underground of coal mining, degeneration, labyrinths, and gender anxiety. The beginning of the description evokes the cramped discomfort of the miner's descent: "We had to wriggle into the tombs on our bellies, over the mounds of rubble, going down into holes like rats, while the bats flew blindly in our faces. . . . It is like being in a mine, narrow passages winding on and on, from nowhere to nowhere" (193–94). This tumulus is unlike any other, for its passages lead nowhere; it is like a pyramid, Lawrence writes, with some very important personage resting in some hidden chamber. It is at this point that Lawrence records his frustration with the whole experience, frustration with the vandalism that has stripped the tombs of many of their features, frustration with scrambling in and out of damp holes and underbrush, frustration with the unfixed meanings, fragmentation, and mystery of it all. The space of the tombs constantly undermines any attempt to control its meaning; it is difficult to determine if this occurs as part of Lawrence's strategy or in spite of it.

The concluding image of Vulci sums up this ambivalence, identifying the space of the Etruscans with a matriarchal underworld that Lawrence seems to desire but is unable wholly to disentangle from other associations:

We looked round once more at the vast mound of the Coccumella, which strange dead hands piled in soft earth over two tiny death-chambers, so long ago: and even now it is weirdly conspicuous across the flat Maremma. A strange, strange nut indeed, with a kernel of perpetual mystery! And once it rose suave as a great breast, tipped with the budded monuments of the cippi! It is too problematic. We turn our back on it all as the *carretto* jolts over the tomb-rifled earth. There is something gloomy, if rather wonderful about Vulci. (195–96)

Unlike the "easy and friendly" Cerveteri, with "phallic stones and lingams" at the doors of its tombs, the other sites resist such easy perspectives. The ideal city quickly settles back into a more conflicted space, atavistic and feminine, but also urban and industrial in its figures.

The constant in Lawrence's tour is the conviction that truth is to be found buried in these ruins, in nature. Once found here, however, it can change the way one sees wherever one is. The nineteenth-century underground combined the ancient with the modern, using the former to cloak the novelty of the latter. In this form of pastoral modernism, the underground is mythologized through its antiquity. While the surrealists, for example, mythologized the urban detritus of the previous century's capitalism, these modernists scoured the landscape for metaphors of prehistory, pre-Christianity, pre–Greco-Roman period, prerationality. In the city, high modernists totalized the contemporary world as an underworld of alienation; in the country, they sought ways to outflank that same totality.

Where Laura Wing could simply descend into the crypt of Soane's Museum, in *A Passage to India* both Mrs. Moore and Adela Quested must betake themselves all the way to India for an experience that provides them less with conscious insight than with the consciousness of a failure to achieve insight. As Mrs. Moore realizes in the aftermath of her visit to the caves:

> The crush and the smells she could forget, but the echo began in some indescribable way to undermine her hold on life. . . . It had managed to murmur, "Pathos, piety, courage—they exist, but are identical, and so is filth. Everything exists, nothing has value." . . . Devils are of the North, and poems can be written about them, but no one could romanticize the Marabar because it robbed infinity and eternity of their vastness, the only quality that accommodates them to mankind.[128]

The famous echo of the caves reverberates through the characters' lives as the still point around which the novel's plotting revolves, and the disastrous excursion around which their fragile social veneer crumbles. Like Lawrence's ruins, it promises a profound reconciliation, but only negatively, in the way it points toward what is missing, the source of the promise. Just as urban modernism addressed the metropolis as a space of thoroughgoing alienation, pastoral modernism documented a search for meaning in a subterranean world as far removed from that space as possible. One reason that the avant-garde was famously unproductive in London by comparison with Paris or Berlin was this severed link in the verticalized conception of its space.

How the Dead Live Today

A young woman appears from nowhere in particular to "help" these drudges; she impinges upon Masterman's son Eric, and they go to the "catacombs," which, in spite of the gas mains, steam mains, cables and drainage, have somehow contrived to get over from Rome, skeletons and all, and burrow under this city of "Metropolis."

> H. G. WELLS, "The Silliest Film: Will Machinery Make
> Robots of Men?" (*New York Times*, 17 April 1927)

It took the Battle of Britain to restore direct meaning to subterranean London, as the city and the symbolizing country as a whole rediscovered an ambivalent rather than a negative component in its urban spaces. The Tube shelters in London during the Blitz became genuinely underground cities, forcibly reclaimed by the shelterers even before authorities finally capitulated by making the nightly occupation official. The story is too well known to require retelling here, but certain details are worth another going over. As a lived space, the Tube shelter restored the nineteenth-century conflict over the underground and renewed the attempt of a few decades earlier to adapt the space of the trenches to that of everyday life. Rather than the traumatic need to find something recognizable in a wholly alien space, however, the shelters constituted an underground space that was readily, almost eagerly, assimilated to the urban world above. The possibility of sudden, terrible death remained always present; there were several direct hits on Tube shelters, including Marble Arch, Balham, and Bank. But the assertion of everyday life over random violence was possible in a way in which it never had been in the world of the trenches. In Evelyn Milland's highly patriotic three-act play, *Underground,* performed in 1943 at Vagabonds Hall, a representative group of Londoners is trapped in a West London station on the Piccadilly line when a bomb seals them off. Pulling together out of utter darkness, they manage to escape in the elevator, aided by a personification of the armed forces, which turns out to have been the heroic spirits of two men killed in the initial blast. The only casualty is a Mrs. L., who begins the play selfishly complaining that she must get to Knightsbridge and ends it killed by a live wire, after it has been revealed, fatally, that she is both a Freudian and a Communist. No need to gloss the ideological details; what is noteworthy is the rediscovery of the material underground as an explicit location for the conflicts embedded in those details.

London had become once again a city defined by its subterranean spaces. This no more implied social reconciliation than it had in the previous century; there were grumblings about the swank shelters beneath the West End hotels just as there were about the foul conditions in the heavily hit East End. What it did provide was an overriding spatial metaphor for social unity, along with a potent means for expressing the operation of that unity. Perhaps the most impressive realization of that expression was the private shelter created in the ancient underground quarries known as Chislehurst Caves in the outer stretches of South London. Converted into a veritable underground city from its previous commercial exploitation for the cultivation of mushrooms, Chislehurst Caves provided penny-a-night accommodations for tens of thousands of Londoners, many of whom commuted daily into the city, others of whom lived there continuously for years on end. At the height of its popularity, Chislehurst Caves boasted a chapel, a cinema, a hospital, and a canteen. Its premises were highly rationalized and controlled, with assigned bunks in numbered, designated quarters and neighborhoods, governed by wardens and subwardens. Needless to say, as this author learned from a fellow visitor to the caves who had sheltered there with great pleasure as a child, there were good neighborhoods and bad, coveted, capacious grottoes, and dreaded, low-ceilinged holes bereft of privacy.

In their compendium *London under London,* Richard Trench and Ellis Hillman argue that London had no underground mythology before the Blitz shelters; it would be more accurate to say that it had no positive underground mythology to mitigate its long-standing negative lore.[129] It could also be said that only with the Blitz shelters did Londoners rediscover the representational space of the apartment building, the ambivalent experience of close quarters, mixed-use habitation so fundamental to the experience of space in modern Paris. That London rediscovered that space only in the mid-twentieth century may partly explain the signal failure of the postwar attempt to resettle the urban poor in council housing tower blocks.[130] As much as the positive resonance of the shelters was due to their assimilation to archaic images of the sociability of the organic underground, the simple pleasures of the cave dweller, normally limited to the English countryside, council housing still could not avoid the negative associations of the rationalized space and spatial attitudes requisite to the operation of the twentieth-century city.

Rather than assaulted from above as London was, Paris, as in the previous century, was invaded and mined from within by a combination of the German occupation and the local collaboration. The underground city had been a primary component of the failed strategy to repel the Germans—the fortified border along the Maginot Line—and then of the equally unsuccessful occupation line along the Normandy coast. The country itself was figuratively split between two underground identities: Resistance fighter or *collabo.* Maintaining the myths of this strict subterranean separation would dominate the nation's representation of itself for many decades following the war. The identity of the underground was characteristically split: German forces did fortify a network of carrières beneath the Odéon theater and Luxembourg Gardens (giving rise to legends that some remnants of the force continued to survive there), while the regional head of the Free French Forces was established in the tunnels beneath the place Denfert-Rochereau, from where he organized the insurrection of the FFI (French Forces of the Interior) in August 1944.[131] Still, the subterranean space of Paris per se played probably a smaller role in the city's spatial representation than it had at any time since the Revolution. Rather than the sustained literary and cultural reflection characteristic of the previous 150 years, wartime and postwar Paris souterrain have been pretty much limited to the spheres of tourism, popular culture, and counterculture. The sewers and Catacombes are prime destinations for foreign visitors but little remarked by Parisians except in mystery novels and *bandes dessinées* (comics), where, as everywhere else in the developed world, they are omnipresent (figure 2.24).[132] Meanwhile, the carrières are a popular destination for local thrill seekers, urban explorers, and cataphiles, not least for the illicit thrill of breaking into them, a much simpler prospect (at least until recently) than that presented by the heavily sealed and jealously guarded sewers and disused Tube stations of London.[133] In the late 1950s and early '60s, the situationists rediscovered the revolutionary heritage and utopian promise of the hidden depths of the city for their theories—recommending wandering in the forbidden Catacombes as an example of the urban *dérive*—and slogans: "The situationists are in the catacombs of known culture"; "beneath the paving stones, a beach."[134] Numerous parties involving hundreds of students were held in the Left Bank carrières, especially in the cavernous space known as "Salle Z" near the bowels of the Val-de-Grâce Hospital. The following decades saw something of a revival of an antitechnological, organic underground primed to emerge from beneath the city, although its principal survivors today seem to be bands of young men (and a few women) content just to hang out down below for a while before emerging to take their places in the adult world.[135]

This conflict between natural and technological space was seldom explicitly evoked in artistic records of the London shelters, which tend to stress one side or the other, but it can still be glimpsed there. In Bill Brandt's photograph of the platform at Elephant and Castle, for instance, we see the overlap graphically visualized (figure 2.25): riders step over and around a line of sleeping shelterers on the platform of an operative Tube station in order to board the train behind. It was as a normal commuter, passing through one of the Tube-station shelters, that Henry Moore first conceived his celebrated series of shelter sketches. Lee Miller's 1943 photograph of Moore's preparation for one of his sketches in Holborn station shows the same contrast in use of space (figure 2.26): the artist is captured leaning against a narrow wall between the exit staircase and the train tunnel, with sleeping persons lined against the left wall and up the stairs.[136] They inhabit different worlds: Moore is fully awake, dressed in a suit, as if a member of the daytime, normal world above; the shelterers appear as if in a nighttime, nightmare world, uncomfortable, haggard, haphazard in their arrangements and activity. One woman is sitting up, staring at Moore, who appears to be sketching. Like

Facing page

2.24. *Notre Dame de dessous la terre*: the climax of the historical romance *Les Fées noires* pits Romantic poet Gérard de Nerval and the Parisian lamia, or fallen angel, Aurélia (*in the labyrinth*) against Alexandre Dumas père, the colonel Henri d'Herlon, a Prussian zombie, and a Polish lamia, the Countess Norodna, in the Left Bank carrières (*top and bottom frame right*). The artist is a former cataphile, and the series is replete with subterranean history and folklore. The dialogue (*top*): "What's that?—A maze . . . A labyrinth . . .—Like in Chartres?—That's right . . . The first Christians built their cemeteries on top of ancient labyrinths . . . They blocked the threshold . . . But this is Notre Dame beneath the earth . . . The last one still open." (*bottom*): "It looks like someone is walking inside it . . .—To open the threshold, a mortal must lay the scarab in the center of the labyrinth." Reproduced by permission from *Notre Dame de dessous la terre*, vol. 3 of *Les Fées noires*, with text by Jean-Pierre Pécau, artwork by Damien (Paris: Delcourt, 2001): 40. © Guy Delcourt Productions–Pécau–Damien.

2.25. Tube shelter: the natural and the technological undergrounds overlap. Bill Brandt, "Elephant and Castle," IWM negative no. D1571. Courtesy of the Imperial War Museum, London.

2.26. Henry Moore: the artist as commuter. Photograph by Lee Miller of Moore at Holborn Underground station during the filming of *Out of Chaos*, September 1943. Reproduced by permission from the Henry Moore Foundation, © Lee Miller Archive, England 2004. All rights reserved.

most of the artists who depicted the shelters, Brandt stressed the humanity and aboveground nature of the Tube and other underground shelters; Moore, by contrast, stressed their underground connection to other subterranean spaces—cemeteries, mines, tunnels—as images of alienation. Neither for the most part captured the ambivalence of the space, the coexistence of above- and underground, conceived and lived space that appears to have been characteristic of the shelters.

Brandt's photos stress everyday activity in unusual settings, shot by him as picturesque scenes: one group of shelterers play cards; a circle of Orthodox Jews read from the Torah; women sit in rows of chairs set among support poles, knitting and reading, wide awake. They sleep anywhere: in a bed made on top of a row of barrels; next to a miniature doll's bed; inside an unused sarcophagus. Brandt individualized his subjects, focusing on particular faces and personalities and on diversity: we see men, women, and children, Jews and Sikhs, West End,

East End, and South London, wine cellars, garage shelters, Tube stations, church crypts, shop basements. In these photos—and this is the dominant image of the Blitz shelters—we are shown a space repossessed by the everyday. The photograph is the most potent means for this argument; paintings by artists such as John Farleigh, Lawrence Scarfe, and Edward Ardizzone by necessity and by aesthetic convention abstracted their subjects more than Brandt's photographs. Nevertheless, they resembled peacetime scenes and stories rather than the disruptions of wartime: a warden with shelterers in Scarfe's *South Kensington Scene 1940,* group scenes with stories to tell; Ardizzone's *In the Shelter 1940,* looking more like figures in a waiting room than those in a bomb shelter. In a symbol of the city's resistance to the dehumanization of war, the most potentially alienating experience of all, the forced habitation of rationalized, public, undifferentiated underground space was recorded as an affirmation of human tolerance, resistance, and resilience. Even the potentially charged image of the man in the sarcophagus cannot be read otherwise than as gently humorous.

Although his drawings—wax crayon, pencil, ink, and chalk under a watercolor wash—have usually been assimilated to the same "London can take it" portrayal of the Blitz, Moore seems in fact to have been after something else entirely. Just as his assertion that he sketched afterward, from memory, denied the possibility of any interaction between artist and subject, so the drawings stress the isolation, alienation, and interchangeability of the figures. Moore's is a quintessentially modernist underground. In *Tube Shelter Perspective: The Liverpool Street Extension* (1941; figure 2.27), we see the familiar nineteenth-century underground view of a receding tunnel, bodies lining it on either side, with a space in the middle. A yellow wash provides the only color, but instead of giving life to the figures, it unites them as a structural motif; the bodies appear as if they are the track ties of the twin railings, barely alive. Other large group scenes suggest a similar dehumanization, as in *Pink and Green Sleepers* (1941), where the horizontal rows of bunks align the bodies as in a barracks or prison. Other sleepers, in more contorted positions on the floor, suggest more sinister associations, as does the only restful figure, in the center bunk, its head drawn as if a skull, emblem of the mass death hovering over the entire group.

While the large-scale groups tend toward frightening images of modern rationalization, bodies placed in the space dictated by the architecture of the Tube station and tunnels, Moore's drawings on a more intimate scale hearken back to Victorian iconography of underground life. The composition of *Grey Tube Shelter* (1941; figure 2.28) shows a group huddled together like the poor in one of Doré's pictures of the homeless. The foreground figure in *Woman Seated in the Underground* (1941; figure 2.29) is bent in the familiar Victorian pose of passive acceptance of one's fate. The modern version of underground suffering has not disappeared from these drawings, either: in the above right corner of *Grey Tube Shelter* Moore added a gray UndergrounD insignia; in the background of

2.27. The familiar nineteenth-century underground vista of a receding tunnel. Henry Moore, *Tube Shelter Perspective: The Liverpool Street Extension* (1941). Pencil, ink, wax, and watercolor wash on paper support, 483 x 438 mm. HMF 1801. Reproduced by permission from the Henry Moore Foundation.

Woman Seated we see another of Moore's receding tunnels, a line of bodies along its right-hand side. The message of these drawings is quite bleak: neither on an individual nor on a social level is there any possibility of reconciliation within such an urban environment.

What is unusual about Moore's series, however, in addition to its divergence from the main line of shelter art, is the insistence on the continuity of the Victorian and the modernist experiences of underground space, and, hence, of the city

2.28. Tube shelterers as the Victorian poor. Henry Moore, *Grey Tube Shelter*, 1940. Water-color, gouache, and drawing on paper support, 279 x 381 mm. HMF 1724. Reproduced by permission from the Henry Moore Foundation.

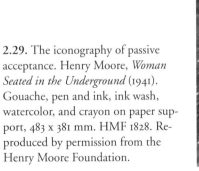

2.29. The iconography of passive acceptance. Henry Moore, *Woman Seated in the Underground* (1941). Gouache, pen and ink, ink wash, watercolor, and crayon on paper support, 483 x 381 mm. HMF 1828. Reproduced by permission from the Henry Moore Foundation.

itself. This becomes quite clear with a comparison to the series of sketches made of workers in the coal pits near Moore's home in Castleford, Yorkshire, during the same war years. The mine remains a closed, claustrophobic space, but there is no trace of the diffuse, passive alienation of the city dwellers. Moore's miners are resolutely different, subterranean—supporting figures are drawn with skull-like features resembling those of the shelterers—but they always appear powerful and alive. *At the Coalface: Miner Pushing Tub* and *Coalminer with Pick* (both 1942; figures 2.30–31) show dynamic figures in action, as indicated already by the titles. These bodies are bent with exertion, not with impotency. Rather than the diffuse, artificial light of the shelters, emphasized by the single-color wash, these sketches contain specific light sources, as if life still remained in the Yorkshire Dales, if not in the London Tube. Certainly modernist in their focus on the alienation of the underground and their distinction between the subterranean spaces of the country and the city, Moore's drawings are instructive in the ways they ground that alienation and those spaces within history. The mine is no more a simple pit than the city is merely an urban hell.

Perhaps the most forceful and influential literary assertion of the country-city split within a renewed consciousness of the underground dynamics of the previous century was J. R. R. Tolkien's allegorization of England and midcentury Europe in *The Hobbit* (1937) and *The Lord of the Rings* (conceived during the same period as *The Hobbit,* written over the next couple of decades, and first published in 1954–55). The greater or lesser applicability of the terms of the allegory are of less interest here than the way in which they cast the narrative dynamics and the social relationships of the history of Middle Earth in terms of subterranean

2.30. The Yorkshire miner as an alien species in an alien environment. Henry Moore, *At the Coalface: Miner Pushing Tub*. HMF 1991. Courtesy of the Henry Moore Foundation.

2.31. Underground space: a study in contained energy. Henry Moore, *Coalminer with Pick* (1942). HMF 1987. Reproduced by permission from the Henry Moore Foundation.

space. *The Hobbit* lays out a traditionally English division between the positive underground space of the hobbit-hole (figure 2.32), highly reminiscent of the aristocratic spaces of Badger's dwelling (itself recast as Bjorn's aboveground house on the wild edge of Mirkwood) and of Toad Hall in *The Wind in the Willows,* and the perilous subterranean spaces of the goblins and Gollum's lair in the Misty Mountains, the storage chambers of the Elves in Mirkwood, and Smaug's lair deep within the tunnels of the Lonely Mountain in the East. Indeed, Bilbo's experience on the quest for dragon's treasure is figuratively nothing other than a long, if comically drawn, descent into the otherworld of lands beyond the safe confines of his comfortable hole in the comfortable, protected, provincial Shire,

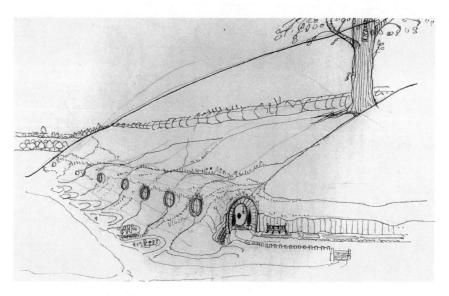

2.32. Bag End, Underhill: the English country cottage par excellence. Drawing by J. R. R. Tolkien, *Bag End, Underhill*. Bodleian MS Tolkien Drawings 3, © The Tolkien Trust, 1987. Reproduced by permission from the Bodleian Library, University of Oxford.

a descent from which he will emerge with knowledge, confidence, treasure, and life experience in a classic update of the traditional medieval romance as an adventure tale for children.

Where Kenneth Grahame fairly unproblematically contrasted the pastoral world of his animals with the deadly detritus of the city, Tolkien's midcentury fantasy allegorized the difficulty of remaining atavistically and ignorantly within one's safe and cozy burrow, the necessary experience of other forms of the underground, and the good and evil to be found out in them. This philosophy of humanist engagement against ancient and modern forces of evil was expressed through the topography and demography of the land he imagined. The final episode in the War of the Ring is not the defeat of the devil Sauron by penetrating the depths of his subterranean forge at Mount Doom to melt down the Ring of Power, cast for good and turned to evil, but the lasting penetration of that evil into the safest space of all, home. It comes in the form of the forces of progress, for the defeated renegade Saruman knows that his sweetest revenge will come from spoiling the pristine landscape, the subterranean shelters, and picturesque villages of the Shire hobbits, Middle Earth's refraction of the myth of Englishness.

Like *The Hobbit, The Lord of the Rings* is built upon a challenge to the pleasures and desires of insularity, and its narrative is a string of ever more perilous and more mythic descents into underworld spaces: the hobbits captured by the barrow wight in their greed for its treasure; the descent of the fellowship of the ring into the Mines of Moria, once a legendary stronghold of the dwarves, now possessed by orcs under the command of a powerful spirit of evil; the subterranean and haunted Paths of the Dead walked by Aragorn as he reclaims his lost kingship; the secret entrance into Mordor through which Frodo and Samwise are led by Gollum before being betrayed to Shelob, the giant guardian spider; and the Cracks of Doom deep within Sauron's own mountain, Oroduin, where Frodo finally destroys the ring. In addition to these passages, thresholds of initiation and knowledge and mystical cruxes to Tolkien's epic plot, there are the subterranean and hidden dwellings that mark the innate kinship of the hobbits and the other races of Middle Earth, with the exception, perhaps, of mankind, the only natural surface dweller. The forces of evil are wholly identified with underground space in a consistently Mumfordian manner. Not only do they choose to live underground and at night as much as possible, but they transform whatever space they possess, whether dwarven halls or human fields, into a desolate wasteland, pocked with trenches and tunnels, which in Tolkien's descriptions resonate powerfully with the wasted battlegrounds of the Great War.[137] Theirs is the scourge of modernity at its most satanic and corrupt. Dwarves, like the evil orcs, inhabit the mountainous caverns in which they mine the gems and metals on which they live and to the allure of which they all too frequently succumb. Unlike the misshapen orcs, many of them products of Sauron's and, later, Saruman's experiments with cross-breeding and genetic modification, the dwarves are the surviving traces of miners and underground races of old; like Wagner's Nibelungs, they are ambiguous figures, capable of both magnificent feats of workmanship and base acts of greed. In Tolkien's underground scheme, they are the most closely tied to the mineral underground and the earth. The elves, by contrast, inhabit an otherworld realm of paradise on earth. The hidden valley of Rivendell, the treetop colony of Lothlorien, even the Elven King's halls under the trees of Mirkwood, are otherworldly rather than physically underground; the elves themselves profess an almost insurmountable aversion to the literally subterranean and base aspects of life, just as they appear to exist somewhere beyond the need to labor for their subsistence.

Tolkien thus based his argument for English engagement in the outside world on a spatial metaphor of resemblance. By virtue of their very insularity—their attachment to their hobbit-holes—the Shire-dwellers are shown to be intrinsically similar to the other inhabitants of the land. The use of underground space underlines the central symbolism of the rings of power, their meaning dependent not on their intrinsic value but on the uses to which they are put by those that wield them. While, on the one hand, Tolkien naturalized national difference as a rather dubious set of racial distinctions between peoples—dwarves, elves, orcs, men—on the other hand, he was thereby able to make material his humanistic argument about the society formed by those peoples. Like Henry Moore, he resurrected the nineteenth-century range of affiliated underground spaces as a way of asserting a unified theory of space and of modern life; unlike Moore, Tolkien increased the complexity of this depiction with recourse to the other period when underground space dominated the conception and perception of the world: the Middle Ages. Tolkien's conscious recourse to the whole range of ancient and medieval journeys and underworld myths is exemplary of a postwar reaction to the primary traumas of the Second World War: the Holocaust and the atomic bomb. The modern experience of alienation and of technologized space could be fruitfully addressed through a return to the concrete subterranean experiences of the previous century; the incomprehensible rationality and technology of two new forms of mass death brought the old myths back to the fore. They had been prominent in modernism, but only mythically; postwar, as in Tolkien, they would be rejoined with the material underground of the nineteenth-century city, spawning a new form of apocalyptic we will examine in the concluding part of this book.

It was the postwar demographic that spurred Tolkien's popularity in the 1960s, establishing a London underground of primarily figurative character, except for the basement clubs and derelict squats that were the main settings for the countercultural aspects of swinging London. This subculture envisioned an organic, utopian space within an urban setting counter to the cozy Blitz myths it rejected, but a lack of attention to the physical underground can again be taken as symptomatic of its failure to harness the politically charged social forces that would explode into the violent riots and nihilistic punk rock of the 1970s. As long as the vertical trope remains the dominant representation of urban space, the negative energy of the underground city and the utopian desires of the natural underground seem unable to converge within the bounds of the English metropolis. This situation showed some signs of changing during the 1990s, which saw the radical appropriation of the pastoral underground through the excavation of tunnels and bunkers to halt the construction of highways through the British countryside, and of the urban terrain through a network of tunnels to link the squatted houses of Claremont Road in East London in a failed attempt to halt a development project.[138] While generally unsuccessful locally, such protests did have an important symbolic effect, although to what degree they will be able to accomplish more than representing a radical wing of the recent vogue for the material underground of Victorian London remains to be seen. Renovated church crypts in London and Paris house cafes and theaters; subterranean clubs and galleries dot the landscapes of both cities; the counterculture nostalgia of Camden Market now includes the "Catacombs," a labyrinth of shops set up in disused railway arches (figure 2.33); the more genteel Viaduc des Arts, east of the place de la Bastille in Paris, combines a planted promenade atop a disused train embankment with antique shops and boutiques in the arches below; third-world chic is on prominent display in Brixton Market beneath the railway arches of South London, or Portobello Road and Ladbroke Grove, along and beneath the Westway. Unlike Reclaim the Streets in London or the heyday of situationism in Paris, however, the mainstream part of the underground vogue represents less a new attention to the spatial dynamics of the city than a commodified spectacle different only from the properly middle-brow Victoriana dominating the rest of London in being geared toward another demographic.

Rather than staggered between the 1940s and 1960s as in London, the '60s revival of underground metaphorics in Paris was accompanied by the nineteenth-century city's acute awareness of spatial dynamics. This revival was related not only to the broad political upheaval of '68 but also to specific changes in the development of Paris. The events of May '68 began in the new banlieue campus at Nanterre before moving to the streets of the Left Bank, and in large part they were a response to the forced relocation of working-class and student culture to concrete high-rise cités, or housing projects, beyond the traditional boundaries of the metropolis that had given a physical face to the phenomenon of modernization.[139] Popular films such as *Les Gaspards* (The Rats, 1973) and *Subway* (1985) cast the battle over the inner city in terms of inorganic and organic underground space, specifically the transformation of the central market of Les Halles into a

2.33. Marketing Victorian subterranea: "The Catacombs" at Camden Market. Photo by author, 1998.

subterranean shopping mall and metropolitan and suburban railway station. Luc Besson's film, discussed in chapter 1, depicted the world above as a superficial realm of empty values, the new underground as an alienated space of mechanization and surveillance, and the deep underground and the new Les Halles at night as a countercultural playground of misfits, eccentrics, and romantics, safe and nurturing except when its inhabitants crossed paths with the inorganic world around them. Scripted by director Pierre Tchernia and René Goscinny (the writer half of the *Astérix* team), *Les Gaspards* was made after the market halls had been demolished but before the new mall complex had been built, while Les Halles was an enormous hole in the center of Paris. Rather than historian Louis Chevalier's virulent surface polemic, *The Assassination of Paris, Les Gaspards* tackled the situation in cartoon fashion as a satire pitting the forces of vieux Paris against those of heartless progress.[140] When his daughter disappears, M. Rondin (Michel Serrault), an old-style bookseller and author of a study of Paris souterrain, descends into the carrières, where he discovers Gaspard (Philippe Noiret), a Captain Nemo–type eccentric leading a cultured utopian community below while waging a subversive battle against the modernizing world above. The mayor of Paris has determined to make his mark on the city through a series of holes, mainly for underground parking garages; Gaspard and his "rats" respond by blowing holes under the city's government buildings and taking hostage a busload of tourists, who are quite pleased at their chance to catch a glimpse of local life below the surface of the city. *Les Gaspards* demonstrates a comprehensive knowledge of underground Paris both mythic and material, and a keen awareness of the symbolic potential of those spaces for its inhabitants.

The two cities' different representations of their spatial dynamics thus mirror the different forms taken by the upheavals of the 1960s and '70s, and the different relationship of those events to urban renewal. In both Paris and London, however, there was less and less physical connection between the cities of the poor—now high-rise concrete agglomerations set in isolation usually far from the city center—and any space that was physically underground. No longer linked to conditions of labor or to fantasies of decomposition, the new cities had severed their inhabitants from any connection to organic space, just as they had severed them from their traditional social networks. To be sure, council housing and the cités de banlieue continue to generate infernal metaphors to describe their conditions, but those metaphors are hopeless, no longer relating in any way to the potential for change and desire for security that could still be found intertwined with them in the nineteenth-century necropolis. Those positive urges have been left to the tourists and to popular culture where, revisiting the subterranean ruins of the urban past, they see only the spectacle, for the material connection to the accompanying experience is no longer present. Having ceased to be the economic and industrial centers they were before the war, Paris and London as cityscapes have ceased to generate a discourse of urban experience capable of bearing any substantial meaning beyond the purely local. Before delving further into the broader significance of the underground revival of the end of the twentieth century in the final chapter, however, we need to address another piece of the nineteenth-century puzzle, the primary source for the negative image of the city, the principal continuity with ancient and medieval subterranean myths, and the mother lode for the longtime dominance by Paris and London of that image: the pathological city, its sewers, its diseases, its parasites, and its demons.

3

CHARON'S BARK

All that they boast of Styx, of Acheron,
    Cocytus, Phlegethon, our have proved in one:
The filth, stench, noise; save only what was there
    Subtly distinguished, was confusèd here.
Their wherry had no sail, too; ours had none;
    And in it two more horrid knaves than Charon.
Arses were heard to croak instead of frogs,
    And for one Cerberus, the whole coast was dogs.
Furies there wanted not; each scold was ten;
    And for the cries of ghosts, women and men
Laden with plague-sores and their sins were heard,
    Lashed by their consciences; to die, afeard.

BEN JONSON, "On the Famous Voyage" (ca. 1610)

Although the underground railway established the urban underground as a site for everyday travel, the sewer has been closely linked under capitalism with another sort of journey, the epochal trip most vividly imagined in the classical figure of Charon, the ferryman on the river Styx who carries dead souls into the afterlife. This is an important subtext, I suggest, for the popular late nineteenth-century boat rides in the Parisian égouts, for the many narratives of sewer discovery in the popular literature of London, and for the paradigmatic journey of Jean Valjean in the 1830 revolution of Hugo's *Les Misérables* (1862). It is a subtext unique to the modern city, although it stretches back as far as Ben Jonson's mock-epic poem "On The Famous Voyage" down the polluted river Fleet, and forward at least to filmmaker Andrzej Wajda's imagination of the end of the Polish Resistance as a journey into Dante's Hell in the sewers of Warsaw in *Kanal* (1956). The journey metaphor is rooted in the construction of the sewers as the mirror image of the metropolis above, an otherworld just beneath the city streets. Equally essential is the identity of the sewer as a threshold or passage; like the rivers whose beds and streams it incorporated into its subterranean networks in London and Paris, the drainage system is defined by its state of flux.

Modeled on the celebrated engineering and imperial order of the Roman *cloaca maxima*, the city sewer in its modern incarnation pioneered arched-tunnel construction.[1] As a drainage system carrying waste away from the inhabitants, it represented the rational control of the archaic underground, the essence of modern society. "Civilization," Lacan pronounced, "is the spoils: the *cloaca maxima*."[2] At the same time, it retained a strong symbolic resonance as a stubbornly irrational space, the most organic, primitive, and uncontrollable part of the modern city. Sewers accumulate waste, not only excrement and offal but the cast-off and outmoded remains of things, places, people, techniques, and ideas for which physical and conceptual space no longer exists in the world above. As such, they are a primary locus of decomposition and disease, tied to fear of and desire for death, decay, and dissolution. As Jonson's "Famous Voyage" suggested as early as 1610, the sewer had incorporated the river Styx into the topography of London. Consequently, the figures associated with the sewer became not only marginal but mythical as well, analogous to the imaginary beasts that inhabit them: the alligators of late twentieth-century Manhattan, the black swine of London, the dog-sized sewer cats and cat-sized sewer rats of every major system (figure 3.1).[3]

Like the shades ferried across the Styx into the underworld, these creatures have been not only removed from the world above, but transformed by that removal. Bloated by the sewage on which they feed, their excess size reveals the paradoxical fecundity of waste, just as the souls in hell are damned for eternity but still possessed of frightful power in the eyes of the living. The underworld follows neither the standard rules of time—for it endures eternally and mingles every

3.1. The endurance of sewer mythology: to suggest there is no vermin left in the Paris system, the Musée des Egouts puts a pair of pet rats on display at the entrance to its exhibition. Photo by author, 1995.

epoch in its depths—nor those of space—for it is dark, supernatural, and labyrinthine in its construction. Yet because every element of it was once a part of the
world above, it maintains the power of that connection, its former meanings re-
combined in unforeseen ways. Those who ply their trades in the literal or figurative proximity of the sewers become both powerful and alien, and serve as per-
sonifications of the powerful and alien qualities of the modern city for which the
world above can find no place: the *égoutiers* and *tafouilleurs* of Paris, and the toshers and mudlarks of London gain their own mythology as epitomes, for good or
for ill, of urban labor (figure 3.2); prostitutes become identified as the sewers
of the city, transmitters of disease and immorality, disposal systems for excess
male libidos, thresholds between above and below, between purity and filth.
Cholera is held to come from and to be resolvable through the sewage system. In
popular London melodrama, the sewer is where emblems of crisis and status col-
lect: poorly disposed corpses, proofs of nobility, and evidence of malefaction.
Rarely, but significantly, the sewer can express utopian dreams as well, if of a conventionally regressive nature: dark, womblike, warm and safe. In sum, whether
viewed positively or negatively, the sewer is the conduit of the archaic and the
atavistic in modern urban society.

THE MUD-LARK.

3.2. Emblems of the urban poor:
the Mud-lark. Drawing by Archibald Henning, *The Mud-lark*, from
a daguerreotype by Richard Beard,
in Henry Mayhew, *London Labour
and the London Poor*, 4 vols. (London: Griffin, Bohn & Co., 1861–
62): facing 2:139.

We begin with an analysis of the sewer's role in the conceptual and material development of the nineteenth-century city, and the different ways in which that role was manifested in the discourse of waste in London and in Paris. Although a powerfully totalizing vision of urban decay, the conceptual space of the vertical city nevertheless allowed scattered traces of less negative forms of experience to persist. We can glimpse such spaces in Valjean's flight and also in Hugo's and other Parisian writers' reveries of ways to make use and money out of excrement and sewage, to recycle every part of the waste products of society; in the Phantom's sanctuary beneath the Paris Opéra; in the child's dream of a hidden clubhouse in the infamous 1860s serial, *The Wild Boys of London*. The topographical analysis of waste can be fruitfully applied to two key concerns of modern urban history: the changing nature of contact between the middle and the so-called lower classes, and the debate over prostitution. Rather than a comprehensive history of either of these heavily studied topics, my goal in this chapter is to sketch some ways in which the physically and metaphorically verticalized spaces of London and Paris have contributed, and continue to contribute to the production of that history.

Underworld Journeys

I tell Viktor there is a curious connection between weapons and waste. I don't know exactly what. . . . He says maybe one is the mystical twin of the other. He likes this idea. He says waste is the devil twin. Because waste is the secret history, the underhistory, the way archaeologists dig out the history of early cultures, every sort of bone heap and broken tool, literally from under the ground.

DON DELILLO, *Underworld* (1997)

The sewer's role as conductor of waste can be distinguished from the analogous place of the necropolis as its repository by recourse to Voltaire's *Dictionnaire philosophique* (1764), published at a time when underground space was being newly reimagined to respond to the pressures of the modernizing city. Voltaire complained about the irrationality of the Parisians, who maintained the Cemetery of the Innocents in the midst of the city while transporting their waste as quickly as possible outside its limits: "We transport filth from the privies a league away from the city while we have heaped all together the decomposed corpses which had produced that filth in the same city for twelve hundred years."[4] Although both cemetery and sewage systems were modernized during the nineteenth century, the irrational separation pinpointed by the pragmatic philosophe has always been retained. The sewer shares with the necropolis a primordial link to the experience of the body in space; for the undeniable perceptions of material existence can be reduced to the triad of birth, excretion, and death. But unlike the catacomb, which represents mortality as a finished, static, and sanitary process—cleaned and ordered bones in Paris, lead-lined compartmentalized coffins in London—the sewer collects everything that is messy about the line between life and death, health and disease, the tolerable and the *immonde,* .a French term of extreme negativity that literally means that which has no place in the world, and is usually translated as vile, filthy, or unclean. It is fluid and mobile: when imagined to be functioning well, it appears as a healthy circulatory system; when it is not, an entire vocabulary of putrefaction, liquescence, and stench must be mobilized to express what it contains.

The modernizing nineteenth-century cities enacted in the renovation of their subterranean infrastructures a specific form of a traditional process of purification, creating order by articulating a place for whatever did not fit that order. The anthropologist Mary Douglas has argued that dirt is simply "matter out of place . . . the by-product of a systematic ordering and classification," and that "pollution behaviour . . . condemns any object or idea likely to confuse or contradict cherished classifications."[5] While Douglas tends to underplay the complex identities retained by the detritus of any social system, her structural analysis implies the crucial point that filth and pollution do not exist in static oppositions to cleanness and purity, but rather that in their quality as categories they are wrought with contradiction. "Seeing 'dirt' as contradiction," writes anthropologist Michael Taussig, "allows us to deepen our understanding and to move beyond the spellbinding surface of the sensational keywords."[6] The cherished principles and categories that define the world above mask their inherent instability by placing underground as dirt anything that does not fit those definitions.[7] But the underground, too, has its "spellbinding" quality, the allure of the forbidden, the taboo, the real. In precapitalist cultures, the contradictions expressed through dirt are assuaged through purification rites; in capitalism, Taussig argues, dirt continues to mark the contradiction of a different formulation of purity, the ideal of equality, composed of two irreconcilable concepts—the qualitative equality of use-value, of each person's intrinsic worth, and the quantitative equality of exchange-value, of equal value for equal work: "Filth is the contradiction that assails the *idealized* principles of equality."[8] The fundamental right to equality is guaranteed within capitalism by the equal opportunity of all to earn money. Whatever exposes the contradiction between this principle and the truth of social inequality, or the lack of equivalence between wages and happiness, is consigned to the underworld as unclean.

"Where there is dirt there is system," writes Douglas; the closest to such a system in the modern world is the concept of money and the liberal ideology that underpins it. Money represents simultaneously the highest expression of power in the developed world and the greatest level of corruption. Flooding, noxious gases, and clogged drainage passages trouble the equilibrium of rational and controlled cityscape; pollution and disaster follow in the wake of the money-making process, reminders of its cost. Excrement, disease, and death have always belied the assurance of a cohesive, unchanging, and incorporeal human body, isolated in space. Because they expose the dual nature of money, prostitution, crime, and foreignness belie similar principles of the body politic in the modern world. As Lynda Nead has observed, the prostitute presents a frightening reflection of and threat to the economic system of which in many ways she occupies the center: "She is able to represent all the terms within capitalist production; she is the human labour, the object of exchange and the seller at once. She stands as worker, commodity and capitalist and blurs the categories"[9] (figure 3.3). It is an argument that has been made since the nineteenth century in various forms: because the prostitute employs as exchange value what capitalist ideology tells us is reserved for use-value only—her sexuality in general and her sexual organs in particular— she makes palpable the inherent contradictions in the conventional divisions between public and private, business and leisure, exterior and interior.[10] Criminal behavior similarly challenges conceptions of equality, demonstrating that not all are content or able to earn a living through wages, that not all are content or able to dwell within the unforgiving constraints of the abstractly perfect space of the

3.3. The Haymarket—London: the equivocal image of the prostitute in one of the most notorious stretches of West End nightlife. *The Haymarket–Midnight* Engraving in Henry Mayhew, *London Labour and the London Poor* (London: Griffin, Bohn & Co., 1861–62): 4:260.

capitalist economy. Finally, foreignness must equally be cast as dirty because it brings alien cultures and customs that challenge the myth of a single system of social equality. Just as they are fixed conceptually, so these categories are placed in particular spaces within a verticalized conception of the city, in spaces consequently identified as more or less subterranean, alien in nature although spatially proximate to the world above.

The conception of the city as a vertically divided space began to dominate urban representations as the lives of the inhabitants and the spaces they inhabited began to be divided in increasingly manifest ways. The industrial city posed several problems for the smooth functioning of mainstream society; nineteenth-century Europe was primarily concerned with resolving them. Large population groups had to be brought together and rationally organized in as efficient a manner as possible. Homogenization and regulation were the primary means of this organization. At the same time, the new concentration of bodies created new problems relating to health, sanitation, and control. The more that the proper operation of capitalism required the denial of the material facts of life, the more the material facts of life pressed themselves upon the public eye. The nineteenth-century metropolis was the first in which rich and poor did not live cheek to jowl in a mixed-use urban space. Growing spatial segregation and the increase of single-use space went hand in hand with a changed sense that the underground carried specific identities applicable only to certain, now unseen, spaces.

Two primary discourses grew up around these strategies of sanitation and underground spaces, one focused on the disposal of waste and conventionally identified with London, the other on its transmutation and identified with Paris. As we shall see, neither discourse fully accounts for the space of either city, nor can the two models be fully understood separately. The London model articulated a strategy of flushing out of sight whatever was defined as dirt; what was not suitable to the world above was to be repressed, if not eliminated altogether. The Paris model naturalized the urban space, viewing it holistically and striving to contain, recycle, and profit from what could not be directly incorporated into the world above.

As the many remaining traces of precapitalist social structures were relocated underground literally and metaphorically as filth, they did not simply disappear. Instead, they gained further power—as allure and as threat—from the act of distancing and rejection, especially as acceptable outlets for the fears and desires they had once expressed licitly became increasingly constrained. Peter Stallybrass and Allon White have interpreted this process through a model combining Bakhtin's ideas with psychoanalysis, arguing that the "bodily lower stratum," repressed as the bourgeois subject matured, was "transcoded" onto the analogous stratum in the city, its lower depths, "the slums, the labouring poor, the prostitute, the sewer."[11] Hence the nineteenth-century trope of filth as truth, and its end-of-the-century Freudian correlative, the unconscious as the locus of truth.

The psychoanalytic model provides a persuasive explanation for the Victorian obsession with all things subterranean, but the focus on a symbolic topography also risks hypostasizing a change in spatial production as an aspect of individual, middle-class experience. One may well argue, for example, as Charles Bernheimer does, that "the complex fascination [of prostitution] is posited in the denial of what is beneath the female body, which . . . the majority of male writers in 19th century France associated with animality, disease, castration, excrement, and decay."[12] Nevertheless, the bourgeois male, if the carrier of the dominant ideology and the test case for the new subjectivity being worked out through the new urban underworld, was only one among many groups involved in the production of the nineteenth-century city. The category of filth cannot be reduced to a single quality without being reabsorbed as an idealized counterpart of the ideology determining that which is clean. Put another way, animality, disease, castration, excrement, and decay are alluring not merely because they represent everything denied in the maturation of the bourgeois male, but because they are dialectical categories; they are, in essence, both positive and negative. The underground fascinates not merely because it contains all that is forbidden but because it contains it as an unimaginably rich, albeit inchoate and intoxicating, brew of other times, places, and modes of being in the world, and because that brew intimates the fragility of the unity claimed by the world above.

It may well be that the underworld continued to function as the locus of truth in the nineteenth century in large part because many of its writers were working through a desire for the lost connection to their own nether parts. Nevertheless, this argument does not account for the mythic component of the descent to the underworld in search of truth as that desire was generally figured, nor for those individuals and social groups that experienced filth in a completely different, if no less conflicted manner, including, among others, prostitutes, the working classes, the criminal classes, and the many individuals only partially or not at all accounted for by any particular category. It does not account for the ambivalence that lurks within even such an apparently straightforward statement as early Socialist Eugène Buret's assertion in 1840 that "the destitute resemble the bands of Anglo-Saxons who took to a nomadic life in the forests to escape the Norman yoke. They are outside society, outside the law, outlaws, and almost all criminals come from their ranks."[13] The evocation of the legend of Robin Hood to characterize the criminality of the laboring classes makes evident the atavistic dream of a life lived freely under natural conditions, even if those very conditions by the nineteenth century could be identified within the confines of the industrial city only in the language of nature befouled and perverted. Stripped of their pastoral romanticism, such fantasies were the closest that mainstream discourse could come to representing the contradictory pulls of poverty toward middle-class respectability and toward underground criminality. Only in the early twentieth century would mainstream discourse begin to replace extreme ambivalence with a more reasoned account of both the mind-numbing drudgery of working-class labor and the complex networks of sociability and fluctuating identities that characterized working-class culture. These phenomena finally became available to mainstream discourse, however, primarily because the primacy of physical labor and degree of cultural heterogeneity that had made them so difficult to apprehend by outsiders had to a large degree been replaced by homogenized cliches of working-class culture safely contained within such mainstream and ostensibly universal forms as the new narrative cinema of the teens and twenties.[14]

The Foucauldian model that dominated readings of the nineteenth-century city over the last two decades of the twentieth century has established that there was a conventional discourse on filth that served primarily to solidify culturally the physical changes created by capitalist exploitation of underground and urban space in the nineteenth century. In its abstract form, the ideology of this discourse is straightforward and, on its own terms, holds an uncomplicated view of filth and the underground. As another look at Bakhtin reminds us, however, this is the simplest and least informative image available of a far more complex and conflicted underworld:

> The image of the underworld also bears this ambivalent character; it contains the past, the rejected and condemned, as unworthy to dwell in the present, as something useless and obsolete. But it also gives us a glimpse of the new life, of the future that is born, for it is this future that finally kills the past. All these ambivalent images are dual-bodied, dual-faced, pregnant. They combine in various proportions negation and affirmation, the top and the bottom, abuse and praise.[15]

The moment we cease viewing the underground from the viewpoint of a unified ideology, the moment we look past the spellbinding surface words that describe it, we find a dialectic between aboveground and belowground whereby each term opens up the contradictions within the other, and whereby the apparently cohesive and universal system formed by the pair presents itself as only in fact a partial explanation of the world. The vertical model, whether mobilized affirmatively or inverted critically on its head, will be able to generate a comprehensive image of the modern city in all its contradictions only when also read laterally through traces of those other, nonvertical organizations of space for which it no longer has any use.

The terms of this dialectic change not only over time, as the Foucauldian account would uphold, but over space, for they are always also local, uneven, and incomplete. The examples Stallybrass and White muster for their equation of filth with truth derive from Paris's *Les Misérables,* London's Mayhew, and Vienna's Rat Man; however, each equation is fundamentally different because each version is consistent with the social space of the city from which it emerged. In the example from Mayhew, it is the physical infrastructure of the main drainage system that explains the city's functioning. For Hugo, Jean Valjean's descent into the sewers metonymically links social truth with individual salvation: in mythic fashion, the descending hero returns with both personal and universal revelations about the nature of waste. For Freud's Rat Man, the truth is one of sexual fantasy, "horror at pleasure of his own of which he himself was unaware"[16]; the figure of the rat reveals a psychic trauma in the patient. Freud's Vienna was the ideal model for the transcoding discussed by Stallybrass and White, as it was for the invention of psychoanalysis, with its expansive and elaborate mansions fronting onto narrow and poorly paved streets in the cramped inner city.[17]

Freud related the symbolic significance of the rat both to its ambivalent character—"in legends generally the rat appears not so much as a disgusting creature but as something uncanny—as a chthonic animal . . . and it is used to represent the souls of the dead"—and to the contemporary enunciation of that character, referring as evidence of the rat's identity as "a dirty animal, feeding upon excrement and living in sewers" to the creatures' appearance in the 1832 collection of obscene illustrations by Le Poittevin, *Diableries érotiques.*[18] One of the Rat Man's most horrifying memories was of seeing an enormous rat that he imagined as having emerged from his father's grave, where it had been gnawing on the corpse.[19] There had been no clean sweep of the past meanings of the rat figure any more than the nineteenth-century city had eliminated prior cityscapes. The social meaning, the interpretation given it by Freud, was indeed new, but it is precisely this aspect of the case history that was specific to the space of Vienna. By contrast, the updated chthonic connection of the rat to the uncanniness of the underworld can be found, inflected differently, in every modern city, and generates the power of the application to a particular space. It is important to distinguish between the different components of the Freudian discourse, between what could be generalized about Western bourgeois culture, about the modern city, and about Vienna, respectively, not to mention those components derived from irreducibly personal experience, such as the eccentric delineations of the Rat Man's obsessions.

While equally fascinated by the underside of city life, Mayhew's "scopophilia" (to use Stallybrass and White's term) is a far cry from the Rat Man's tormented fantasies. Mayhew was intrigued by the social system of the "nomadic tribes" of London as a challenge to middle-class society. The authorial voice in *London Labour* alternates between shock at the costermongers' lack of knowledge of religion, disinterest in marriage, and refusal to save money and envy at their freedom from the constraints those very institutions placed on his own social class.[20] In this ambivalent model, occupations such as pure-finding (scavenging "pure," or dogs' dung, for, paradoxically, cleansing and purifying leather), mudlarking (scavenging the polluted mudflats and drainage entrances of the Thames at low tide), and toshing (scavenging within the sewage tunnels for objects and money that had fallen through the drains) were emblematic not simply for their function as an abstract "truth" hidden beneath the veil of filth, but as specific spatial practices within the cityscape of London that, because representable only as filth, more directly expressed the contradictions of the rapidly rationalizing city.

Mayhew divided the various occupations of street-finding and collecting spatially: those who limited their finding to the London streets, those whose labour was confined to the river or "that subterranean city of sewerage" that drains into it, and those who removed waste from the houses as well as the streets.[21] At times, he outlines a social hierarchy between the lumpen grubbers, "vacuous of mind"; the intrepid sewer-hunters, "intelligent and adventurous," working in gangs; the "small master" dredger-men; the working-class dustmen, "of the plodding class of labourers, mere labourers"; and even, although not interviewed, the "wealthy contractor for the public scavengery . . . as entirely one of the street-folk as the unskilled and ignorant labourer he employs."[22] At other times, he appears to regard all of them as a challenge to mainstream society, as in his characterization of grubbers as "with a few exceptions stupid, unconscious of their degradation, and with little anxiety to be relieved of it."[23] Finally, there is a temporal specificity to this spatial practice, for Mayhew implied the eventual disappearance of these "outcast" occupations, since each of them was subject to rationalization into "the occupation of a wealthy man, deriving a small profit from the labour of each particular collector."[24] Mirror of a complex social system, image of underground deviance, metaphor of loss of tradition to progress: these different discourses and different conceptions of a marginal space of the city coexist in the pages of Mayhew.

It is difficult to reconcile the romantic nostalgia for the vanishing occupations of a previous order of capitalism documented in *London Labour* with the conventional Victorian discourse on the lower depths deployed by Stallybrass and White, or by French historian Alain Corbin, who characterizes it as "the incessant vacillation between fascination and repulsion."[25] Nor should we dismiss Mayhew's ambivalence simply because it romanticized the nomadic life of the "dirty" Londoners; rather, we should use that contradiction in the category of London filth to crack open the categories that he was purportedly defending.[26] The life-altering truth with which Mayhew returned from his descent into the underworld of London life was the half-expressed realization that he had viewed not merely something sublimely, terrifyingly true, but something that he could both recognize and express as a material desire in himself. In the italicized words of a tosher he interviewed, a former blacksmith's apprentice and veteran of the sewers for over twenty years: "*The reasons I likes this sort of life is, 'cause I can sit down when I likes, and nobody can't order me about. When I'm hard up, I knows as how I must work, and then I goes at it like sticks a breaking;* and tho' the times isn't as they was, I can go now and pick up my four or five bob a day where another wouldn't know how to get a brass farden."[27]

Whereas Freud formulated the Rat Man's relation to filth through the city's subterranean fauna, and Mayhew formulated his through identification with a different social organization and a different practice of urban space, Hugo metaphorized the city of Paris as a living organism, a "Leviathan," whose history could best be understood through the study of its "entrails." As befits a city whose inhabitants have always been supremely conscious of its representational spaces, Hugo traced the fifteen years leading up to the 1830 revolution and presented his solution to the rift between les misérables and the rest of France, between the ideals of the Revolution and its execution in history, by means of the actual space of its drainage system:

> Paris throws twenty-five million francs a year into the water. This is no metaphor. How, and in what way? . . . By means of what organ? By means of its intestine. What is its intestine? It is its sewer. . . . A great city is the most powerful of stercoraries. To use the town to manure the plain is to ensure prosperity. If our gold is dung, then, conversely, our dung is gold. . . . These heaps of filth around the stone bollards, these tipcarts of muck rattling along the night streets, these frightful *refuse barrels, these fetid streams of underground slime that the pavement* hides from you—do you know what they are? They are the meadow in flower, the green grass, thyme and sage; they are game, cattle, the satisfied mooing of great cows in the evening, perfumed hay, golden wheat, bread on your table. They are warm blood in your veins, health, joy, life. Thus is the desire of that mystery of creation which is the transformation on earth and the transfiguration in heaven.[28]

"This is no metaphor," insisted Hugo, and, indeed, it is not, for the Paris sewer does in fact contain grain, herbs, and cattle, the "warm blood" and the life of the French countryside within its tunnels, transmuted into filth through the excretory systems of the city's inhabitants, primarily the wealthy with their water closets. It required not an alchemical process but a simple change in perspective for the filth described in the first half of this passage to transmute into the pastoral vision purportedly its opposite. Hugo provided practical directions for this transformation by urging the recycling of Parisian sewage as fertilizer; the first experiments in "manure-spreading fields" were conducted only four years after the publication of *Les Misérables*.[29]

What remains a metaphor, however, is the degree to which Hugo assimilated France's poor into this natural cycle of consumption, digestion, and excretion; the metaphor is actualized by the religious language with which the passage concludes, the "mystery" of creation, and especially of the transfiguration of wine and bread into flesh and blood. For the burden of Jean Valjean's character, the ideology with which he emerges from his odyssey through the sewers, is to persuade the middle-class reader that the same natural relationship inheres between the classes as between nourishment and the nourished. As Fred Radford has suggested, Valjean links the worlds of above and below through the mythography he performs as well as through his representation as digestive matter:

> His underworld flight is also a journey of salvation which preserves the life of Marius. It is a harrowing of hell: one chapter of the episode is even called, "He Also Carries his

Cross." . . . His identity with the underworld of the sewers is reaffirmed at the same time as he earns a new life. The duality is also there biologically . . . Valjean is digested, that is, transformed into both nutriment (he saves Marius) and excrement (his convict identity is reconfirmed when he is arrested by Inspector Javert at the sewer exit).[30]

Radford does not, however, draw the final conclusion of Hugo's social program, whereby even the convict, even the excrement of the system, can be converted into something of value to the body politic. Whether emerging from the Leviathan as Jonah from the whale in his individual quality as social prophet within the novel's structure, or excreted from it as fertilizer for generations to come, Valjean closes the circle of a perfected and benevolent capitalism in which nothing would go to waste. Paris as Leviathan would feed on the rich produce of the surrounding country, digesting what was of immediate value and excreting through its sewers as fertilizer to be returned to the countryside what it could not make immediately useful. As one supporter eulogized the process in verse in 1866:

> Into an enormous pit
> Goes what we collect there,
> Nothing perished, all is transformed:
> None knows this better than we.
> Tomorrow, this vile refuse
> Will be changed into the ripe grape,
> Into flowers, into fruits, into amber grains
> Of barley and pure wheat.[31]

This is the representational identity of the Paris underground, subsumed within its social space as useful rather than, as in the London model, being carried away as waste product.

The transformation of dirt into gold is a common socialist fantasy, a familiar metaphor for the obscured processes of early capitalism. This is the means whereby Mayhew's scavengers subsist on the margins of the new economy; in the full-fledged ideology of monopoly capitalism, the metaphor disappears in favor of the creation of money ex nihilo, without the necessity of dirtying one's hands, of processing it through the digestive system first. Exchange value in its purest form uses capital to create more capital, eliminating the material altogether. Hugo, by contrast, recovers the material processes of urban capitalism through the transformative metaphor. So, whereas Radford, for example, writes critically that "even in Hugo the final agent of purification is money,"[32] I would argue that we must read the image dialectically: in comparison with precapitalist systems, this is indeed a frightening process; in comparison with the dematerialized capitalism and the cleansed underground that was developing in the late nineteenth century, it actually provided a critical reminder that the process of purification was in fact not yet completed.

There was a British tradition of sewage recycling, based, as Christopher Hamlin has documented, in a theory of "cosmic sanitary dualism": "As Henry Austin put it, 'the great cycle of life, decay, and reproduction must be completed, and so long as the elements of reproduction are not employed for good, they will work for evil.'"[33] This tradition was important, Hamlin argues, in motivating the great labor and cost of the midcentury drainage works, although it was superseded in the late 1870s by a new focus on bacteria.[34] The adoption of this natural theology as a metonymy for the poor is beyond the scope of Hamlin's essay, but it is evident in Austin's language ("so long as the elements of reproduction are not employed for good, they will work for evil"); its distance from the conciliatory tone of Hugo's theology is especially apparent in the passage Hamlin cites from chapter 15 of Charles Kingsley's 1850 novel, *Yeast: A Problem.* Lancelot looks down from a Thames bridge

> at that huge, black-mouthed sewer, vomiting its pestilential riches across the mud. There it runs . . . hurrying to the sea vast stores of wealth, elaborated by Nature's chemistry into the ready materials of food; which proclaim, too, by their own foul smell God's will that they should be buried out of sight in the fruitful, all-regenerating grave of earth; there it runs; turning them all into the seeds of pestilence, filth, and drunkenness.[35]

The use of sewage to personify the poor is clearest in the concluding triad of terms; what is striking in comparison to Hugo is the apocalyptic language: whereas in *Les Misérables,* the recycling of sewage was local, practical, and above the ground, scattered over fields outside Paris, Kingsley called for a Noah's flood to wash the scum off the face of the city.

The nearest to the Hugolian model to be found in a London setting is probably the socialist utopia of William Morris's *News from Nowhere* (1890). In Morris's vision, London has been transformed into an idealized medieval town in the aftermath of a cataclysmic conflict. The emblematic urban figure is a transformed version of that Victorian icon, the dustman, who made his living collecting and scavenging "dust," the desiccating Victorian euphemism for urban waste, which was primarily composed of horse manure and human excrement (figure 3.4). Morris's "Golden Dustman" is a utopian version of his namesake, Boffin, in Dickens's *Our Mutual Friend,* who becomes a conventional millionaire when he inherits the immensely valuable piles of dust accumulated on his master's estate. In Dickens's less holistic and more cynical vision, however, Boffin was counterbalanced by Gaffer Hexam, the sinister riverman, who makes his meager living by scavenging corpses out of the Thames. Meanwhile, Boffin is unable to rest easily with the gold that comes out of his dust; it threatens to ruin his life by undermining his innate petit-bourgeois values. For Dickens, unlike for the Catholic Hugo, the transmutation of dust into gold, of negative filth into positive value, was not a miracle of holistic nature but a token of the parasitic, unnatural space that was London. Filth, for Dickens, as for the conventional Victorian, was at best worth a salutary warning before being flushed out of sight. A good Protestant, Dickens saw in excessive money only the moral taint of filthy lucre.

Morris argued, conversely, that the city could truly be cleansed, but only by changing its very nature in a process of historical alchemy. His Golden Dustman is so named not because of his worth in gold but because of the beautiful, gaudy clothing in which it pleases him to ply his trade. In this utopian future, the past —that other waste product traditionally carried through the sewers—has been eliminated except in the memories of eccentrics such as the curmudgeonly old man who inhabits the former British Museum and ruminates on the bad old days like a latter-day Mayhew. Even in the socialist utopia of Morris, however, not everything can be made useful and beautiful. Rather than recycled to fertilize the good that is to come, the dust of the new city of London is symbolically dis-

3.4. "Dusty Bobs": "There are none, we think, so essentially, so peculiarly, so irretrievably *Londonish*, as our 'London Dustmen.'" Front cover illustration, *London Dustmen*, in *London Saturday Journal* no. 7, n.s. (13 February 1841).

posed of in another filthy and irredeemable institution, the houses of Parliament, relegated to the status of monumental dustbin in the London of the future. Too hopelessly contaminated by centuries of corruption, the houses of Parliament cannot be made beautiful. Unable to be reincorporated à la Hugo into the political economy, they could at least, Morris suggested, be made useful as containers.

The equation of a political center with filth has been a commonplace of invective for millennia; what is unusual in the case of London is that, following the Great Stink in 1858, when the sewers were flushed into the Thames by order of the Metropolitan Board of Works, contaminating the river and disrupting the functioning of the government with their stench, the satirical metaphor materialized in the space of the city. A Christmas pantomime of that year, *Harlequin Father Thames and the River Queen,* staged the Great Stink, as an article of the time put it, as a "war between impurity and purity."[36] The play opens under the arches of Waterloo Bridge, where a chorus of mudlarks welcomes Father Thames and his allies in filth, the houses of Commons and Lords—"allegorical representations" of the city's various sewers and bridges, respectively. Father Thames himself is an unrepentant slummer, filthy, malodorous and drunken; his fellow merrymakers include such luminaries as the Lord Mayor, the chairman of the Metropolitan Board of Works, and assorted aldermen; joined by Gog and Magog, they take a vow to be "foul together ever more."[37] *Harlequin Father Thames* drew its humor from a vertical division of the city whereby high and low became analogous to cleanliness and filth: the opposition is led by Sanita and her lieutenant, the River Queen, from Richmond, extra-urban, upstream, and royalist, with support from the city's parks.

Playing on the same long tradition of political satire and Thames filth, the broadsheet poem *Father Thames and the Builders' Strike* put the river god in the more conventional position of complaining about his current state, playing on the potential for scatological humor in the Great Stink (figure 3.5). Sitting at home, suffocating on the "pestilent air," Old Father Thames complains about the miserly governing bodies of the city: "Commissioners squabbled, the Commons debated, / But giving the cash was a measure they hated."[38] He concludes with a lament struck at the heart of a nation obsessed with flushing away its waste: "I am dos'd with quick-lime, and the doctors are clever, / But my bottom, I fear, will stink for ever." The analogy of Thames and toilet has been enduring, as demonstrated by pop artist Claes Oldenburg's *Proposed Colossal Monument for Thames River: Thames Ball* (1967), which took a typical image of monumental London—a postcard of the houses of Parliament and the riverside—and added two toilet floats balancing on the water, attached by long arms to Lambeth Bridge: the Thames is the tank, the houses of Commons and of Lords a pair of toilet bowls (figure 3.6). The adolescent impulse of scatological graffiti gains a deeper resonance through the sanitary history of the river.

3.5. The long history of London filth: George Cruikshank's 1832 satire, *Salus Populi Suprema Lex* (The Welfare of the Public Is the Supreme Law), depicts John Edwards, owner of the notoriously unsanitary Southwark Water Works, occupying Father Thames's customary place amid sewers gushing effluvia and customers and onlookers shouting complaints and abuse. Illustration by George Cruikshank, *Salus Populi Suprema Lex* (London: Samuel Knights, 1832). Reproduced by permission from the Guildhall Library, © Corporation of London.

While satire would create figures such as the joyfully corrupt villain of *Harlequin Father Thames,* and feuilleton novels would proffer criminals who reveled in the filth of their underworld life, seldom in London or in Paris does one encounter an extended representation of the positive potentialities of the organic underground. Those that exist are quite instructive to examine, for they help to delineate the peripheries of the central discourses. One such representation can be found in *The Wild Boys of London* (1866), an infamous penny-dreadful serial that so scandalized because of its sex and violence that reprints of it were seized by the police.[39] In fact, *Wild Boys* was no more pornographic than many less vilified serials; it did, however, paint an unusually sympathetic portrait of the band of homeless lads that provides its title. The description of the sewer hideout of the so-called Children of the Night is bereft of the protestations of filth and foul odors that were (and remain) de rigueur for accounts of organic underground urban dwellings. Instead, we find something more akin to an adolescent, makeshift imitation of that Regency invention, the London club:

> It was built in a style of architecture which is rarely seen now; the walls were stone, the roof vaulted, and supported by large pillars. It was furnished with innumerable piles of mats of every description, from the rough rope to the luxurious woolen. On these a number of boys reclined in various attitudes, each according to his inclination. Several lamps hung from chains fixed to the roof, and gave a smokey aspect to the place. A square iron stove stood in the centre, and the smoke was conducted out by means of a pipe, which, with considerable ingenuity, was so placed as to lead downward into an adjacent sewer. A box formed of rough planks, served them for a table, and completed the domestic arrangements, since it also served as a receptacle for provisions.[40]

The introductory architectural note is important, as it grounds the boys'-club fantasy in nostalgia for an earlier urban space, "which is rarely seen now." Traces of what might be considered discomfort remain, as in the "smokey aspect" of the lamps, but they contribute to a picturesque effect in keeping with the nostalgic tone.[41] It is an ingenious, comfortable, and safe space.

It is not so much that the sewer has been elided but that the passage has drawn on the positive aspects of dirt instead of the more conventional negative ones. Rather than assimilated as filthy by the sewers in which they live, the wild boys move through them at will, in contrast to the streets above, where they continue

3.6. The iconography of Thames filth modernized for the late twentieth century. Claes Oldenburg, *Proposed Colossal Monument for Thames River: Thames Ball* (1967). Crayon, ink, watercolor, on postcard, 8.9 x 14 cm. © Claes Oldenburg and Coosje van Bruggen.

to be pursued and harassed. "It's nothing when you get used to it," explains Dolphin to the newly arrived refugee, Dick. "We gets wet, and we gets dry again; the mud makes us dirty, and the water makes us clean. And when we gets in, we has a warm bed and a good fire, with something to eat in the bargain."[42] Unusually in descriptions of underworld dwellers, the boys' identity is in no way fixed by the space in which they shelter. There is a physical ordeal to undergo, a frightening dive and swim through flooded tunnels, but the otherworld within, just under the streets but worlds away, is everything not being offered to these boys in the world above: escape from the authorities, along with "a warm bed and a good fire, with something to eat in the bargain."

The sensational space the reader expects from the serial's title and from his or her prior knowledge of penny-dreadful filth is there as well, in spades, matched by the lurid scene gracing the cover of each issue. One of the newly arrived boy's first adventures in the sewers is the discovery of the body of a man being consumed by rats; not surprisingly, this iconographic sensation scene was the one chosen for the week's illustration (figure 3.7). Visual representation tends even more strongly to the typical than the more abstract mode of language. Indeed, at the low end of the publishing market it was not unusual for stock illustrations to be recycled: the same rescue scene beneath a river bridge found here would soon grace the cover of the *Wild Boys of Paris*. The plotting meets all expectations of a verticalized space as well: the clean-at-heart boys—those worthy of being salvaged from the sewers—are eventually filtered out and rehabilitated; the dirty-to-the-core ones are shipped off to Australia, which often functioned as a continental garbage dump in the Victorian imaginary (not to mention in the historical fact of its prison colonies). But this should not lead us simply to dismiss the original idyll as pure ideology or simple fantasy, for then we must perforce dismiss the same idylls when they appear as pure ideology or pure fantasy in their more familiar place in middle-class discourse. Instead, they can remind us that the utopian aspects of bourgeois desire are no more necessarily joined to capitalist ideology than the negative aspects of filth are inherently lower class.

The dialectic between the safe haven and the familiar spectacle is not the same as the play between attraction and repulsion to which the underworld is generally reduced in accounts of nineteenth-century dirt, where the boys would have to be represented as unthinking if pitiable animals in their lair or as abovegrounders temporarily and criminally misplaced in the world below. In neither case is the sewer the haunt of the unrepentant villains of the genre, who generally dwell in the figurative underworld of the slums (not to mention the heavenly mansions). The sewer offers shelter and knowledge to those with the misfortune of finding themselves in it. In *The Mysteries of Old Father Thames* (1848), for example, a misplaced youth who will eventually make good is taken in and trained by an old mudlark, who leads him through the tunnels to the abandoned thieves'

3.7. *The Discovery in the Sewer:* a conventional visual representation of the sensational underworld illustrates a less conventional text. Illustration from *The Wild Boys of London or The Children of the Night. A Story of the Present Day* [London: Newsagents Publishing Co., 1866], 1:25. BL shelfmark 12620.h.27. Reproduced by permission from the British Library.

house on West Street above Fleet Ditch where he has a derelict squat, little better than the sewer running just below its floor (figure 3.8). Both tunnel and room are equally pervaded by "noxious and pestilential vapours" and "darkness and filth."[43] This view from below is not bereft of critical impetus, but it is expressed solely through the negative formulation of dirt. The old mudlark, it turns out, is actually something of a hermit in retreat from the world above, where, as a shop-

3.8. The nadir of underground labor: the sewer-hunter. Illustration by Archibald Henning, *The Sewer-Hunter*, from a daguerreotype by Richard Beard, in Henry Mayhew, *London Labour and the London Poor* (London: Griffin, Bohn & Co., 1861–62): facing 2:388.

keeper with a loving family, he had experienced, as he puts it, "the turpitude with which the competitive system of production and distribution is rife, but the frightful extent of which is known only to those engaged in it."[44] By contrast to the compromised, vitiated survival of the old mudlark, too beaten down even to be granted a name, *The Wild Boys of London* gives us brief glimpses of dispossessed individuals participating on their own terms in a world from which they have otherwise been excluded. Here, the lower depths exhibit the same range of experience as any other social space.

Similar spaces in the literature of Paris are more frequent, although they tend, as in the case of *Les Misérables,* to be more ambivalent than this London exception. Dating from the early twentieth century, Gaston Leroux's depiction of subterranean Paris epitomizes the discourse of the previous century. In his first novel, *La Double vie de Théophraste Longuet* (1903), Leroux reported that the "bedroom" of the famous eighteenth-century bandit Cartouche had been discovered in the sewers when they were being cleaned during the 1820s.[45] The better-known but equally apocryphal apartments of Erik the Phantom in an underground lake beneath the Paris Opéra have much in common with the Wild Boys' London crib in terms of safety and comfort. Although never described wholly from Erik's point of view, we see even from the kidnapped Christine's description how it could be regarded as a banal space, made sinister only by its subterranean location and her position as prisoner: "No doubt I was dealing with some awful eccentric who had mysteriously come to live in these cellars, like others, out of necessity, and, with the silent complicity of the administration, had found a definitive shelter."[46] As with so much in the novel, which plays on dual identities and reflected spaces, the angelic voice and the demonic face, we are given a dual perspective on Erik and his home, and he is allowed to assert an irreducible identity: "I am neither angel, nor genie, nor phantom . . . I am Erik!"[47] Once his mask is lifted to reveal a hideously scarred face, however, Erik, unlike the Wild Boys, is indelibly marked as other, the physical evidence reflected in his underworld life and his ever more twisted behavior. This otherness renders the space romantic, an aristocratic fantasy rather than the homey comfort of the Wild Boys' space, and consequently closer to the conventional discourse of the sewer as otherworld.

As such an otherworld, it has lent itself to reveries both physical and metaphysical. Ben Carré's subterranean sets for the 1925 Lon Chaney film version of *The Phantom of the Opera* were based, among other sources, on the façade of L'Enfer, a popular Pigalle nightclub, which presented an art-nouveau mouth of hell (figure 3.9). The last vestige of the bodily was removed as Erik's world was wholly recuperated as diabolic novelty in the world above. The space could also be reduced to its material base: an early twentieth-century tour of the Opéra would include not only the stage itself, from high above the wings to four stories deep in the cellars beneath, but a look "down through the trap-door in the pavement [to] the black waters of a river, a subterranean river that loses itself in the soil underneath this part of Paris," including, no doubt, the fait divers that inspired Leroux's novel.[48] A 1940s paperback edition included a convenient map on its back cover (figure 3.10). In its elimination of any representational component, the landscape description or mapping mirrors the rational discourse of the nineteenth-century sewer tour; in its resonance as the Phantom's realm, it reminds us of the traces of the underworld journey that emerge from even the cleanest tour of the London or Paris sewers.

3.9. *The Entrance to "Hell"*: The underworld as nightlife entertainment. Drawing by Edouard Cucuel of the Cabaret de l'Enfer, boulevard de Clichy, in *Bohemian Paris of To-day*, by W. C. Morrow from notes by Edouard Cucuel (London: Chatto & Windus, 1899): 277.

3.10. The Phantom's realm mapped for sensation seekers in rationalistic postwar America. From the jacket cover of *The Phantom of the Opera* by Gaston Leroux, © Used by permission of Bantam Books, a division of Random House, Inc.

Public Utilities in London

The metropolitan area covers more than a hundred square miles and contains approximately thirty thousand streets, or about six hundred thousand houses. . . . No man knows every quarter of the capital. But its dingiest alleys as well as its most fashionable avenues are cared for at stated times by the municipal scavengers.

P. F. WILLIAM RYAN, "London's Toilet," *Living London* (1901–3)

There is a genre of sewer writing in which the space itself appears bereft of all assertions of filth, disease, and stench: the scientific and journalistic narrative of the sewer worker and the space in which he works. In exchange for such underground utopianism, however, we find no recognition of physical discomfort whatsoever: these workers are invariably healthy and happy, the perfect mirror of the worker desired in the world above. This rationalizing discourse of the organic underground is expressed differently in London and in Paris. In the former, the sewer has always been sealed off as a public utility, requiring, as one account put it, that "in order to investigate that world thoroughly special arrangements will have to be made, and special permissions obtained from various authorities."[49] In the latter, the sewer and its workers have always held their own mythology, with the sewer tour a requisite of any visit to the French capital from 1867 on, and the égoutier occupying a privileged place in the mythology of the Parisian worker.[50] In either case, reconciliation with the working classes is the underlying message.

The rhetoric of rationalized sewage and healthy sewer workers began in the mid-nineteenth century; as the novelist and travel writer Fanny Trollope complained during her visit to the Continent in 1835, "almost the only thing in the world which other men do and the French cannot, is the making of sewers and drains."[51] Earlier tours had a different resonance: a good example is Jonson's "Famous Voyage," discussed above. While Jonson's allusions to the classical underworld descents in Aristophanes' *Frogs* and Virgil's *Aeneid,* and the mythical journeys of Theseus, Hercules, and Castor and Pollux establish the river Fleet as an underworld, there is no sense that the polluted river is anything more than a synecdoche for the corruption and filth of the city as a whole; nor does the passage through the not-yet-subterranean river explicitly verticalize the cityscape beyond the general danger of "showers" from the houses above. As Stephen Copley and Ian Haywood have characterized two celebrated eighteenth-century depictions of cloacal imagery in London, Swift's "Description of a City Shower" and the Fleet Ditch diving competition in book 2 of Pope's *Dunciad,* the river provided scatological imagery of impropriety and disgust as well as "an emblem of cultural, moral and social corruption" (figure 3.11).[52] The Fleet had originally

3.11. The Fleet Ditch diving competition, from Pope's *Dunciad* 2: "Here strip my Children! Here at once leap in, / Here prove who best can dash thro' thick and thin." Illustration by Francis Hayman, engraved by Charles Grignion, *View of the Fleet Ditch with Bathers*, ca. 1750. Reproduced by permission from the Guildhall Library, © Corporation of London.

been a navigable waterway, but already by the time of Jonson's poem it had become so full of debris and garbage as to be impassable; hence the mock-epic tone of the difficult return. Where Aeneas had departed the underworld with prophetic knowledge revealed him by the shade of his father, Jonson's intrepid wherry reaches the drainage of the Fleet into the Thames at Holburn with the mundane experience of any unwary pedestrian in London, a "shitten" head and a tormented nose:

> How dare
> Your dainty nostrils (in so hot a season,
> When every clerk eats artichokes and peason,
> Laxative lettuce, and such windy meat)
> 'Tempt such a passage? When each privy's seat
> Is filled with buttock, and the walls do sweat
> Urine and plasters?[53]

In retrospect, such a synthetic attitude seemed incomprehensible to the rational nineteenth-century encyclopedist. As the article "Underground" in *Knight's London* put it in 1841, "London generally must have been then almost as bad as St. Giles's is now!"[54] The eighteenth-century writer was still able to view the city as a whole, including the Fleet, which was partially bricked over in 1737 and not fully covered until 1766. The same period saw a great increase in subterranean drainage. Between 1756 and 1834, 114 sewers were built either wholly or in part in the City, a third of them after 1824 (figures 3.12 and 3.13). When the architect John Nash cut Regent Street in the 1820s, not only did he make the cut so as "to leave out to the East all those bad streets," but he also linked the new suburban development around Regents Park to the existing sewer main under St. James's Park by means of a drainage tunnel running beneath the new street.[55] The tradition of the sewer tour that would become synonymous with late nineteenth-century Paris persisted in London only in the odd satire, as in the 1850s suggestion that boating excursions should follow the Fleet Ditch through the main collector sewer to take in the "*véritable eau de Smithfield*," where the waste from the slaughterhouses was dumped, with the added allure for nature lovers of the "land rat and water rat" (figure 3.14). Targeting opposition to the demolition of Smithfield Market, the satire's several allusions to the French capital emphasized the underlying distinction between urban images: such perverse pleasure trips were suitable only to the decadent Continent.

The newly expanded and renovated underground became a symbol of the newly divided city at the same time as it was being adapted to represent the underworld on a different level of representation. Platt and Saunders cited Dr. Southwood Smith's tracing of a map of disease onto the network of tunnels:

> If . . . you were to take a map and mark out the districts which are the constant seats of fever in London, as ascertained . . . and at the same time compare it with a map of

3.12. *Opening a Sewer by Night*: a hint of enchantment in the portrayal of nocturnal technology. Drawing in J. C. Platt and J. Saunders, "Underground," in *London*, ed. Charles Knight (London, 1841–44): 1:225.

3.13. *Fleet Ditch, 1841.—Back of Field Lane*: The stretch of the sewer richest in subterranean London lore. From an etching by John Wykeham Archer, in J. C. Platt and J. Saunders, "Underground," in *London*, ed. Charles Knight (London, 1841–44): 1:230.

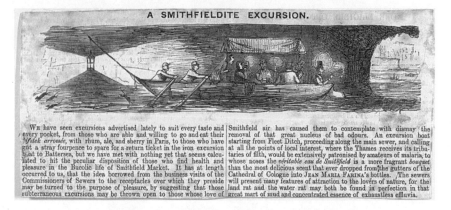

3.14. "A Smithfieldite Excursion": a modern sequel to Jonson's "Famous Voyage." Woodcut ca. 1850. Courtesy of the Guildhall Library, © Corporation of London.

the sewers of the metropolis, you would be able to mark out invariably and with absolute certainty where the sewers are and where they are not, by observing where fever exists; so that we can always tell where the commissioners of sewers have been at work by the track of fever.[56]

Although less sanguine about the drainage works, Dr. John Snow also linked the water system to disease: his cholera maps charted the incidence of death that grouped around specific pumps, demonstrating that the disease was transmitted via contaminated water and food rather than miasma in the air (figure 3.15).[57] In the scientistic accounts, the sewers traced the progress of sanitation; in the sensational literature, they traced the persistence of filth.

Early Victorian concern over deteriorating public health and skyrocketing mortality rates in the cities was galvanized by the publication of Edwin Chadwick's *Report on the Sanitary Condition of the Labouring Population of Great Britain* in 1842.[58] Chadwick's report eventually led to the passage of the Public Health Act of 1848 and the consolidation in London of the local government authorities into the Metropolitan Commission of Sewers, with the exception of the City of London, which appointed its own medical officer, Dr. John Simon. Following Chadwick's recommendation, the commission proceeded to flush out the city's sewers, which by then numbered 369, totally contaminating the Thames and contributing to the cholera epidemics of 1848–49 and 1854. Nothing substantive would be done until, in 1855, the Metropolitan Board of Works was finally formed and ordered to design and construct a main drainage system to dissipate the sewage. Joseph Bazalgette, chief engineer of the Board of Works, submitted a comprehensive proposal to intercept and drain off the sewage from the Thames, and to embank the mudflats along its shores. The final impetus to pass the plan was provided by the Great Stink, which in June 1858 disrupted even the functioning of the House of Commons. The Main Drainage Works at Crossness were opened in 1865; the Embankment was completed in 1870; the whole scheme was realized by 1875.

The ceremony at Crossness, presided over by the Prince of Wales and attended by members of the nobility and the high clergy, was a landmark in the representation of the drainage system as a rational space. The members were taken to visit the very culvert that would soon be receiving the city's sewage: "There was nothing about it to remind one of the purpose for which it had been built. It was sim-

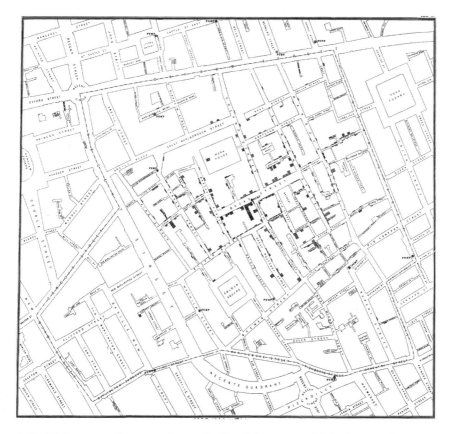

3.15. Cholera mortality mapped onto the Broad Street area of Soho by Dr. John Snow. Local pumps are marked; deaths are marked by black rectangles. Map 1 in John Snow, *On The Mode of Communication of Cholera* (London: J. Churchill, 1855). Reproduced by permission from Ralph R. Frerichs and the John Snow site: http://www.ph.ucla.edu/epi/snow.html.

ply a long, lofty, wide tunnel of excellent brickwork."⁵⁹ This is the ideal of the rational underground: spatial anonymity, interchangeability of use. Conversely, the reservoir, the next step on the tour of inspection, presented instead a backward-looking spectacle, the industrial sublime of the infinity of receding lights, as the vast space had been "illuminated for the occasion by myriads of coloured lamps."⁶⁰ This is the dual representation of the new underground during the waning of the age of heroic engineering: the just-reassuring-enough spectacle of the artificial infinity, trace of the old mode of spatial representation; and the endlessly reproduced sameness of the utilitarian space, the underground equivalent of the "mean streets" of late nineteenth-century working-class housing.

Rather than simply rejecting the traditional tropes of the organic underworld, sanitation writing sought ways of sanitizing the metaphors themselves, just as the ceremony at Crossness found a compromise between outmoded and novel ways of representing an unfamiliar space. In "Sanitary Science," an 1860 article in Dickens's *All the Year Round* serial, it was the discourse of science that would erase remaining traces of the otherworldly:

> There are many houses in Great Britain which have inherited evil reputations; there is a "ghost's room", or a "ghostly corridor", or a "ghost's tower", or a "ghost's terrace." The true ghost's walk is, however, in the basement, amongst and through foetid drains and foul sewers, the ghost's reception-chambers are ancient cesspools, and the ghost's nectar is drawn from tainted wells and neglected water cisterns. . . . Your only exorcist is the sanitary engineer.⁶¹

In *Underground London,* first published as a series of articles in the same weekly journal, and primarily devoted to the sewer, John Hollingshead suggested the genre of science writing as a replacement for romance, with its own denatured tropes, the excess imagination that led to "impracticable proposals" and the shock of the technical language: "His [Sir John Denman's] report is very elaborate and very learned, and while some readers may think that a plain translation ought to have been given, others will doubtless feel that half the horror lies in the language."⁶² If the sewer could not be represented without the otherworldly tropes proper to it, then at least those tropes should be employed as humorously and harmlessly as possible.

As the heroic gave way to the utilitarian in the aboveground representation of the construction and maintenance of the drainage system, the narrative of the London sewer visit stressed more and more the normality of the world below. The residual hint of the otherworld would be contained primarily within the separate, working-class identity of the space of the sewers. Just as the rational city had no room for a dangerous or disruptive underclass, so would its more permeable underground spaces be cleansed of any hint of organic matter. In the 1870s, Edward Walford produced a lurid account of "A Modern Golgotha," the charnel house of St. Enon Chapel, north of the Strand near the eastern entrance to

Clement's Inn.[63] Its vaults were filled to the rafters with corpses by the 1830s, so the practice was discontinued in 1844 when the commissioner of sewers sealed it off while creating a drainage tunnel beneath the building. The bodies continued to fester in this "dust-hole" for several years until the premises were purchased by a surgeon in 1847–48 with the purpose of removing the remains "to a more appropriate place." As the exhumation proceeded, a pile of human bones and one of decaying coffin wood accumulated, and until carted off to Norwood were viewed by some six thousand persons. Walford concluded in properly rational 1870s manner, "It is indeed strange to think that such foul abuses were not swept away until the reign of Victoria." It is a token of the power of the utilitarian discourse that he failed to notice that the "Golgotha" sensation was raging a good decade into the queen's reign and had even then been undertaken out of private philanthropy rather than public initiative—the commissioner of sewers had tried simply to wall it in.

By the start of the twentieth century, the rationalizing discourse dominated, but its inherent instability is readily evident in traces of the old underworld mythology that seeped into the otherwise watertight new sanitation system. Take, for example, the concluding description of the "dust destructor" in an otherwise perfectly standard document of the order and cleanliness of "London's Toilet."[64] After an impersonal catalog of the city's dustmen, watering carts, horse brooms, orderly boys, street and crossing sweepers, and scavengers, the author introduces the Edwardian garbage incinerator in terms that reveal that its inhuman scale and mechanical mode of destruction remained alien enough to require the rhetoric of the medieval underworld rather than that of the new underground. "Had Dante but known the dust destructor," he begins, "to what exquisite agonies could he not have condemned some of the wretches of his 'Inferno'! It is grand, ugly, choking, diabolical; it is a place to fly from. But its very ugliness, while repelling, holds you fast."[65] The industrial sublime of nearly a century before is resurrected to come to terms with the irrational power of the technology of filth. For this is not yet the sanitary, hermetically sealed image the twentieth century would come to associate with incineration and cremation in its view from without. For Ryan, the dust is part of the machine and the torture mechanism as frightening as the dust. The stokers are "black as negroes," the air around them is "dust, nothing but dust; it shuts out the roof, you blink it into your eyes, it enters your nostrils, it settles on your lips." As with the torments of Dante's Hell, however, the visitor cannot tear his eyes away from the awful spectacle: "Everything is big, coarse, forbidding; and yet the gloomy, brown pavilion of fire holds the eye; its ugliness redeemed by the majesty and power of the mysterious force within—the god of Zoroaster, a very slave in the service of despised Bumble!" (figure 3.16)[66] The two men in front of a furnace in the accompanying photograph show up the disjunction between early industrial awe and late industrial matter-of-factness; what remains is the insistence on the power of dust to evoke the demons of the underworld, even when the language of technology had already relegated them to the realm of poetic fancy, the atavistic city visions of expressionist poetry and cinema (figure 3.17).

Given that each discourse had its rhetorical weaknesses, we can trace the change in the dominant scientific discourse over the nineteenth century. Although the period around Chadwick's report, during which the good surgeon G. A. Walker had cleaned up Enon Chapel, was dominated by the rhetoric of danger, filth, and alienness that has echoed ever since in the literature of sensation, there were already dissenting London voices asserting the healthiness of sewer gases. In an 1848 letter to the new Commission on Sewers, Mr. Edward D'Anson reported that, "a woman, who *lived near one of the open street-gratings,* had . . . never been *well till she came there.* And it certainly was a fact, that when London was ravaged by the cholera, *no case* occurred *among workmen employed in the sewers.*" In addition to being safe from disease, he continued, the sewer workers "are strong, hearty men; they live more than the ordinary duration of life"; their work affected only their complexions.[67] The example of the woman belongs to an older representation of urban space in which individuals do not necessarily take

3.16. A modern, industrial-style Moloch. Photograph titled "In a Dust Destructor (Shoreditch)," P. F. William Ryan, "London's Toilet," in *Living London,* ed. George R. Sims, 3 vols. (London: Cassell & Co., 1901–3): 3:32.

3.17. Moloch in *Metropolis*: an image sublime enough to fit the inflated rhetoric. Frame enlargement from *Metropolis*, directed by Fritz Lang (Universum-Film A.G., 1926). BFI Films: Stills, Posters and Designs.

on the identity of the space they inhabit; her relationship to the open sewer, whether beneficial or detrimental to her health, remained circumstantial. The worker, by contrast, is physically marked by the space in which he works; like the miner, he becomes hereditarily identified with the underground. Mayhew likewise noted of sewer-hunters that, contrary to expectations, they were "strong, robust, and healthy men, generally florid in their complexion," some long-term practitioners were between sixty and eighty years of age, and all of them had "a fixed belief that the odour of the sewers contributes in a variety of ways to their general health."[68] Such claims were likely adapted from the Paris discourse to suit the new claims of London rationality. Across the Channel, by contrast, such beliefs were part of urban folklore. According to Reid, popular wisdom had long asserted the beneficial qualities of raw sewage. Such beliefs persisted even in more scientistic accounts such as Parent-Duchâtelet's influential *Essai sur les cloaques, ou, Egouts de la ville de Paris* (1824), which displaced blame for disease from the space of the sewers to the behavior of the workers: only the morally strong could survive.[69]

The sewers and the mythology and vocabulary associated with them have clung persistently to discourses of urban poverty ever since the latter came to embody urban crisis and urban solutions in the mid-nineteenth-century city. In his study of what he calls the "myth of the dreadful enclosure," E. V. Walter has identified four stereotypes regarding poverty that emerged from the language of social science as urban populations for the first time became spatially segregated according to wealth: the use of animal metaphors, such as those of rats, to describe the effect of living in densely populated spaces; the interpretation of chronic problems as moments of crisis requiring crisis intervention rather than long-term solutions; the "culture of poverty," the belief that poverty traps a person into a certain, common lifestyle; the "pathological imperative," the conception that lower-class life is pathological in and of itself.[70] The gist of Walter's argument is that it will be impossible to identify why the inhabitants of projects and slums do not live well until one has identified the stereotypes that have to a large degree driven unsuccessful attempts at comprehension thus far. Each of these four clichés of representation is recognizable in the metonymy of the sewer with the slum; what Walter's analysis does not recognize is that, along with its particular myth, each of these clichés equally embodies both a truth about why people do not live well and an image of how they might come to do so. For example, as emerges in another study of the "dreadful enclosure," there has more often than not been a fair degree of spatial truth in the equation of the slum with the sewer: "Tenants in Eastern City are quick to point out that 'City Cape', the largest project, was literally built on a city dump right next to an archaic sewage disposal plant. Other projects, too, stand on or near dumps or waste lands."[71] In addition to being sandwiched among the cul-de-sacs and no-man's-land created by transport infrastructure or near drainage outfall and treatment facilities of the sewage system, housing that has been either built for or devolved to low-income occupants has usually occupied the least salubrious and most poorly serviced parts of the cityscape. From the polluted mudflats of Jacob's Island, the riverside districts of Bermondsey, Ratcliffe, and Shadwell (which were singled out for attention in 1883 by Andrew Mearns in *The Bitter Cry of Outcast London*), and the Fleet Ditch frontage of Clerkenwell in London to the depths of the old Marais, the Quartier Saint-Marcel along the Bièvre, or Belleville around Montfaucon in Paris, to the favelas that now creep up the unserviced hills around the metropolises of Latin America and the families that gain their livelihood from the urban garbage dumps they also inhabit, the lower-depth location may not physically hold true in the vertical framework, but it remains a blatantly inferior space. The lack of sanitation has remained a constant of slum dwelling over several centuries, and whether built above and around sewers or in total isolation from them, the spaces inexorably take on the associated qualities of filth. It does not necessarily follow—and this is where Walter's argument is instructive—that the inhabitants of those spaces experience them exclusively in those terms or permit their everyday identities to be determined by them without stiff resistance.

By contrast with sensationalistic representations of the slums, which freely invoke the sewer metonymy whether or not the spatial justification exists, the rationalizing account extends its argument to the entire working class only by implication. The presumption is analogous, however; "dreadful labor" defines identity as much as it denotes the habitation of a "dreadful enclosure." The difference in representation is explained by the difference in social role: working-class labor is associated with the modern underground, necessary and controlled; working-class leisure and everyday life with the organic underground, atavistic and alien. Both maintain an intense fascination for the world above, but as the definition of labor became ever more identified with the inorganic underworld over the course of the twentieth century, it shed much of its glamour. The allure of slumming, by contrast, did not, and the voyeuristic descent to the lower depths has still lost none of its power or popularity as a mode of representing poverty.

In the London discourse during the late nineteenth century, we find tropes of the *katabasis,* or journey of descent, continuing to punctuate rationalist reportage that was otherwise wholly invested in depicting the sewers as a highly controlled world apart. There is, for example, the sewer worker's costume, which must invariably be donned by the investigator before the descent, and which invariably brings on anxiety over a change of identity. In "A Gloomy Ramble" (1881), for example, the author is informed by his guide that, "'Your own twin brother wouldn't know 'ee.'" The narrator confesses his relief in such anonymity, for "instead of creeping down into the sewers I had come to explore somewhere just outside the premises . . . our party had to go half a mile or so through the crowded streets of the city."[72] The article concludes less with an appreciation of the sewers than with some implicit advice to the young reader: "It is a repulsive way of earning a living, and as I emerge again into the world of sunshine and fresh air, I feel deeply thankful that I am not a regular hand, but only an *Amateur Sewerman.*" An 1888 piece begins with the reader's hypothetical sighting of a man in "strange clothing . . . emerging through an aperture in the pavement from depths of mysterious darkness below," before continuing with the author's giving thanks for his own outfit's protection against "slimy moisture"; what was healthy for the worker was not necessarily so for the reader.[73] A journalist in 1902 writes of the kit he dons to explore the world of the "Human Mole": "If I didn't look weird, I certainly felt so!"[74] (figure 3.18). The analogous moment in a slumming narrative such as Jack London's *People of the Abyss* (1903) duplicates the loss of identity, but here the ambivalent pleasure of the experience could be more clearly enunciated. Dressed in the costume for which he has just overpaid an old-clothes merchant on Petticoat Lane, the author discovers that "I had become one of

3.18. Human moles: *Sewermen going below*. Photograph in Eric Banton, "Underground London," in *Living London*, ed. George R. Sims (London: Cassell & Co., 1901–3): 2:127.

them." In place of fawning servility he finds hearty comradeship from his newly adopted class counterbalanced by a life "cheapened" in relation to anyone else, such as policemen or railway attendants. The "compensation," as he terms it, comes in terms of "escape" from the "pestilence of tipping," and in anonymity and natural intercourse with his fellow men.[75]

Notwithstanding the protestations of odor and disgust, articles of this genre never fail to assert the health of sewer workers, even in times of epidemics. Although we find such rhetoric echoed in the later admiration of such left-leaning writers as George Orwell and Jack London for the "toughness" and "noble bodies" of the "young gods," that admiration was tempered in their reportages by the knowledge that such working-class fortitude was short-lived, extremely fragile, and born of hardship and exploitation.[76] Nor, as their narratives made clear, did it necessarily extend to women or children; as with Mayhew's depiction of the passing of old-fashioned capitalism, London and Orwell found what they regarded as the positive attributes of working-class life to be rapidly giving way to the ravages of disease and mindless toil. In *The Road to Wigan Pier*, Orwell recorded what he saw as the degeneration of the urban poor from a combination of poor nutrition, lack of light, and sheer monotony. He had made a similar argument in *Down and Out in Paris and London* (1933), a novelization of his actual, rather than journalistic, experience as a member of the underclass. For Orwell—and this is characteristic both of the decade in which he was writing and of his political orientation—poverty was bad not so much in itself as for its dulling and deadening routine and its function as a support of the undeserving world above. Underground spaces and dirt recur obsessively in the novel as emblems both of the materiality of working-class life and of what the world above does not want to see of the mechanism that makes its life possible. Hence, Orwell summarizes the routine of his work as dishwasher in a fancy Paris hotel as a model of this life:

> For what they are worth I want to give my opinions about the life of a Paris *plongeur.* When one comes to think of it, it is strange that thousands of people in a great modern city should spend their waking hours swabbing dishes in hot dens underground. The question I am raising is why this life goes on—what purpose it serves, and who wants it to continue, and why. . . . I think we should start by saying that a *plongeur* is one of the slaves of the modern world. . . . At this moment there are men with university degrees scrubbing dishes in Paris for ten or fifteen hours a day. One cannot say that it is mere idleness on their part, for an idle man cannot be a *plongeur;* they have simply been trapped by a routine which makes thought impossible. . . . The question is, why does this slavery continue? People have a way of taking it for granted that all work is done for a sound purpose. They see somebody else doing a disagreeable job, and think that they have solved things by saying that the job is necessary. Coal-mining, for example, is hard work, but it is necessary—we must have coal. Working in the sewers is unpleasant, but somebody must work in the sewers. And similarly with a *plongeur's* work. Some people must feed in restaurants, and so other people must swab dishes for eighty hours a week. It is the work of civilisation, therefore unquestionable. This point is worth considering.[77]

In its physical difficulty, its drudgery, and its dirtiness, underground toil epitomizes working-class labor in general: unpleasant, out of sight, but justified as necessary to allow everything above to function, no matter how gratuitous it may appear; hence the conclusion of the passage with the emblematic occupations of mining and sewer work. This represents a different inflection of the same spatial representations invoked by the sewer visits discussed above. For Orwell, however, it was not the ingrained layers of dirt and grime that caused members of the underclass to take on the identity of the spaces in which they live and work, nor did the descent retain anything of the sensational; both aspects were overwhelmed by the monotony and the grinding sameness of underground labor. While there was more tolerance and more social space available to the down-and-out in Paris than in London, the main argument, in characteristic *entre-deux-guerres* fashion, focused on the overriding alienation of the city in general as epitome of the modern condition.

Jack London followed a similar strategy in *People of the Abyss,* masquerading as a down-and-out Londoner, his only concession to his status as outsider the emergency funds he sews into his outfit of slumming rags. London's city is not yet the rationalized metropolis of Orwell's 1930s; Jack London's experience is primarily based on waiting and frustration—at the workhouse, for a job—rather than endless mindless work. Except for the degree of his immersion in the culture, London's discourse is identical to that of turn-of-the-century tracts on degeneration. What is most frightening to him is the physical condition of the poor; they are "people of the abyss" because they are sickly and pale, like vitiated cave dwellers. When they emerge into the daylight of the countryside in search of work picking hops, they reveal the full extent of their "withered crookedness": "As they drag their squat, misshapen bodies along the highways and bodies, they resemble some vile spawn from underground."[78] Whereas in both of his books on poverty Orwell maintains his distance and proper identity through irony and intellectual analysis of his condition, for London it is his fit, young, and strong body that prevents his outfit and his activities from marking him indelibly as a person of the abyss. Mary Higgs's reportage, *Glimpses into the Abyss* (1906), reveals the analogous fear for the female slummer—bereft of the protection of her middle-class clothing, her body is exposed to the sexual predation of the men around her—and, as Deborah Nord has observed, a consequently diminished sense of the freedom to be had from the temporary experience of vagabond wandering.[79] Gender conventions permitted London to be more explicit about the risk to his body: the navel point of his descent comes when he suddenly realizes the danger of contagion from the naked, diseased bodies around him in the workhouse. Preparing to recount the episode, he begins, "I must beg forgiveness of my body for the vileness through which I have dragged it, and forgiveness of my stomach for the vileness which I have thrust into it."[80] The episode concluded, he hastily sheds his disguise and rushes to a Turkish bath, desperately trying to "sweat out whatever germs and other things had penetrated my epidermis," praying that the return to the upper world would leave no deeper traces than the matter for a sensational book.[81]

While it uncomfortably evokes turn-of-the-century discourses of eugenics, criminology, and other means whereby the language of science identified poverty's sufferers as a "race apart," London's book, like Orwell's (which also touches on such issues), is extremely effective in using that discourse against its grain to cause the reader to identify with poverty as a holistic experience rather than as a spectacle. In other words, the moment at which London signals the danger of contagion, of permanent damage from his journalistic descent, is an intensified version of the same frisson of danger in the underworld journey provided by the sewer tour for the middle-class lady, the apache tour of Paris's criminal underworld, or the slumming tour in London that Orwell was able to scorn from the insider's perspective: "Presently the slummers gave it up and cleared out, not insulted in any way, but merely disregarded. No doubt they consoled themselves by thinking how brave they had been, 'freely venturing into the lowest dens,' etc. etc."[82] The journeys share the identification of the destination as underworld; the frisson varies in proportion to the perceived danger. London and Orwell require the same mythic structure in order to authorize the truth-value of their reportage; the greater the risk they run, the more persuasive the conclusions with which they return from the land of the dead. All underground space retains some measure of this trope; the pathological underground retains it most forcefully because it materializes the threat as one of contact and contamination.

Public Filth in Paris

And the endlessly renewed flood of voyagers that bursts forth at certain hours from the depths of Paris can be regarded as symbolizing the un-quenchable—and practically unsuspected—resources that give the Grand' Ville its marvelous power of attraction and its splendid vitality.

EMILE GÉRARDS, *Paris souterrain* (1908)

Just as the test of fire in the slumming narrative is whether or not the voyager will shake hands with the denizens and share their food, so the sewer narrative plays with two threats: the contact of skin with excrement and the encounter with rats.[83] That the thrill is partially a pleasurable one is demonstrated not only by the anodyne apache outfit and shared glass of mulled wine of the "grand duke's tour" through the bas-fonds of fin-de-siècle Paris but by the encounter with the prostitute, in which an equivalent—and probably riskier—physical contact is defined positively rather than negatively. The key to the shifting attitude toward these underground spaces lies in the principle of control—control from above, resistance to control from below. According to the grand historical narrative of shifting epistemes, such as rendered, for example, by Corbin, in the eighteenth century, putridity began to be localized spatially. Subterranean prison grounds, charnel houses beneath churches, and slaughterhouses such as Mont-faucon took on a mythic identity as inherently dangerous places. Incompletely sealed gaps in the earth—wells, quarries, plowed fields—must also be carefully monitored: "A multitude of beliefs that will engender an obsession with fissures, interstices and imperfect joinings. Of all the dangerous terrain, above all it is important to keep watch on the borders. These are the sites of contact through which mephitic exhalations filter out."[84] For Corbin, the ambivalence toward these spaces becomes representable through odors, which can be both deadly and beneficial; égoutiers and other subterranean workers, for example, were recommended to wear sachets of garlic and camphor around their necks when descending.[85] Once spaces were identified thus with certain odors, their inhabitants began to be identified with those spaces as well. Representations of the ragpickers' trade centered on the quartier Mouffetard, including the open quarry at the Fosse-aux-Lions (figure 3.19). Odors were transferred from the soil to the social. Once animal odors lost their vogue as scents, Corbin argues, it became possible to distinguish between different social classes according to their tolerance for those odors in everyday life. Those whose occupations brought them in daily contact with dirt—ragpickers, sewer workers—and those metaphorically closest to such thresholds—prostitutes, Jews—formed the first stage of this assimilation. Following the 1832 cholera epidemic in Paris, which killed twenty thousand people, the identification was extended to "the stench of the populace in its entirety."[86] The first stage in control was to cover up odor; the second stage to eliminate it altogether. Corbin sees the conclusion of this process for the bourgeoisie in the new stress on the individual's "permanent confrontation with his odors"; for the working class in its ongoing resistance to deodorization.[87]

Although putatively universal, Corbin's model is clearly confined to France, in particular to Paris and the discourse surrounding it, especially in the role played by popular resistance, which mirrors the generally more ambivalent attitude to the underground and the stronger sense of its revolutionary potential. Popular resistance was rooted in long-standing traditions of the positive aspects of excre-

3.19. The underground economy of Paris: a ragpickers' warehouse. Illustration by F. Thorigny, *A Rag-Warehouse in the Quartier Mouffetard, at Paris*, in *Illustrated London News* (8 June 1861): 542.

ment: a persistent belief in the therapeutic value of excrement; a desire to preserve those professions, such as the *homme-fumier* ("manure man," the Parisian
counterpart of the London dustman) and the ragpicker, depended on urban
waste; and the argument that deodorizing excrement lowered its quality and thus
its value.[88] As late as 1896, an article recording the extraordinary range of waste
that accumulated where the main collector sewer drained into the Seine at Asnières could report not only that a M. Souffrice had found a use for the rotting
corpses of the ten thousand or so dogs and cats that washed up there, but that
"he wanted to make a profit from putrefaction itself," selling by the thousands as
fishing bait the maggots that accumulated on the corpses during the process of
transforming them into stearine and candles.[89]

The more sanitary drainage method of *tout-à-l'égout* (everything into the
sewer) had the advantage of being more easily regulated; however, the disadvan-
tage of wasting waste, of eliminating established distinctions between more and
less valuable excrement, remained an argument to which even Eugène Belgrand
lent credence:

> The cesspool cleaners know this well; they estimate the value of the excrement piled
> up in the pits of the poor much more highly than that of the rich, which has been
> overly diluted. Belgrand established, with the greatest precision, a social scale of the
> product's value. He sketched the topographical distribution of the nitrogen content of
> the excrements of the capital.[90]

Partisans of human fertilizer virulently opposed the loss of this valuable commodity, "the secret of wealth and of public security."[91] Another twist on the familiar paradox of modern space: although in the pre-nineteenth-century metropolis, rich, poor, merchant, and artisan had lived on top of one another, their
excrement had been emptied into distinct cesspools; the newly segregated spaces
created such extreme problems of sanitation due to the population density of the
poor neighborhoods that wholesale solutions of regulation and control needed to
be established. A further paradox: human excrement is the best fertilizer, and the
best of it comes from the excrement of the least well-nourished citizens, because
it is uncontaminated by refined food. There was a material ground to the nineteenth-century Parisian obsession with the most efficient way to use the waste
products of its city, but the desire to make the best use out of it worked at cross
purposes to the need to control and police it.

This was a paradox to which the French were especially attuned; in squeamish
England, tout-à-l'égout had been established by midcentury, as had the individual water closet that flushed into the drainage system; and many of Mayhew's
exotic fauna had consequently fallen by the wayside. As Orwell observed of the
two cities in the 1930s, comparing the East End of London to working-class
Paris, "Everything was so much cleaner and quieter and drearier. One missed the
scream of the trams, and the noisy, festering life of the back streets."[92] Orwell saw

Paris as a mine or a factory, with a settled and reliable social life. London, by contrast, appeared as a police state or a prison, defined by daily "tramping" from one institution of poverty to the next. Although the particulars had changed, the terms of comparison were little different from those employed by Mercier in praising the "tranquil virtues" of Londoners over the "prodigal search for pleasure" of the Parisians.[93] Although singing the praises of its drainage system on paper, London has never allowed public access to its sewers, citing reasons of safety. When Paris had its own "Great Stink" in 1880, twenty-two years after London's, with typhoid and other diseases on the rise, a group of experts journeyed to London to observe its subterranean success story. The *Pall Mall Gazette* took the opportunity to gloat over their continental neighbor's "barbaric system of drainage, the absence of knowledge as to traps, intercepting, ventilating, &c." Even with the vast system constructed by Belgrand, tout-à-l'égout, the author claimed, "would . . . be extremely dangerous, particularly as the Parisians have no notion of protecting their houses from the ingress of sewer gas."[94] The degree to which Paris functioned for this article, as so often it did in London, as its own counterpart in filth, is especially evident if we note that by 1880, at least in Paris, due to Louis Pasteur's research on germs, the belief in the pathogenic role of odors had mostly disappeared; tout-à-l'égout was finally established in 1894. The pleasure in Paris's barbaric underground is particularly striking in that two years later, as we shall see below, the *Pall Mall Gazette* would be running a series of articles decrying the barbaric state of its own city's underworld, not the perfectly regulated sewers but the "maw of the London minotaur," through whose "labyrinth wander[ed], like lost souls, the vast host of London prostitutes."[95]

Like its drainage system, London's public toilets were another source of polemical comparison with Paris. When the crusading engineer George Jennings overcame a combination of apathy and distaste to obtain permission to install public lavatories at the Great Exhibition in 1851, over eight hundred thousand visitors (some 14 percent of the total number) had been willing to pay to use them.[96] He was soon installing his patented six-person urinals all over London; the nominal fee levied to pay for amenities soon gave rise to the expression "to spend a penny," a neat summation of the convergence of sanitary and business principles in their construction and adoption. An enclosed kiosk with outer barriers screening entrances at either end, Jennings's design stressed the "greater privacy" offered by its angled compartments, the greater sanitation offered by its water drainage, and the savings in water use made possible by its "discharge plug."[97] Over the next few decades, the desirability of "public conveniences" would be widely accepted; so too apparently would the utility of placing them underground, first proposed by Jennings in 1858 to strong opposition.[98] Distinctively tiled below, they were marked in the streets above only by iron arches or railings, which, noted one engineering journal in 1894, were "fast becoming landmarks in the principal thoroughfares and centres of population"[99] (figure 3.20).

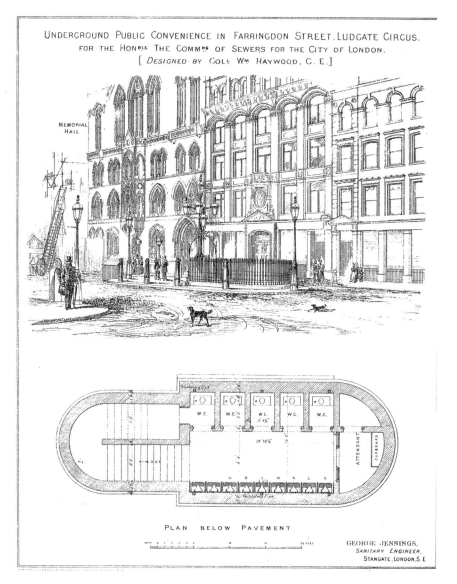

3.20. An example of George Jennings's pioneering "underground public conveniences." William Haywood, designer, George Jennings, engineer, "Underground Public Convenience in Farringdon Street, Ludgate Circus," in George Jennings, *Jennings' Patent Urinals as Arranged for Public Thoroughfares* (London, 1895): 45.

Still, the infrequency with which they appeared in guidebooks of the time suggests that their presence was tolerated rather than celebrated, another late-century addition to the silent control of underground space.[100] The Parisian equivalent, the *urinoirs* (also known as *pissoirs*), first appeared around the city in 1841, as single columns, open at the bottom, and known as *colonnes Rambuteau* after the prefect of the Seine; by 1843, there were 468 of them.[101] In 1877, judged inconvenient and obscene, they were duly removed and replaced by the iconographic double- or multi-compartmented *vespasiennes* (figure 3.21).[102] Planted at ground level on the sidewalks of the boulevards, in the parks, and at other busy locations, the vespasiennes may have been considered an improvement over their predecessors, but they continued to place the bodily function they serviced in plain conceptual view, the narrow bands of metal that encircled the central troughs barely obscuring the physical act itself. There were a few *cabinets inodores* scattered around the city for the use of women, but, as the Guide Joanne warned, most were not in a state to be entered.[103] Joanne did not even mention the urinoirs, the location and use of which would be self-evident to the traveler and the filthiness of which would be less of an issue to his male readers. After nightfall, the urinoirs were a prime site for prostitution, picking pockets, and homosexual meetings as well as blackmail; those of Les Halles were especially frequented by male prostitutes.[104] As one opponent of the street-level facilities insisted, "The sight of these édicules is a suggestive invitation that finishes by creating a habit for the Parisians." The city ought to replace them all, he proposed, with "subterranean refuges" on the model of those in London.[105]

This was the turn-of-the-century battle between an old Paris, with its quasi-mythic belief in the powers of human fertilizer and urine, and the forces of social progress that believed that segregation of bodily functions and waste was the key to social and spatial order and control. The leader of the Socialist Party proposed in 1892 that subterranean conveniences, "as in London," were far more easily surveillable and would prevent the respectable citizen from being exposed to "horrors."[106] Following a fact-finding trip to Britain in 1901, the municipal council made a similar recommendation, urging that the construction of "subterranean galleries of convenience" be undertaken to coincide with the works for the Métro. The subterranean urbanism that had originated in the London discourse was the wave of the future, but it took a different form in Paris. The Society of Subterranean Lavatories did open what Roger-Henri Guerrand terms "a veritable hall of necessity" under the flower market at the place de la Madeleine, but it was not until the 1930s that Paris began to remove the most visible of the vespasiennes; and plenty of urinoirs of various designs were still around long into the postwar decades.[107] The distinction in design and location of public conveniences reflected the dominant attitude in each city toward its waste and the activities associated with that waste; nevertheless, actual physical conditions were

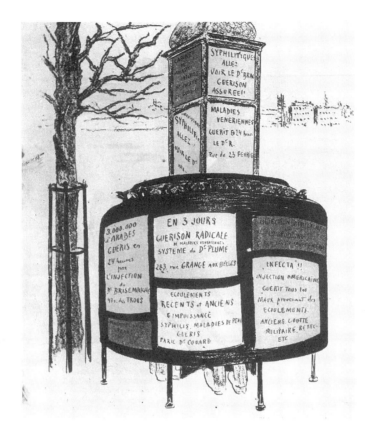

3.21. "A practical means of informing the ladies": a Parisian *vespasienne* is used as a vehicle to satirize the response to Eugène Brieux's banned play *Les Avariés* (1901), a cautionary tale about syphilis. Brieux is quoted as an epigraph: "We must teach women about syphilis." The vespasienne is blanketed with advertisements for quick cures. Illustration titled *Un moyen pratique de renseigner les dames*, in "Les Avariés," *L'Assiette au beurre* (18 March 1905).

more alike than not, and grew more so as the century wore on and the rhetoric of modernization began to structure debate in a more and more abstract manner.

Earlier on, material conditions rather than moral concerns played a formative role in debate in both cities, and the differences were more drastic. For example, while suitably horrifying each in its own way, the scattered burial grounds in London could in no way approach the concentrated effect of the enormous cesspits at Montfaucon to the northeast of Paris, which loomed large in the physical and symbolic landscape of the metropolis. The heaps of waste at what had been since 1781 the city's only dump covered an area of thirty-two thousand square meters, augmented daily by another 230 to 244 square meters of human excreta and the rotting corpses of tens of thousands of horses and other animals from the nearby slaughterhouses.[108] It was a cursed place in the topographical mythology of Paris, spread out around the site of the medieval gallows, and still the dumping ground for the corpses of executed criminals refused the sanctuary of the Catacombes (figure 3.22). As the waste of the growing metropolis and the problems of a burgeoning populace replaced old moral associations with new pressures of disease and disgust, the pits of Montfaucon syncopated the underground identities of the city into a pervasive stench that on a summer day could penetrate even to the Tuileries gardens. As recent historians have noted, the dump blended images of "filth and crime . . . as two aspects of one and the same discharge from the city," just as it merged "deep cultural associations of execrated criminals and society's excretions."[109] The closest analogue in London would be the pits dug to bury the thousands of victims of the Great Plague of 1665, which were often blamed for later outbreaks of disease. Scattered through the city, hidden and half-forgotten beneath the cityscape rebuilt on them after the Great Fire, the fragmentary and repressed plague pits suited the London discourse as monumental Montfaucon suited that of Paris.[110] Although similarly embedded in the city's mythico-historical past, Montfaucon presented a typically holistic and monumental image of Paris's relation to its waste, a source of shame and disgust for foreign visitors, of crisis for the authorities, and of untapped potential for sanitary visionaries.

Notwithstanding its location high above the city, Montfaucon was central to the representation of underground Paris during the first half of the century, inspiring chroniclers to extremes of vitriolic rhetoric. Unlike visits to factories and other industrial locations, however, these accounts all stressed the organic character of a Dantesque underworld, its deep roots in the darkest past of Paris, and its intimate relation with the dirty underbelly of the new city. It had its version of toshers and mudlarks, "totally nude men" who passed "whole days in the middle of basins, searching there, in the mass of fecal matter, objects of value which it might contain."[111] But even this festering wasteland, swarming with rats and other fauna, was recycled back into the city and the land. The cesspools were dried out and aged over the course of several years to produce *poudrette*, or fertilizer.[112] The bones had traditionally been burned and used to build walls in poor neighborhoods such as the faubourg Saint-Marceau and the faubourg du Temple.[113] As with the sewer workers, Parent insisted that the poudrette workers suffered no ill effects from their labor; many others were less sanguine about the threat of contamination.[114] The workers and scavengers who made their living in the area were wholly assimilated to its evil attributes, but that identity easily spread out to encompass the entire northeast of Paris and the entire population of laboring and criminal classes. Whether asserted as a relatively healthy and integrated relationship to the bio-economy of the region or proclaimed to be the "social leprosies" of the urban body, there was no separating the laborer from the labor.[115]

Nevertheless, even the extremity of Montfaucon did not eliminate the deep-rooted association of this same population with dreams of freedom and liberty. Dug out under the massif of the Buttes-Chaumont and closely associated with it

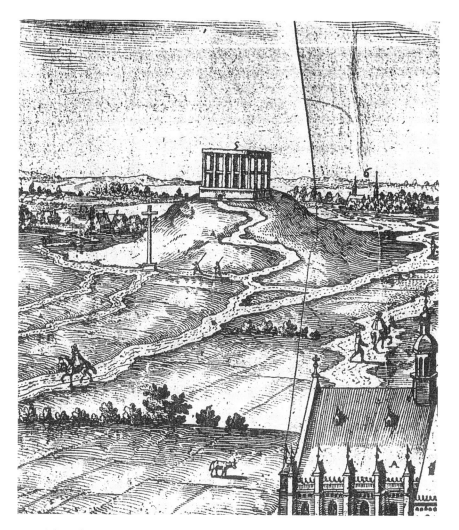

3.22. The infamous gibbet atop Montfaucon: beginning of the site's enduring legacy of crime, death, and decay. Drawing by Claude Chastillon (1612), engraved by Poinssart (1640), *Montfaucon au début du xviie siècle*, in Maurice Vloberg, *De la cour des miracles au gibet de Montfaucon* (Paris: Editions Jean Naert, 1928): facing p. 196.

in the urban imagination were the notorious carrières d'Amérique, subterranean quarries whose plaster kilns provided heat to the homeless and whose tunnels sheltered the lawless. Unlike the quarries of southern Paris, which were assimilated to the macabre but well-contained order of the Catacombes, the carrières d'Amérique were located in the heart of the working-class stronghold of revolutionary Paris, and were wild even in their landscape and their name (figure 3.23). Exuding the heat and life generated by decomposition above and kilns and quarries below, they were closely linked to a set of images that, in however debased a form, still partook of the utopian attributes of underground Paris, as Hugo well knew when he concluded *Notre-Dame de Paris* with the macabre but touching "marriage" of the remains of the outcasts Quasimodo and Esmeralda in the charnel house beneath Montfaucon.[116] Later in the century, a feuilleton novel described the carrières in a language of shelter and comfort quite similar to that of *The Wild Boys of London:* "Profound cavities surrounded the pit from which a gentle heat emerged, and, under its commodious vaults, these gentlemen were perfectly sheltered from rain, wind, and cold. They did not even lack for light, and the circular cavern was illuminated here and there by candles fixed in the plaster or stuck into bottles."[117] To be sure, the description is ironic here, as is the subsequent comparison with the old Court of Miracles so important to Hugo's medievalist Paris (the next action of these "gentlemen" is to threaten the hero with incineration in the plaster kilns), but there is an unmistakable tinge of nos-

3.23. The carrières d'Amérique before their transformation into the parc aux Buttes-Chaumont. Illustration of *Les buttes Chaumont* in Adolphe Joanne, *Les environs de Paris illustrés: Itinéraire descriptif et historique* (Paris: Hachette, 1856): 93.

talgia to it as well. The *pègre*—the criminal underworld—was a source of both fear and envy, just as the clochard was a source of pity and envy. As Joachim Schlör has written of the iconic status of the latter, "'radical homelessness' . . . the condition of vagabondage stands for a fundamental refusal of all ties, for the *choice of freedom.*"[118] In Eugène Sue's *Mystères de Paris,* le Chourineur (the Slasher), who had first worked as a horse butcher near Montfaucon and later slept rough near the plaster kilns and worked as a *carrier* before becoming Prince Rodolphe's faithful henchman, plays a similar role in Sue's attempt to show the potential of recuperating these impulses—to no avail: le Chourineur does not survive the novel. Fortuné de Boisgobey's *Mystères du Nouveau Paris* took an approach better suited to the late nineteenth century, introducing a free (and millionaire) spirit, "le Californien," returned from the United States to seek revenge for ancient injustice, and aided in his exploration of the Paris underworld by a police detective.

The cesspools were eliminated in 1850 by the construction of a ten-kilometer tunnel to pump out the sixty-five thousand bushels of daily waste from the slaughterhouses east of the city to the wood of Bondy by steam power. Liquid matter would eventually be authorized to be flushed through the sewers, and the gelatinous matter of the cadavers extracted from its effluvia for agriculture.[119] During the late 1860s, the entire site was transformed by Haussmann, the engineer Alphand, and Paris's gardener-in-chief Barillet into the parc aux Buttes-Chaumont, eliminating both sources of disease in one fell swoop. Not surprisingly, the very construction of the park inspired a series of sensational plays and novels about the site, exploiting for all they were worth the urban legends while their memory was still fresh. In *Le Drame des Carrières d'Amérique* (1868), as if the park had not opened the previously year, we find the tunnels still there, characterized as a "sewer" into which the human "mud [*boue*]" of the city flows.[120] The construction had evidently piqued public interest, which was satisfied by tales of the horror of a now-vanished threat to order. Emblematic of the transformed character of this space was the reassuring presence of the police, which appeared at the rhetorical depths of the description of the sewer community, shining light into the darkness and rounding up all the vagabonds to be booked at the precinct.[121] The underclass, like the sites it had made its own, was now safely contained within the context of urban spectacle (figure 3.24). Having encountered the pègre and its dens in theater and fiction, foreign visitors could not only glide down the sewers, they could also take the "tour of the grand dukes," with full approval of the authorities. Disguised as an "apache," or member of the underworld, they would be taken on a fixed route of "all the famous bars, cellars and dives of Belleville, Montmartre and Les Halles, and . . . drink a traditional glass of mulled wine with one of the most famous 'apaches.'" Far from objecting to the practice, the locals were supposedly "proud of the attention they were given."[122]

3.24. Policing the underground: Juve and Fandor square off with Fantô-mas at a Seine sewer inlet. Publicity still for *Fantômas: Le Mort qui tue*, directed by Louis Feuillade (Gaumont, 1913). BFI Films: Stills, Posters and Designs.

The new Buttes-Chaumont was the aboveground counterpart to the make-over of the sewers. The latter had been transformed into an icon of underground utility; the former was to transmute a wasteland of filth and crime into a pictur-esque landscape of grottoes, lakes, and bridges (figure 3.25). It was intended, as Baedeker had it, "for the benefit of the artizans of this quarter of the city." They used to be hanged there; now they could come to admire the one hundred–foot

cascade, the Corinthian temple, and the view down to the city below. Local inhabitants did use this "working-class paradise" as a promenade, including the
painter Seurat, who was deeply impressed by the many walks taken as a child
with his mother and siblings in the park.[123] In the broader Parisian imagination,
however, the Buttes-Chaumont remained a wild place best known for the unin-
tended use to which the name of the cable span that linked the two heights alluded: the Suicides' Bridge. Beset by boredom late one night, Louis Aragon, André Breton, and Marcel Noll took a midnight taxi to "the park in which nestles
the town's collective unconscious. . . . This great oasis in a popular district, a
shady zone where the prevailing atmosphere is distinctly murderous."[124] Out in
the banlieue, cloaked in the night, flanked by the tunnels of the chemin de fer de
Ceinture and the métro stations of Bolivar and Botzaris, Buttes-Chaumont represented for Aragon the sacred traces of the mythology of Paris, the remnants of
the organic past, an underworld journey in all its sensory overload rather than a
sanitized boat ride or a guided tour. But Aragon was too self-conscious a surreal-
ist to lose himself completely in the search for the lost authenticity of the working classes, their faits divers and their most sublimely awful spaces. Descending a
"labyrinth of rock, half grotto and half serpent," he comes up against an iron
grill; arrived at the "veritable Mecca of suicide," he summons up the vertiginous
genius of the place, but faced with another iron grille that has led to the "docile"
public abandoning the practice, he loses interest.[125] The surrealists took the organic underground of old and new Paris as their watchword and stalked it, especially in the neighborhood cinemas, winding streets, and storied sites of the
northeast.[126] The trajectory followed by Montfaucon and the Buttes-Chaumont
over the past two centuries demonstrates the potency of representational space to
determine urban renewal and the endurance of spatial association long after its
original impetus may have disappeared. It also demonstrates the tenacious promise offered by filth in the Parisian discourse of an escape from order and disci-
pline, a promise played out in Aragon's attempt to wrest back from his bête noire
Haussmann the meaning of the Buttes-Chaumont. And, finally, it demonstrates
the difficulty with which the actual inhabitants and everyday users of these su-
percharged spaces avoid being sucked into the representations generated by their
roots in the mythic underground.

Fascination with filth of a different order was the theme of the Parisian sewer
tour, which was a permanent public sight following its great success at the 1867
Exposition Universelle de Paris (figure 3.26). Rather than highlighting technological achievement per se, as the London narratives did, the Paris tour promised
integration with the underworld in a system rational enough to be safe but organic enough to thrill. As Maxime Du Camp put it, "It has become a sort of
pleasure trip to visit the sewers."[127] In his panoramic 1867 book, *Les Odeurs de
Paris*, Louis Veuillot archly wrote: "Those who have seen everything say that the
sewers are perhaps the most beautiful sight in the world. The light shines in

3.25. The carrières d'Amérique after their transformation: the parc aux Buttes-Chaumont grotto. Photo by author, 1999.

them, the sludge [*fange*] maintains a mild temperature, people take boat rides through them, undertake rat-hunts in them, organize interviews in them—and, already, more than one dowry has been had there."[128] The photographer Félix Nadar, too, in his description of the sewers, took the tone of a light diversion, addressing a female audience rather than the implicitly male individual of the London tour narratives.[129] Nadar's tour is a series of rhetorical dangers: the "filthy" cascade that falls to the right and left (but never on the ladies); the possibility of rats (but none seen); another boat-wagon turns a corner and threatens to collide (but turns away just in time); in the old part of the sewers the ordure mounts (but only around the égoutiers pushing the boat). In his reading of the piece, Radford stresses the message of the triumph of technology and spectacle over the lower orders;[130] in comparison with the London narrative, we should also note the ongoing desire that each inhabitant experience each and every part of the city he or she inhabits. The underworld is rendered as spectacle, the frisson of otherness is mild, the égoutiers serve double time as tour guides and mules, but there remains a material experience of a working urban space otherwise totally segregated from the world above. That the sewer tour could be more of a material experience of the urban underground than most accounts suggested is further sug-

3.26. A sewer tour in early 1870. Note that women occupy the boat, handily spotlit, while male visitors walk alongside it. (In another part of the tour, the two groups ride together.) Illustration by Jules Pelcoq, *The Sewers of Paris: The Boat*, in *Illustrated London News* (29 January 1870): 128.

gested by Du Camp's remark that a policeman would ride in each sewer wagon to guard against pickpockets.[131]

As is amply evident from an 1870 *Illustrated London News* feature, the sewer tour was an eagerly anticipated aspect of the representational space: "Among the sights of Paris, which provincials and foreigners are most anxious to see, are the gigantic collecting-sewers beneath the city."[132] As Radford observes, the boat in the accompanying illustrations is "entirely filled with ladies."[133] Whether exaggerated or no, the presentation of the tour as a feminine attraction serves to underline the thrill and to suggest that in the space of Paris women could experience a different interaction with the organic underworld than available at home. After all, for any aboveground woman, the only normally available experience of the organic urban underground would be to be mistaken for (or to work as) a prostitute—a fallen woman, to use the English trope.[134] Given the frequency with which the presence of a respectable woman unaccompanied on the city streets leads to an incident of misrecognition in Victorian literature, the Paris frisson takes on practically transgressive proportions.

What could be enjoyed and even treasured in the context of Paris must quickly be flushed out of the space of London: "Sewage," to quote Hollingshead, "whether fluid or solid, mixed or unmixed, is very much like our convicts, everybody wants to get rid of it, and no one consents to have it."[135] Unlike in Paris, neither sewage nor prostitution was ever given extended treatment in Victorian fiction of any literary pretension. As Amanda Anderson has argued about the "social category" of the fallen woman, "The street woman serves as a powerful index of a faulty society yet cannot sustain the status of subject in that society."[136] Even the cognitive gap between the metaphorical term "fallen" and the social fact of a woman living on (and off) the streets was seldom if ever bridged in the novelistic discourse of Victorian London. Just as the fault of Dickens's fallen women, such as Martha in *David Copperfield,* whom David follows along the filthy bank of the Thames, and whom Dickens equates with "plague" and "pollution" and describes as "part of the refuse it had cast out," is never rooted in any social fact or individual autonomy, so does the physical reality of the sewage system never enter directly into the novelistic space of the city.[137] Even a novel such as *Our Mutual Friend,* obsessed as it is with waste in its every aspect, shies away from the physical fact of "dust," as it avoids the physical space of the sewer, displacing its role onto the riverman Gaffer Hexam and the open, flowing surface of the Thames, just as the moral thrust of fallenness glosses over the physical and social facts of prostitution. We do find in the same novel an unfavorable comparison of London with Paris, "where nothing is wasted, costly and luxurious city that it be, but where wonderful human ants creep out of holes and pick up every scrap"; however, even in the comparison, the language remains euphemistic.[138] In Victorian iconography, according to Nead, the river was used to represent the "lowest and most degraded level of prostitution."[139] In respectable London discourse, the

Thames provided a euphemistic shorthand not only for the unspeakable fact of prostitution but for the standard association of that fact with the sewers that emptied into it.[140] Both fact and association were standard currency in the medical debate; the Thames served not only to cover them over rhetorically but to naturalize them just above the threshold of decency, rather than to dredge them up from below it.

In sensational literature, muckraking journalism, and medical writing, the connection was always made. Dickens was dependent for the plot of *Our Mutual Friend* on Chadwick's report that close dung heaps were a means of paying "a considerable part of the rent of the houses. . . . Thus, worse off than wild animals . . . the dwellers in these courts had converted their shame into a kind of money by which their lodging was to be paid"; he was well aware, as were his readers, of the twenty thousand tons of horse manure deposited annually on the streets of London—nevertheless, he called it dust.[141] Moreover, Dickens had visited and interviewed former prostitutes at Urania Cottage, a "Home for Fallen Women" established by Dickens and the philanthropist Angela Burdett Coutts in Shepherd's Bush in 1848.[142] In other words, the conventional London discourse maintained a respectable distance between what was experienced on the streets of the city and discussed among professionals and what could be "known" about that experience through the mode of the middle-class novel.

The division was clearly conventional, not only in positing a gender distinction between these two worlds that was not at all upheld in practice but also because the audience for the lurid serials of Reynolds and others overlapped significantly with that of Dickens. To be sure, that audience may have been less explicitly interpolated within the diegesis of the work, but Dickens was read by much of the same lower-class urbanites who, according to Mayhew, eagerly awaited the newest installment of *The Mysteries of London*. It is surely tempting to draw an analogy between the poorly integrated sewer commissions, the barely institutionalized systems of regulation of prostitution, and the lack of overlap between different discourses in London, as opposed to the centralized metropolitan improvements, the highly regulated (and corrupt) institution of prostitution, and the integrated fictional discourse on the underground in Paris. There is simply no equivalent to Baudelaire's poetic depiction of the whore, Hugo's history of the sewers, Manet's Olympia, Zola's Nana, or Dégas' and Toulouse-Lautrec's prostitutes in English arts and letters. Consequently, it is the Paris sources that are richest in drawing out the ambivalent character of filth and underground space.

This integrated discourse is already evident in the leading article from the 1831 collection *Paris, ou le livre des cent-et-un,* which adapted the panoramic figure of the devil-on-crutches as a chiffonnier in the sewers:

> Later he took up a ragpicker's pannier. He sought out mores and histories in all the
> sewers of Paris. Not long ago he was on brightly lit rooftops, but we have seen him at

the crossroads lantern in hand; the filthy hook had replaced the elegant crutch; formerly he would write his books on the back of Fiction, that pretty prostitute with scented hair . . . presently it is he who has to crouch down—there he is on two knees in the mud writing in his notebooks on the bollard. . . . This time . . . it's the common people who are ridiculous and vice-ridden, since it was the turn of the people to become king.[143]

The French Revolution again serves as dividing line for a change in tropes, from unveiling the vices of the rich by lifting off their rooftops (with an added allusion, no doubt, to the famous letter-writing scene of *Les Liaisons dangéreux*), to satirizing the poor by rooting through the lower depths. Truth is linked to the high and the low; the courtesan is relegated to the sewer: both images serve to encapsulate the character of the city as a whole.

Although it permits a comprehensive grasp of the entire spectrum of the city, the grandiose mythmaking characteristic of the Paris model nevertheless does not approach the integration of urban landscape with the entire social spectrum achieved in the late Dickens by virtue of his far more subdued ideology. Nor has there ever been anything like the sensational depiction of London for rendering the negative potential of the subterranean; indeed, there is almost no penny-dreadful tradition of spectacularly lurid sewer scenes in Paris, perhaps because it has always been a closed system, without the glaring openings into the Thames that so mark the London tradition. The role of sensational setting was played instead by the Catacombes and quarries, and the sewer had to wait until the next century's *Phantom of the Opera* to make even a cameo appearance in something resembling a pulp context. This was true as much for the foreign as for the local use of the discourse: in the *Wild Boys of Paris,* an inferior follow-up to the London prototype, the sewers were replaced by a half-hearted rendering of the Catacombes, some of it cribbed from Berthet, some from Sue (the setting was 1847), and the rest based vaguely on the Roman catacombs and the recently opened Victorian cemeteries of London.[144] Unlike Erik's apartments or the Wild Boys' London clubhouse, the Paris boys do not even possess a permanent lair, meeting instead under an arch of the pont des Arts.

It would be a mistake to privilege one city's space or mode of representation over the other, however, just as it would be a mistake to assume that either space can be comprehended distinctly from the other. To be sure, there are factual arguments to be made about the differences between them, between their social structures and physical spaces, between their political histories and roles as imperial centers: these determine the conventional discourses I have outlined above, and the representations of city space that dominate both internal and external depictions. But they do not delimit the range of representation any more than the facts delimit the experience of the space by each of its inhabitants. Even within middle-class representations, it was common for Parisian writers to adapt

London models to their city, and vice versa. For Maxime Du Camp, writing in 1870 a panorama of Paris wholly different from the popular examples of the 1840s, Paris had become a better version of London, and London more like the bad old Paris. Although his vast survey did not neglect the much-loved folklore and variety of the city, its ideological focus was on the efficiency of its institutions and the inexplicable and inexcusable choice to act contrary to those institutions. The underground, for Du Camp, was not ancient, exotic, or exciting, but technologized, perfectly managed, and useful. Describing the vast cellars of the Banque de France, for example, he compared their contents negatively to the glittering treasures of Ali Baba or of the dragon of the Nibelungenlied, asserting that they were not alluring in the least, but hidden in heavily guarded safes.[145]

As is usual with the rationalized underworld, the sewer in Du Camp's Paris was simultaneously a metaphor for moral and social turpitude and a metaphor for the perfectly regulated urban space. In the early days when the île de la Cité was the center, the Seine had been "both the source of water and the public sewer"; under the lawless times of the Fronde, "Paris was a cloaca without light or water"; the lowest level of society is "society's sewer"; an unsullied girl is warned not to "throw herself into the sewer"; even in the progressive year 1870, in terms of mores, "Paris is the *cloaca maxima* of the world."[146] At the same time, the secret police of Napoleon III was to everyday law enforcement as the circulatory system of the sewer is to the city above: "Like the human body, populous towns have their secret organs that are no less indispensable to life for being hidden. This is one of the most important of them: it polices material things and purges the city of every impure element."[147] Properly functioning drainage below the ground was mirrored by proper lighting above ground; both technologies, Du Camp confessed, came from London, but their proper ideological use dated back to Nicolas de La Reynie, who was responsible in the late seventeenth century not only for promoting public lighting in Paris but for founding the urban police force. La Reynie thus put into action the maxim of his ruler, Louis XIV, "who knew on what basis the moral and physical state of his good city depended, giving him three substantives as watchwords: *cleanness, clarity, security.*"[148]

Du Camp's epic survey is an implicit repudiation of Hugo's equally epic novel, published eight years earlier. For Hugo, every surface phenomenon is possessed of its scarcely plumbable depths, its abyss, its underbelly; for Du Camp, every phenomenon only becomes of social utility when brought to light and controlled. In Du Camp's Paris, nothing was more frightening than the hint that perfect control might not be possible; for all his stress on the extraordinary efficiency of the police, Du Camp was forced to admit that "it is impossible to fix upon" the number of thieves in Paris, that, even though a race apart with its predetermined sites, "they remain in our midst."[149] It is symptomatic that in the course of his thirty-page chapter on the sewers, Du Camp mentions Hugo's name not a single time. Where Hugo is fascinated with the mythic history of the sewers, Du Camp is focused on its future. Both connect it with England, but for Hugo the connection was negative: "Today, the sewer is proper/clean [*propre*], cold, correct. It has nearly realized the ideal embodied in England by the word 'respectable.'"[150] Like the formerly unruly "*peuple de* Paris," the sewer had been cleaned and tamed. Nevertheless, like Du Camp, if from the opposite perspective, Hugo hinted that the "revolution" had not been complete: "Miasmas still live in it [the common people]. It is more hypocritical than irreproachable. The Prefecture of Police and the Health Commission have labored in vain. Despite all the hygienic procedures, the populace exhales a vaguely suspect odor."[151] Down to its lexicon of miasma and smells, *Les Misérables* summarized and epitomized the holistic discourse of the Paris underground; Du Camp inflected the tropes of filth as if he were a proper Englishman, proposing rational and sweeping solutions to the mythic populism he would not even deign to name. For Du Camp, the new sewage system had made Paris "a city unique in the world" to which not even ancient Rome could compare; moreover, "M. Belgrand's works on the subterranean canalization of the city, in order to bring potable water into it and expel soiled water from it, would suffice to illustrate an epoch and a nation."[152] Like the old *îlots insalubres* (unhealthy blocks) and centers of revolutionary fervor swept away by Haussmann, and just put down again in the Commune, so did Du Camp attempt to wish away Hugo's powerful subterranean vision of society, replacing an emblematically organic underground with an emblematically inorganic one.

Near the beginning of his chapter on the sewers, Du Camp asked rhetorically if there was anyone who, "seeing the capital healthy, well-ventilated, and spacious," had not already forgotten the ennui of the years of construction.[153] The allure of metropolitan improvements as a solution to social ills lies precisely in the illusion that a finished product is available, a time when all unsavory neighborhoods, all pockets of disease, all obscure streets will have disappeared, in the myth that the perfect representation of space can be put into practice. Haussmann dreamed of a sewer beneath every street in the city:

> The subterranean galleries, organs of the great city, would function like those of the human body, without showing themselves in the light of day; pure and fresh water, light and heat would circulate in them like the diverse fluids whose movement and maintenance keep us alive. The secretions would take place mysteriously and would maintain the public health without troubling the proper order of the city and without spoiling its external beauty.[154]

By relying on the ancient metaphor of the city as body, Haussmann was couching his vision in tradition; in that vision of a perfectly hidden and autonomous space beyond the reach of human intervention or error, he looked forward to the technological discourse of the next century.

Haussmann's abstract space never quite materialized any more than any other metropolitan plan managed to accomplish the mission its ideology had promised. The first exercise in London of tout-à-l'égout succeeded only in creating the Great Stink; the conclusion of the nineteenth-century obsession with animal odors ended not with the elimination of foul smells but with the recognition during a new stink in 1911 that the source was not organic but industrial;[155] the slum clearances in London, like those in Paris, earned millions for speculators, but did little to ease housing conditions for the poor, who in London continued to crowd together as nearby as possible, and who in Paris, as even Du Camp conceded, were simply forced to the outer arrondissements to the north and east, and beyond the *barrières* (the old toll gates) in all directions, creating the Zone, a ring of shantytowns around the city (figure 3.27).[156] Rationalizing the cityscape improves some conditions for some persons and worsens some conditions for others; what is undeniable is that in the nineteenth century, for the first time, direct change in physical space was equated with direct change in social space, and on a vast scale. It was as if the scope and concentration of the problem required a response on an equal scale. When that response could not be made where it needed to be, it was made where it would be most profitable and most spectacularly visible.

In this sense, the perfect control imagined by Du Camp's Haussmannian reading of Paris, forerunner of the modernist space of the first half of the next century, is the exact counterpart of the modernist celebration of marginality analyzed most pointedly by T. J. Clark in his cultural history of the Second Empire, *The Painting of Modern Life.* For Clark, "modernist painting accepted and reworked a myth of modernity in which the modern equaled the marginal. Shifting and uncertainty were thus taken to be the truth of city life and of perception, the one guaranteeing the other."[157] The impressionists did indeed flock to and celebrate the very spaces of Paris created by Haussmann, but not the rationally conceived infrastructure eulogized by Du Camp: they were attracted by the spectacular culture of the new boulevards and the marginal, unfinished spaces at the city's edges, where everything excluded and displaced by the vast works and their totalizing ideology had resettled willy-nilly. Through the early twentieth century, the Zone expanded outside of any constraints of building code or sanitation, counting forty-two thousand marginal inhabitants by 1926.[158] It is not accidental, then, that Manet planned a painting of Paris souterrain for his series of city canvases.[159] Impressionism adopted as a purely aesthetic strategy the material celebration of the lower depths employed by earlier urban writers from Egan and Mayhew to Hugo and Baudelaire.

The difference, and this is the thrust of Clark's argument, is that impressionism abstracted an aesthetic program from the social phenomenon of uprootedness and change taking place in the cityscape around them without relating that program back to the urban space itself: "It is one thing to argue that the capital

3.27. Paris Zone, ca. 1912: an Atget photograph of a ragpicker's premises off the boulevard Masséna at the edge of the 13th arrondissement. Photograph by Eugène Atget, *Chiffonnier: Bd. Masséna*, No. Atget: 343 (1912). Reproduced by permission from Bibliothèque nationale de France.

city lacks intelligible *form,* and has no coherence to speak of; it is quite another to say that it lacks *order,* that it is uncontrolled or classless."[160] Just as the ideology of metropolitan improvement purports to eliminate social pathology through a transformation of physical space, so the ideology of modernism purports to eliminate social control by representing the city as a free-floating spectacle. Like other modernists, the impressionists mistook, as Clark phrases it, "the real and important margin for error in capitalist society for an overall loosening of class ties," helping to create instead the representational space of a new class, the petit-bourgeois.[161]

Although Clark at times tends overly to reduce cultural phenomena to a status as mere safety valves for economic issues, his argument is especially valuable in showing how the rationalized ideology of a Du Camp can be related to its counterpart, the revaluation of the underground as sewer, as margin, as underworld, that would guide a series of avant-garde movements throughout the twentieth century and be adopted by mainstream culture by the century's end. If the ideology of Haussmann centered on the total control of the city, the actual process known as Haussmannization resulted, as Clark astutely demonstrates, in making the city formally illegible, or, to refine his argument according to my model here, in making it legible only as an inorganic underground, a rational space. What modernist artists seized upon as the illegible by-products of Haussmannization—the Zone, the margins, the underground—were in fact simply those spaces where modernity and everyday life continued to be legible as such. They were the contradictions in the Haussmannian representation of space. Such perceptions were almost invariably distanced as aesthetic stance—witness the fey paradox of Gertrude Stein's account of her and Pablo Picasso's response to a later wave of metropolitan improvement: "We need the picturesque, the splendid, we need the air and space you get only in old quarters. It was Picasso who said the other day when they were talking about tearing down the insalubrious parts of Paris that it is only in the insalubrious quarters that there is sun and air and space."[162] Perhaps Clark's most persuasive example is to be found in Seurat's famous painting *The Bathers at Asnières* (1883–84), which portrays a quintessential moment of the new petit-bourgeois culture celebrated by the impressionists: the suburban bathing excursion.[163] What the painting occluded was the counterpart to this new leisure, the point where the subterranean ideology of Haussmannization emerged into the open air: the emptying of the main collector sewer of the entire Paris system at an unseen point in the middle of the space depicted by the canvas. What ostensibly depicted the enjoyment of nature in fact portrayed the contaminated margin between city and country, the outflow of the new urban culture lauded by Du Camp, the waste necessary for the perfect functioning of the cityscape on the periphery of the painting.

The Seminal Drain

It is a very phenomenal city whose existence can only be determined by its lupanars and its sewers.

ROBERT BUCHANAN, *Pall Mall Gazette* (20 September 1886)

Excremental things are all too intimately bound up with sexual things; the position of the genital organs—*inter urinas et faeces*—remains the decisive and unchangeable factor.

SIGMUND FREUD, *Collected Papers* (IV:215)

The Wild Boys of London proves that even the space of the sewer is not fixed in its range of meanings; this raises the possibility of a similar approach to that obsession of the nineteenth century to which it was most frequently equated: prostitution. To be sure, there are as few resolutely positive nineteenth-century representations of the figure of the prostitute as there are of the space of the sewer. Nevertheless, it is important to recall that the contradictions embodied in the prostitute are positive as well as negative. This is the gist of an argument running through contemporary feminism that stresses the liberating power embedded in the figure, an argument that found its most influential formulation in the character of Juliette in the novels of the Marquis de Sade. In the wake of the Second World War, Max Horkheimer and Theodor Adorno had already made Juliette the standard bearer of the collapse of Enlightenment ideology from within, "*amor intellectualis diaboli,* the pleasure of attacking civilization with its own weapons."[164] As Angela Carter has written of Sade and the tradition of pornography, adapting that philosophical critique to contemporary society, "sexual relations between men and women always render explicit the nature of social relations in the society in which they take place and, if described explicitly, will form a critique of those relations, even if that is not and never has been the intention of the pornographer."[165] Carter may have been willfully optimistic about the transparency of language here, but her analysis neatly captures the dialectic that pornography shares with other underground culture: on the one hand, its "surface falsity"—the fact, for example, that the actual labor of the woman, her "*really* dirty work . . . is unmentionable"[166]—and on the other hand its capacity to play the devil to aboveground ideology. By contrast with her victim sister Justine, clinging to the purity of her bourgeois ideals as she is raped again and again by the representatives of those ideals, Juliette is the consummate whore, "single-mindedly destructive. Her careerist efficiency is a mask for her true subversiveness."[167] Juliette's perfect emulation of the principles of free-market capitalism is simply an elaboration of the paradoxical image of the prostitute, powerless and passive in what she sells but self-sufficient and predatory in the act of selling, simultaneously natural and denatured.

It is an image she shares with that of excrement, a traditional symbol of both the wastefulness of capitalism and its unmatched ability to make waste productive. Both Carter and Jane Gallop regard the disproportionate attention devoted to coprophagia in the Sadeian text as key to deciphering Juliette's role in its economy. For Carter, "the coprophage's taste asserts the function of flesh as a pure means of production in itself. His economic sense . . . insists that even the waste products of the flesh must not be wasted. All must be consumed."[168] Just as the perfect libertine explodes the distinction between natural and unnatural, so he eliminates bodily hierarchies between upper and lower, production and excretion. The circulatory metaphor that would dominate rhetoric on the nineteenth-century city appeared in Sade condensed into the functioning of a single body. For Sade, all social relations, all representations of space could be expressed through the orifices of the body. Carter takes pains to open that condensation back onto twentieth-century representations of women and of sexuality. Gallop, on the other hand, is invested in the "scandal" of the Sadeian system itself, the impossibility of its being made useful: corpses and excrement, she argues, are as the "waste products" of the "life and death struggle of the Hegelian dialectic."[169] In the present context, such a dialectic can equally well describe the London discourse of capitalism: raw material, live bodies, nourishment are fed into the system to produce value; what has no value is excreted and discarded as useless. The "scandal" of Sade's texts is their refusal to dispose of what should already have been left behind by the process of dialectical negation, even though that refusal inevitably results in perversion rather than production: "Coprophagia can only reincorporate the fallen turd into the entire digestive process in the mode of an endless repetition. . . . The turd digested comes out turd, leaving nothing behind."[170]

The same paradox structures Gallop's definition of Juliette as "whore-in-the-major-mode" because she assumes her identity out of desire rather than economic necessity: "Only a 'real whore' would *want to be a whore*."[171] Both Carter and Gallop find positive inspiration less in Sade than through him: for the former, he showed glimpses of "becoming a revolutionary pornographer," but was finally able only to subvert individual roles rather than the class system as a whole; for the latter, he offers a vision of "community" outside of the constraints of modern society, albeit a vision based on the paradox of "the friend as whore."[172] Just as Sade's writings were fundamental to the theorizing of renegade surrealists such as Georges Bataille in Paris, and have for several decades now constituted a threshold of consumption between scholarly criticism and an unspeakable subculture, so the prostitutes and the excrement that defined Sade's own limits not only bring social critique sharply into focus, but they also—not in the same gesture but often at cross-purposes with it—manifest visibly the utopian promise that lies in the waste heaps of the past. It is because that promise is so tightly intertwined with the grimmest and most taboo aspects of the underground that prostitutes and sewers have retained more mythic power than other aspects of the modern underworld. Refusing to flush them away will not make them more meaningful or palatable, for, to paraphrase Gallop, there is nothing left in them of value within aboveground modes of representation. Herein lies the fallacy of the Paris discourse, which addresses the symptoms rather than the disease. As containers of what cannot be seen in the modern world, however, their potency has not been explored enough, wrought as it is with the blind-eye horror characteristic of London. A look through this double rubric at the heavily studied topic of nineteenth-century prostitution can perhaps suggest some different ways of approaching this quintessential emblem of the urban underworld.

Just as the libertine woman became the symbol of the Revolution as well as of the Terror, and the Vésuvienne embodied the simultaneously seductive and uncontrollable *femme-soldat* of 1848, so the prostitute and her arsonist cousin, the *pétroleuse,* figured significantly in representations of the Commune eighty years later.[173] During the siege of Paris, the government had ordered the expulsion of vagabonds and "girls of debauchery" from the city as "useless mouths."[174] The communards did the same, on grounds of freedom from oppression rather than because of public health and morality. Regardless, the underworld identity of the prostitute became firmly associated with the unforeseen force that had taken over the city:

> One reckoned armed prostitutes among the ranks of the insurgents. They were among those who took part in the saturnalias at the barricade of the rue Royale. The world of public debauchery furnished its own contingent of pétroleuses, and it could well believe, along with the wrongdoers and old offenders, that the burning down of the Prefecture of Police, by destroying simultaneously its archives, the Bureau of Morals, and the dispensary [site of regular required medical examinations since 1802], would consecrate their definitive enfranchisement.[175]

Sporting the trademark Phrygian bonnet, drunken, bloodthirsty, and debauched women repeatedly recurred in Versaillais propaganda, a degraded caricature of the spirit of 1789 as a hideous pétroleuse (figure 3.28); other images personified the Commune as a seductive prostitute hiding a serpentine tail.[176] Seldom has the war over urban space taken on simultaneously such powerfully literal as well as symbolic meaning: rebellion against the new order of Napoleon III and Haussmann attacked the instruments of surveillance just as it flaunted the behavior such surveillance was meant to suppress. Writing a year after the Commune, C.-J. Lecour, head of the Brigade des moeurs (also known as the Police des moeurs), followed his portrait of a city overrun by vandalous prostitutes with a boast of the rapid regeneration of the prior mechanism of regulation under the Third Republic: police, arrests of clandestine prostitutes, reopening of licensed houses.[177]

One of the primary fantasies of the siege had been that German troops would invade the city from through the Asnières collector sewer, appearing, as Du Camp imagined it, "in the blink of an eye with arms and equipment . . . in the middle of Paris."[178] The system that guaranteed the healthy circulation of the city had rendered it a porous body; guards and barriers were placed at the offending orifices (figure 3.29). From this perspective, the true danger of infection would turn out instead to come from within. The *fédérés* (pro-Commune members of

3.28. The *pétroleuse*: emblem of the feminine underworld in all of its most powerful—and, for the Versaillais, negative—associations. Illustration by Bertall [Albert d'Arnoux], *La Barricade, Types de la Commune* no. 34, in *Les Communeux, 1871: Types, caractères, costumes* (Paris: Plon, 1880): no. 37.

the national guard) used the carrières for telegraphic communications, and traces were found of an attempt to mine the Catacombes as a trap for the victorious Versaillais.[179] A fair number of fédérés were arrested seeking to flee the city at Asnières, but no matter the wild rumors (see figure 2.5), only bodies and abandoned weapons were found in the Catacombes.[180] More concrete traces of this underworld force were left in the carrières d'Amérique, where the bodies of eight hundred executed fédérés were buried.[181]

The fear of the lower depths overrunning the city can be attributed to other historical experiences in addition to the formative ones of the city's revolutions. For example, Paris was subject to periodic flooding of the Seine, frequently severe, whereas, London was less affected by the tidal fluctuations of the Thames (figures 3.30 and 3.31). Belgrand was ordered by Haussmann to solve the problem of flooding as well as that of sewage; he concluded that only the latter could, in fact, be fixed. "Flooding in Paris," he wrote, "is an endemic problem."[182] Parallel to the fantasies of the implosion of the city through the collapse of its catacombs discussed in the previous chapter was the fantasy of flooding through the same conduit, as in the plan of the "Seine Rats," a band of river pirates in the 1852 melodrama *Les Nuits de la Seine*.[183] Paris equally suffered from a series of epidemics of disease through the early twentieth century, when the last of its densely populated îlots insalubres were demolished. It was after the cholera epidemic of 1832, writes Bernheimer, "that the connection between that specifically sexual contagion and the diseased organism of Paris itself was established in the imagination of many bourgeois observers."[184] Although Bernheimer exaggerates the degree to which the Paris as prostitute metaphor was at work in discourse of the time, there are certainly moments when the view from below that generally operates in the descent narrative merged with the moral and satirical view from above. Baudelaire, for instance, included an extended comparison in the draft of an epilogue for the second edition of *Les Fleurs du mal* (1861), which he characterized in a letter as an "ode to Paris seen from the height of Montmartre":

> Your salvaged principles and shouted-down laws
> Your haughty monuments to which the mists cling,
> Your metal domes enflamed by the sun,
> Your loins, theaters with voices that enchant,
> Your alarms, your guns, a deafening orchestra,
> Your magical paving-stones raised into fortresses,
> Your petty orators with their baroque swellings,
> Preaching love, and then your sewers full of blood,
> Opening a pit into hell [*s'engouffrant dans l'enfer*] like the Orinoco.[185]

Baudelaire personifies the city according to the medieval tradition of the body politic, updated to meld the failed revolution of 1848—barricades, guns, orators—with the iconography of the prostitute in Louis Philippe's Paris—towers as

3.29. Soldiers keeping watch at a collector sewer opening during the siege of Paris in 1870. Their attention is distracted by the rat in the foreground that one of the men has speared with his bayonet. *Inside Paris: Keeping Watch Underground (Sketch by Balloon Post)*, in *Illustrated London News* (26 November 1870): 541.

her breasts, theaters as her hips, and sewers as her infected veins, savage and coursing with blood. To cap off the prosopopoeia, the poem imagines her genitals as the navel point of the topography, a pit opening all the way to an inferno defined by the final simile as that fluvial outpost of slavery dear to the Romantic imagination, the Orinoco.

3.30. "The Boulevard Haussmann after the Bursting of a Sewer: This famous boulevard was flooded by water, which forced its way upwards through the sewers beneath the roadway." Photograph in "Paris Submerged. Special Supplement Illustrating the Disastrous Floods in the Heart of the French Capital," *The Sphere* (5 February 1910): iv.

3.31. Images of a flooded Paris reach London. "Water, Water Everywhere: Flood water flowing out of underground drains." Photograph in *The Sphere* (5 February 1910): 121.

This is the infernal imagination of Paris as prostitute that Baudelaire would make dialectical by reintegrating its powerful allegory of bodily corruption with the material space of the city itself. In Baudelaire's poetry, the resonance of this earlier, purely mythic image of the whore persisted in the background, while she was simultaneously reduced to the status of an inhabitant of Paris. Rather than eliminated or glossed over, the misogyny and colonial exoticism were made to project a truth about their dark power in the economy of the city. Strong proponents of modernism such as Baudelaire might make the metaphor dialectic, but elsewhere, and especially later in the century, the scientific discourse generally required a strictly verticalized city in which the pestilential and excremental would always be contrasted with the clean city they threatened. The mythic imagery did not disappear entirely, but it went underground, as can be glimpsed in the otherwise rational discourse of Du Camp's description of the sewers, when he writes that the metallic conduits "extend under each lane of the pont au Change two pipes that split off from a common trunk and resemble the legs of a black giant lying on its back."[186] The black giant, even if putatively male, introduces a hint of atavistic, colonial menace to the technologized sewer.

A similar process was used explicitly in Zola's novel of the end of Second Empire Paris, *Nana* (1880), in which the eponymous courtesan represents not the city as a whole but the deadly threat surging out of its depths. The ruling metaphor emerges midway through the novel out of an article *à clef* in the *Figaro* read by one of her lovers as Nana admires her naked body in a mirror. Entitled "The Golden Fly," it chronicles the life of a daughter of "four or five generations of drunkards" who rose like a fly out of the ordure of the bas-fonds to infect the entire city.[187] The image is executed with Zola's customary thoroughness as a full-fledged sociohistorical argument: "With her the rottenness that is allowed to ferment among the populace is carried upward and rots the aristocracy," the narrator asserts. "She corrupts and disorganizes all Paris between her snow-white thighs."[188] While the description of her body counters the Romantic image of dark seduction from abroad by stressing her rise from the "boue de Paris" itself, the final verb, "disorganizes," clarifies the connection between sex, ordure, and order in that shift: Nana is not merely a moral but a political threat. Her power lies in her body; this power is tied to the underground not only through the metaphorical equation with waste but to her nude presentation in subterranean tableaux at the beginning and end of the novel, and her association with the threshold demimonde of the *passages* and boulevard theaters throughout. Zola thus first introduces his destructive force in the seductively scandalous context of a tableau at the théâtre des Variétés on the boulevard Montmartre next to the entrance to the passage des Panoramas: Nana debuting as a "Blonde Venus" nude in a sparkling grotto carved out of a silver mine in Mount Aetna; Nana remembered as she appeared equally nude amid "cascades of diamonds" in a crystal grotto in *Mélusine*.[189] Like the River Queen, Sanita's servant in *Harlequin Father Thames,* who rises out of a fountain in her Crystal Caves to perform a ballet, Nana's appeal is framed as an organic, feminine image of nature controlled. The movement of Zola's narrative, however, exposes that image as a façade concealing the counterimage of the organic underground, the equally feminine filth. The dual meaning is already encapsulated in the leitmotif of the first chapter, the manager's insistence on calling his theater a "bordello." It is expanded in the final chapter, for the reminiscence introduces a very different spectacle of organic femininity—Nana's corpse, ravaged by smallpox: "Venus was decomposing. It seemed as if the virus caught by her in the gutter, carried by carcasses, this ferment with which she had poisoned a populace, had just made its way up to her face and had rotted it through."[190] The novel presents the dialectic of the feminine underground, only to argue that it is a false dialectic: the positive aspect is an immobile and deceptive illusion; the negative aspect is a powerful and destructive truth with potentially deadly consequences for the city itself. The last words of the novel associate Nana's death with the inception of the Franco-Prussian War and the spectacle of a Paris eaten away from within that accompanied it.

The metaphorical armature of Zola's naturalism merely unpacked what had long been the lexicon of urban crisis. Over twenty years earlier, William Acton had asserted of London in a tract on prostitution that "as a heap of rubbish will ferment, so surely will a number of unvirtuous women deteriorate."[191] Although Jonathan Swift could unproblematically imagine the streetwalker Corinna having nightmares of being pursued by constables through eighteenth-century London, "Or, near Fleet-Ditch's oozy brinks, / Surrounded with a hundred stinks,"[192] the image of the prostitute as both a product of the sewer and an actor on the social stage would never appear as such in the discourse of Victorian London fiction, where the dunghill is represented as the dustheap, dry as a bone. Even in the popular, Surreyside production *Harlequin Father Thames,* Sanita, as befits her name, is a force of sanity and sanitation, a progressive Amazon who arrives in a shower of electric sparks; it is Father Thames who is corrupt, wet, and foul. By contrast, the French equivalent of the Victorian English euphemism *dust* is *boue;* both words signify waste, dung, shit, sewage, garbage, dirt, but the centuries-old phrase of "boue de Paris" retains the denotation of wet and damp elided by the London dust. As one inhabitant complained about the Paris streets, "I find myself humiliated . . . because obliged to walk on uneven paving stones, covered with mud [*boue*] which makes me slip if I want to go quickly and fall if I hesitate for too long."[193] The same image of fluidity could equally be employed more pragmatically; Parent argued that "prostitution . . . is similar to a torrent that one cannot stop, but [one] that it is possible to a certain point to direct."[194] Such a lexicon for urban London is easily found prior to the nineteenth century, in the scatological humor of the poems by Jonson and Swift discussed above, but Victorian waste is dried out.[195] Just as the Thames was a metonymy for the sewers, so when novelistic London is damp, as in the famous opening of *Bleak House,* it is foggy rather than effluvial, an atmospheric moisture that comes from above and connotes mental and moral confusion rather than disease and decay. Mud and mire there may be, but their animal origin is occluded.

It is unimaginable that one would find an organic image of ordure in Victorian London to match the infamous and influential apology by Parent-Duchâtelet in his study of prostitution, a sequel to his exploration of the Paris sewers:

> If I have been able, without scandalizing anyone at all, to penetrate into the sewers, handle putrid matter, pass part of my time in dumps, and live after a fashion in the midst of all that is the most abject and disgusting among groups of men, why should I blush to approach a sewer of another sort (a sewer filthier, I admit, than all the others) in the well-founded hope of doing some good while examining it in all its aspects?[196]

The effect of defining the prostitute as a sewer was to naturalize her profession. As Parent expressed this conclusion, "Prostitutes are as inevitable, where men live together in large concentrations, as drains and refuse dumps."[197] This was the conventional nineteenth-century French discourse; most succinct, perhaps, was the military and medical historian Louis Fiaux's denomination of the *maison de tolerance* (brothel) as "the seminal drain."[198]

The French "regulatory system" sought to enclose prostitution as it did its other waste products, with regular inspections to guarantee healthy circulation, just as the égoutiers spent their day sweeping out the tunnels to make sure nothing solid remained to fester into effluvia. There were heated arguments as to the best means of achieving this enclosure and regulation. Parent believed houses of prostitution should be placed only on main thoroughfares, for those on narrow, deserted streets would pose a threat to passersby and be more difficult to control. Others maintained that authorities should always seek to locate such houses on "little frequented and noncommercial streets, as much to make less visible the scandal that trails the exercise of prostitution as to cause as little prejudice as possible to retail commerce."[199] If prostitution were truly necessary to service a natural bodily function, and if it were truly as well regulated as one desired, than surely, implied Parent, it should be as public and visible a utility as the fountain or street drain. Writing twenty years later, Parent's followers were less sanguine than their utopian master as to the perfectibility of the regulatory system, opting for something closer to the English convention of hiding it as much as possible out of sight.

The primary cause for concern, notwithstanding the high level of surveillance and documentation, was the difficulty of identifying who was a prostitute (*fille publique*) and who a woman on the street (*débauchée*), even though public solicitation had been forbidden in 1830. Parent attempted to address the problem of identification through definition: a fille publique was a member of the "debauched" class that should be followed and documented with the utmost care; a débauchée was a woman who had "passed into that state of scandalous brutality whose excesses the authorities must repress."[200] Needless to say, Parent never specified a boundary for his fluid definition of the distinction between legal and illegal debauchery. Writing thirty-five years after the pioneer in the field, Lecour confronted a similar contradiction, expressed this time spatially: filles publiques were now apparently simple to define, they were the ones registered and confined to maisons de tolérance. Unfortunately, there was an undefined number of *insoumises* or *non inscrites* ("incorrigibles" or "unrecorded"), who were "everywhere." This caused two problems for the authorities: because insoumises used codes and signs rather than open solicitation, they were difficult to identify and thus to control. At the same time, and paradoxically, their presence "on the most attractive boulevards," circulating as prostitutes, scandalized members of the public, "who take them for inscribed prostitutes under infraction of the regulations, and . . . are shocked by the inaction of the police toward them."[201]

The same experience can be found echoed from the perspective of the connoisseur in Knox's global survey of life underground, for Paris stood as the world capital of prostitution no matter what the authorities thought. According to Knox:

Everyone and everything appears so proper that inexperienced and innocent souls have expressed their astonishment at the ill fame the city has acquired, and have concluded that its bad name is undeserved. Promenading on the Boulevards or riding on the Champs Elysées, they are unable to distinguish the Faubourg St. Germain from the Quartier Latin—the upper-world from the under-world.[202]

Disinterested in a simple distinction between above and below, Knox went on to detail what he termed the six "circles" of the demimonde, from the "educated and rather refined women," unable to marry into the rank to which they naturally belong, to "the lowest and last of the semi-mundanes . . . who accost strangers at night on the Boulevards. . . . When they have reached this grade of degradation they cannot go back; they cannot stand still; they cannot fall lower."[203] Taxonomies of the Paris demimonde were popular both in literature and in guidebooks; particularly alluring were the nebulous middle ranges of the scale, such as Knox's second circle, inhabited by types such as the *grisette*, "half-married, and yet wholly independent."[204] The figure of the grisette was often invoked to represent the quintessential Parisian: frivolous, gay, and addicted to the amusements and luxuries that defined the city. In the literature of prostitution itself, however, such a fluid range of identities was generally impermissible, even in Paris. Nevertheless, we do see its negative traces in the anxiety with which the insoumises were regarded, the ones who disrupted even Knox's easy assertion that the upper-world and the under-world could not be distinguished.

To the Parisian scheme of inscription, as imperfectly as it might work, the French opposed the disastrously "free" system of London, using their attacks on it to express fears about their own system. "The comparison," maintained Dr. Gustave Richelot, "is terrible for England."[205] Citing statistics from the English medical journal *The Lancet,* which labeled prostitution in London "the worst" in Europe, Richelot wrote that the unregulated, unsupervised traffic in London was "a hideous stain . . . an open wound." Unsurprisingly, the behavior that shocked Richelot most about London was found recorded by Knox about Paris above: the overtness of the solicitation. Richelot quoted an English tract, *The Great Sin,* which asserted of France and Germany, "There, you never notice the audacious stares, gaudy attire, and shocking solicitations so habitual at home."[206] While Richelot perhaps exaggerated the London situation to make it all the easier to ignore the analogous problem of the insoumises in Paris, the language he used and the reception of that language is more instructive here than its precise relation to the facts.

Facts and figures, "authoritative accounts," eyewitness reports, lurid anecdotes, and overheated moral rhetoric all circulated, intermingled, throughout the century. There is no doubt that the prostitute was an omnipresent urban experience as well as an important symbolic figure. Hence, the midcentury calculation by certain authors of some fifty thousand to eighty thousand active prostitutes in London cited by Lecour is likely to be exaggerated; on the other hand, the official count in Paris in 1830, the year public solicitation was outlawed, did give the extraordinary number of sixty thousand, just as the statistical tables in the 1857 edition of Parent-Duchâtelet's work showed that the number of prostitutes inscribed monthly between 1812 and 1854 never averaged fewer than one thousand, increasing steadily to over four thousand monthly by the 1850s.[207] Arguments over more debatable facts frequently took the form of argument about the type of discourse to be used. The study of prostitution in volume 4 of *London Labour* gives a good example of this phenomenon.[208] Bracebridge Hemyng complained about the circulation of a particular anecdote first reported in Michael Ryan's frequently quoted study, *Prostitution in London, with a Comparative View of That of Paris, and New York* (London, 1839), and subsequently reproduced in Richelot's survey as a factual account of London: "An *enlightened medical gentleman* assured me that near what is called the Fleet Ditch almost every house is the lowest and most infamous brothel. There is an aqueduct of large dimensions, into which murdered bodies are precipitated by bullies and discharged at a considerable distance into the Thames, without the slightest chance of recovery." Hemyng continued, "Mr. Richelot quotes this with the greatest gravity, and adduces it as a proof of the immorality and crime that are prevalent to such an awful extent in London. What a pity the enlightened medical gentleman did not affix his name to this statement as a guarantee of its authenticity!"[209] Since Clerkenwell had been cleaned out in the 1840s, the anecdote could no longer possibly be true; on the other hand, when Ryan was writing—as Mayhew, and we can assume Hemyng also, well knew—the existence of such establishments elsewhere was quite likely, as had been verified during the 1844 demolition of the area. What was being contested was a particular image of London even more than a particular truth about London, and it was contested especially against the Parisian authority, Richelot.

While we do not know exactly how recently the thieves' dens along the Fleet Ditch had been in operation up to 1844, there is no doubt at all that they had flourished in the previous century. Indeed, the most lurid nineteenth-century accounts of London do not exceed what was taken as given for eighteenth-century London, except that they are limited to the medical genre, and rarer in England than on the Continent. In the eighteenth century, prostitution in London had been out in the open both in the cityscape and in the cultural representation of that space.[210] As Georg Lichtenberg, the German physics professor and commentator on Hogarth, had reported, women were readily to be found, "got up in any way you like, dressed, bound up, hitched up, tight-laced, loose, painted, done up or raw, scented, in silk or wool, with or without sugar, in short, what a man cannot obtain here, if he have not money, upon my word, let him not look for it anywhere else in this world of ours."[211] One can only assume that prostitution continued to follow such free market principles in the following century, even if the prevailing discourse did not.

As in the Fleet Ditch anecdote to which Mayhew took such exception, both the French and the English discourses relied on a vertical segmentation of space in which the prostitute constituted the primary threshold between above and below. To again cite the formative language of Parent-Duchâtelet, "debauchery" would constitute the "passage from an honest life to the state of abjection of a class which is cut off from society."[212] The goal of Parent's study, as of most such works, was to cross that threshold in order to determine how to eliminate it. In the Parisian model, this meant determining a hard and fast distinction between what Parent called "public prostitution" and "public debauchery," between what could be regulated and what could not. In the London model, this meant venturing over the threshold in order to determine which individuals were worthy of salvation and which belonged below. If the police-guided nocturnal sally into the criminal underworld was the paradigmatic narrative of crossing the threshold into the lower depths, the prostitute was the figure who personified distance and proximity simultaneously:

> The symbol of female vice, the prostitute established a stark contrast to domesticated female virtue as well as to male bourgeois identity: she was the embodiment of the corporeal smells and animal passions that the rational bourgeois male had repudiated and that the virtuous woman, the spiritualized "angel in the house," had suppressed. She was also a logo of the divided city itself. . . . In these accounts, prostitution appeared in two guises: as disorderly behavior on the part of "soiled doves," sauntering down the city thoroughfares, dangerous in their collectivity; or as the isolated activity of the lone streetwalker, a solitary figure in the urban landscape, outside home and hearth, emblematic of urban alienation and the dehumanization of the cash nexus. In both cases, they stood in stark opposition to the classical elite bodies of female civil statuary that graced the city squares: they were female grotesques, evocative of the chaos and illicit secrets of the labyrinthine city.[213]

Walkowitz's description of the "'soiled doves' . . . dangerous in their collectivity" suggests one explanation for the resistance in the English discourse to a naturalizing, holistic image of prostitution: it was too redolent of the revolutionary power of the lower depths of Paris. Mayhew, for example, could tolerate the Fleet Ditch as a site of robbery and murder in the context of a penny-dreadful serial such as *The Mysteries of London,* but not in relation to prostitution, and not in a discourse of fact. The analogy between streetwalker as "urban grotesque" and female civil statuary as "classical and elite" nicely brings out the underlying spatial threat: statuary fixes space abstractly; the streetwalker makes space fluid and contradictory. As a cultural historian, Walkowitz aims her methodology at dissecting the power dynamics of the divided city and demonstrating how those same dynamics motivate present-day nostalgia for the structured world of the Victorians as well as present-day pleasure in tearing down that structure. What her methodology does not permit is a recognition of the streetwalker as a dialectical counterpart of the male flâneur, not simply in her wandering but in the power she embodies as an oppositional urban figure, even if this oppositional power is expressed through negative clichés of femininity. A comprehensive understanding of the varieties of spatial practice in the nineteenth-century city must be able to unify the repressed fluidity of the streetwalker with the overemphatic and equally confining solidity of the caryatid. As Orwell wrote of the place of the coal miner in the "metabolism of the Western world": "He is a sort of grimy caryatid upon whose shoulders nearly everything that is *not* grimy is supported."[214] The London streetwalker, as Walkowitz's use of the imported term "flâneur" suggests, requires a reading through the Parisian discourse; conversely, the hordes of Paris require humanization and monumentalization through the London discourse.

What are the consequences of naturalizing prostitution as in the Parisian discourse? For one, it brings out into the open many guiding assumptions of the nineteenth-century city, in particular that the inhabitant of it is defined as a heterosexual male, while the women are defined as part of the infrastructure; discursively, no other permutation can exist. It allows prostitution to be treated as a question of engineering, a matter of the proper organization of abstract space rather than a social issue. It deflects one moral definition of prostitution—a sinful activity that should be eradicated—by means of another: prostitution defiles those who are by nature assigned to practice it. On the more positive side, one could argue that, like the horrors of the fiction of urban mysteries, naturalizing prostitution acknowledges it as a material social phenomenon and takes some account both of its power in the urban imagination and of the social cost of its dehumanizing aspects. It is certainly a brutal gesture to define women as drains, but it does succeed in expressing a truth of sexual labor absent from the English discourse of the fallen woman.

What are the consequences of individualizing prostitution? It is a discourse well suited to the laissez-faire capitalist system with which London was identified in the nineteenth-century. If each fall is individual, then it is the individual that is blamed or the individual that is a victim, and it is individually that the fallen woman must be saved or damned. As William Stead argued in *The Maiden Tribute of Modern Babylon,* it may be inevitable that "London's lust annually uses up many thousands of women. . . . But I do ask that those doomed to the house of evil fame shall not be trapped into it unwillingly."[215] London regulation of prostitution, such as it was, and London reform of prostitution would operate on a piecemeal basis. On the more positive side, we could argue that the refusal to acknowledge the downside of prostitution, the horrors emblematized by the sewage analogy, along with the possibility of casting prostitutes as victims, made available the rare argument that prostitution was caused by the desire of men rather than the corruption of women. This is especially evident in the case of Josephine Butler and the Ladies National Association of which she was the leader in their nearly twenty-year battle against the amended Contagious Diseases Act of 1869, which permitted the police to detain and subject to medical examination any woman they deemed suspicious. The LNA "rejected the prevailing social view of prostitution as pollutants of men, and instead depicted them as the victims of male pollution."[216] The source of their insight, as Walkowitz phrases it, was "spiritual identification with the fallen-sisterhood"; the opposition responded in kind by symbolically thrusting them back into the lower depths, attacking Butler while she was speaking in Manchester, tearing her clothes, and covering her in flour and excrement.[217] As Flora Tristan had put it several decades earlier in her *London Journal,* "Prejudice, poverty and servitude combine to produce this revolting degradation. Yes, for if you men did not impose chastity on women as a necessary virtue while refusing to practice it yourselves, they would not be rejected by society for yielding to the sentiments of their hearts, nor would seduced, deceived and abandoned girls be forced into prostitution."[218] Tristan remains wholly within the discourse of the fallen woman, individualizing responsibility and blaming prostitution on seduction, but she mobilized this discourse to combat its primary assumptions.

Tristan also incorporated an economic argument that partakes of a Marxian discourse that would eschew the vertical segmentation of space altogether. Although her language was cast in the moral terms well-nigh inescapable in the nineteenth-century discourse, it nevertheless asserts a plausible material cause: "Prostitution is a blight on the human race, the most hideous of all evils caused by the unequal distribution of wealth."[219] Marx's critique of the character of Fleur-de-Marie in Sue's *Mystères de Paris* elaborated a more detailed argument about the way in which the ideology of the modern economic system worked to fix social identity.[220] Where the vertical model, whether mobilized critically or affirmatively, identifies the inhabitant of the city and that person's occupation with the space he or she inhabits, thus reinforcing the physical and social segregation of the city, Marx's argument assumes that individual identity is not fundamentally determined either by where one lives or by what one does. For Marx, the clichéd depiction of Fleur-de-Marie as the innocent prostitute as Sue introduces her in the novel presents a far more critical image than after she has been informed that her occupation is sinful and that she is permanently sullied, fallen—for this is indeed an example of what I have called the London discourse. Marx prefers here to privilege the possibility that one may one day escape one's exploitative labor and one's oppressive dwelling, that one is only passing through the underworld, even if it requires accepting the fantasy of happiness or complicity in that exploitation in the process. This was a contextualized polemic on Marx's part against the common acceptance of Sue's program as socially progressive; elsewhere, he generally preferred, as did his collaborator Engels, to focus on the easy mobilization of horrors available to the verticalized model of the descent into hell.

In the copious nineteenth-century literature on prostitution, the nonvertical model of analysis is as rare as the protofeminist focus on male agency in the phenomenon. The vertical model is seductive, as can be witnessed by the accumulation of examples of the "bodily lower stratum" applied to every aspect of the nineteenth-century urban underground by later writers and critics: it offers a potent model for presenting crisis and contradiction but no means of assigning agency or resolution. In this sense, the dialectic identified by Clark as quintessential to modernity can be applied to the experience and representation of underground space: the exclusive focus on modern incarnations of the ancient underground myths—corruption, death, putrefaction—precludes recognition of the genuinely new underground—rational, ordered, and supremely verticalized—introduced to the city through those myths. Because derived from actual spatial practice—albeit primarily past practices—the tropes of the urban underworld continue to function as if they still determined spatial practice in the modern city: "Capital devises a set of orders and classifications which makes the *city* unintelligible, but does not thereby make modernity so, or everyday life. . . . It is part of that fixing that the city itself should vanish, since the city was precisely a site of unfixity—uncontrol—in the previous social order."[221] Although to my mind the final sentence takes abstract space—the representation of the city as perfectly controlled—at face value, Clark's argument still captures well the paradox of modernity. The tropes of the organic underworld are particularly seductive here because they in fact give a simultaneously real and aesthetically pleasing representation of the social costs of modernization. Part of that pleasure is the equally real assurance that the world above provides an answer to those costs. The paradox is that the enunciation of the problem through underground space and underground metaphors precludes a full understanding of the problem and, consequently, a correct appreciation of the solutions. What it does provide is the space wherein to reintegrate aspects of above and below, to construct a dialectic out of the contradictions in the representation of both spaces that would allow the construction of the space in its actual rather than its aesthetic complexity.

A document such as Yves Guyot's *Prostitution under the Regulatory System French and English,* published in France in 1882 and translated into English two years later, provides one tool for taking apart the verticalized city of prostitution. In a rhetorical move similar to those employed by Marx, Guyot took the French discourse on prostitution and turned it on its head. For Guyot, it is the police administration that creates and maintains the institution of prostitution, and the police, consequently, that are the problem: "This police administration, which affirms that prostitution is an evil—a necessary evil, it is true—has only one aim: to manufacture 'common prostitutes,' who can be nothing else but prostitutes, and who are condemned to remain prostitutes for life."[222] Guyot took exception not only to the *police des moeurs,* which he called "a nocturnal institution," but to the social hypocrisy that would label as evil and fix in that identity for life a fluctuating social group indistinguishable by any rational criterion from the remainder of society.[223] He demolishes the moral issue exemplified in Emile Littré's definition in his dictionary of prostitution as "abandonment to immodesty" by arguing that the prostitute is debauched only because her trade requires her to be so; under the same criteria, the male client is far more debauched, because out of volition. He discards naturalizing the argument that the prostitute is a race apart by arguing that if "a prostitute is any woman for whom sexual relations are subordinated to the question of gain," then nearly any woman in contemporary society must be considered a prostitute.

Guyot's model comes closer to dealing with the statistical facts of prostitution than anything to be found in the vertical model. Although, as Harsin has observed, Parent did not choose to draw conclusions from facts with which he did not agree, he nevertheless faithfully recorded them.[224] According to Harsin, his data suggests that the primary factor for women becoming prostitutes was economic, an argument echoed for London by Mayhew and later by Stead, who hypothesized in the *Pall Mall Gazette* that the majority of women took up prostitution not because they had been seduced or because of abject poverty but "occasionally as a means of supplementing scanty wages."[225] The figures confirm that prostitution is seldom a permanent occupation and that it is not necessarily full time. According to inscription dates for individual women in Paris, for example, over half were prostitutes for fewer than four years.[226] Picturesque and complex hierarchies of prostitution are not only a Victorian eccentricity but also a distorted reflection of the fact that contrary to the prevailing representation there was no single identity, just as the space of filth is a multifaceted, fluid, contradictory space. One can conclude, as Guyot and many following him have, that moral policing simply perpetuates a false identity rather than controlling a concrete phenomenon.

What is striking in Guyot's book is not the arguments per se; they had been made in bits and pieces by previous Marxist writers, and have since become a cornerstone of Foucauldian readings of the nineteenth century. Rather, it is the way in which the different discourses of the verticalized city he uses actually shift his discussion into a different register of urban space. As he wrote of the "common prostitute," giving a different turn to the sewage trope: "Society throws this woman in the river or the sewer, and has no metaphor coarse enough to express all its scorn."[227] The essence of waste lies not in its status as the degraded, debased detritus of society, but in its quality of valuable resources. Guyot expresses the fundamental truth of capitalist exploitation: it uses and discards without regard for what it is that it has used. If waste is indeed the devil-twin of weapons, as Don DeLillo has suggested, the way to eliminate weapons is neither simply to decry the horrors they commit nor to defend those horrors as necessary, but to remember what is differently wasteful about weapons, and what in waste can be turned into a weapon of a different sort.

4

URBAN APOCALYPSE

Each epoch not only dreams the next, but also, in dreaming, strives toward the moment of waking. It bears its end in itself and unfolds it—as Hegel already saw—with cunning. In the convulsions of the commodity economy we begin to recognize the monuments of the bourgeoisie as ruins even before they have crumbled.

WALTER BENJAMIN, "Paris, Capital of the Nineteenth Century" (1935)

The apogee of underground space as an urban spectacle arrived, fittingly, in 1900, at the Exposition Universelle de Paris. As usual, the catacombs and sewers were listed as major sites to be visited; what was new was that in the old quarries beneath the palace of the Trocadero two vast exhibits were mounted, Le Monde Souterrain and L'Exposition Minière Souterraine; together, they provided a summa of the underground world. Le Monde Souterrain presented "natural or artificial curiosities found under the earth," including reproductions of archaeological finds and wonders of ancient civilizations—Phoenician mines, Mycenaean tombs, the necropolis of Memphis; dioramas showing the aspects of the earth during each geological age; and natural curiosities—grottoes of southern France and Naples, and of Dead Sea hermits; the marble mountains of Annam, complete with pagodas.

The mining exhibition was even more sensational, including "a real descent into a mine, or rather into a series of working mines," by means of an elevator with a seating capacity of eighty persons, where one could witness "the most diverse substances, such as coal, gold, silver, copper, iron, salt, diamonds, etc., in the course of extraction."[1] The galleries of the subterranean mine gave the illusion of being a thousand feet below the ground, reported one guide, and extended horizontally for nearly one thousand yards, including a functional extracting engine and a "life-size" reproduction of a Transvaal gold mine, "where real Kaffir miners excavate the real mineral."[2] As you ascended the passage to daylight, you could trace the entire process of refinement—"the factory for treating gold ore, with its crushing machinery, its cyanuration tubs, etc., and visitors are able to follow the operation till the moment the ingots of gold are extracted from the ore"—until emerging into the streets of Paris, the final destination, after all, of so many of the fruits of subterranean labor.[3] The entrance to the exhibition was located in the east section of the Trocadero gardens, reserved for foreign countries, under the buildings of the regions associated with archaeology—Egypt—and with subterranean riches—the Transvaal.[4] It is the clearest statement one could find of the range of meaning brought together under the nineteenth-century rubric of the underground; its perfectly packaged, disenchanted form as pure spectacle signals the waning of its material hold over the aboveground space of the city. When Emile Gérards went to photograph the sites a few years later for his mammoth volume *Paris souterrain,* they were already in ruins (figure 4.1). Constructed in one of the most ancient sections of subterranean Paris, this pair of subterranean exhibits was presented as if it were already part of the past.

Elsewhere in the Exposition, the experimental big-screen cinema caused a sensation that would only bear fruit a number of years later, but the most novel sight of the day, equally inaugurating the twentieth century, was line no. 1 of the Métro, running east-west as the hub of the Exposition, which had provided the incentive finally to begin its construction after decades of debate. It was unfinished, but precisely in its unfinished state it remained open to the world above, pointing the way to the material future of subterranean space. In the nineteenth century, the novel exploitation of the underground had cloaked itself in ancient images of the devil, just as the novel experiences of urban crises had been enunciated through mythic tropes of the underworld. As these once novel experiences

4.1. The Subterranean World in ruins: remains of the Chinese pagoda beneath the Trocadero gardens. Photograph by J. Passoir. Reproduced by permission from Photo Ville de Paris, Inspection générale des carrières.

were incorporated into the abstract space of the city as second nature, what did not fit into that streamlined space was relegated metaphorically to the underground as ruin. What capital could make simple use of was redefined as the inorganic underground; what had proved unusable was recast as the organic underground. As Benjamin wrote, the meaning of works of art is never more visible than when they are dead and their skeletal structure has become evident.[5] He coined the aphorism in the context of the Baroque theater's obsession with death; he found new meaning for it in the detritus of nineteenth-century Paris that remained scattered about the city between the wars: the run-down *passages,* the now seldom-visited Catacombes and sewers, the forgotten popular culture of the previous century. Detached from its direct connection to the quotidian, to its role as mediator between the abstract representation of space and the representational space of everyday life, underground space in the twentieth century generally manifested itself either in the rational form discussed in chapter 1 or in the apocalyptic mode; for what the inorganic underground most violently represses is precisely the meaning that has always been most closely connected to subterranean space: death, destruction, and decomposition.

Notwithstanding their mythic unity of meaning, such images have continued to take specific form in relation to specific historical events and specific urban spaces. The first such event was the trench warfare of the First World War, which sounded the death knell of the multifarious nineteenth-century underground, opening up the space to the unitary theories of meaning characteristic of the period between the wars. Where the underground imagery of Paris and London had rooted mythic imagery in specific cityscapes, the imagery of modernism tended toward an abstract myth of a modernist city that had exceeded the spatial framework of any individual metropolis. The Second World War gave those unitary theories a different inflection. As the nineteenth-century capitals of Europe were either bombed into rubble or, as in the case of Paris, occupied by a foreign power, and as a traditional inhabitant of the imaginary urban underworld, the Jew—as well as homosexuals, gypsies, and other minority populations—was systematically eliminated from those same cities, the ruined metropolis imagined throughout the previous century took material form for the first time.

With the European city in tatters both physically and economically, the focus of rationalized underground space shifted away from Europe altogether in order to address the new mode of apocalypse made concrete in Hiroshima and Nagasaki. At the same time, as symbolic center of American economic power, and possessed of an eminently verticalized space, postwar Manhattan, like Paris and London before it, began to generate images of postwar urban apocalypse, mobilizing through its subway and sewage systems a new discourse of race and colonialism to overlay the old vertical depiction of class. The densely packed and visibly segregated space of New York helped to conceptualize a global North-South divide that was rapidly coming to present similar social problems to those faced by nineteenth-century Paris and London, except that the economic motor was operating from outside rather than from within the space it exploited.

The model of rational space now dominates the representation of the space of the developed world because it is able to displace any trace of the organic onto the distant horrors of the third world. The new mode of apocalyptic that has gained in visibility since the end of the cold war insists upon the dialectical link between these two representations of underground space, belying the assertion of absolute segregation between all the wonders of technology, embodied in the inorganic underground, and all the horrors of the lack of technology, embodied in the organic underground. Information technology makes them more integrated than ever before; the underground imagery contradicts that representation, as a reminder of the extraordinary inequality of the world economy; on the other hand, when pushed, it reveals the truth of that insistence, that the world is in fact more integrated than ever, but only in terms of the baldest forms of exploitation. It is a truth, however, that, because underground space as such no longer occupies the margins of capitalist exploitation, it can be expressed through the vertical model only via the extreme imagery of apocalypse.

The City in Ruins

From high up you can see the population of palaces, monuments, houses, and hovels, which seem to have gathered in expectation of some cataclysm . . . I have spent hours on Fourvièvres looking at Lyons, on Notre-Dame de la Garde looking at Marseilles, on Sacré Coeur looking out at Paris. . . . And, yes, at a certain moment I heard in myself something like a tocsin, a strange admonition, and I saw these three magnificent cities . . . threatened with collapse, with devastation by fire and flood, with carnage, with rapid erosion, like forests leveled en bloc. At other times, I saw them preyed upon by an obscure, subterranean evil, which undermined the monuments and neighborhoods, causing entire sections of the proudest homes to crumble. . . . What astounds one is that Paris, Lyons, and Marseilles have endured.

LÉON DAUDET, *Paris vécu* (1930)

During the nineteenth century, ruin was still expressed from both extremes of the vertical city, in the view from above—the satanic overview of the city in flames, and the look back of the lone survivor—and in the view from below—the perspective of the ragpicker, the melancholic sorting through the discarded dust and fragments at street level or below. We have seen examples already of the biblical imagery of moral ruin, the rhetoric of the metropolis as Babylon, Sodom, or Rome. For ruin as a sentiment rooted in a particular urban experience, however, there is no doubt that the discourse belonged to Paris. As Giovanni Macchia has argued in *Paris in Ruins,* his evocative gloss of Benjamin's theory of disaster in the *Arcades Project,* the Revolution gave Paris a uniquely concrete sense of itself as already a ruined city, a city that had achieved greatness only at the cost of its own destruction. The properly Parisian consciousness of history, Macchia writes, is one of tragic grandeur:

> When, after the massacres and violence of the Revolution, this city was, in an accumulation of monuments, going to become the capital of modern civilization, the wounds of its ruins assailed the poets of the early nineteenth century as if in a nightmare. Become an antique city like Rome, Athens, Memphis, or Babylon, Paris also seemed obliged to testify to its own grandeur through the spectacle of its own destruction.[6]

Not only the revolutionary cycles that punctuated the century but the material history of Paris underlay this sentiment. The very stone with which the city was built had been dug out from beneath its streets; by the time of the Revolution, Paris had undermined its foundations to such a degree that cave-ins were a regular occurrence.[7]

At the end of the eighteenth century, Count Volney's influential world history, *Les Ruines d'empire* (1791), had popularized a neoclassical moral vision, which asserted that all great empires reach their term and collapse. The nineteenth century revised this dictum to mean that a city could be truly certified as great only once it could be excavated from its ruins. This meant that a true vision of Paris had to be constructed, first of all, by a sense of its relation to antiquity, to the past. As Charles Péguy wrote, "When Hugo saw a beggar on the road . . . he saw him for what he is, for what he really is in reality: the ancient mendicant, the ancient supplicant, . . . on the ancient road. . . . When he looked at a door to the street, and at a doorstep . . . he distinguished clearly on this stone the ancient line, the sacred threshold."[8] Benjamin labeled this attitude Hugo's chthonic conception of antiquity and associated it with the author's affinity for subterranean Paris. Macchia further relates it to Hugo's description in *Les Misérables* of the revolutionaries' taking up of paving stones to create barricades: constructing a future Paris by taking apart its past piece by piece, an image that would echo through utopian visions of the city at least as far as the situationists.[9]

Macchia does not distinguish this mode of perception of catastrophe from that of the city as Sodom; however, in its grounding in the paving stones and Catacombes of the city, Hugo's vision, like Baudelaire's, was resolutely allied to the view from below, the ground-level experience of the city's ruins as its dirt. This was the vision Haussmann most especially attacked in his own creation out of destruction; what he aimed for was not the return of a vision based in antiquity but a rational city that would eliminate all vestiges of the past, of cycles, and of revolutions in favor of an eternal present. Faced with the destructive spectacle of Haussmannization, and puzzling over the conundrum that the land of Paris was worth more razed and swept clean than piled with the accumulated clutter of centuries of urban living, the novelist, playwright, and journalist Edmond About could not wholly persuade himself that the world would be better off without the bas-fonds:

> When I think back on these worthy people before the ruins of their old nest, I wonder if the insalubrious streets, the narrow tenements, the dark alleyways, and the spiral staircases haven't their own destiny and utility in the world. This filth of the poor quarters being swept disdainfully outside the barrières, wasn't it once civilization's fertilizer? Didn't the most beautiful fruits of Parisian industry emerge from this dunghill?[10]

The organic underworld grounds the imagery of catastrophe by analogy to the cycles of nature and fosters an attitude of passive observance; the inorganic strives to be linear, if not to negate temporality altogether, and must actively combat any encroachment of natural disorder.

The aspect of the Paris discourse that was applied to London was the view from above. Just as social-problem reportage always availed itself of the vision of the metropolis as hell, so we also find the "last man" vision, most famously perhaps in Gustave Doré's illustration for *London: A Pilgrimage* depicting a New Zealander high above the river Thames, looking down on the ruined city, a reverse image of colonial exploration (figure 4.2).[11] As we saw in chapter 1, the catastrophe was equally the necessary catalyst for the underground utopia, whether in Paris or in London. There, however, we found a focus on the view from below, the descent to the underworld predicated on the fact that the city above has been blasted, rendered unusable. When the future traveler did venture into the ruined city, as in most of Wells's future visions, as well as those of Forster and others, the vision invariably complicated itself, establishing various links between material reality and utopian desires rather than predicating the latter on the elimination of the former. It is here that apocalypse, as in the simultaneously forward- and backward-looking visions of Hugo and Baudelaire, is at its most critical, when it treats the underground as both negative and utopian, as repository of past remains and of future possibilities.

While the Paris discourse grounded this dialectic in the layered and contradictory history of its cityscape, the London discourse worked a different dialectic whereby the positive effect of ruin lay in the enforced return to the rural past, and negative knowledge lay in the ruined city. In *The Wind in the Willows,* Badger's safe home in the center of the forest is burrowed out of the subterranean ruins of a great city. In *News from Nowhere,* the narrator begins with a vision of London transformed into a medievalist collective, but finds true reconciliation only through an autobiographical journey up the river Thames to his childhood home. In "The Machine Stops," Forster's young hero discovers the hills of Kent as a pastoral alternative only after escaping the regimented life belowground,

4.2. The ruins of empire. Illustration by Gustave Doré, *The New Zealander*, in *London: A Pilgrimage*, by Doré and Blanchard Jerrold (London: Grant & Co., 1872): 188.

soon to be cataclysmically destroyed. London, the underground city, provides knowledge, but only negatively.

Perhaps the most striking example of this London dialectic is Richard Jefferies's novel, *After London* (1885), which imagined a postapocalyptic England returned to a form of medieval feudalism, with the buried remains of London poisoning Southeastern England like a toxic-waste dump. Notwithstanding the resolutely negative imagination of the metropolis as an imploded sewer, it is to this blasted space that the hero, Sir Felix Aquila, is drawn on his wandering quest. Only two attributes of the vanished city persist amid the waste of its ancient situation: money and rats, the latter ranging the land in terrifying hordes, the former buried deep under the marsh that covers the ruin, luring treasure seekers to their deaths. Jefferies's extraordinary description of the end of London turned its nineteenth-century identity on its head: the empire that had been built on the circulation the world over of goods to and from its waterway has choked on the clogged circulation of its own waste; it now blocks the rest of England from access to the sea, creating a cultural backwater.

In Jefferies's dialectic, the medievalist, pastoral lifestyle is viable and natural but brutal and uncivilized; the world of 1885, projected as ruin into the future, is poisonous but essential. In his wanderings, Felix finds himself inexorably drawn to the wasteland, around which have accumulated not only pestilential vapors but traditional otherworld myths:

> He had penetrated into the midst of that dreadful place, of which he had heard many a tradition: how the earth was poison, the water poison, the air poison, the very light of heaven, falling through such an atmosphere, poison. There were said to be places where the earth was on fire and belched forth sulphurous fumes, supposed to be from the combustion of the enormous stores of strange and unknown chemicals collected by the wonderful people of those times. . . . Ghastly beings haunted the site of so many crimes, shapeless monsters, hovering by night, and weaving a fearful dance. Frequently they caught fire, as it seemed, and burned as they flew or floated in the air. . . . The earth on which he walked, the black earth, leaving phosphoric footmarks behind him, was composed of the mouldered bodies of millions of men who had passed away in the centuries during which the city existed.[12]

The traces of the industrial city are joined with preindustrial mythology; the lure of both draws the adventurer to the site. At great risk to his life, Felix retrieves from the other world a sack of gold coins and a diamond, triumphantly returning, in conventional fashion, with the wherewithal to lay claim to his inheritance and marry Aurora, his beloved.

Signaling the end of the Victorian city, Ford Madox Ford concluded a 1905 fantasy on the economic decline of London with a stark choice between two future cities: one, buried by sewage as in Jefferies's reverie; the other, clean, white, and continually in motion, an inorganic dynamo. In the fragmentation of the modernist city, the two systems are no longer conceptually compatible. Each is a picture of isolation; the first, a city caved-in on itself, undermined by the very river and drainage works that made it great:

> And indeed this picture of an immense Town, shut off from the rest of the world, black, walled in, peopled by gibbering neurasthenics, a prey to hysterias, useless for work, getting no pleasures from horrible self indulgences—this image of a City of dreadful Night is appalling enough. . . . And, as trade ebbs and ebbs from this city of neurasthenics, the Vestries, the Corporations, the Conservancies, will lack the money with which to fight the Thames, that great friend that made London, that great enemy that ultimately shall overwhelm it. A very little want of attention to the sewers, the embankments and the up-river locks would swamp at each tide all the City and all London. The sliding sands would get into motion beneath St. Paul's; all the hidden streams and rivulets that London has forgotten would swell, burst their bonds, and beneath the ground eat into the foundations of the houses.[13]

The other option is a "London with its portable houses, its masked and numbered inhabitants," the same order, cleanliness, and tedium bemoaned by Orwell some twenty years later:

> It will . . . become a gigantic, bright, sanitary and sane congeries of little white houses that can be folded up and carried off in the night. On the one hand, there will at last be Rest in London; on the other—humanity being redeemable—there will never be rest at all, but the great city will go staggering along through a series of changes in the nature of man.[14]

In the twentieth-century discourse of London, rest can no longer be imagined except in its primordial place in the organic underworld—as death. Social life within the city, conversely, can be imagined only as sterility—the inorganic underworld.

Apocalypse between the Wars

> Lice, rats, barbed wire, fleas, shells, bombs, underground caves, corpses, blood, liquor, mice, cats, artillery, filth, bullets, mortars, fire, steel: that is what war is. It is the work of the devil.
>
> OTTO DIX, *War Diary 1915–1916*

Within the mythology of the trenches, the conception of rest, of escape from the space of death, was available only in a similarly extreme picture of the organic underworld, the legend of cannibalistic deserters inhabiting the blasted no-man's-land between the lines. As the cultural historian Paul Fussell records it: "A battalion-sized (some said regiment-sized) group of half-crazed deserters from all the armies, friend and enemy alike, harbored underground in abandoned trenches and dugouts and caves, living in amity and emerging at night to pillage corpses and gather food and drink."[15] The wild men—a distorted picture of pacifist communalism as well as of international working-class solidarity—not only broke down conceptions of nationality but also the fundamental (and fundamentally abstract) divisions of warfare, living in amity although originating from different sides of the struggle. The order of the city—its street signs, its grids and patterns—provided, conversely, the only means of making the inhuman trench into a social space comprehensible to the outside world. Trenches were named after the streets of London, temporary landmarks after the monuments of Berlin. Rather than the forbidden desires of peace and freedom, city images took a jocular form of urban survivalism.

In the wartime coda to his otherwise nineteenth-century roman-fleuve, Proust imagined Paris under attack as a different sort of apocalyptic space. Both Prendergast and Macchia have read the aerial bombardment as the final episode in the nineteenth-century fascination with, respectively, the underground and the city as Sodom. As Marcel wanders through the pitch-black night, like a refugee from the past century due to his long absence from the city, we witness the ultimate peeling away of the veil that had separated the visible, daytime, aboveground Paris from the invisible, nighttime, underground city, where sodomites "celebrated . . . their secret rites in the shadows of the catacombs."[16] Macchia sees in the Pompeian frescoes of Jupien's house of vice and in Proust's language a reworking of the biblical Sodom to announce the destruction of Paris by German planes, "the 20th-century form of the exterminating Angel."[17] Here we glimpse the limits of Macchia's nineteenth-century model, for Proust's vision of destruction equally leaps forward, an entre-deux-guerres version of Hugo's dialectic of antiquity and futurity: the vision of Sodom to be destroyed looks back through the long-standing metropolis of vice and immorality and forward to a city menaced by a mechanical, man-made angel. Paris is reduced simultaneously to a cauldron of sin and a network of muddy trenches.

Following his eye-opening wandering through Jupien's homosexual brothel, Marcel emerges onto the darkened streets to seek shelter in another forward-looking space, the Métro. This space, too, is both shelter and Sodom, as the dark permits all manner of fortuitous physical encounters, such as the one he observes between the two men next to him. Prendergast regards this episode as a conclusive example of the potential for hidden pleasure opened up by the Parisian sense of underground space.[18] Although one might want to correct his utopianism with the apocalypse of Macchia's reading, it is certainly striking that the space that is repossessed for pleasure in this episode is not a nineteenth-century French house such as Jupien maintains, but the putatively safe, rational, and nonperverse space of the underground railway. Just as memory for Proust is a dialectical tool, reaching back to retrieve experience out of the ruins of the past as it looks forward to the ordering of that experience into art, so does the unveiling of Paris as Sodom and Gomorrah recapitulate the apocalyptic mode of the nineteenth-century city, while positing it in the future as an unforeseen mode of experience, loss paired with insight.

As Proust sensed in *Le Temps retrouvé*, apocalypse had been given a new set of meanings by the First World War, becoming one of the privileged modes of representing the trench experience, and, consequently, a key mode of modernism. Henri Barbusse's novel *Le Feu* ended allegorically in a modern, infernal flood. The German painter Max Beckmann saw the Western Front at Ypres as a collection of necropolises, "all those holes and sharp trenches. Those ghostly passageways and artificial forests and houses. . . . Strangely unreal cities like lunar mountains, cities of the dead."[19] Beckmann's *Resurrection* (1918) depicted a landscape pocked with holes, with naked and distorted bodies emerging from, or perhaps sinking into, them; other paintings and drawings interwove biblical themes and sociopolitical satire into the dreamscape of the trenches and the trench experience. As Jay Winter has persuasively argued, the religious iconography of Revelation and the Last Judgment not only dominated popular representations of the war but was an important component of the discourses of modernism usually considered as being wholly secularized.[20] Whereas the Parisian discourse had generally regarded ruin as belonging either to the past or to an impending future, for the soldier at the front, as well as for the civilian trying to make sense of the war, hell had arrived with an immediacy only certain miners and subterranean workers had ever experienced before: "The otherworldly landscape, the bizarre mixture of putrefaction and ammunition, the presence of dead among the living, literally holding up trench walls from Ypres to Verdun, suggested that the demonic and satanic realms were indeed here on earth. . . . To all too many Englishmen and women, Hell was indeed just across the Channel."[21] Winter's concluding remark reminds us that apocalypse remained, with good reason, more closely identified with France than with England.

The proximity of Paris to the Western Front gave rise not only to the literally underground experience recorded by Proust but also to the greater assimilation of one space with the other. As the center of the French government, Paris also became associated with the world above responsible for what was occurring or had occurred in its nether world of the trenches. The march of the risen dead onto the capital was a repeated trope in literature and film. In Roland Dorgelès's 1926 novel, *Le Retour des morts*, a host of the dead marches on Paris to besiege the city in anger; in the first version of Abel Gance's film, *J'accuse* (1918–19), they march in order to question whether their sacrifice had been in vain; in the second version of *J'accuse* (1937), they march to prevent another war. Winter traces the image back to a popular, religiously inflected legend recounted by Maurice Barrès and enshrined in *Debout les Morts!*, a best-selling *image d'Epinal* (popular color illustrations produced by the Imagerie of Epinal since the eighteenth century). Attacked by some soldiers for its clichés and its appropriation of the dead for propaganda, the patriot mythmaking of *Debout les Morts!* told of a slaughtered troop that, on hearing the command of a dying survivor, arose to turn back the enemy.[22]

Apocalypse surfaced in the melancholic and misanthropic modes of urban modernism in iconic places such as the "unreal city" of T. S. Eliot's *Waste Land,* peopled by the alienated souls of modern Londoners; in the shell-shocked suicide, Septimus Smith, in Virginia Woolf's *Mrs. Dalloway,* whose visions of London as an inferno connect the events of the war to the society world of Clarissa Dalloway's party; in Wyndham Lewis's art and novels from *Blast* through the war art to the epic rewriting of Dante in *The Human Age* (1928–56); in the nihilism of Céline's first novels, framed by the trench experience as epitome of modern life; in key moments such as the Proustian episode above, or the conclusion of Thomas Mann's *Magic Mountain* down in the trenches. The epistemological mode of apocalypse determined the revolutionary gestures of avant-garde art and the theoretical extremism of a Walter Benjamin, whose work was bracketed by his experiences of evading the draft in 1914 and fleeing Berlin for Paris when the Nazis took power in 1933, and which was predicated on the historical catastrophe that would usher in the Messiah. The infernal space of the trench, layered onto the tradition of urban apocalypse, drove a generally satanic view from above in which the verticalized space could be righted only by wholesale elimination of the world above.

The trench experience and the early century urban crises equally galvanized the opposing discourse, which would resolve both disasters through drastic measures of order and rationality rather than chaos and disorder. A critique by Clough Williams-Ellis put the two discourses together, claiming that he

> would certainly sooner go back for another year in wartime Ypres than spend a twelve month in postwar Slough. Should that sound like an overstatement I should explain that it is merely the prudent desire of one who desires to remain happily alive, and who would therefore assuredly choose an eighty per cent risk of being shot, gassed, or blown up in heroic company to the certainty of cutting his own throat in surroundings of humiliating squalor.[23]

When Peter Hall wrote that "twentieth-century city planning, as an intellectual and professional movement, essentially represents a reaction to the evils of the nineteenth-century city," he might have added that those "evils" found their most symbolically potent representation in the trench as the culmination of the apocalyptic city.[24] The preeminent American urbanist of the time, Lewis Mumford, was a prophet of urban doom, who saw a direct and unwavering descent from the mine to the modern city to the trench to the next world war. For Le Corbusier, too, "historic Paris" was identical to "tubercular Paris"; for him and many other modernists after the Great War, the past was something to be eliminated.[25]

Utopias of the late nineteenth century had tested the potential of subterranean space to contain the contradictions of the modern city; cinema between the wars posited the inorganic underground as a new solution to those contradictions. Fritz Lang's *Metropolis* (1926) combined the verticalized cityscape of Manhattan with the mythic underworld of Paris and the contemporary concerns of Berlin into an allegory of a stratified future highly derivative of Wells's visions.[26] What was new in the film, beyond the visual impact of the spectacular sets and the expressionist manipulation of the crowds of workers, was the cataclysmic explosion of the workers in revolt under the prompting of the robot-woman, Maria. Destroying the machines that render their subterranean city habitable, the crazed workers flood their own apartment blocks, nearly drowning their children in the bargain, before rampaging through the city above, rioting and looting (figure 4.3). Reconciliation is at hand, however, and it arrives through the graces of the surviving remnants of an organic underground derived from the legends of Paris. Beneath the workers' quarters are organic tunnels that predate the new city above; in these catacombs, the good Maria leads clandestine reli-

4.3. The uncontrollable forces of the underground bursting out of their oppression to destroy the city of Metropolis. Frame enlargement from *Metropolis*, directed by Fritz Lang (Universum-Film A.G., 1926). BFI Films: Stills, Posters and Designs.

gious services and preaches to the workers of a mediator to come. The final confrontation takes place in another archaic site of the city, an ancient cathedral copied from Paris's Notre-Dame. The robot-Maria is burned at the stake in front of the cathedral, there is a rooftop confrontation out of *Notre-Dame de Paris* by way of Lon Chaney and Hollywood, and, having saved the good Maria, the master's son reconciles the workers' leader with his father. Notwithstanding (and probably because of) its reactionary mythmaking, *Metropolis* was effective in demonstrating the dehumanizing potential of the inorganic underground on both the world above and the workers below; its division of the organic underground into an archaic, benevolent force and a futuristic, wild force grafted a soothing, nineteenth-century solution onto that critique.

Two English science-fiction films of the 1930s, *Things to Come* (1936) and *Transatlantic Tunnel* (1935), also posited a new relationship between urban apocalypse and the inorganic underground, but from a much more pragmatic, London point of view. Based as it was on a screenplay by H. G. Wells, it is not surprising that *Things to Come* was very much in the tradition of the turn-of-the-century utopia. It begins with the prophetic destruction from the air of a London-based Everytown (figure 4.4). The second episode shows an interim society, bereft of the accoutrements of civilization, reverting to a more savage version of Jefferies's pastoralism. The third episode details the construction of a new subterranean city by a resurgent civilization. Everytown is the epitome of Le Corbusian ideas, rational and flooded with light, with clean, white lines (figure 4.5).[27] The goal of this town is to launch a rocket into the unknown sky, a fitting image for the conquest of irrational space. The only threat left to this regulated space, the only hint of an organic underground, is a malcontent revolutionary who attempts to sabotage the rocket. *Things to Come* beautifully updated heroic engineering for the twentieth century, but with no more sense than the nineteenth-century utopias as to how that engineering would work without a wholesale destruction of the existing city, the same fate Le Corbusier had projected for central Paris in his Voisin Plan.

Transatlantic Tunnel was equally invested in heroic engineering, in this case a subaqueous thoroughfare between London and New York as necessary for the assurance of world peace. The allegory of Anglo-American cooperation was filmed on studio sets that rendered the tunnel and its construction as amplified versions of the London Tube, while the futuristic New York at one tunnel entrance was once again based on the modernist concepts of Le Corbusier (figure 4.6). The plotting pits heroic engineering against the forces of nature—an underground volcano that erupts, killing the engineer's son—and femininity—the English engineer's wife loses her sight during a visit to the tunnel construction site. The antiseptic, streamlined, masculine underground of the transatlantic tunnel cannot coexist with the organic, uncontrollable, feminine underground it is replacing.

4.4. A 1930s dream palace presides over the destruction of Everytown in an aerial bombardment in *Things to Come*. Frame enlargement from *Things to Come*, directed by William Cameron Menzies (London Film Productions, 1936). BFI Films: Stills, Posters and Designs.

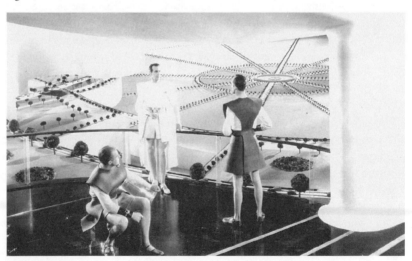

4.5. The Corbusian Radiant City realized in the rebuilt future of Everytown in *Things to Come*. Frame enlargement from *Things to Come*, directed by William Cameron Menzies (London Film Productions, 1936). BFI Films: Stills, Posters and

The film was based on a 1913 German novel by Bernhard Kellermann, and identical German and French versions were filmed two years earlier with a few alterations, locating the European entrance at an unspecified Continental location and downplaying the heroic engineering and plot of personal sacrifice in favor of straightforward industrial espionage and sabotage (figure 4.7). Pan-European production schemes echoed the pan-European thematic of the tunnel itself. By the end of the '30s, modernist space was as fully established a mode of representation as urban apocalypse, each predicated on the nonexistence of the other.

The entre-deux-guerres polarization of underground spaces reduced the distinction to a contrast between two views from above: the world as order and the world as chaos. The view from below, the everyday details of representational space, was obscured in both models. Just as the First World War had united all of Europe in destruction, and modernism had fostered a pan-European set of aesthetic ideologies, so was urban imagery from before the war opened out to encompass the continent as a whole, to make a spatial metaphor large enough to

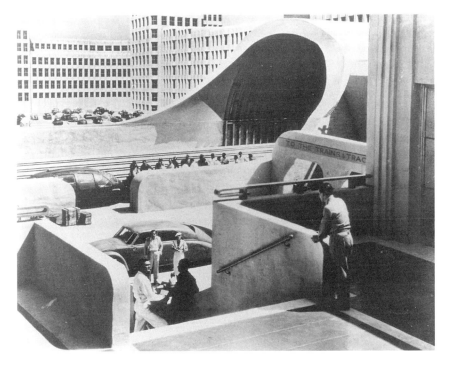

4.6. The clean, curved contours of the New York entrance to the Transatlantic Tunnel, with a modernist office block in the background. Frame enlargement from *Transatlantic Tunnel*, directed by Maurice Elvey (Gaumont, 1935). BFI Films: Stills, Posters and Designs.

4.7. Action scene from one of the two Continental adaptations of Bernhard Kellermann's novel, an early starring role for Jean Gabin. Publicity still from *Le Tunnel*, directed by Kurt Bernhardt (Vandor Films, 1933). BiFi: Bibliothèque du film.

deal with the war. Consequently, while London and Paris were still primary producers of subterranean representations, those representations were attached to abstract city types rather than to particular cityscapes. Other topographies, in particular the skyscraper/subway pairing of New York, emerged in their place. But there too, as also in Berlin, the focus was on the urban as symbol of modernist categories of alienation, order, or apocalypse rather than everyday experience.

This is not to say that such views did not exist and cannot be retrieved, but that theory as such dominated the intellectual and cultural life of this period, and theory privileges the representation of space over its practices. Consequently, the reception of the entre-deux-guerres has tended to keep the different spaces as far apart as possible, and to lean far too heavily on theoretical pronouncements and not heavily enough on the relation of those pronouncements to the spatial experience of their authors and the spatial practices expressed within their texts. Because the majority of present-day theories of culture as well as of present-day criteria of aesthetic valuation descend directly from the period of modernism between the wars, this incomplete reception remains an important issue of interpretation.

Modes of Hell in Postwar Europe

The concentration and death camps of the twentieth century, wherever they exist, under whatever régime, are *Hell made immanent.* They are the transference of Hell from below the earth to its surface. . . . To have neither Heaven nor Hell is to be intolerably deprived and alone in a world gone flat. Of the two, Hell proved the easier to recreate. (The pictures had always been more detailed.)

GEORGE STEINER, *In Bluebeard's Castle* (1971)

The polarized theorization of modernist space was transformed in practice by the Second World War, although its categories have continued to resonate as ruins long after their immediate historical application has passed. The trench had established a potent metonymical connection to the modern city; the bombing of Europe and the occupation of Paris made the connection literal: the modern city was indeed, for the first time, in ruins. While apocalyptic space became concrete and everyday, rationalized space was twisted to the infernal purpose of the final solution. The old myths of the underworld became newly tailored from city to city, while the image of hell on earth was grafted onto the methodical slaughter of the concentration camps.

The first modern urban apocalypse was the Battle of Britain. Unlike the Great War's uneasy combination of nineteenth-century battle order and hierarchy with modern weapons of slaughter, the response to the Blitz stressed the quotidian fabric of the city, a fact demonstrated by the resurgence of representational space in the London underground, a wholly understandable fondness for the shelter and society of what until then had been primarily an inorganic, utilitarian space. Not only were the tube stations taken over early on by shelterers in defiance of regulations, but makeshift subterranean space all over the city was appropriated as shelter, from Chislehurst Caves to church cellars and hotel basements to purpose-built deep shelters. By no means were these spaces egalitarian: West End hotels served champagne and caviar; Brompton Road featured motion pictures projected on the wall. But it is undeniable that one of the effects in London was to endow urban apocalypse with an everyday, experiential meaning as well as a metaphysical, cataclysmic one. In this light, the slogan "London can take it" of the celebrated documentary by Humphrey Jennings was not merely propaganda but a popular assertion of representational appropriation rather than merely abstract control over a disintegrating urban space.

Carol Reed's adaptation of Graham Greene's screenplay, *The Third Man* (1949), provided a characteristically displaced image of the Blitz as an allegory of postwar Europe. Shot in the rubble of a Vienna where it is always nighttime and every building seems a ruin, the film used the vertical topography of the city graphically to depict the psychic and material cost of the war. The city above is divided into four zones ruled by the Allied powers; the sewers below are the province of racketeer Harry Lime, played by Orson Welles as a Mephistophelean tempter able to traverse the muck-filled tunnels between the different sectors with nary a stain on his gleaming shoes (figure 4.8). The film is framed by Lime's two funerals, the first faked, the second real, as if its true subject were how to lay to rest the ghost of a past and vanished life. As Major Calloway (Trevor Howard), the hardened English officer working to shut down Harry's penicillin racket, comments upon the discovery that Lime is using the sewers to navigate the zones, "We should have dug deeper than the grave." For Harry's two friends, Holly Martins (Joseph Cotten), his naive childhood companion from America, and Anna Schmidt (Alida Valli), his tragically romantic lover from Prague, he represents not only a dark underworld of evil to which they cannot be reconciled but a past grown utopian in a memory that they will not give up. Anna's suicidal refusal to taint her memories with the knowledge of Harry's crimes is no more viable than Holly's betrayal of his friend in the name of an abstract justice that more than likely is merely screening a desire for his girl. When he steps off the train into 1949 Vienna, Holly has not seen his friend for ten years—since, that is, the declaration of war. When he finally shoots the wounded Harry dead, trapped like a rat by a sewer grate, the network of tunnels signifies less a triumph of law and order over filth—even though the extended chase scene stresses the organization and mobilization of the armed forces and their newfound control of the underground—than a recognition of an irrevocable fall from a moral certainty that has a place for loyalty and emotion. In an existentialist conclusion that would be echoed in other postwar sewer films such as Andrzej Wajda's *Kanal,* the underground is the only remaining refuge for human sentiments, but it is a filthy and degrading labyrinth that always results in death. To survive the war intact you had either to accept the flat new world it had left behind or to cling to a past haunted by horrible ghosts.

The experience of Paris took a different form than that in London, or for that matter the rest of Europe, for its apocalypse was psychological rather than physical. France and its capital were occupied with barely a shot fired, rather than bombed into submission. As Céline implied in his 1950s trilogy about the experience of occupation and collaboration, Paris during the war saw itself as a collection of shades waiting to be ferried down the river Seine by Charon into the afterlife. They were stuck, like the souls in Limbo, neither dead nor any longer alive. It was a potent metaphor, and it struck home in a France still resisting the degree of its responsibility for what had transpired during the war years. In its repudiation of the quotidian, it threw a blanket over the specific experiences and decisions made, a blanket of which Céline, for one, was desperately in need.[28] In the second volume of the trilogy, *North,* Céline opened out the scope of his vi-

4.8. Harry Lime (Orson Welles) finally about to get his shoes dirty in the climactic chase through the Vienna sewers in *The Third Man*. Frame enlargement from *The Third Man*, directed by Carol Reed (London Films Production/British Lion, 1949). BFI Films: Stills, Posters and Designs.

sion to the blasted landscape of Germany in defeat, rehearsing the apocalypse of the previous war all over again.

An even greater degree of abstraction is evident in Jean Giraudoux's play *The Madwoman of Chaillot,* written in 1942 but not performed until three years later. Although concretely set in the quartier of Chaillot right around the pont d'Alma, Giraudoux's play staged the threatened ruin of his beloved city as a metaphysical battle between what Reid terms "Paris *profonde"*—the so-called *folles* of the different quartiers, the ragpicker, the sewerman, a *plongeuse* (dishwasher)—and the forces of modernization—unscrupulous financiers and their henchmen, who believe the subsoil of Paris is rich in oil and plan to tear it to pieces to find it.[29] "Their newest edifice is nothing but the mannequin of a ruin," the madwoman complains. "They build quays by destroying the banks . . . towns by destroying the country . . . the palace of Chaillot by destroying the Trocadero. . . . Humanity's occupation is nothing but a universal enterprise of demolition."[30] In a denouement so broadly allegorical as to apply equally to the occupation, capitalist speculation, and modern urbanism, the eponymous Countess Aurelia lures the entire unwanted world above into a magical sewer-otherworld cul-de-sac from which no return is possible. The cityscape cleansed, vieux Paris returns, and a lost populace of smiling and courteous figures emerges from a different otherworld, transformed from animals, plants, and the madwoman's long-lost love. The use of a morality play quid pro quo and a conventional opposition between a whimsical, pastoral antiauthoritarian collective and a soulless and evil overclass betrays the inability to gain any distance on the wartime experience.[31] The filth is not even flushed out of the city—the positive space of the sewers would be tainted by it—much less transmuted into something comprehensible. Instead, it would be locked away in a subterranean closet from which it would slowly but inevitably seep out again during the subsequent half century.

Perhaps the most evocative demonstration of how this war had been different from the last, and of how collaboration had functioned, was the Parisian documentarist Chris Marker's short fiction film *La Jetée* (1962), which allusively addressed the occupation through a vision of the Third World War. Told almost entirely in still photographs, with a voiceover narration bridging the gaps between images, the film begins with a specific, obsessional memory: a man shot on the observation jetty at Orly Airport, watched, horrified, by a woman. This childhood memory is all that the unnamed protagonist possesses with which to remember the period he lived before nuclear war destroyed Paris, making the surface of the planet uninhabitable, and sending the survivors underground, where the victors conducted experiments on the losers. The film's subterranean spaces were photographed in the area beneath the Trocadero that housed the Monde Souterrain exhibit in 1900, and Marker included images of broken statues stored there as if mementos of that time.[32]

Now, while nineteenth-century narratives of the subterranean future seldom established a direct link between the city before and the civilization after the apocalypse, *La Jetée* is concerned with nothing else. The scientists of the future, seeking to find a way to survive in a postnuclear wasteland, experiment on their prisoners, sending them into the past so as eventually to learn how to send them for help to the future. Although it is never certain whether the time travel is mental or physical, the scenes in the present, in which the prisoner lies in a hammock, eyes covered, injected with drugs by sinister scientists who whisper in German, undeniably resonate both with images of Nazi camp doctors and with reports of French army torture of members of the FLN, the Algerian forces conducting a guerrilla war of independence at the time *La Jetée* was made.

Yet the journey into the past is driven as much by the prisoner's obsessive memory as by the force of his captors. He rediscovers images of Paris, he finds the woman on the jetty, he meets her in department stores, in parks, and in the Museum of Natural History. Piecemeal and transitory as it is, this past is happier by far than the subterranean present. At the same time, the use of still photographs creates an eerie distancing effect for the viewer. And while the single instance of movement, when the sleeping woman opens her eyes to stare at the camera, momentarily transcends the constraints of time and space, the lengthy subsequent sequence at the museum works in the opposite direction. Accumulated images of stuffed, dead animals, vast collections enclosed behind glass, suggest the mortification inherent in memories as snapshots, without movement, past and dead.

Following the museum sequence, the traveler is brutally pulled into the present, never to return to the past of his memories, and sent instead into the future, a Paris thousands of years hence. Unlike the analogous space of Everytown, however, this is a city unnavigable and unrecognizable, represented by magnified stills of plant cells, as if it were an organic organism beyond the comprehension of human perception. The inhabitants of the future hover in black space, a dark circle at their pineal eye indicating their ability to travel freely through time, just as, we assume, they have the perceptual ability to navigate a city neither above-nor underground. They send the traveler back to the Catacombes of Paris with the dynamo required to restart civilization. They then appear to the prisoner, offering him a place in the future; he chooses the past instead, and finds himself back on the jetty, running toward the woman in his memory, and shot down by a captor who had followed him. "The image he had remembered from his childhood," the voice-over concludes, "was an image of his own death."

Faced with the linear trajectory of apocalypse and the verticalized space of the prison, *La Jetée* proposes a circular vision of memory. It is not simply a solipsistic retreat from the pressures of history, however; the prisoner's story resonates both with the experience of a Parisian under the occupation seeking any escape from limbo, and with the ordeal of a concentration camp victim, whose very memories can be appropriated by his captors. Each resonance falls under the film's deathlike spell, the former a death of the spirit, the latter a mortification of the body. Moreover, in the moment of its production during the Algerian crisis, the film pointedly raised the question of the importance of remembering, whether for good or for ill, what had occurred in the past and been pushed underground, out of sight but not forgotten.

Narratives of and writing about the Holocaust have many times raised the question of how such an experience could even be represented. The postwar problem of the representation of hell is analogous to the problem of underground space in the nineteenth century, the choice between an individual experience, a view from below that would impart the raw violence and brutality of the events, and a view from above that would place it within an overarching but ameliorative framework of meaning. Many indeed are the memoirs of the Holocaust that have borrowed the infernal metaphor as the only possible framework with which to contain such an experience.[33] But the traditional inferno is insufficient precisely because the concentration camp was organized not as a conventional underworld but as an inorganic one. If it was indeed, as Steiner wrote, "hell made immanent,"[34] it was hell as it had never been seen before; not, perhaps, a worse hell in terms of numbers or suffering than that suffered during any other genocide, but a hell different in meaning because it realized for the first time the globally destructive potential of what most still believed to be the inherently utopian nature of the rational organization of space.

The traditional underworld was a perfectly suitable form with which to narrate, for instance, the Polish resistance, as in *Kanal* (1956). A surviving detachment of fighters flees the rubble aboveground for the sewers that will connect them to the sector of the city still held by the local forces (figure 4.9). As in the nineteenth-century sewer narrative, the city below retains the memory of vanished streets, a mirror image not of the present but of the past; the sewers of Warsaw remain partisan longer than the streets whose patterns they trace. This conviction is quickly overturned, however, as the force becomes lost in the labyrinth below, overwhelmed by the horror of the war its sewage transmits. The analogue to Harry Lime is Daisy, who navigates the sewers between the surrounded partisans and the other spaces of resistance; she is not morally compromised like Lime, but she is indelibly marked by her task. "You stink of the sewer" are the first words her lover, Jacek, says to her. She survives the final odyssey through the

4.9. Daisy (Teresa Izewska) and Jacek (Tadeusz Janczar) trapped in the infernal sewers beneath occupied Warsaw in *Kanal*. Frame enlargement from *Kanal*, directed by Andrzej Wajda (ZRF [Vereinigung der Film Regisseure] Gruppe "Kadr," Warsaw, 1956). BFI Films: Stills, Posters and Designs.

tunnels, only to be trapped with the dying Jacek at an iron grate blocking a drainage opening out of the sewer; a poet loses his way mentally and wanders the tunnels playing a sorrowful tune on his ocarina and reciting Dante; the leader of the group finds his way to what he believes to be the desired exit, emerges into the light, and is immediately taken prisoner by the Germans. The historical underpinnings are joined to an existential tone common to the '50s underworld, especially in narratives of Communist resistance: there was simply no way out.

Part of the problem with representing the Holocaust within this model is that there always was a way out of hell, because the narrative is generally based on or told from the point of view of a survivor who must, consequently, also account for the horror of surviving. Since the underworld had for several centuries been employed almost solely for the negative portrayal of subterraneans, almost always considered responsible whether morally or otherwise for their position, it is extremely difficult to appropriate those metaphorics to render the story of an innocent victim. At perhaps the only moment where Primo Levi allowed a poetic sentiment into his memoir of Auschwitz, it was to recite, translate, and explain the speech by Ulysses in Dante's *Inferno,* but he left no doubt that the noble sentiments and essential humanity of the damned soul were as nothing to the all-powerful authority beyond him: "And over our heads the hollow seas closed up," concludes the chapter.[35] As Levi makes painfully clear, the very fact of having survived implies the temporary denial of a basic humanity—clinging to it would have brought extinction. As he put it in a wrenching calque of the ancient dictum that the way to hell was easy but difficult the return, "If the drowned have no story, and single and broad is the path to perdition, the paths to salvation are many, difficult and improbable."[36] With the "third way" of middle-class life eliminated, the dehumanizing, degrading effects of life in society's hell to which the drowned have always fallen victim must be confronted for what they always were: intolerable and insufferable. The conventions of representation mitigate against that very realization, having no mode for giving meaning to the guiltless but by definition inhuman "paths to salvation." Levi's solution was to treat the camp as he would have any other social system; the resultant strain on conventional assumptions about identification and morality in some measure analogizes the strain on him as narrator, his eventual survival as unexpected as the accomplishment of the narrative gesture, and the otherworldly knowledge with which he returned from hell as undesired as the descent had been to begin with.

Other strategies could also be adopted beyond the katabasis, such as the act of remembering the humanity one had had before, the life aboveground, the countless heartbreaking narratives of lives cut short by the camps, a temporal verticalization with no return. Or there is the indirect approach of Alain Resnais' short documentary *Night and Fog* (1955), recounted solely through the contemporary space of the camps themselves and the traces of the prisoners left behind, the inhuman piles of hair, eyeglasses, shoes, modern reflections of the nineteenth-century dust piles, reminder that the Germans, like the inhabitants of the Victorian city, wasted nothing material (figure 4.10). More recent, more distanced versions such as Art Spiegelman's comic book diptych, *Maus: A Survivor's Tale* (1978–91), made evident what the movies already knew: that the only sphere of discourse where vertical representation of history might still work was in the pulp language of popular culture. While the high culture tradition of the descent to the underworld was laden with the epistemological assumption that descent and redemption, suffering and knowledge, were intertwined, Spiegelman's cat-and-mouse story not only borrowed the raw emotion and freedom from classical linear narratives characteristic of low culture, but neatly sidestepped the conventional subterranean scheme by making the concentration camp prisoners mice rather than rats. The complex formal structure and self-reflexivity of the narration allowed Spiegelman to negotiate the traditional perils of Holocaust representation on the one hand and the risk of sensationalism and reductionism on the other. While the narrative revolves around the *descensus ad inferos* of Auschwitz that closes the first volume, a series of miniature subterranea prepares the reader for the horror to come: the key chapter, "Mouse Holes," details a succession of hidden bunkers —a false coal hole, a false attic corner, the corner of a courtyard dustbin, the end of a tunnel through a mound of shoes—with the accompanying explanatory diagrams seeming to mock the objective distance of spatial representation. The same chapter mirrors these physically repugnant but dearly needed shelters with the psychological underground of the narrator's (and author's) 1973 account of the 1968 suicide of his mother (a Holocaust survivor) in *Prisoner on Hell Planet*, drawn in a mannerist style that partakes equally of Munchean expressionism and pulp postwar comic books. An expanded repertoire of subterranean spaces and associations lends depth and context to the central inferno, heightening its emotional power while urging a broader analysis of its implications.

Hiroshima posed fewer problems for representation, because it was such a clean, universal apocalypse, an instant obliteration of what had been. This, too, is a fantasy of the rational underworld, of the clean bomb dropped from the well-lubricated B-52. The greatest horror of Hiroshima is the lingering traces on those that did survive, the organic margins outside the perfect center. Why else did the bomb shelter present itself in '50s America as the perfectly individualized replication of the inorganic space, stocked with tinned foods, plastics, and hermetic seals? This was the rationality satirized in Stanley Kubrick's film *Dr. Strangelove*, which traced the fear of the organic through General Jack D. Ripper's obsession with fluoridated water, and drew out the organic lure of the underground in the American powers' happy retreat to a luxury shelter stocked not for short-term protection but for the long-term indulgence of every pleasure with no responsibility, the resurrection of a traditional fantasy of underground utopias. Back in Japan, the most powerfully resonant representation also turned out to be a comic

4.10. The Nazi version of Victorian dust piles, all too recognizable for what they really are. Frame enlargement from *Nuit et brouillard*, directed by Alain Resnais (Cocinor–Comptoir Cinématographique du Nord/Como Films [Paris]/Argos Films, 1955). BFI Films: Stills, Posters and Designs.

book, Keiji Nakazawa's *Hadashi no Gen* (*Barefoot Gen*, 1972–73), which used black-and-white drawings to capture the minutiae and the enormity of the horror of a city reduced to rubble and a populace transformed into "monsters" in a matter of seconds (figure 4.11). In the second volume, Nakazawa specifically drew out both the futility and the ancient resonance of subterranean space, introducing a wild band of orphaned children, pitiful bullies, who have transformed the air raid shelter into a clubhouse cum shelter, the last remnant of a perverted nationalistic innocence.[37]

The traumatic shock effects of Hiroshima and Nagasaki do seem partly to explain a national penchant for imagining verticalized urban spaces matched only in postwar global culture by the case of New York discussed below. Particularly in the last couple of decades, Japanese *manga* and anime have made futuristic, apocalyptic cities, either literally or figuratively buried belowground à la *Metropolis* and *Blade Runner,* into a stock element. The work of probably Japan's best and certainly its most popular living novelist, Haruki Murakami, has made the connection of this obsession with the meanings of underground space to the history of Japan during the war and to the contemporary cityscape of Tokyo a funda-

4.11. *Barefoot Gen*: using the comic book format and the child's perspective to render the immediacy of an intolerable experience. Keiji Nakazawa, *Barefoot Gen: A Cartoon Story of Hiroshima*, tr. Project Gen, 1987 (San Francisco: Last Gasp of San Francisco, 2003): 244–45. Reproduced by permission from Keiji Nakazawa and Last Gasp of San Francisco.

mental component of his oeuvre. In his oral history of the sarin gas attacks on the Tokyo subway that killed eleven and injured over five thousand persons in 1995, Murakami noted that his two novels most concerned with underground spaces, *Hard-Boiled Wonderland and the End of the World* (1991) and *The Wind-Up Bird Chronicle* (1994–95), bracketed a self-imposed exile and sense of estrangement from his own culture.[38] The earlier novel had imagined a battle beneath Tokyo to contain the mysterious Inklings, "horrible creatures, they have no eyes and feed on rotting flesh." The later book took on the Japanese past directly, reaching back to the war in Manchuria through the medium of a deep well in a Tokyo backyard and a more metaphorical sense of a dreamworld of other dimensions. The well is dried up, blocked, and in darkness; it must be made to flow again to restore equilibrium and memory, both personal and historical. Dealing with the preponderance of what he called "comic strip" memories of the gas attacks that rejected the Aun cult members as incomprehensible Inklings inhabiting an "impenetrably dark world," rather than products of Japanese culture, Murakami seemed to question the utility of his own narratives, where the vertical division between a proper social surface and a repressed id has always been taken for granted. His culture was trapped, he implied, between a periodic need for "the gentle healing embrace of darkness" and a set of narratives, including his own, that could portray the underworld only in terms of alienness and apocalypse. The underground was the most powerful image for bringing trauma to the surface but could not be imagined outside of the framework of those traumas. In Murakami's fiction, this dilemma manifests itself in an assertion that the only mode of access to social space, memory, and history is through wholly individualized undergrounds and similarly private spaces: the solipsistic, dream-like worlds into which his characters so frequently lose themselves in their search for something beyond the banality of everyday life. The two spheres could be separated, as in the polarized title images of *South of the Border, West of the Sun* (1993), but never fully dissociated from a sense of uncanny forces and a more or less tragic resolution.

A similar dilemma emerged from Emir Kusturica's controversial allegorical film of postwar Yugoslavia, *Underground* (1995), which opened on an apocalyptic sequence of the bombing of Belgrade during World War II and concluded with a second, less defined sequence of war and chaos related to the breakup of Yugoslavia and the war in Bosnia. In between, an entire community is kept sealed up in a vast cellar under the belief that they are producing arms for the wartime resistance. As with Don Delillo's novel *Underworld* (1999) and Murakami's *Wind-Up Bird Chronicle,* the subterranean is employed as a spatial metaphor to unite a disparate and otherwise incoherent set of secret and repressed histories of the second half of the twentieth century, as if the war had managed to hide everything of importance out of sight. Kusturica's film differs from the pair of fin-de-siècle summas in two important ways. First, it materialized its underground in the half-utopia half-prison of the munitions workshop. Moreover, as the complex deception of the arms dealer Blackie crumbles, and the subterraneans surface, Kusturica opens up his perspective to incorporate a brilliant spatial metaphor of the new European community, a network of vast sewer and drainage tunnels crisscrossing the continent for a new generation of Harry Limes to travel at will. Aboveground, economic refugees die daily trying to cross the boundaries of fortress Europe; hidden from view, illegal business has no trouble at all. His underground vision had no basis in historical or architectural fact, just as it was wide open to criticism for its polemical reading of postwar Yugoslavia, but Kusturica's phantasmagoric take on a vertically split Europe took full advantage of the still powerful resonance of the spatial representation.

These late twentieth-century recourses to the archetypal underground to frame a rereading of postwar culture were willing to embrace cliché in order to overturn what they regard as complacency and received ideas. For most of the second half of the century, the legacy of World War Two was a set of infernal experiences, the most enduring ideology of which was that they were unique events. Faced with the irresolvable contradiction of the concentration camps between rationalized slaughter and individual survival, the twentieth century revealed what had always been the plight of the urban poor and the underground worker, as well as the brutal illusion of the simple elimination of any past whatsoever in Hiroshima and Nagasaki. To be sure, this was a necessary ideology at the time: it focused attention on horrors that would otherwise have been glossed over as every other horror of the modern world is quickly glossed over. But it became a compromised ideology as time passed; for it obscured ways in which both events did in fact also fit with perfect and easy logic into the space of the modern world, and could be viewed on a continuum with those other phenomena that had been principally regarded as infernal. This begins, certainly, with the material experience of the ruined cities of Europe, but it extends in terms of mass extermination to the experience of the Stalinist Soviet Union, and in terms of individual responsibility to the many details of collaboration and betrayal that never can be accounted for in a global framework.

It extends to the more recent genocidal wars in Europe and Africa, which have instead primarily been received in terms of the degradation model of the nineteenth-century underground, all knowledge of world complicity and responsibility that had been made available by the Holocaust crisis in representation once again conveniently forgotten because it was not part of the underground space of savage lands and dark continents. And it extends to the cultural and economic genocide waged, as it was in the prior century, by capitalist exploitation all over the globe, which follows the same rationalized exploitation of space perfected by the Nazi camps, and no less visibly, nor with any lower a threshold of denial. Herein lies one reason for the other problematic raised by the Holocaust as the events and those who remember them as lived experiences recede into the past: the primary iconography has become dissociated from the events that so powerfully galvanized it, and has itself become spectacle and cliché, full of visceral horror but bereft of historical insight. This is amply demonstrated, for example, by the nine tableaux of model death camps that constitute English artists Jake and Dinos Chapman's *Hell* (1998–2000).[39] Arranged on tables supported by green planks and arranged in the shape of a swastika, these fiendishly intricate sculptures of tiny, sexually mutated, and physically mutilated plastic soldiers and prisoners take the representation of the Holocaust to a pitch of graphic violence heretofore seen only, if anywhere, in the extremes of exploitation cinema. Pits of mangled bodies frozen in resin, individual couplings realizing the wildest fantasies of the Marquis de Sade, thwarted prison escapes, death trains, killing fields and torture chambers, all cut away to provide a clear sight line to the enterprising viewer with an eye for detail, looking down from the Olympian heights of the sheltered present. Rather than limit their palette to the Holocaust, however, the Chapman brothers toss in iconography from the trenches, from Vietnam, and from the many ways in which the horrors of war have lent themselves in the so-called postwar era to the pleasures of spectacle. The underlying visual metaphor references the adolescent male in his playroom, building model railroads and imagining ever more recondite ways to destroy his toy soldiers. This is less a jejeune satire on the machismo of warfare than a reckoning with the inevitable allure of violence. Most of us neither act out our repressed fantasies nor suffer directly from the acting out of others; instead, we are simultaneously drawn to and repulsed by the subterranean impulses of others whenever they are exposed to the world, the more spectacularly the better.

It is far easier, in other words, realistically to represent the point of view of the perpetrator than the point of view of the victim. What the Chapmans' *Hell* suggests is the degree to which the latter has receded from view while the former has been quite successfully streamlined to the quality of spectacle. Indeed, the only thing that could be said to rescue these tableaux from the status of exploitation is the very adolescent obsessiveness and verve with which they have been painstakingly executed. Their modeling subtext captures the imagination of war in the unrefined rawness of the adolescent who has not yet learned to channel his fantasies in a socially mature fashion; only as art could these images in this form appear in public, and the fact that they can appear at all testifies to the replacement of the shock of the experience they represent with an iconography of horror no longer associated directly with that experience. The seductive imagery of underground space can no longer, as it did in the nineteenth century, place us in direct contact with the spaces of exploitation and contradiction; for these spaces are no longer literally underground for the most part. What it can do is provide contrasting as well as resembling images for those spaces that are at the current margins, both beneath our feet, where we no longer look for them, and far away, where we no longer see them. The vertical model is unlikely to lose its efficacy and potency either as a weapon of disenchantment or as a tool of exploitation; what we must not forget is its fundamental incommensurability with the actual shape of the world in which we live.

The Mole People and Global Space

There were people in the late seventies who used the tunnels occasionally to get high or whatever, but it wasn't until the eighties that people started settling in, living down here.

Tunnel dweller SEVILLE WILLIAMS (quoted by Jennifer Toth in
The Mole People: Life in the Tunnels beneath New York City [1993])

There were times, travelling on the Tokyo subway after writing this novel, when I'd fantasize seeing Inklings "out there" in the darkness. I'd imagine them rolling a boulder into the path of the train, cutting off the power, breaking the windows and overrunning the carriages, ripping us to shreds with their razor-sharp teeth.

HARUKI MURAKAMI, *Underground: The Tokyo
Gas Attack and the Japanese Psyche* (1997)

The comic book and the imagery of popular culture have at times been able to deal with the legacy of the Second World War in innovative and effective ways because their tropes tend to universalize everyday experience and eschew dominant representations of space. For them, no taboo is off limits: witness for instance Walter Moers's recent series, *Adolf* (1998–2002), in which it is revealed that "the Nazi-swine" has spent the past fifty-odd years hiding in the sewers until he decides it is safe to emerge to "start a new life" (figure 4.12).⁴⁰ There is no need to press the allegorical undertones; because its characters and situations are based in cliché, they wear their symbolism neither lightly nor heavily, but simply on the surface. The sewers of history breed monsters, and within them Adolf has survived perfectly well, as a short bit of Web surfing through the less savory zones of the Internet easily demonstrates. Moreover, Moers's Adolf takes his place alongside a whole pantheon of misbegotten creatures of the deep, properly organic and atavistic in character, and deeply subversive and dangerous to boot. It is fitting, then, that he is first glimpsed stealing a spoonful from a soup pot in the "Cooking-Hell of Dr. Biolek," forecasting perhaps a genetically modified future or a biotech nightmare descendant of Nazi eugenics. Such apocalyptic fantasies ran rampant in the aftermath of the Second World War in a nuclear mode, and the cities were always the target, both in the patently cold war–inspired monster movies of the 1950s, such as *Them!* (1954), where mutated ants took over the storm drains of Los Angeles (figure 4.13), and in *Godzilla* (1956) and the host of monster movies that followed it in Japan through the '60s. It was not until the 1970s, however, that this postwar urban mythology uneasily reconnected with the urban population with which it had been joined in nineteenth-century Paris and London. In a bankrupt New York City blanketed with graffiti, awash in crime and drowning in poverty, the sewer monsters recovered their old under-world referents beneath the streets of Manhattan.

From the end of the 1970's until they were driven out by transit police and other authorities in the late 1990s, there were over five thousand people living either permanently or transiently in the vast network of subway and railway tun-

4.12. The sewers of history breed monsters: Frame 1: "Adolf, the Nazi swine. No. 1—I'm back!" Frame 2: "In the Cooking-Hell of Dr. Biolek.—Hmmm! Delicious! Delicious!" Frame 3: "Let's recall the events: unfortunately, Adolf had lost the Second World War and was forced to go underground. For years he has been living in the sewers with time to reflect on his mistakes . . .—I ought to have attacked Russia harder on the flanks." Frame 4: "Then finally the statute of limitations for his crimes expires.—Ah . . . fresh air." Frame 5: "However—can Adolf overcome the shadow of the past . . . !? Here begins his struggle for a new life . . . 'Sein Kampf,' as it were." From Walter Moers, *Adolf* (Frankfurt am Main: Eichborn Verlag, 2000): [5]. © Eichborn AG, Frankfurt am Main, 1998, S. 5.

4.13. In the film *Them!*, monstrous ants born of cold war obsessions leave their irradiated nests in the Nevada desert for the inhospitable but well-provisioned storm drains of Los Angeles. Frame enlargement from *Them!*, directed by Gordon Douglas (Warner Brothers, 1954). BFI Films: Stills, Posters and Designs.

nels below Manhattan.[41] Until the first journalistic reports and sympathetic studies on this population appeared in the early '90s, however, they were an urban myth—the "mole people"—and their presence was more visible in a series of horror movies and television dramas than as a phenomenon of homelessness. Their representation derived primarily from two earlier literary images: the legend of giant alligators living in the sewers popularized first by Thomas Pynchon's novel *V* (1963) and then by the horror movie *Alligator* (1980), and the fictional depiction by Richard Wright in "The Man Who Lived Underground" (1944) and Ralph Ellison in *Invisible Man* (1952) of blackness in America as a subterranean condition. The class-based vertical metaphorics of Victorian Paris and London returned in New York City as a representation of race relations.[42] In the view from below, they came to the surface as a potent but monstrous and brutal force of destruction: neo-Morlocks mutated by toxic waste into "Cannibalistic Humanoid Underground Dwellers" in *C.H.U.D.* (1984), or the reptile glutted with biohazardous waste in *Alligator* that took particular pleasure in its revenge on the CEO of the company whose corruption had produced it. In the view from above, they took a kinder and gentler but well-contained form, as in the cult fantasy-drama television series *Beauty and the Beast* (1987–90), in which a neo-Victorian cum medievalist pastoral community beneath the hills of Central Park provides the perfect setting for an unrequited interracial romance between Vincent the "Beast" (Ron Perlman) and Catherine the "Beauty" (Linda Hamilton). Although traces of both modes of representation would manifest themselves in the oral history collected in the 1990s, neither came close to even suggesting that there was a material basis for the twin popular fantasies.

As that material basis finally surfaced in the '90s, it became clear that what had happened beneath New York in the previous decade was unprecedented except in times of war. Somewhere beneath Grand Central Station was an underground community with its own mayor, certified teachers and nurses, laundry and bathing facilities, its members repeating the familiar litany of subterranean utopia: an ethics based on "caring and protecting our brothers and sisters, on communication and love."[43] In an Amtrak tunnel under Riverside Park on the West Side was a more loosely knit group of tunnel dwellers seeking the basic necessities of life—shelter and security—down where they have always been sought.[44] Scattered throughout the system were the underground city's loners and its own "underworld," like the Dark Angel, a white man with glowing red eyes, feared by all who journeyed underground, either because he was dangerously insane or because he wielded satanic powers.[45] The population was diverse in age, sex, and ethnicity, just as it varied in modes of living and degrees of permanence. It engaged in squatting and scavenging to a degree that would appear ridiculous if not for the dignity and humanity with which most of the subjects carry themselves throughout the documentation.

The material manifestation of an appropriation of space wholly opposite to the rampant gentrification and corporate greed occurring in the streets and skyscrapers above it proved as irresistible to the imagination as the convergence of space and representation in London and Paris had done during the previous century. What was striking about the New York episode, and what has given it such mythic resonance, is its stark realization of the proximity of the privileged world above and the desperate world below. The willingness of thousands of New Yorkers to live under conditions that contradicted what are held to be the basic requirements of human beings—light and air—gave the lie to the ideology that such requirements were, in fact, available to all aboveground. It equally demonstrated that other necessities—shelter and independence—could be held even more dearly than those basic requirements. After all, working and living conditions for common laborers have for centuries proven that light and air are not in the least necessary for survival (at least in the short term). There is no need, one hopes, to accumulate evidence of ways in which living conditions in many contemporary cities exceed in horror even those recorded in the nineteenth-century metropolis. Pictures of shantytowns and favelas, however, are not what shock most these days; they are familiar to the point of having become second nature, and feel like a permanent part of the natural landscape, an acceptable if unpleasant way of living. What has maintained the capacity to shock in the current turn of the century are accounts of the appropriation of inorganic space, especially underground, for habitation. The mole people lived in conditions no worse than plenty of the inhabitants of New York slums, but they did so in space normally represented as being uninhabitable. They lived in no more squalor and filth than plenty of slum dwellers, but they did so in space identified as suitable only for waste. Consequently, the only urban representational mode available was the apocalyptic: if human beings can accept such conditions, either they as individuals are monstrous or the society in which they live must be so.

Single men in Hong Kong rent cages stacked on top of one another in windowless rooms, sleeping in shifts. Illegal immigrants desperate to enter the developed world travel for days sealed in the holds of ships or in the backs of trucks, materializing their identity as human waste, yet hoping at the same time to escape from their underworld journey transmuted into something else. More and more children live in sewers and subway tunnels all over the world.[46] In Bogotá, Colombia, petroleum engineer Jaime Jaramillo discovered an entire community of homeless children in the drainage tunnels of the city's sewers. In his book on this community, he unconsciously echoed the rhetoric of *The Wild Boys of London,* entitling his account, *Los Hijos de la oscuridad.* The central episode of the book was the story of the rescue of an "authentic child of darkness," Milton, the son of thirteen-year-old sewer dweller Blanca, who had been born and spent every moment of his two-year-old life underground.[47] In one sense, the story of Milton is no different from that of any other child born in a threshold space, a space not intended as the setting for any significant event—on a bus, in a taxi—except that those human-interest stories seek the heartwarming effect that comes from the transformation of a threshold space into a positive, lived space. Milton's story employs the opposite effect: the horror that the natural event most associated with purity and life should take place in the space most associated with filth and decay: "Human refuse floated past. . . . Fleas, cockroaches, and rats were the other witnesses of Milton's birth."[48] In its direct appeal to the emotions and charity of his readers, Jaramillo's rhetoric testifies to the enduring power of such clichés of contradiction.

Even in the claim to the novel extremity of its shock effect, the rhetoric duplicates the mid-nineteenth-century language of Reynolds's *Mysteries of London,* in which each terrible space can be distinguished from the others only by further superlatives. The limits of such rhetoric lie in the fact that Jaramillo's direct appeal can hope to work only by finding a new extreme of degradation, the child born in the sewers. The more the object of pity and fear is transmuted into a mythic image—the sewer alligator, the mole people, the end of the world as we know it—the greater chance it has of persisting in the cultural imagination, and the greater chance of attracting both charitable and institutional attention, for better or for worse. At the same time, the more it is mythified, the more it also loses its humanity, the attachment to everyday life that makes it recognizable to us as an equal.

There is in fact very little that one could qualify as purely abstract space in what is generally called the developing world; nothing is wasted, and nearly every space is appropriated in myriad ways by the sheer weight of poverty and numbers. There is also little that one could call an empty space, and little that one could term an inorganic space, for there are always, everywhere visible, pressing traces of the organic experience of human life at its most material. The myth of this discourse is that, like that of Paris in the previous century, it is distinct from the discourse of its counterpart, the developed world, where the illusion of inorganic, rational space can for the most part be maintained precisely because the developing world functions in this manner. Abstract space does exist in the developing world, but only in its most invisible, speculative form as finance capital. The media representation in the developed world of the crises of the developing world proffers the same absolute truths as the nineteenth-century sewer—birth, excretion, death—but only in their negative image as disaster, the very scale of which renders them abstract and apocalyptic. It follows the conventional pattern of the urban mystery: the crises *are* in the developing world, the situation *is* apocalyptic, it is just that the real causes and the real solutions lie elsewhere, in a different grasp of space that would refuse the separation between above and below.

The urban crises of the developed world duplicate in microcosm the global spatial division, and the progress is the same. Whereas the last decades of the twentieth century saw the Western city, particularly New York and Los Angeles, in full-fledged apocalyptic mode, with entire urban zones given over to underworld identities, the reclamation of downtown as spectacle has asserted a different sort of space. Christine Boyer has well documented the Victorian revival that remakes urban communities as preservation zones, fixing the downtown into an abstract concept of the past. Just as the inorganic underground space of the mall replaces the traditional urban underworld, so the "old town" fixes a specific image of the past in place of a complex and unprofitable quotidian present. Disney's Times Square pushes out the seedy, teeming vice of the past, which is not eliminated but relocated out of the tourists' sight in Long Island City and Sunset Park. Even that quintessentially transitional space, the public toilet, has gotten a makeover. When not eliminated, like the old pissoirs in Paris—which were far too exposed to continue functioning as the subterranean space they so clearly were—underground conveniences have been converted, as in London or in Eastern Europe, into cafés, bars, nightclubs, and boutiques. The brief descent and the elaborate tiling summon up enough Victorian ambiance to make a nice blend with the frisson of underworld perversion and filth.

The full consequences of this transformation can be grasped only with a comprehensive account of the spaces involved.[49] The Victorian revival has economically revitalized derelict downtowns in a repetition of the pattern of Victorian metropolitan improvement. The former residents get pushed out, the space gets cleaned up, the investors get rich. What is novel is that instead of constituting the particular form of the spectacle in which the new space is packaged, it is the underworld itself that provides the primary spectacle. It's a rare urban blockbuster film that lacks an action sequence (what the Victorians used to call a sensation scene) in a derelict urban underground completely at odds with the inorganic space presented by the city itself. That is, if Manhattan has never been safer, cleaner, and more orderly, its sewers, subways, and slums have never been more present in pop-culture spectacle, and never depicted as more dangerous, degraded, or explosive. Where the arches in Victorian London sheltered underworld occupations, now they shelter nostalgia for the underworld: the London Dungeon, an exhibition of atrocities in English history, occupies the arches under London Bridge station (figure 4.14); down the road a renovated prison competes for leftover tourists; clubs beneath the South London arches pump drum-and-bass through the night; Vinopolis renovates the wine storage vaults of Southwark as a paradise of consumption with just a hint of the hells of old London; even old public toilets have been imbued with a new cachet.

But while turn-of-the-century capitalism appears to have hit upon the efficient formula for packaging the outmoded cityscape, the other side of the Victorian underground—its role as a symbolization of the novel crises of the modernizing city—has been pressed into service in visualizing and containing the rest of the world, the conditions of which resemble nothing more than the stratified society of nineteenth-century London and Paris. There is little that is seductive about the Victorian underworld as applied to the developing world, however, for there is no longer anything powerful or utopian attached to it. In this, it is closer to the London discourse, in which the positive underground could be located only in the country. The twin to the developing world as apocalyptic drainage system is the rain forest as a vanishing pastoral underworld. Neither image is wholly false any more than are Boyer's and others' analyses of the alienated space of the contemporary city as entertainment, but each is incomplete without the other.

The view from above dismisses the urban dreamscape as satanic alienation, the decadence and death of the traditional city; the view from below reveals the horrible physical destruction being wrought throughout the developing world as an image of primitivism and savagery. At the representative centers of capital, meanwhile, a different revolution is underway, the revolution of information technology, which promises a total transformation of global space of a different order. The representational space proper to this revolution has turned out to be the inorganic space first developed in the transport revolution at the end of the nineteenth century, a space hermetically sealed from the outside world, a purely practical but also purely theoretical space. Even as more and more persons are finding shelter below in the now naturalized, partially ruined forerunners of this space—in the

4.14. "Enter at Your Peril": the visible face of the Victorian revival under the viaduct just south of London Bridge station in Southwark. Photo by author of the entrance to the "London Dungeon," Tooley Street, Southwark, 2000.

subway tunnels and sewage ducts built a hundred years ago or more—more and more surface dwellers are spending their lives in the artificial undergrounds of the office cubicle, bereft of the same qualities—natural air and natural light—they bemoan in horror to be lacking in the lives of the mole people.

Like previous revolutions in spatial practice, the information technology revolution threatens to solidify an even greater segregation between the haves and the have-nots, between those who are networked and those who are not. In its metaphors, however—cyberspace, networks, online, Web pages, e-commerce—the Internet has thus far avoided a vertical conception of space. Even the underworld of cyberspace is not localized as such; hackers and disseminators of computer viruses have not for the most part either embraced underground identities or been labeled with them. Underground space no longer represents positive utopia but only negative, regressive fantasies: cyberspace has in fact been embraced by real-world underground organizations around the world eager to spread information and raise money and awareness of their causes; Luddite antiglobalization movements have similarly embraced the technology of the Web to forward their alternative causes. The attributes of the Web—the anonymity promised by its enormity, the staggering multiplicity of its offerings, the impossibility of fixing the truth of anything offered on it—are highly reminiscent of representations of the nineteenth-century city as simultaneously the center of power and wealth and the center of opposition and difference of every kind. But the IT revolution has eschewed the urban metaphors that go along with the vertical representation of space. It is an inescapable if undesirable conclusion that the city is no longer the repository of mainstream utopia.

The city, which had long been identified as an underground space, has instead acquired the imaginary status of a ruin. The capitals of the developed world are being transformed into packaged, aestheticized relics akin to the Subterranean World exhibit of the previous turn of the century; the capitals of the developing world are being transformed into literal ruins. In contemporary representations of space, the city has moved to the periphery of abstract space. It is a pretty picture: one set of cities as amusement parks, one set as garbage dumps, and the world above them a set of computer screens seamlessly linked one to another in a different space entirely. The same split is reproduced, albeit with far less media attention, within the United States as well. Witness the tradition of "Devil's Night," which began on the night before Halloween in 1983 in Detroit, when pranksters set fire to the old houses and warehouses of the all-black inner city, most of them vacated in the flight to the suburbs or to somewhere with jobs.[50] The annual conflagration, mixing underground rage with large-scale vandalism, was soon drawing crowds from all over the world to the artificial spectacle reproducing the physical effects of the race riots of earlier decades with none of the political charge. Photographer and urbanist Camilo Vergara has painstakingly documented the physical disintegration of the American inner cities, cities like Detroit, Newark, or Camden that have none of the symbolic weight of New York or Los Angeles, where the submerged truths currently representable only as urban apocalypse emerge with a clear and unadulterated reckoning of their human and economic costs.[51] The only thing new to grow in these blasted spaces is an inorganic underground: the fortress architecture of policing and social services designed to be impregnable from the crumbling cityscape around it.

Cyberspace is the most nearly perfect repudiation yet produced of those irreducible facts of life that have always been associated with subterranean space, and that were attached for the past few centuries to urban space: death, destruction, and decomposition. The Internet promises freedom from fixed identity, from fixed corporeality, from lived space. The utopian aspirations of this promise should not be underestimated: a freedom from physical necessities that would eventually result in immortality. The inorganic underground has always promised freedom from the organic, and, like the physical counterparts of cyberspace—the material spaces in which even the most addicted net surfer must still deposit his or her body, the overtaxed urban-based power grids that fuel the information age—it aspires to the condition of an absolute space, a space that need not be verticalized because there is no outside from which it needs to be distanced.

The much discussed end-of-the-century blockbuster film *The Matrix* (1999) took as its eminently plausible premise the identity of this fantasy of cyberspace as the newest allegory for capitalism. The city of the future—and it is important to its meaning that the film renovated both the city and the organic underground as setting and counterimage to the Matrix—is a computer-generated mass illusion fed through cable ports into human bodies fixed in vast pod communities beneath the surface of the planet. The bodies are kept mentally alive by the images of the Matrix while being harvested by robots that use the heat generated by the bodies to produce the power necessary to fuel their own society. As no system, however perfect, is without its contradictions, so here a rebel movement has somehow emerged, peopled by individuals who have been freed from their pods and inhabit a secret city deep within the earth's core, where the last dissipating traces of natural heat can still to be found. The rebels travel through the vast sewage network that seams the planet's interior, plugging in and out of the Matrix with their own hacking programs, waiting for a messiah, the foretold One who will have the ability to see through and thus manipulate the complexity of the Matrix's program for what it is, a stream of encoded numbers, a pattern of meaning rather than a material reality.

As at least one reviewer noted, two fundamental truths are asserted during the course of the film that mitigate its otherwise wholly traditional narrative of underground revolution: first, the traitor's preference for a wholly persuasive illusion of happiness over the filthy, hard, and unrewarding life of the rebel; and two, the robot-agent Smith's assertion that humans are like a virus on the planet, sowing destruction wherever they go, disrupting the natural system as no other species has done. These two truths enunciate the double meaning of capitalism: its seductive promise of absolute happiness, even if one knows that that promise is in the final analysis illusory and comes at the cost of physical and mental enslavement; and its practice of absolute exploitation and destruction of everything it encounters.

The Matrix used the now-obsolete metaphorics of the underground to resurrect a traditional tale of revolution from below, but it cleverly adapted that tale to the obsolescence of the city itself, self-consciously playing on its own appropriation of the imagery of the contemporary cinematic spectacle. Transport out of the Matrix is initiated through the contemporary technology of product-placed cellular phones, but achieved through the archaic technology of derelict pay phones and rotary dialers in seedy hotels. The urban illusion of the Matrix, in keeping with turn-of-the-century aesthetics, presented the city to its wards in all of its nostalgic multiplicity. The oracle to which the hero, Neo, is taken by his mentor, Morpheus, is an African American matriarch ensconced in a burnt-out housing project high-rise. When on their way to an exit phone in another old hotel, the rebels are trapped by a change in the Matrix's program, transforming the organic ruin into a sealed-off, bricked-up cul-de-sac; they escape by finding the contradiction in the space, shimmying down through the shaft between two walls normally traversed only by the cockroaches and rats of decaying housing stock. Neo's penultimate battle with agent Smith occurs when he is trapped within a crumbling subway station.

Although it cloaked its narrative and visuals in the familiar and comforting mythology of the urban underworld, *The Matrix*, like its rebels, equally appropriated and innovated upon the cutting-edge technology of the computing world that its ideology attacked.[52] Through the skills of their alternative programmers, the rebels can both materialize and instantly master any military or other technology needed to survive in the Matrix. The film itself, analogously, won Academy Awards for the computer graphics whereby it simulated the effects of Neo's growing mastery of the system of the Matrix, his ability to bend around flying bullets and to manipulate the space around him in any manner he pleases. The basis of this skill, however, derived not from computers but from the martial arts, and not from Hollywood but from the alternative entertainment industry of Hong Kong, whence the directors, Andy and Larry Wachowski, recruited the celebrated action director Yuen Woo-Ping to lend the film an acrobatically physical component rarely seen before then in Hollywood fare.

Although its conclusion fell into the predictable utopian apocalypticism of the absolute freedom following the destruction of the entire system of oppression—Neo ends the film by crashing the Matrix—the film's overall message is more conflicted. While it certainly embodied with utter self-consciousness the very system of illusion its narrative demolished, to the point of engendering two over-hyped sequels that attempted unsuccessfully to duplicate its tightrope walk between critique and commodification, its analysis of the system in which it participated was as sophisticated as the technology it so skillfully manipulated for the expression of that analysis. Its resolution may have been facile, but its portrayal of the interconnection between the contemporary space of the inorganic underground and the outmoded but still present organic underground, of the ideology of new technology and its allures and disadvantages, was unusually sophisticated and persuasive.[53] In place of the hand-wringing media response to the confusion between fiction and reality perpetrated by the Matrix-world onto its fans, or critiques of the Wachowski brothers' complicity with the system, I prefer to hypothesize a global audience enthralled with a vision of the contemporary world that could be so entertaining and so on-target at the same time. No underground movement will ever succeed that cannot combine these two inimical qualities, even if the ill-judged (if eye-pleasing) spectacle of Zion's multiethnic rave culture in *The Matrix Reloaded* can serve as an object lesson in how transitory the analytical effect of such a vision can be.

To take another example of the way in which the seductive apocalyptic of the organic underground can be meshed with the spaceless ideology of information technology, witness how the quickly forgotten mass hysteria over the Y2K bug succeeded both in uncovering the tenuous hold of the representation of the computer world as a perfectly controlled, rational space, and in showing the degree to which that space was in fact rational and controlled. More money was spent controlling a cyberspace that turned out to be in no particular need of control than has been spent doing anything at all about a global underground for which the computer remains an alien object. Apocalyptic fantasies of the reversion of a computer-led world run rampant saw the inorganic space quickly degenerating into the worst nightmare of an organic underground, the negative image of the utopian revolution envisioned by *The Matrix* and so much speculative fiction before it. When the real-space analogue of Y2K manifested itself nearly four years later, it took the eminently material form of the blackout of 2003, when a chain-reaction crashed the entire power grid of the northeast corridor, crippling nearly every aspect of an urban infrastructure whose every facet (and faucet), from ATMs to cell phones to the water supply, turned out to be powered by electricity. The only surprise greater than the realization at how easily cyberspace could be grounded and how decrepit the system providing for it had become was the nearly total absence of any of the negative activities so closely associated with urban night—there was no apocalypse, no Devil's Night, just relief that it was only a blackout and nothing worse.

What has become clear through these events is that the information revolution, while eschewing any metaphorical relation to the urban underground, exhibits the same crises and contradictions as the space of the nineteenth century, or as any space does that must be absolutely controlled in order for its ideology to function. The promises of the Internet have served only to separate further those who can afford the ever more expensive and sophisticated technologies of high-speed access from the billions of people who do not even have access to electricity, much less a home computer. Moreover, in practice, the Internet has lent itself just as well, if not better, to illicit as to licit commerce. Every activity traditionally relegated to subterranean space has found a use for the Internet, from child pornography to terrorism to organized crime. Saboteurs generate new viruses at a rate slightly faster than antivirus programs can be written to counter them. Control, surveillance, and privacy are combative and irresolvable issues just as they were in the previous centuries. Nothing has changed but the representation of the terrain of combat.

The era in which the industrial city and its social and spatial divisions dominated the representation of capital appears to have passed. More recently, the movement of capitalism into the exploitation of everyday life has also been completed and left behind. Cultural criticism of the spectacle from the situationists on must now reckon with the incompleteness of that development, and begin sifting through the cracks and rifts in the now firmly established spatial representations of the quotidian. Movies such as *The Matrix* suggest that the center of development is currently shifting into spaces that an earlier critic like Lefebvre would scarcely have recognized as possible. The appropriation of underground space to a global division along Lefebvre's tripartite scheme suggests that the information revolution has made possible a global conception of the world as an exploitable space. The city, the underground, the quotidian are no longer effectively applicable categories of critique because the system of capital has exceeded their boundaries, developing a hitherto invisible space. Due to its very invisibility, however, this global space also provides the most accurate representation yet of the function of capitalism, a fact testified by the end-of-the-century availability of that image to such mainstream entertainments as *The Matrix, Dark City, The Truman Show, eXistenZ,* and their myriad pop-cultural progeny in America and abroad.

One may take this rapprochement of image with truth either as a sign of the nearly complete domination of capitalism or of its increasing disenchantment, or, dialectically, as both at once. What the global application of underground space and the global division of urban space can tell us about this new development of capitalism is where its peripheries are and where its contradictions arise. Witness antiglobalization guru Naomi Klein's characterization of the so-called free trade zone as "a tax-free economy, sealed off from the local government of both town and province" established in developing countries to produce goods solely for export: "If Nike Town and the other superstores are the glittering new gateways to the branded dreamworlds, then the Cavite Export Processing Zone [a 682-acre walled-in industrial area housing 207 factories 90 miles from Manila in the Philippines] is the branding broom closet."[54] Apocalypse, the primary form taken by the devil in the post-nineteenth-century developed world, marks those spots, and remains one of the few points of intersection between the outmoded urban system and the new global one. At the same time, the ruined utopian impulses mobilized by the aestheticized cityscape and the repackaged urban underground need to be reconnected with those newly peripheral spaces to which the living counterparts of those impulses have migrated. The spectacle tells us the meaning of the space that is adequate for the inorganic uses of capital; the scattered ruins out of which the spectacle emerged can tell us the potentially more important uses which failed to be adequate to that system. There is no global space of truth that can be represented as such and persist as true; nevertheless, the insights buried within images of underground space suggest the incomplete truths that are the best we can hope for. These fragmentary truths can suggest ways of glossing the various ways in which they remain incomplete, and can help to construct a provisional and always changing but fairly accurate image of the lived spaces of the material world, an increasingly difficult, but nevertheless eminently desirable goal.

Notes

Introduction

1. I adapt the term "fortress architecture" from Camilo José Vergara, whose photo-essay *The New American Ghetto* (New Brunswick, N.J.: Rutgers University Press, 1995) documents the rise of such building strategies in urban slums.

2. Sewage tunnels were in use in the city of Mohenjo Daro in the Indus Valley as early as 2500 B.C.E. Other early underground construction includes irrigation tunnels dug by the Babylonians through the plain separating the Euphrates and the Tigris rivers, rock-cut water channels in ancient Etruria, and, in 750 BCE, a 1,750-foot channel from the concealed Springs of Gihon to the city of Jerusalem to provide water for the people of Judah if attacked by the Assyrians (Benson Bobrick, *Labyrinths of Iron: Subways in History, Myth, Art, Technology, and War* [New York: Henry Holt, 1986], 26–27).

3. Burton Pike discusses the ancient topos of the city as a site of symbolic ambivalence in chapter 1 of *The Image of the City in Modern Literature* (Princeton: Princeton University Press, 1981), 3–26. The argument was especially urgent between the wars in the context of the modernist city. In his influential treatise, *The Decline of the West*, Oswald Spengler argued that all history was made by the "world-city," from Babylon and Thebes onward, but that those cities were also "the monstrous symbol and vessel of the completely emancipated intellect," the source of a rootlessness that led to their own downfall (1926–28, tr. Charles Francis Atkinson, 2 vol. [New York: Knopf, 1947], 2:98–99). For the American cultural critic Lewis Mumford, "only one symbol can do justice" to life in ancient Rome: "an open sewer" (*The City in History: Its Origins, Its Transformations, and Its Prospects* [New York: Harcourt Brace Jovanovich, 1961]). While Rome epitomized the early "megalopolis," Mumford argued that even the earliest cities offered not only protection and security but also the expectation of "outward assault" and of "intensified struggle within," a struggle that both he and his teacher, the Scottish town planner Patrick Geddes, maintained could end only in the destruction of all concerned (*City in History*, 52–53; *The Culture of Cities* [New York: Harcourt, Brace, 1938], 292). As Geddes wrote, "When they asked Dante, 'Where didst thou see Hell?' he answered, 'In the city around me'"(*Cities in Evolution: An Introduction to the Town Planning Movement and to the Study of Civics* [1915; New York: H. Fertig, 1968], 87).

4. Mary Douglas, *Purity and Danger* (London: Routledge & Kegan Paul, 1966), 40.

5. There exist many side-by-side discussions of the two cities, especially in terms of architectural history, but there has been surprisingly little direct or in-depth comparison of representations of London and Paris. Most studies assume the model of modernity of their subject metropolis to apply equally everywhere else; where there is comparison, it tends simply to echo the polarizing discourses of the time. In *Cities and People: A Social and Architectural History*, Mark Girouard contrasts the "black Babylon" of London with the "bright Babylon of Paris" (New Haven: Yale University Press, 1985), 343–48. In *Victorian Babylon: People, Streets, and Im-*

ages in Nineteenth-Century London, Lynda Nead proposes London's fragmentary and scattered modernity as a countermodel to the Parisian treatment of urban space as a "totality" (New Haven: Yale University Press, 2000), 55–56. Sharon Marcus makes the opposition and "points of intersection" between modes of dwelling in the two cities a leading argument in *Apartment Stories: City and Home in Nineteenth-Century Paris and London,* but never develops the comparison as such (Berkeley: University of California Press, 1999), 4, 83–85. In their brief investigation of the street as a unit for historical study, François Bédarida and Anthony Sutcliffe make an instructive comparison between the vibrant street life of Paris and the fragmented experience of sprawling London ("The Street in the Structure and Life of the City: Reflections on Nineteenth-Century London and Paris," in *Modern Industrial Cities: History, Policy, and Survival,* ed. Bruce M. Stave [Beverly Hills: Sage Publications, 1981], 21–37). Joachim Schlör makes some helpful distinctions in passing, especially in relation to prostitution, in *Nights in the Big City* (1991, tr. Pierre Gottfried Imhoff and Dafydd Rees Roberts [London: Reaktion Books, 1998], 193–94, 202). Andrew Lees has collected many useful contemporary reactions to the two cities in *Cities Perceived: Urban Societies in European and American Thought, 1820–1940* (Manchester: Manchester University Press, 1985).

6. On the view from Saint Paul's and the panorama, see Richard Maxwell, *The Mysteries of Paris and London* (Charlottesville: University Press of Virginia, 1992), 126, 267–68, 348–49; Martin Zerling, "London as a Panorama," unpublished essay. The locus classicus of the view from Notre-Dame de Paris is the celebrated chapter, "Paris à vol d'oiseau" (book 3, chap. 2), in Victor Hugo's eponymous novel of 1831; on its relation to mapping the city from above and below, see Priscilla Parkhurst Ferguson, *Paris as Revolution: Writing the Nineteenth-Century City* (Berkeley: University of California Press, 1994), 67–68.

7. On the "Asmodeus flight" and the view from above in city guides, see Ferguson, *Paris as Revolution,* 59–65; on its use in the realist novel, see Jonathan Arac, *Commissioned Spirits: The Shaping of Social Motion in Dickens, Carlyle, Melville, and Hawthorne* (New Brunswick: Rutgers University Press, 1979), 22, 85–86, 111–13; and Marcus, *Apartment Stories,* 10.

8. J. Collin de Plancy, *Dictionnaire Infernal,* 6th ed. (Paris: Henri Plon, 1863), 152.

9. Salman Rushdie, *The Ground beneath Her Feet* (London: Vintage, 2000), 73. For a comprehensive treatment of the descent journeys in Rushdie's novel in terms of East–West relations, see Rachel Falconer, *Hell in Contemporary Literature: Western Descent Narratives since 1945* (Edinburgh: Edinburgh University Press, 2005), 200–219.

10. For the classic reading of this experience in its literary and philosophical context, see Marshall Berman, *All That Is Solid Melts into Air: The Experience of Modernity* (New York: Simon and Schuster, 1982).

11. Piero Camporesi, *Bread of Dreams: Food and Fantasy in Early Modern Europe* (1980), tr. David Gentilcore (Chicago: University of Chicago Press, 1989), 79.

12. Ibid., 22–23.

13. Edward Bulwer-Lytton, *Asmodeus at Large* (Philadelphia: Carey, Lea & Blanchard, 1833), iii.

14. Karl Marx and Friedrich Engels, "Manifesto of the Communist Party," in *The Marx-Engels Reader,* ed. Robert C. Tucker, 2nd ed. (New York: Norton, 1978), 469–500, at 489.

15. Henri Lefebvre, *The Production of Space,* 1974, tr. Donald Nicholson-Smith (Oxford: Blackwell, 1991), 129.

16. Edward W. Soja, *Third Space: Journeys to Los Angeles and Other Real-and-Imagined Places* (Cambridge, Mass.: Blackwell, 1996), 46.

17. Lefebvre, *Production of Space,* 174.

18. Ibid., 33.

19. Ibid.

20. Ibid., 362.

Chapter 1. The New Life Underground

1. H. G. Wells, *When the Sleeper Wakes* (1899; London: Everyman, 1994), 85.

2. E. J. Hobsbawm, *Behind the Times: The Decline and Fall of the Twentieth-Century Avant-Gardes* (New York: Thames and Hudson, 1999), 38–39.

3. Ford Madox Ford, *The Soul of London,* 1905, ed. Alan G. Hill (London: Everyman, 1995), 15.

4. Benson Bobrick, *Labyrinths of Iron* (1981; New York: Henry Holt, 1994), 131.

5. According to Pick, head of London Transport, "If London grew beyond the magic 12 to 15-mile limit set by the economics of the tube, it 'must cease to be intrinsically London'"(Peter Hall, *Cities of Tomorrow* [London: Blackwell, 1988], 85).

6. H. P. White, *Greater London,* vol. 3 of *A Regional History of the Railways of Great Britain* (Newton Abbot: David & Charles, 1963), 105.

7. Bobrick, *Labyrinths of Iron,* 165.

8. *The Times,* 30 November 1861; qtd. in T. C. Barker and Michael Robbins, *A History of London Transport,* 2 vols. (London: George Allen & Unwin, 1975), 1:118.

9. Walter Benjamin, *The Arcades Project,* tr. Howard Eiland and Kevin McLaughlin (Cambridge: Harvard University Press, 1999), 84; Convolute C1a,2.

10. G. E. Haussmann, *Mémoires du Baron Haussmann,* 3 vols. (Paris, 1890–93), 2:53; qtd. in Peter Jukes, *A Shout in the Street: An Excursion into the Modern City* (New York: Farrar, Straus, Giroux, 1990), 71. For further detail, see David P. Jordan, *Transforming Paris: The Life and Labor of Baron Haussmann* (New York: Free Press, 1995), 170–76; and David Pinkney, *Napoleon III and the Rebuilding of Paris* (Princeton: Princeton University Press, 1958), 25–31.

11. Bobrick, *Labyrinths of Iron,* 85.

12. Ford, *Soul of London,* 23.

13. On the iconographic appeal of Jean Gabin and Mireille Balin, see Ginette Vincendeau, *Pépé le Moko* (London: BFI Film Classics, 1998). For a sustained analysis of poetic realism in the context of '30s France, see Dudley Andrew, *Mists of Regret: Culture and Sensibility in Classic French Cinema* (Princeton: Princeton University Press, 1995). I adapt the term "populist melodrama" from Alan Williams's "populist tragedy," in his discussion of poetic realism in *Republic of Images: A History of French Filmmaking* (Cambridge: Harvard University Press, 1992), 232–42.

14. For more on the Thames Tunnel, see Pike, "'The Greatest Wonder of the World': Brunel's Tunnel and the Meanings of Underground London," *Victorian Literature and Culture* 33, no. 2 (2005): 341–67.

15. Bobrick, *Labyrinths of Iron,* 92.

16. Qtd. in W. J. Passingham, *The Romance of London's Underground* (London: Sampson Low, Marston & Co., [1932]), 11.

17. Richard Trench and Ellis Hillman, *London under London: A Subterranean Guide,* new ed. (1984; London: John Murray, 1993), 131–32.

18. Henry Mayhew, "The Metropolitan Railway," in *The Shops and Companies of London and the Trades and Manufactories of Great Britain,* ed. Mayhew, 2 vols. (London: Strand, 1865), 1:142–53, at 144.

19.Sir Joseph Paxton to the Select Committee on Metropolitan Communications 1854–55 (415) X, qq. 716 seq., p. 84.

20. "By Underground!" *Punch* (17 January 1885): 34. My thanks to Joseph McLaughlin for bringing this item to my attention. The previous year, a plot had been uncovered by the Dynamiters, an anarchist group associated with the Fenians, to blow up four London railway stations.

21. Ibid.

22. Barker and Robbins, *London Transport,* 1:124.

23. Trench and Hillman, *London under London,* 147.

24. John Betjeman, "Coffee, Port and Cigars on the Inner Circle," *London Times,* "Supplement on the Centenary of the London Underground" (24 May 1963).

25. John Galsworthy, *The Man of Property* (1906; Harmondsworth: Penguin, 1951), part 3, chap. 4; 269.

26. R. D. Blumenfeld, *R. D. B.'s Diary 1887–1914* (London: William Heinemann, 1930), 6–7. It was not unusual for American visitors to exaggerate the negative underground that was characteristic of the London discourse. Melville's *Redburn* (1849) chronicled a descent into a hell of poverty in Manchester and an underworld of gambling; Hawthorne found the Thames in 1855 to be "bordered with the shabbiest, blackest, ugliest, meanest buildings I ever saw; it is the backside of the town" (*The English Notebooks,* ed. Randall Stewart [New York: Modern Language Association of America, 1941], 216).

27. Edward Rose and "Captain Coe," *Orpheus and Eurydice,* Aquarium, Great Yarmouth (20 July 1891) Add. 53479 H (The Lord Chamberlain's Plays), Department of Manuscripts, The British Library, London.

28. Alice Meynell, "The Trees," *London Impressions: Etchings and Pictures in Photogravure by William Hyde and Essays by Alice Meynell* (Westminster: Archibald, Constable and Co., 1898), 12–15, at 15.

29. Elizabeth Robins Pennell, "London's Underground Railways," *Harper's New Monthly Magazine* 92, no. 548 (January 1896): 278–87, at 287.

30. Galsworthy, *Man of Property,* 266–67.

31. Mayhew, "Metropolitan Railway," 145.

32. Qtd. in Barker and Robbins, *London Transport,* 1:148.

33. George R. Sims, *The Mysteries of Modern London* (London: C. Arthur Pearson, 1906), 72. Sims had first made his mark with a series of articles on the lives of the poor in 1883 in the *Pictorial World,* for which he was dubbed "Dante of the London slums" (Anthony S. Wohl, introduction to Andrew Mearns, *The Bitter Cry of Outcast London, with other selections,* ed. Wohl [Leicester: Leicester University Press, 1970], 12).

34. Sims, *Mysteries,* 11.

35. Ibid.

36. Passingham, *Romance of London's Underground,* 32.

37. Qtd. in Trench and Hillman, *London under London,* 139.

38. Bobrick, *Labyrinths of Iron,* 102.

39. Qtd. in Barker and Robbins, *London Transport,* 1:118.

40. Eric Banton, "Underground Travelling London," in *Living London: Its work and its play. Its humour and its pathos. Its sights and its scenes,* ed. Sims (1901–03), rpt. as *Edwardian London,* 4 vols. (London: Village Press, 1990), 4:60–63, at 62.

41. Ibid., 62–63.

42. Ibid., 63.

43. Betjeman, "Coffee, Port and Cigars."

44. Rose Macaulay, *Told by an Idiot* (1923; Garden City, N.Y.: Doubleday, 1983), 200–202.

45. Ibid., 200.

46. Pennell, "London's Underground Railways," 278.

47. Anthony Trollope, *The Way We Live Now,* 2 vols. in 1 (1874–75; London: Oxford University Press, 1962), chap. 91, 2:382.

48. Henry James, *A London Life* (1889; New York: Grove, [n.d.]), 82.

49. H. G. Wells, *Tono-Bungay* (1909; London: J. M. Dent-Everyman, 1993), 107.

50. H. F. Howson, *London's Underground* (1951; London: Ian Allan, 1967), 20.

51. Alexandre Ossadzow, "Les Pères du métropolitain: L'Intervention des ingénieurs," in *Métro-Cité: Le chemin de fer métropolitain à la conquête de Paris 1871–1945,* exhibition catalog (Paris: Paris musées, [1997]), 57–72, at 63.

52. Norbert Lauriot, "La Genèse d'un réseau urbain: La Logique des tracés," in *Métro-Cité,* 33–46, at 41. Lauriot's figure is somewhat deceptive. The average length of the journey was and still remains much shorter for the Parisian traveler than for the Londoner (H. C. P. Havers, *Underground Railways of the World: Their History and Development* [London: Temple Press Books, 1966], 145).

53. Qtd. in Roger-Henri Guerrand, *Mémoires du Métro* (Paris: Editions de la Table Ronde, 1961), 30.

54. Qtd. in Passingham, *Romance,* 23–24; qtd. in Guerrand, *Mémoires,* 29.

55. Guerrand, *Mémoires,* 30.

56. Qtd. in Bobrick, *Labyrinths of Iron,* 103; qtd. in Guerrand, *Mémoires,* 30.

57. Qtd. in Norma Evenson, *Paris, a Century of Change: 1878–1978* (New Haven: Yale University Press, 1978), 94.

58. Bobrick, *Labyrinths,* 142–43.

59. Guerrand, *Mémoires,* 44.

60. Lauriot, "La Genèse," 37.

61. Emile Gérards, *Paris souterrain* (Paris: Garnier Frères, 1908; rpt. Torcy: DMI, 1991), 563–64.

62. Qtd. in ibid., 563.

63. Qtd. in ibid., 568.

64. Banton, "Underground Travelling," 62.

65. Jules Romains, *Les Hommes de bonne volonté* (1932–46); "The Sixth of October," vol. 1 of *Men of Good Will,* tr. Warre B. Wells (New York: Knopf, 1933), 7. On the acrimonious disputes leading up to the construction of the Left Bank route of the line, see Sheila Hallsted-Baumert, "Une Ligne peu académique: La Ligne 4 et l'Institut de France," in *Métro-Cité,* 86–98.

66. Qtd. in Guerrand, *Mémoires,* 44.

67. *Ibid.,* 175.

68. On this and the other cave-ins in modern Paris, see Laurence and Gilles Laurendon, *Paris Catastrophes* (Paris: Parigramme, 1995), 84–91.

69. Gérards, *Paris,* 582.

70. Henri Duvernois, "La Parisienne et le métropolitain," *femina* 5, no. 99 (1 March 1905): 120.

71. André Chaignon, "La Parisienne en électrique," *femina* 5, no. 99 (1 March 1905): 121.

72. Guerrand, *Mémoires,* 179–81.

73. Qtd. in ibid., 180.

74. Louis Aragon, *Paris Peasant* (1926), tr. Simon Watson Taylor (1971; Boston: Exact Change, 1994), 130.

75. For the story of the title of *Fantômas* and the influence of its violent excess and unmotivated plotting of events on the surrealists, see Robin Walz, *Pulp Surrealism: Insolent Popular Culture in Early Twentieth-Century Paris* (Berkeley: University of California Press, 2000), 43–75. Walz is excellent on the historical context of popular culture of the time, but reductive in his assessment of the admittedly mixed qualities of that culture.

76. Pierre Souvestre and Marcel Allain, *Fantômas III: Le Mort qui tue* (Paris: Fayard, n.d.), esp. chaps. 4–5, 11, 15. See also Richard Abel, *The Ciné Goes to Town: French Cinema, 1896—1914,* 2nd ed. (Berkeley: University of California Press, 1994), 376–77.

77. Guerrand, *Mémoires,* 176–78.

78. Ibid., 117.

79. Marcel Proust, *Time Regained* (1927), in *Remembrance of Things Past,* 3 vols., tr. Andrea Mayor (New York: Vintage, 1982), 3:707–1107, at 864.

80. Ibid., 870.

81. José de la Colina and Tomás Pérez Turrent, *Objects of Desire: Conversations with Luis Buñuel,* ed. and tr. Paul Lenti (New York: Marsilio, 1992), xi–xii. The image endured: this volume was originally published in 1986 as *Prohibido asomarse al interior.*

82. Louis-Ferdinand Céline, *Entretiens avec le Professeurs Y* (Paris: Gallimard, 1955), 117–18; *Conversations with Professor Y,* tr. Stanford Luce (Hanover, N.H.: University Press of New England for Brandeis University Press, 1986), 106–9.

83. Simonetta Fraquelli, "Montparnasse and the Right Bank: Myth and Reality," in *Paris: Capital of the Arts 1900—1968,* exhibition catalog (London: Thames & Hudson, 2002), 106–17, at 110. On *Nord-Sud* and its relationship to avant-garde poetry of the time, see Maurice Nadeau, *Histoire du surréalisme* (Paris: Seuil, 1964), 20. Apollinaire mourned the review's passing in 1918, "Echos," *L'Europe nouvelle* (6 April 1918), rpt. *Chroniques d'art 1902–1918,* ed. L. C. Breunig (Paris: Gallimard, 1960), 539. The Nord-Sud (or "A," now line no. 12) and two other shorter lines were run by a separate company until it merged in 1930 with the Compagnie du chemin de fer métropolitain, which controlled the rest of the network. On the construction and history of the line, see Yann Dronne, "La Seconde compagnie parisienne: La Société du chemin de fer électrique souterrain Nord-Sud de Paris," in *Métro-Cité,* 134–44.

84. Gino Severini, "The Plastic Analogies of Dynamism—Futurist Manifesto 1913," in *Futurist Manifestos,* ed. Umbro Apollonio (1970), tr. Robert Brain, R. W. Flint, J. C. Higgitt, and Caroline Tisdall (1973; Boston: MFA Publications, 2001), 118–25, at 125. Severini (1883–1966) had first settled in Paris in 1906; he helped the group to make contact with the Paris art world and hold an important exhibition there in 1912.

85. Umberto Boccioni, Carlo Carrà, Luigi Russolo, Giacomo Balla, and Gino Severini, "Manifesto of the Futurist Painters 1910," in *Futurist Manifestos,* 24–27, at 27, 25.

86. According to the director, "I thought it would make the character of Valentine more interesting and a little mysterious to suggest in the song that she had once been a prostitute" (qtd. in Alexander Sesonske, *Jean Renoir: The French Films, 1924—1939* [Cambridge: Harvard University Press, 1980], 208).

87. Guerrand, *Mémoires,* 225.

88. The endurance of this myth in a sanitized version is evident in Jean-Pierre Jeunet's recent Montmartre-centered paean to *vieux* Paris, *Le Fabuleux destin d'Amélie Poulain* (2001). A moment of lovelorn despair finds the eponymous heroine skipping rocks at sunset on the canal

St.-Martin, while the métro aérien flies over a bridge in the background: poetic-realist short-hand applied to a modern feeling of inability to escape the confinement of one's neuroses.

89. Raymond Queneau, *Zazie dans le métro* (1959; Paris: Gallimard, 1975), 14.

90. Compare Gary Sherman's cult horror film, *Raw Meat* (1973), about the cannibalistic descendants of London navvies trapped in underground while digging the Piccadilly Line in the late nineteenth century. The degenerate and diseased surviving male and his dying pregnant mate prey on passengers in the Russell Square Tube station. A warped sympathy for the pitiful monsters is the best the London scene could muster to depict its own counterculture in a subterranean setting."

91. On the centrality of "feminine terms" in the depiction of the urban crowd and the "'second city,' the underworld or urban labyrinth," see Elizabeth Wilson, *The Sphinx in the City: Urban Life, the Control of Disorder, and Women* (Berkeley: University of California Press, 1992), 5–8.

92. Henri Lefebvre, *The Production of Space,* 1974, tr. Donald Nicholson-Smith (Oxford: Blackwell, 1991), 36, 262.

93. J. C. Platt and J. Saunders, "Underground," in *London,* ed. Charles Knight, 6 vols. in 3 (London, 1841–44), 1:224–40, at 225.

94. Ibid., 225–26.

95. Rosalind Williams, *Notes on the Underground: An Essay on Technology, Society, and the Imagination* (Cambridge: MIT Press, 1990), 97.

96. Platt and Saunders, "Underground," 226.

97. Passingham, *Romance,* 84.

98. Banton, "Underground Travelling," 63.

99. Frederick Etchells, introduction to *The City of To-morrow and Its Planning,* by Le Corbusier (1929; New York: Dover, 1987), v–xviii, at x.

100. Ibid., 62. On Kemble's 1827 visit, see Frances Ann Kemble, *Record of a Girlhood* (London, 1878); Humphrey Jennings, *Pandaemonium 1660–1886: The Coming of the Machine as Seen by Contemporary Observers,* ed. Mary-Lou Jennings and Charles Madge (London: Picador, 1987), 168–69; Williams, *Notes,* 96–98; Pike, "Greatest Wonder."

101. F. L. Stevens, *Under London: A Chronicle of London's Underground Life-lines and Relics* (London: J. M. Dent and Sons, [1939]), 50–51.

102. Gérards, *Paris,* 2.

103. Ibid., 525.

104. Ibid., 521.

105. Sims, *Mysteries,* 120, 122.

106. Williams, *Notes,* 108.

107. Ibid., 211.

108. Michel Ragon, *Histoire de l'architecture et de l'urbanisme modernes,* 2 vols. (1986; Paris: Seuil, 1991), 1:10.

109. Williams, *Notes,* 102.

110. Ibid., 98.

111. Qtd. in ibid., 128.

112. Edward Bulwer-Lytton, *The Coming Race* (1871; rpt. Santa Barbara, Calif.: Woodbridge Press, 1979), 22.

113. Ibid., 6–7.

114. Ibid., 2–3, 45. John Martin's *The Bridge over Chaos* was inspired by plans for the Thames

Tunnel, for which excavations had begun in 1825. The twenty-four mezzotints for *Paradise Lost,* executed between 1823 and 1827, were first published in folio form in London in 1827.

115. Raymond Williams, "Utopia and Science Fiction," in *Problems in Materialism and Culture* (London: Verso, 1980), 196–213, at 201.

116. Bulwer-Lytton, *Coming Race,* 60.

117. Ibid., 1–2.

118. Ibid., 2.

119. Ibid., 66.

120. H. G. Wells, *The Time Machine* (1895; London: Everyman, 1993), 49.

121. Ibid., 52.

122. Ibid., 63.

123. Wells, *When the Sleeper Wakes,* 67.

124. Williams, *Notes,* 176–77.

125. C. F. G. Masterman, *The Condition of England* (London: Methuen, 1900), 105. Masterman (1873–1927) was a member of the Liberal government.

126. Ibid., 119–20.

127. Lefebvre, *Production of Space,* 341–42.

128. E. M. Forster, "The Machine Stops" (1909), in *Collected Short Stories* (Harmondsworth: Penguin, 1954), 109–46, at 138.

129. Ibid., 125.

130. Ibid., 126.

131. Ibid., 133.

132. Ibid., 143–44.

133. Forster, "Introduction," in ibid., 5–7, at 6.

134. William Morris, *News from Nowhere* (1890), in *News from Nowhere and Other Writings,* ed. Clive Wilmer (Harmondsworth: Penguin, 1993), 41–228, at 41.

135. Auguste Villiers de l'Isle-Adam, *L'Eve future,* intro. and notes Pierre Citron (Lausanne: Editions l'Age d'Homme, 1979), 140.

136. Williams, *Notes,* 135.

137. Ibid.

138. Gabriel Tarde, *Fragment d'histoire future* (1896; Paris: Séguier, 1998), 41–53.

139. Ibid., 85.

140. Ibid., 69.

141. René Schérer, preface to Tarde, *Fragment,* 7–37, at 27.

142. Ibid., 123.

143. Ibid., 112.

144. Ragon, *Histoire,* 2:56.

145. Peter Hall, *Cities in Civilization: Culture, Innovation, and Urban Order* (London: Weidenfeld & Nicolson, 1998), 611.

146. Ibid., 612–13.

147. George E. Chadwick, *The Works of Sir Joseph Paxton 1803–1865* (London: Architectural Press, 1961), 209–10.

148. Ibid., 210.

149. Charles Fourier, *Oeuvres complètes,* 12 vols. (1841; Paris: Anthropos, 1966–68), 4:462–64; *The Utopian Vision of Charles Fourier: Selected Texts on Work, Love and Passionate Attraction,* ed. and trans. Jonathan Beecher and Richard Bienvenu (London: Jonathan Cape, 1975), 243–44.

150. Barker and Robbins, *London Transport*, 1:66. On both schemes, see also Felix Barker and Ralph Hyde, *London As It Might Have Been* (London: John Murray, 1982), 137–39.

151. Ragon, *Histoire*, 1:58.

152. Lefebvre, *Production of Space*, 124.

153. Le Corbusier, *Urbanisme* (1925), tr. Frederick Etchells, *The City of To-morrow and Its Planning* (1929; New York: Dover, 1987), 244.

154. Le Corbusier, *City of To-morrow*, 275–89.

155. Ibid., 254.

156. Ibid., 280.

157. Ibid., 284.

158. The phrase is from Siegfried Giedion, *Building in France, Building in Iron, Building in Ferro-Concrete*, 1928, tr. J. Duncan Berry (Santa Monica, Calif.: Getty Center for the History of Art and the Humanities, 1995), 68.

159. Ragon, *Histoire*, 2:49.

160. To be sure, Le Corbusier was less of a social radical than many of his contemporaries, unselfconsciously detailing the luxurious life in one of his residential high-rises with all cooking and cleaning taking place far below the apartments so that the latter could remain pristine living machines.

161. Ragon, *Histoire*, 2:49.

162. Antonio Sant'Elia, "Manifesto of Futurist Architecture 1914," in *Futurist Manifestos*, 160–72, at 170.

163. Jukes, *Shout in the Street*, 54.

164. Ibid.

165. Giedion, *Building in France*, 68, 65.

Chapter 2. The Modern Necropolis

1. "Une pyramide, un immense caveau, / Qui contient plus de morts que la fosse commune. / . . . un cimetière abhorré de la lune." Charles Baudelaire, "Spleen II," *Les Fleurs du mal*, 1857, *Oeuvres complètes*, ed. Claude Pichois, 2 vols. (Paris: Gallimard, 1975–76), 1:73.

2. Kenneth Grahame, *The Wind in the Willows* (London, 1908), 39.

3. *Ibid.*, 40.

4. Gaston Leroux, *La Double vie de Théophraste Longuet* (1903), vol. 3 of *Romans fantastiques* (Paris: Laffont, 1970), 163–478.

5. Vicomte de Launay [Delphine de Girardin], *Lettres parisiennes*, 1843, ed. Anne-Martin Fugier, 2 vols. (Paris: Mercure de France, 1986), 1:342–43 (24 November 1838). The grotto of Posilippo was a nearly mile-long, thirty-foot-high tunnel executed (according to the ancient Greek geographer Strabo) for the emperor Augustus to link Pozzuoli with Naples. It was part of the tour of Roman ruins and was painted by Hubert Robert, among others (see below).

6. Victor Hugo, *Les Misérables* (Paris: Garnier, 1957), pt. 5, bk. 7, chap. 1; 854.

7. Philippe Muray, *Le XIXe siècle à travers les âges* (1984; Paris: Denoël, 1999), 22. Emile Gérards, *Paris souterrain* (Paris: Garnier Frères, 1908; rpt. Torcy: DMI, 1991), 445.

8. Gérards, *Paris souterrain*, 445.

9. Félix Nadar, "Le Dessus et le dessous de Paris," in *Paris-Guide par les principaux écrivains et artistes de France*, 1867; ed. Corinne Verdet (Paris: La Découverte/Maspero, 1983), 154–75, at 156.

10. Louis-Sebastien Mercier, "L'Air vicié," *Tableau de Paris*, 12 vols. (Amsterdam, 1783), 1:43; 120–29, at 121–22.

11. Elie Berthet, *Les Catacombes de Paris*, 4 vols. (Paris: L. de Potter, rue Saint-Jacques 38, 1854), 1:3.

12. Ibid., 10.

13. Muray, *Le XIXe siècle*, 35.

14. Qtd. in Gérards, *Paris souterrain*, 293.

15. Ibid., 381.

16. Ibid., 383.

17. Ch. Depeuty and E. Bourget, *Les Carrières de Montmartre*, Théâtre de la Porte-Saint-Martin, 10 May 1855.

18. Gérards, *Paris souterrain*, 384.

19. Sigmund Engländer, *Geschichte der französischen Arbeiter-Associationen*, 4 vols. (Hamburg: Hoffmann und Campe, 1864), 2:314–15; qtd. in Walter Benjamin, *The Arcades Project*, tr. Howard Eiland and Kevin McLaughlin (Cambridge: Harvard University Press, 1999), 89 (Convolute C3a,1).

20. Gustave Flaubert, *L'Education sentimentale* (Paris, 1869), pt. 3, chap. 2.

21. Michel Ragon, *L'Espace de la mort* (Paris: Albin Michel, 1981), 233.

22. Ibid., 106.

23. Thomas Carlyle, *The French Revolution* (1834–37), pt. 3, bk. 5, chap. 1.

24. "Catacomb," *Encyclopaedia Britannica*, 11th ed., 490.

25. L. Knab, "Catacombes," in *La Grande Encyclopédie* (Paris: H. Lamirault, 1898), 788–97.

26. P. L. Jacob [Paul Lacroix], *Les Catacombes de Rome* (1845; Verviers: Marabout, 1975), 65, 71. The original subtitle was *Episode de la vie d'un peintre français*.

27. Robert, who lived in Rome from 1754 to 1765, was nicknamed "Robert des ruines" for his drawings of the city, including several of the catacombs and other subterranean sites. He also made a series of sketches of the nocturnal transport of remains from the Cemetery of the Innocents to the Catacombes of Paris. In the fourth canto of his *L'Imagination* (Paris, 1806), the preeminent poet of the day, the abbé Delille, celebrated Robert's miraculous escape when lost in the catacombs of Rome; later Robert also escaped being guillotined during the Terror when another person was mistakenly executed in his place. Fragonard studied at the Académie de France in Rome from 1756 to 1761; he and Robert were friends and frequently drew together. For a catalog and analysis of the paintings and drawings they produced there, see *J. H. Fragonard e H. Robert a Roma*, exhibition at Villa Medici, 6 December 1990—24 February 1991 (Rome: Fratelli Palombi, 1990).

28. Jacob, *Catacombes*, 191.

29. Ibid., 276. Lacroix probably based himself here on Delille's account, which occupied the last 119 lines of the first volume of *L'Imagination* (see n. 27 above), a final "Impression de Lieu," which the poet claimed in a note was based on events that had actually occurred to "M. Robert" in Rome (1:275–76). The narrative was a standard underground adventure, progressing from losing one's way to losing one's light to utter despair just before the fortuitous escape (he rediscovers his Ariadne's thread). The only variation was a nod in the direction of the sublime, as the artist, "Safe from danger, his soul still trembling / Wants to savor this place and his fright. / He feels, in his heart, from the lugubrious sight, / A pleasure stirred up by a remnant of terror" (250).

30. Jacob, *Catacombes*, 277.

31. Ibid., 220.

32. Ibid., 10. Delille's epic poem similarly read the Paris carrières into the catacombs of Rome: "Under the ramparts of Rome and beneath her vast plains / Are deep caverns, subterranean domains / Which, for two thousand years, excavated by men, / Gave their rocks to the palaces of the Romans" (*L'Imagination,* 1:245).

33. J. C. Catnach, *Green in France; or Tom and Jerry's Rambles through Paris. Attempted in Cuts and Verse* (2, Monmouth-court, Seven Dials, London: J. C. Catnach, 1822).

34. In Louis Etienne François Héricault de Thury, *Description des Catacombes de Paris, précédée d'un précis historique sur les catacombes de tous les peuples de l'ancien et du nouveau continent* (Paris, 1815), 315.

35. Gérards, *Paris souterrain,* 472–73. The soirée was reported in *Le Matin* (3 April 1897). Leroux used the concert as the means of his characters' escape from the city of the Talpa in *La Double vie,* commenting of the occasion that it "surpassed . . . the funerary carnival of Montmartre" that was the rage at the time (462–64).

36. Qtd. in Gérards, *Paris souterrain,* 462–63.

37. Lilian Herbert Andrews, *Marie: A Story of the Morgue and Catacombs of Paris* (New York: Peter Fenelon Collier, 1893), 3.

38. For a history of the morgue and an insightful analysis of the relation of its spectacle of death both to the policing of the city and to "revolutions, accidents, crimes and suicides," see Vanessa R. Schwartz, *Spectacular Realities: Early Mass Culture in Fin-de-siècle Paris* (Berkeley: University of California Press, 1998), 45–88.

39. Andrews, *Marie,* 175.

40. Berthet, *Catacombes,* 2:35.

41. Ibid., 1:217.

42. Ibid., 2:42.

43. The four volumes of the 1854 edition at the British Library and the Bibliothèque Nationale contain around half of the complete text included in later editions. This passage is cited from a reprint of the original serialization (Paris: Bureaux du Siècle, 1856), 134.

44. Ibid.

45. Berthet, *The Catacombs of Paris,* trans. M. C. Helmore (Westminster: A. Constable & Co., 1900), 481.

46. Alexandre Dumas, *Les Mohicans de Paris* (1854–59; Paris: Gallimard, 1998), 62.

47. An editor's note on p. 1569 of the modern edition records the facticity of Dumas' offer of an underground guide: "Giverny was a *limonadier* at number 308, rue Saint-Jacques (*Almanach du commerce,* 1855)."

48. Jules Verne, *Paris au XXe siècle* (Paris: Hachette, 1994). Submitted after the success of his first novel, *Five Weeks in a Balloon,* the book was rejected by Verne's editor Hetzel and remained unpublished until 1994. The editor, Piero Gondolo della Riva, dates the manuscript to not before 1863.

49. Ibid., 47.

50. Ibid., 166.

51. Ibid., 168.

52. Gérards, *Paris souterrain,* 479–80.

53. Ragon, *L'Espace,* 112.

54. Ibid., 219.

55. Nestor de Lamarque, "Les Catacombes," in *Paris, ou le livre des cent-et-un,* 15 vols. (Brussels: Louis Hauman, 1831–34), 6:19–34, at 24.

56. Ragon, *L'Espace,* 101.

57. James Steven Curl, *Egyptomania: The Egyptian Revival; A Recurring Theme in the History of Taste* (Manchester: Manchester University Press, 1994), 175–77.

58. Philippe Jullian, *Le Cirque du Père-Lachaise* (Paris: Fasquelle, 1957); qtd. in Ragon, *L'Espace*, 52.

59. Ragon, *L'Espace*, 51.

60. Philippe Ariès, *The Hour of Our Death* (1977), tr. Helen Weaver (New York: Vintage, 1982), 64–65.

61. Arsène Houssaye, "Rue et Faubourg-Saint-Denis," in *Les Rues de Paris. Paris ancien et modernes. Origines, histoire, monuments, costumes, moeurs, croniques et traditions,* ed. Louis Lurine, 2 vols. (Paris: Kugelmann, 1844), 2:1–16, at 5.

62. Ibid., 6.

63. On the morgue as spectacle and urban theater, see Schwartz, *Spectacular Realities,* 45–88. Accounts of the morgue were a fixture of the Paris discourse, figuring prominently in foreign travelogues and guides.

64. Gérards, *Paris souterrain,* 481.

65. Ibid.

66. T. W. Wilkinson, "Burying London," in *Living London: Its work and its play. Its humour and its pathos. Its sights and its scenes,* ed. Sims (1901–3), rpt. as *Edwardian London,* 4 vols. (London: Village Press, 1990), 3:287–93, at 289.

67. "London Burials," in Knight, *London,* 4:161–76, at 162.

68. Ibid., 161.

69. Ibid., 162. See, for example, the outraged report in the *Morning Herald* of the death of two "able-bodied" men in Aldgate churchyard (8 September 1838).

70. Charles Dickens, "The City of the Absent," in *The Uncommercial Traveller* (1860, 1865, 1875, 1890); rpt. in *The Uncommercial Traveller and Reprinted Pieces etc.,* Oxford Illustrated Dickens (Oxford: Oxford University Press, 1958), 233–40. "The City of the Absent" first appeared in the second, 1865 edition.

71. Ibid., 240.

72. Ibid., 233.

73. Ibid., 234. The church, recognizable by the Dutch motif of skull and crossbones, was St. Olave, Hart Street, built in 1450, destroyed during the Blitz, and rebuilt afterward. St. Olave's was Samuel Pepys's church, and he and his wife are buried within.

74. Baedeker reports the tradition about the skulls over the gate, but adds that it is not supported by the burial registers (Karl Baedeker, *London and its Environs* [1878; Leipzig: Karl Baedeker Publishers, 1905], 153)

75. Dickens, "City of the Absent," 238–39.

76. Ibid., 240.

77. Alice Meynell, "The London Sunday," in *London Impressions,* 1–3, at 2–3.

78. Ibid., 2.

79. Ibid., 1.

80. Ibid., 2.

81. Ibid.

82. Augustus Welby Northmore Pugin, *An Apology for the Revival of Christian Architecture in England* (London: J. Weale, 1843), 41; for more on Pugin's polemic and commercialism, see Curl, *Egyptomania,* 181–82, and John Morley, *Death and the Victorians* (Pittsburgh: University of Pittsburgh Press, 1971), 41–51. Giovanni Belzoni (1778–1823) was a circus giant, showman,

and Egyptian expeditioner whose collections were exhibited to great success in 1821 at the Egyptian Hall, Piccadilly. See Curl, 158–59; Joseph McLaughlin, "Out of Egypt: Moses, Belzoni, Boz," conference paper, Monuments and Dust Conference, April 1998, The Institute for Historical Research, London.

83. Thomas Barker, *Abney Park Cemetery: A Complete Descriptive Guide . . . etc.* (London, 1869); qtd. in Hugh Meller, *London Cemeteries: An Illustrated Guide and Gazeteer,* 3rd ed. (Hants: Scolar Press, 1994), 32.

84. Mrs. Basil Holmes, *The London Burial Grounds: Notes on Their History from the Earliest Times to the Present Day* (London: T. Fisher Unwin, 1896), 255.

85. The catafalque at Kensal Green Cemetery has been preserved and is still in use, as are the catacombs beneath it.

86. Felix Barker, introduction, *Highgate Cemetery: Victorian Valhalla,* photographs by John Gay (Salem, N.H.: Salem House, 1984), 13. On the cost of cemetery burial, see also Morley, *Death,* 41–42.

87. Barker, *Highgate Cemetery,* 14.

88. For a comprehensive and well-illustrated account of the house, see John Summerson, *A New Description of Sir John Soane's Museum* (London: published by the trustees, 1955). Summerson was the museum's curator.

89. Elisée Reclus, *Londres Illustré* (Paris: Hachette, 1865), 149.

90. Baedeker, *London,* 239.

91. Robert Harbison, *The Built, The Unbuilt and the Unbuildable: In Pursuit of Architectural Meaning* (London: Thames and Hudson, 1993), 103–4.

92. Henry James, *A London Life* (1889; New York: Grove, [n.d.]), 86–88.

93. Ibid., 87.

94. Ibid., 91.

95. Ibid., 83.

96. Ibid., 86.

97. For Mumford's argument that "the nineteenth century town became in effect—and indeed in appearance—an extension of the coal mine," see *Technics and Civilization* (New York: Harcourt, Brace, 1934), 157–59.

98. Thomas Wallace Knox, *Underground; or, Life below the Surface* (London: Sampson, Low & Co., 1873), 34.

99. Louis Simonin, *La Vie souterraine: Les Mines et les mineurs* (1867; rpt. Seyssel: Editions du Champ Vallon, 1982), 138.

100. Ibid., 139.

101. Ibid., 138–39.

102. *Half Hours Underground: Volcanoes, Mines, and Caves,* The Half Hour Library of Travel, Nature and Science for Young Readers (1878; London: James Nisbet & Co., 1900), 193.

103. Ibid., 187.

104. John Leech, "Capital and Labour," *Punch* 5 (May 1843): 48.

105. *Jane Rutherford; or, The Miner's Strike,* by A Friend of "The People," *The True Briton* 1 (n.s.), no. 55 (21 July 1853): 883.

106. Ibid., 884.

107. Ibid.

108. Ibid.

109. Ibid.

110. On the reformist elements of the episode and its reliance on the parliamentary blue book, *1842 Report of the Children's Employment Commission,* see Janet L. Grose, "Social Reform through Sensationalized Realism: G. W. M. Reynolds's 'The Rattlesnake's History,'" in *Caverns of Night: Coal Mines in Art, Literature, and Film,* ed. William B. Thesing (Columbia: University of South Carolina Press, 2000), 63–70.

111. G. W. M. Reynolds, *The Mysteries of London,* 4 vols. (London: John Dicks, [1846]), 1:355.

112. Ibid., 357.

113. Emile Zola, *Germinal* (1885; Paris: Garnier-Flammarion, 1968), pt. 3, chap. 1, 152.

114. Ibid., 3:1; 156.

115. James used the vocabulary of the anarchist as "Subterranean" throughout his novel; the connection to mining is invoked periodically, as in the humorous context of the Poupins' revolutionary fantasies: "'I mean a force that will make the bourgeois go down into their cellars and hide, pale with fear, behind their barrels of wine and their heaps of gold!' cried M. Poupin, rolling terrible eyes. 'And in this country, I hope, in their coal-bins. *La-la,* we shall find them even there,' his wife remarked." (*The Princess Cassamassima* [1886; Harmondsworth: Penguin, 1977], 94). In *The Secret Agent* (1907) Conrad drew on a bomb attack on the Greenwich Observatory in 1894 to depict a London beset by a group of anarchists who, unlike the conventional, "working-class" underworld, were unpredictable in their behavior and resisted detection and surveillance. This alien underground, a parasite on productive society, is embodied in the figure of the Professor, who makes his very body into a bomb ready to be detonated to avoid arrest and imprisonment.

116. In the final, "Future History" part of Anatole France's satirical novel, *Penguin Island* (1908), the giant metropolis of skyscrapers and tunnels is similarly shaken by a series of anarchist bombings that concludes in a massive conflagration.

117. Zola, *Paris* (1898), in *Les Trois villes,* vol. 7 of *Oeuvres complètes,* ed. Henri Mitterand (Paris: Cercle du Livre Précieux, 1968), 1175–1567, at 1539.

118. Zola, *Germinal,* pt. 7, chap. 5, p. 453.

119. Jules Verne, *Les Indes noires* (1877; Paris: Hachette, 1967), 4.

120. Mammoth Cave had been discovered in the late eighteenth century, and by 1816 was the second major tourist attraction in the United States, after Niagara Falls. For an example of the ongoing London interest in the site, see "A Tour in Mammoth Cave," *All the Year Round* 4, no. 96 (19 January 1861), 343–47. Visits to and mishaps in the caverns, as with the Paris Catacombes, were a staple of underground tourist writing in particular and travel literature in general.

121. Verne, *Indes noires,* 88.

122. George Orwell, *The Road to Wigan Pier* (1937; New York: Harcourt, Brace, 1958), 22–23.

123. Walter Pater, *Marius the Epicurean: His Sensations and Ideas* (1885; London: Penguin, 1985), 229.

124. D. H. Lawrence, *Sons and Lovers* (1913; Harmondsworth: Penguin, 1994), 19.

125. Ibid., 152.

126. Ibid., 364.

127. Lawrence, *Etruscan Places,* 1932; in *Mornings in Mexico and Etruscan Places* (Harmondsworth: Penguin, 1960), 97–215, at 102.

128. E. M. Forster, *A Passage to India* (1924; New York: Vintage, 1954), 149–50.

129. Richard Trench and Ellis Hillman, *London under London: A Subterranean Guide,* 1984, new ed. (London: John Murray, 1993), 9.

130. Moreover, as Roy Porter has observed, by making so many Londoners homeless and necessitating so much reconstruction on such a large scale, "the war rendered London a less rooted place" (*London: A Social History* [Harmondsworth: Penguin, 1996], 342). The vast majority of the homeless were those inhabitants of the eastern and southern areas conventionally troped as belowground in the social topography of the city, and financially unable subsequently to reroot themselves through sheer purchasing power.

131. René Suttel, *Catacombes et carrières de Paris: Promenade sous la capitale* (1986; Châtillon: PICAR, 1993), 194–95. According to the author, who mapped the tunnels from 1943–45 for possible use by the FFI, before the war the Cagoule, a secret organization of the extreme right, also made use of the northern and southern carrières, as well as the sewers, in its plot to overthrow the Popular Front government in 1937 (192–93).

132. For an informed survey and catalog of bandes dessinées images of the Catacombes, see the Web page, http://www.lhermine.com, maintained by a member of KtaBreizh, a collective of Breton cataphiles, or *ktaphiles,* as they prefer it.

133. *La cataphilie* continues to be a wide-ranging underground phenomenon in France, visible in numerous Web sites laying claim to a dialect, sharing information on sites and means of entry, outlining a philosophy of life, documenting numerous subterranean adventures in Paris and afield, and, most recently, beginning to write the history of the movement and its protagonists.

134. Guy Debord, "Théorie de la dérive" (1956), rpt. *internationale situationniste* 2 (December 1958): 19–23; "L'aventure," *internationale situationniste* 5 (1960): 3–6, at 3.

135. An opinionated but detailed history of postwar cataphilie can be found on the Web site of Zedou Connection, at http://www.catacombes.info/histoire/index.php?subCAT=3.

136. Moore recreated his sketching of a couple of years earlier for Jill Craigie's thirty-minute 1944 documentary about wartime artists, *Out of Chaos.*

137. Tolkien had gone to the front with the Lancashire Fusiliers in July 1916, where he fought in the Battle of the Somme, and was sent home four months later with trench fever. By 1918, he later wrote, "all but one of my close friends were dead" (Jenny Turner, "Reasons for Liking Tolkien," *London Review of Books* [15 November 2001]: 15–24, at 18). See also John Garth, *Tolkien and the Great War: The Threshold of Middle-earth* (New York: Houghton-Mifflin, 2003).

138. See the Web page of Reclaim the Streets, the direct action group that emerged from these protests, at http://rts.gn.apc.org.

139. For a reading of the events and their political and cultural aftermath, see Kristin Ross, *May '68 and Its Afterlives* (Chicago: University of Chicago Press, 2002).

140. Louis Chevalier, *The Assassination of Paris,* 1977, tr. David P. Jordan (Chicago: University of Chicago Press, 1994).

Chapter 3. Charon's Bark

1. For a history of the London sewers, see John Hollingshead, *Underground London* (London: Groombridge & Sons, 1862); Francis Sheppard, *London 1808–1870: The Infernal Wen* (London: Secker & Warburg, 1971), 249–96; and Dale H. Porter, *The Thames Embankment: Environment, Technology, and Society in Victorian London* (Akron, Ohio: University of Akron Press, 1998). On Paris, see Eugène Belgrand, *Les Travaux souterrains de Paris* (Paris, 1873–77); Emile Gérards, *Paris souterrain* (Paris: Garnier Frères, 1908; rpt. Torcy: DMI, 1991), 483–515;

David Pinkney, *Napoleon III and the Rebuilding of Paris* (Princeton: Princeton University Press, 1958), 127–50; and Donald Reid, *Paris Sewers and Sewermen: Realities and Representations* (Cambridge: Harvard University Press, 1991).

2. Jacques Lacan, "Conférences aux Amériques," *Scilicet* 6–7 (1975); qtd. in Dominique Laporte, *History of Shit* (1978), tr. Nadia Benabid and Rodolphe el-Khoury (Cambridge: MIT Press, 2000), 56.

3. On the "monstrous breed of black swine . . . that Hampstead sewers shelter," see the *Daily Telegraph* editorial of 1859 reproduced in Thomas Boyle, *Black Swine in the Sewers of Hampstead: Beneath the Surface of Victorian Sensationalism* (New York: Viking, 1989), 204–6. On alligators in the New York sewers, see David L. Pike, "Urban Nightmares and Future Visions: Life beneath New York," *Wide Angle* 20, no. 4 (October 1998): 8–50.

4. Voltaire, "Enterrement," *Dictionnaire philosophique* (1765), vol. 17–20 of *Oeuvres Complètes de Voltaire,* 52 vols. (Paris: Garnier Frères, 1878; rpt. Nendeln/Lichtenstein: Kraus Reprint, 1967), 18:551–52.

5. Mary Douglas, *Purity and Danger* (London: Routledge & Kegan Paul, 1966), 35–36.

6. Michael Taussig, *The Devil and Commodity Fetishism in South America* (Chapel Hill: University of North Carolina Press, 1980), 112.

7. Laporte makes the similar argument in *History of Shit* that "*Waste* is caught in the crossroads" of the goals of "socially profitable production" and "the gain-in pleasure" (14). Consistent with his psychoanalytic reading, Laporte stresses the way in which "the gain-in-pleasure must be made to *enrich* civilization in a *sublimated* form"—that is, recycled on the order of the Paris discourse. I follow Douglas and Taussig in preferring a more dialectical reading of the underground as a conceptually distinct sphere of social space.

8. Taussig, *The Devil,* 117.

9. Lynda Nead, *Myths of Sexuality: Representations of Women in Victorian Britain* (Oxford: Blackwell, 1988), 99.

10. See, for example, Baudelaire's equation of the prostitute with the poet in the alluring sordidness of their relation to the marketplace; Benjamin's analysis of this equation vis-à-vis the 1930s, particularly in Convolute J of the *Arcades Project* (to which Nead's feminist interpretation is strongly indebted); Peter Brooks's argument that the prostitute raises the difficulty of distinguishing between labor and crime, between "the sold body" and "the socially aberrant body," in *Reading for the Plot: Design and Intention in Narrative* (New York: Vintage, 1985), 168; and Amanda Anderson's summary and critique of contemporary versions of this analysis in *Tainted Souls and Painted Faces: The Rhetoric of Fallenness in Victorian Culture* (Ithaca: Cornell University Press, 1993), 5–9.

11. Peter Stallybrass and Allon White, *The Politics and Poetics of Transgression* (London: Methuen, 1986), 125.

12. Charles Bernheimer, *Figures of Ill Repute: Representing Prostitution in Nineteenth-Century France* (Cambridge: Harvard University Press, 1989), 1–2.

13. Eugène Buret, *De la misère des classes laborieuses en Angleterre et en France* (Paris: Paulin, 1840), qtd. in Louis Chevalier, *Laboring Classes and Dangerous Classes in Paris during the First Half of the Nineteenth Century,* 1958, tr. Frank Jellinek (Princeton: Princeton University Press, 1973), 144.

14. On the "democratisation of leisure" and its relation to popular culture, see especially Peter Bailey, *Popular Culture and Performance in the Victorian City* (Cambridge: Cambridge University Press, 1998); T. J. Clark, *The Painting of Modern Life: Paris in the Art of Manet and His*

Followers (Princeton: Princeton University Press, 1986); and Joachim Schlör, *Nights in the Big City,* 1991, tr. Pierre Gottfried Imhoff and Dafydd Rees Roberts (London: Reaktion Books, 1998).

15. Mikhail Bakhtin, *Rabelais and His World,* 1965, tr. Hélène Iswolsky (1968; Bloomington: Indiana University Press, 1984), 409.

16. Sigmund Freud, "A Case of Obsessional Neurosis," *Standard Edition* 10 (1909), 153–320, at 166–67; qtd. in Stallybrass and White, *Politics and Poetics of Transgression,* 144.

17. On the particular character of the Viennese house and the old city, see Donald J. Olsen, *The City as a Work of Art: London, Paris, Vienna* (New Haven: Yale University Press, 1986), 58–68.

18. Freud, "A Case," 214. "Le Poittevin" was the pseudonym of Eugène Modeste Edmond Poidevin. Freud most likely knew the illustrations through the collector Eduard Fuchs's various histories of morality, of erotic art, and of caricature. See, for example, Fuchs's *Geschichte der erotischen Kunst* (Berlin: A. Hoffmann, 1908), 345–51. Fuchs does not mention any connection with rats, sewers, and excrement—this seems to have been Freud's late-century sense of Le Poittevin's obscenely playful devils.

19. Ibid., 215.

20. For an excellent analysis of this ambivalence in Mayhew in the context of the different versions of *London Labour,* see Richard Maxwell, "Henry Mayhew and the Life of the Streets," *Journal of British Studies* 17, no. 2 (spring 1978): 87–105. For a more critical view of the different impulses and generic qualities mixed up in *London Labour,* see Gertrude Himmelfarb, *The Idea of Poverty: England in the Early Industrial Age* (New York: Vintage, 1985), 312–70. On Mayhew's definition of the poor in terms of their "affirmation of an alternative ethos that was more profoundly radical than anything proposed by the radicals of the time," see Himmelfarb, 369.

21. Henry Mayhew, *London Labour and the London Poor,* 4 vols. (1861–62; New York: Dover, 1968), 2:136.

22. Ibid., 137.

23. Ibid., 136.

24. Ibid.

25. Alain Corbin, *Le Miasme et la jonquille: L'Odorat et l'imaginaire social 18e–19e siècles* (Paris: Flammarion, 1986), 172.

26. Among the many examples of prominent Victorians eccentrically obsessed with aspects of the Victorian underclass or underworld, I cite only Arthur Joseph Munby, champion of the right of women to work in the mines, not least because of his attraction to women in men's clothing covered with coal dust. The many layers of displacement denote not only an association between "dirt, coal dust, and working-class sexuality," as Martin A. Danahay describes Munby's fetish ("The Aesthetics of Coal: Representing Soot, Dust, and Smoke in Nineteenth-Century Britain," in *Caverns of Night: Coal Mines in Art, Literature, and Film,* ed. William B. Thesing [Columbia: University of South Carolina Press, 2000], 3–18, at 13), but also a broader and even less well-defined desire for the alien social space produced and inhabited by those associations. See also Derek Hudson, *Munby: Man of Two Worlds; The Life and Times of Arthur J. Munby 1828–1910* (London: John Murray, 1972); Hannah Cullwick (the servant Munby secretly married), *The Diaries of Hannah Cullwick, Victorian Maidservant,* ed. Liz Stanley (New Brunswick, N.J.: Rutgers University Press, 1984).

27. Mayhew, *London Labour,* 2:154.

28. Victor Hugo, *Les Misérables* (1862; Paris: Laffont, 1985), vol. 5, book 2, chap. 1; tr. Nor-

man Denny, *Les Misérables* (Harmondsworth: Penguin, 1980); modified with reference to Fred Radford, "'Cloacal Obsession': Hugo, Joyce, and the Sewer Museum of Paris," *Mattoid* 48 (1994): 66–85.

29. Georges Verpraet, *Paris, capitale souterrain* (Paris: Plon, 1964), 143.

30. Radford, "Cloacal Obsession," 79.

31. Frère Jean [E. Vaughan], *Du neuf et du vieux* (1866); qtd. in Roger-Henri Guerrand, *Les Lieux: Histoire des commodités* (Paris: Éditions la Découverte, 1986), 113.

32. Radford, "Cloacal Obsession," 75.

33. Christopher Hamlin, "Providence and Putrefaction: Victorian Sanitarians and the Natural Theology of Health and Disease," *Victorian Studies* 28, no. 3 (spring 1985): 381–411, at 397.

34. Ibid., 409–10.

35. Qtd. in ibid., 403.

36. Announcement for *Harlequin Father Thames and the River Queen,* in *The Era* (26 December 1858): 12.

37. C. J. Collins, *Harlequin Father Thames and the River Queen; or Ye Lorde Mayore of London,* Surrey Theatre, 27 December 1858, Add. 52977 B (The Lord Chamberlain's Plays), Department of Manuscripts, The British Library, London.

38. R. B. P[itman], "Father Thames and the Builders' Strike" (London, 1859).

39. For a history of the penny dreadful in England, see E. S. Turner, *Boys Will Be Boys: The story of Sweeney Todd, Deadwood Dick, Sexton Blake, Dick Barton, et al.,* 1949, rev. ed. (London: Michael Joseph, 1957). See also John Springhall, "'A Life Story for the People'? Edwin J. Brett and the London 'Low-Life' Penny Dreadfuls of the 1860s," *Victorian Studies* 23, no. 2 (winter 1990): 223–46.

40. *The Wild Boys of London; or The Children of the Night. A Story of the Present Day* (London: Newsagents' Publishing Co., 1866), 8.

41. In her study of responses to the Victoria Embankment, Michelle Allen has noted that criticism of the project generally took the form of laments for the loss of the picturesque quality of what was otherwise decried as the dirty and disordered riverside ("The Contest for Salubrity: Embanking the Thames, 1862–1870," conference paper, 17 April 1998, University of Virginia).

42. *Wild Boys,* 8.

43. *The Mysteries of Old Father Thames. A Romance* (London: W. Caffyn, [1848]), 48–49.

44. Ibid., 179. A similar economic critique couched in the moral Manichaeism and sensational plotting of the view from below is evident in Charlton Carew's account of an explorer who underwent perils "greater than Belzoni's," a "treasure seeker of the sewers" who discovers a valuable ring in his journeying, only to be arrested on suspicion of theft. The moral fortitude he and his wife demonstrate in the course of the story (she even ventured into the tunnels to rescue him after he had collapsed in exhaustion) is rewarded when the grateful owner of the diamond ring gives them respectable employment in the pastoral confines of his country house as gardener and maidservant, respectively ("The Searchers of the Sewers: A Tale of the Modern London Underground," *Ainsworth's Magazine* 8 [November 1845]: 447–55). My thanks to Marc Bare for bringing this story to my attention.

45. Gaston Leroux, *La Double vie de Théophraste Longuet* (1903), vol. 3 of *Romans fantastiques* (Paris: Laffont, 1970), 163–478, 320 n. 2; see Reid, *Paris Sewers,* 190 n. 17.

46. Gaston Leroux, *Le Fantôme de l'Opéra* (1911; Paris: Livre de Poche, 1959), chap. 13, 240–41.

47. Ibid., 241.

48. Burton Holmes, *Travelogues,* 2 vols. (New York: McClure, 1910), 2:125–26.

49. Eric Banton, "Underground London," in *Living London: Its work and its play. Its humour and its pathos. Its sights and its scenes,* ed. George R. Sims (1901–3), 2:127–32, at 127.

50. For a comprehensive history of the mythology and the reality of the Parisian sewer worker, see Reid, *Paris Sewers.*

51. Frances Trollope, *Paris and the Parisians in 1835,* 2 vols. (London: Richard Bentley, 1836), letter 15, 1:112–19, at 117.

52. Stephen Copley and Ian Haywood, "Luxury, Refuse, and Poetry: John Gay's *Trivia,*" in *John Gay and the Scriblerians,* ed. Peter Lewis and Nigel Wood (New York: St. Martin's, 1989), 62–82, at 66.

53. Ben Jonson, "On the Famous Voyage," in *The Oxford Authors: Ben Jonson,* ed. Ian Donaldson (New York: Oxford University Press, 1985), 276–81, at lines 164–70.

54. J. C. Platt and J. Saunders, "Underground," in *London,* ed. Charles Knight, 6 vols. in 3 (London, 1841–44), 1:224–40, at 230. In the next edition, St. Giles's, having been plowed under by New Oxford Street, was replaced in the comparison by Clerkenwell.

55. For Nash's language on the placement of the cut, see J. Mordaunt Crook, "Metropolitan Improvements: John Nash and the Picturesque," in *London—World City, 1800–1840,* ed. Celina Fox (New Haven: Yale University Press, 1992), 77–96, at 90; see also Olsen, *City,* 16–19.

56. Platt and Saunders, "Underground," 231.

57. John Snow, *On The Mode of Communication of Cholera* [London, 1849; enlarged ed., 1855]). For more on Snow, see the maps and articles at the Web site of Ralph R. Frerichs and the UCLA Department of Epidemiology, ; and Pamela K. Gilbert, "'Scarcely to Be Described': Urban Extremes as Real Spaces and Mythic Places in the London Cholera Epidemic of 1854," *Nineteenth Century Studies* 14 (2000): 149–72; and "The Victorian Social Body and Urban Cartography," in *Imagined Londons,* ed. Pamela K. Gilbert (Albany: State University of New York Press, 2002), 11–30.

58. For the background surrounding Chadwick's report, see R. A. Lewis, *Edwin Chadwick and the Public Health Movement, 1832–1854* (1952; New York: Augustus M. Kelley, 1970); M. W. Flinn, intro to Edwin Chadwick, *Report on the Sanitary Condition of the Labouring Population of Great Britain* (1842), ed. Flinn (Edinburgh: Edinburgh University Press, 1965), 1–73; and Anthony S. Wohl, *Endangered Lives: Public Health in Victorian Britain* (Cambridge: Harvard University Press, 1983), 80–116; for the results of Chadwick's report specifically in London, see Sheppard, *London,* 247–96, and Wohl's somewhat divergent reading of the facts (107). The following account is drawn primarily from Sheppard, and the article "Drains and Sewers" (in *London Encyclopaedia,* ed. Ben Weinreb and Christopher Hibbert, 1983, rev. ed. [London: Macmillan, 1993], 243–45). See also Roy Porter's summary in *London: A Social History* (London: Penguin, 1996), 257–66; and Dale Porter's in-depth study, *Thames Embankment.*

59. "The Prince of Wales at the Metropolitan Drainage Works," *Illustrated London News* (15 April 1865): 342.

60. Ibid.

61. "Sanitary Science," *All the Year Round* 4, no. 78 (20 October 1860): 29–31, at 31.

62. Hollingshead, *Underground London,* 4, 130. It is quite probable that Hollingshead was also the author of "Sanitary Science."

63. "A Modern Golgotha," Walter Thornbury (vol. 1–2) and Edward Walford (vol. 3–6), *Old and New London,* new ed. (1873–78; London: Cassell, [1879–85]), 3:31–32.

64. P. F. William Ryan, "London's Toilet," in Sims, *Living London,* 3:27–32.

65. Ibid., 32.

66. Ibid.

67. *A Few Words on the New Commission of Sewers: with Comments on the Reports and Evidence of the Sanitary Commission, by a Farmer, a Lawyer, and an Ex-Commissioner* (London, 1848), 7, 18.

68. Mayhew, *London Labour,* 2:152.

69. Reid, *Paris Sewers,* 98–99; Alexandre-Jean-Baptiste Parent-Duchâtelet, *Essai sur les cloaques, ou Egouts de la ville de Paris* (Paris: Crevot, 1824), 98–99.

70. E. V. Walter, "Dreadful Enclosures: detoxifying an urban myth," *European Journal of Sociology* 18, no. 1 (1977): 151–59, at 157.

71. Ibid., 153.

72. "A Gloomy Ramble," *The Boy's Own Paper* (17 September 1881): 817–18.

73. Columbus, Jr. "How It Is Done. X.—the Draining of the City," *Cassell's Saturday Journal* (1888): 225.

74. H. Jenner-Fust III, "The Human Mole—The Strange Life and the Stranger Perils of the Men Who Work in the London Sewers," *The Royal Magazine* (1903): 121–28, at 121.

75. Jack London, *The People of the Abyss* (1903; Oakland: Star Rover House, 1984), 13–15.

76. London, *People of the Abyss,* 39; George Orwell, *The Road to Wigan Pier* (1937; New York: Harcourt, Brace, 1958), 22–23.

77. Orwell, *Down and Out in Paris and London* (1933; New York: Harcourt, Brace, 1961), 115–16.

78. London, *People of the Abyss,* 168.

79. Mary Higgs, *Glimpses into the Abyss* (London: P. S. King & Son, 1906); Deborah Epstein Nord, *Walking the Victorian Streets: Women, Representation, and the City* (Ithaca: Cornell University Press, 1995), 230–35.

80. London, *People of the Abyss,* 91.

81. Ibid., 112.

82. Orwell, *Down and Out,* 181.

83. Needless to say, the experiences overlapped, as when London records being awakened from a "frightful and sickening" night in the workhouse by "a rat or some similar animal on my breast" (*People of the Abyss,* 107–8).

84. Corbin, *Miasme,* 26.

85. Ibid., 75–76.

86. Ibid., 173.

87. Ibid., 110.

88. Ibid., 247–49.

89. Louis Paulian, "La Richesse des égouts," in *Archives de Paris,* ed. Jacques Borgé and Nicolas Viasnoff (Paris: Balland, 1981), 87–89.

90. Corbin, *Miasme,* 140.

91. Guerrand, *Lieux,* 99.

92. Orwell, *Down and Out,* 114.

93. Mercier, "Contraste des Parisiens avec l'habitant de Londres," *Tableau de Paris,* 12 vols. (Amsterdam, 1783), 7:238–43, at 241.

94. "The Sewers of London and Paris," *Pall Mall Gazette* (2 April 1883): 3–4.

95. "The Maiden Tribute of Modern Babylon," *Pall Mall Gazette* 42, no. 6336 (6 July 1885): 1–6, at 2; 42, no. 6337 (7 July 1885): 1–6; 42, no. 6338 (8 July 1885): 1–5; 42, no. 6339 (9 July 1885): 1–6; 42, no. 6340 (10 July 1885): 1–6.

96. Lawrence Wright, *Clean and Decent: The Fascinating History of the Bathroom and the W.C.* (London: Routledge & Kegan Paul, 1960), 200.

97. George Jennings, *Jennings' Patent Urinals as Arranged for Public Thoroughfares* (London, 1895), 9.

98. Wright, *Clean and Decent,* 200.

99. *The Surveyor & Municipal & County Engineer* (11 January 1894), rpt. in Jennings, *Jennings' Patent Urinals,* 42.

100. Many of the Victorian facilities have survived, but few still serve their original function, as they have become costly for borough councils to maintain and have long raised questions of security and morality, a reputation played upon in recent films about the lives of gay Londoners such as the playwright Joe Orton (*Prick Up Your Ears,* 1987) and the painter Francis Bacon (*Love Is the Devil,* 1998). The combination of Victorian heritage and the underground cachet of their origins has made them popular for conversion, including a tiny Manchester club, Temple of Convenience; the twelve-seat Theater of Small Convenience in Great Malvern; and Public Life, a bar/Internet café/art venue in trendy Spitalfields about which the artist owner predictably opines, "Underground thoughts, underground agendas . . . staying below the surface . . . Mainstream ideas don't really interest us" ("Are Britain's Public Toilets an Endangered Species?" 3 November 2000, http://www.cnn.com/2000/TRAVEL/NEWS/11/03/britain.toiletstransf.ap/; see also Melissa Viney, "Penny Pinching," *Time Out London* [July 17–24 2002]: 26–27).

101. Claude Maillard, *Les Vespasiennes de Paris, ou les précieux édicules* (Paris: Editions de la Jeune Parque, 1967), 24.

102. Ibid., 34–35.

103. Adolphe Joanne, *Paris Illustré, nouveau guide de l'étranger et du parisien* (Paris: Hachette, 1863), 29.

104. Guerrand, *Lieux,* 117.

105. Jules Armengaud, *Nettoyons Paris* (Paris: M. Bauche, 1907); qtd. in Guerrand, *Lieux,* 165–66.

106. Guerrand, *Lieux,* 164.

107. Ibid., 170, 188. It is interesting to note that the borough council of Westminster has revived the old Parisian tradition for weekend nights in Soho, installing portable, open-air urinals for use when the pubs empty out, to be removed for cleaning during the daytime hours. It is perhaps not surprising that the practice has taken root in a neighborhood long known for the visibility of its underworld life and identified during the late nineteenth century as the most foreign area of central London.

108. Parent-Duchâtelet, *Les chantiers d'équarrissage de la ville de Paris* (Paris: Crochard, 1832), qtd. in Chevalier, *Laboring Classes,* 210. Chevalier uses Montfaucon as a material symptom of the crisis caused by the overcrowded city (210–14); Reid covers the replacement of Montfaucon by tout-à-l'égout (*Paris Sewers,* 10–12 and 71–83); Bernheimer traces the links between Parent's different objects of study (*Figures of Ill Repute,* 8–15); Richard Maxwell unpacks the significance of the site as the concluding emblem of Hugo's *Notre-Dame de Paris* (*The Mysteries of Paris and London* [Charlottesville: University Press of Virginia, 1992], 52–54).

109. Chevalier, *Laboring Classes,* 212; Reid, *Paris Sewers,* 11.

110. Daniel Defoe's seminal account was written half a century after the fact; for the pits, see *A Journal of the Plague Year* (1722), ed. Louis Landa (Oxford: Oxford University Press, 1990), 58–63.

111. Henri Joseph Gisquet, *Mémoires de M. Gisquet, ancien préfet de polices, écrits par lui-*

même, 4 vols. (Paris: Marchand, 1840), 4:306–7; in Reid, *Paris Sewers,* 72. Gisquet had been prefect of police during the 1830s.

112. Reid, *Paris Sewers,* 72.

113. Chevalier, *Laboring Classes,* 210–11.

114. Bernheimer, *Figures of Ill Repute,* 9–10; Chevalier, *Laboring Classes,* 213.

115. The language is from Angelo de Sorr, *Le Drame des Carrières d'Amérique* (Paris: Ferd. Sartorius, 1868), 3.

116. In *The Mysteries of Paris and London* (52–54), Richard Maxwell gives a superb reading of the way in which Hugo used the medieval and modern associations of the site to bridge the space between his novel's setting and its Parisian audience.

117. Fortuné de Boisgobey, *Les Mystères du Nouveau Paris,* 3 vols. (Paris: E. Dentu, 1876), 2:125.

118. Schlör, *Nights,* 158.

119. *Galignani's New Paris Guide, for 1855* (Paris: A. and W. Galignani and Co., 1855), 272.

120. De Sorr, *Drame des Carrières,* 5. Later sensational fictions such as Charles Deslys's *Les Buttes Chaumont* (Paris: C. Marpon & E. Flammarion, [1890]) would take the more plausible route of contrasting the present with the past they were luridly reconstructing.

121. Ibid., 23.

122. Leo Schidrowitz, ed., *Sittengeschichte von Paris: Die Großstadt, ihre Sitten und ihre Unsittlichkeit* (Vienna [1927]), 260, 264; qtd. in Schlör, *Nights,* 138. The tours evidently dated back to "long before the war" (ibid.). See also Alfred Morain, *The Underworld of Paris: Secrets of the Sûreté* (New York: E. P. Dutton, 1931), 39. Morain was prefect of the Paris police.

123. Albert Boime, *Art and the French Commune: Imagining Paris after War and Revolution* (Princeton: Princeton University Press, 1995), 149–50.

124. Louis Aragon, *Paris Peasant,* intro. and tr. Simon Watson Taylor (London: Cape, 1971), 136, 133.

125. Ibid., 179–80, 173.

126. For an account of the relationship between the surrealists and the popular culture of Paris, see Robin Walz, *Pulp Surrealism: Insolent Popular Culture in Early Twentieth-Century Paris* (Berkeley: University of California Press, 2000); for a more general study of the fait divers and popular culture in a similar context, see Adrian Rifkin, *Street Noises: Parisian Pleasure, 1900–1940* (Manchester: Manchester University Press, 1993).

127. Maxime du Camp, *Paris: Ses organes, ses fonctions et sa vie jusqu'en 1870* (1870; Monaco: Rondeau, 1993), 606.

128. Louis Veuillot, *Les Odeurs de Paris* (Paris: Palmé, 1867), vi.

129. Nadar, "Le Dessus et le dessous de Paris," in *Paris-Guide, par les principaux écrivains et artistes de la France,* 1867, intro. and ed. Corinne Verdet (Paris: Editions La Découverte/ Maspéro, 1983), 154–75. On the female addressee of Nadar's description, see Radford, "Cloacal Obsession," 72–73.

130. Radford, "Cloacal Obsession," 74.

131. Du Camp, *Paris,* 607.

132. "The Sewers of Paris," *Illustrated London News* (29 January 1870): 129.

133. Radford, "Cloacal Obsession," 74.

134. On the uses to which the more respectable new space of the underground railway could be put by women in the society novel, see 45–46.

135. Hollingshead, *Underground London,* 11.

136. Anderson, *Tainted Souls and Painted Faces,* 9.

137. Although not concerned with Dickens's lack of representation of the drainage system, Nead provides a persuasive analysis of the association between filth and prostitution within the discourse of London, including a reading of Martha in the text of *David Copperfield* and accompanying illustrations (*Myths of Sexuality*, 118–34).

138. Charles Dickens, *Our Mutual Friend* (1864–65; Harmondsworth: Penguin, 1971), bk. 1, chap. 12, 191.

139. Nead, *Myths of Sexuality*, 125.

140. My thanks to David Trotter for sharing his thoughts on the role of the Thames in the representation of underground London.

141. Chadwick, *Sanitary Condition*, 98. On the relation between dust, money, and death in Dickens's novel, see Catherine Gallagher's Foucauldian reading of filth in general and corpses in particular as counters to the doctrine of political economy ("The Bio-Economics of *Our Mutual Friend*," in *Fragments for a History of the Human Body*, vol. 3, ed. Michael Feher [New York: Zone, 1989], 344–65). On the representation of dust in literature, and the nonrepresentation of dung heaps in Victorian photography, see Ellen Handy, "Dust Piles and Damp Pavements: Excrement, Repression, and the Victorian City in Photography and Literature," in *Victorian Literature and the Victorian Visual Imagination*, ed. Carol T. Christ and John O. Jordan (Berkeley: University of California Press, 1995), 111–33.

142. Anderson, *Tainted Souls*, 77–79. See also Jane Rogers, "Dickens and Urania Cottage, the House for Fallen Women," http://www.victorianweb.org/authors/dickens/rogers/contents.html.

143. Jules Janin, "Asmodée," *Paris, ou le livre des cent-et-un*, 15 vols. (Brussels: Louis Hauman et Compe, 1831), 1:17–30, at 25–26.

144. *The Wild Boys of Paris; or, The Mysteries of the Vaults of Death* (London: Newsagents' Publishing Company, 1866).

145. Du Camp, *Paris*, 230–31.

146. Ibid., 565, 584, 251, 344, 713.

147. Ibid., 599.

148. Ibid., 585. Because they have retained their double meaning more than their English equivalents have, the French words—*netteté, clarté, sûreté*—give a better sense of the combination of physical and moral directives they impart.

149. Ibid., 233.

150. Hugo, *Les Misérables*, vol. 5, book 2, chap. 5.

151. Ibid.

152. Du Camp, *Paris*, 605, 727.

153. Ibid., 605.

154. Baron Haussmann, *Mémoire sur les eaux de Paris* (1854); qtd. in Guerrand, *Lieux*, 112.

155. Corbin, *Miasme*, 265.

156. Du Camp, *Paris*, 246.

157. Clark, *Painting of Modern Life*, 259.

158. Norma Evenson, *Paris: A Century of Change, 1878–1978* (New Haven: Yale University Press, 1978), 206.

159. For a discussion of Manet's plans, see Antonin Proust, *Edouard Manet: Souvenirs* (Paris: H. Laurens, 1913), 94; qtd. in Christopher Prendergast, *Paris and the Nineteenth Century* (Oxford: Blackwell, 1992), 74.

160. Clark, *Painting of Modern Life*, 23.

161. Ibid., 258.

162. Gertrude Stein, *Paris, France* (New York: C. Scribner's sons, 1940), 17–18; qtd. in Evenson, *Paris,* 314.

163. For Clark's discussion of the painting, and the paradoxical presence/absence of the collector sewer in its setting, see *Painting of Modern Life,* 161–63, 201–2.

164. Max Horkheimer and Theodor W. Adorno, *Dialectic of Enlightenment* (1944), tr. John Cumming (1972; New York: Continuum, 1987), 94.

165. Angela Carter, *The Sadeian Woman: An Exercise in Cultural History* (London: Virago, 1979), 20.

166. Ibid., 13.

167. Ibid., 103.

168. Ibid., 88.

169. Jane Gallop, *Intersections: A Reading of Sade with Bataille, Blanchot, and Klossowski* (Lincoln: University of Nebraska Press, 1981), 44.

170. Ibid., 47.

171. Ibid., 121 n. 19.

172. Carter, *Sadeian Woman,* 132–33; Gallop, *Intersections,* 113–14.

173. On the Vésuvienne, see Laura S. Strumingher, "Les Vésuviennes: Les femmes-soldats dans la société de 1848," in *La Caricature entre République et censure,* ed. Raimond Rütten, Ruth Jung, and Gerhard Schneider (Lyons: Presse Universitaire de Lyon, 1996), 234–48.

174. C[harles]-J[érôme] Lecour, *La Prostitution à Paris et à Londres 1789–1871,* 2nd ed. (Paris: Librairie de la Faculté de Médicine, 1872), 337.

175. Lecour, *La Prostitution à Paris et à Londres,* 337.

176. On the pétroleuse, see Boime, *Art and the French Commune,* 38–39, 108–9, and Marie-Claude Schapira, "La Femme porte-drapeau dans l'iconographie de la Commune," in Rütten et al., ed., *La Caricature,* 423–34; for the seductive *diablesse,* see Schapira, 430–32.

177. Lecour, *La Prostitution à Paris et à Londres,* 338.

178. Du Camp, *Paris,* 610. See also René Suttel, *Catacombes et carrières de Paris: Promenade sous la capitale* (1986; Châtillon: PICAR, 1993), 186–88.

179. Suttel, *Catacombes,* 189–90.

180. Ibid., 190–91.

181. *Guide de Paris mystérieux,* ed. François Caradec and Jean-Robert Masson (Paris: Tchou, 1966), 183.

182. Ch. Eggimann, ed., *Paris inondé, la crue de janvier 1910* (Paris: Editions du Journal des débats, 1910), 28–29.

183. Marc Fournier, *Les Nuits de la Seine, mélodrame en cinq actes, neuf tableaux, dont un prologue,* Théâtre de la Porte Saint-Martin, 12 June 1852.

184. Bernheimer, *Figures of Ill Repute,* 33.

185. Baudelaire, *Oeuvres complètes,* 1:191–92; *Correspondance,* 2 vols., ed. Pichois (Paris: Gallimard, 1973), 2:59; qtd. *Oeuvres complètes,* 1:1175.

186. Du Camp, *Paris,* 606.

187. Emile Zola, *Nana* (1880; Paris: Flammarion, 1968), chap. 7, 215.

188. Ibid.

189. Ibid., chap. 1, 52–53; chap. 14, 429–30.

190. Ibid., chap. 14, 439.

191. William Acton, *Prostitution Considered in its Moral, Social and Sanitary Aspects, in London and Other Large Cities* (London, 1857), 29.

192. Jonathan Swift, "A Beautiful Young Nymph Going to Bed" (1731).

193. Catherine de Silguy, *Histoire des hommes et leurs ordures du moyen âge à nos jours* (Paris: Le Cherche Midi, 1996), 27–28.

194. Parent-Duchâtelet, *De la prostitution dans la ville de Paris, considérée sous le rapport de l'hygiène publique,* 2 vols. (Brussels: Société Belge de Librairie, 1836), 1:336; qtd. in Jill Harsin, *Policing Prostitution in Nineteenth-Century Paris* (Princeton: Princeton University Press, 1985), 127. For more on Parent-Duchâtelet (1790–1836) and his formative role in nineteenth-century debates over prostitution, see Harsin, *Policing Prostitution,* 96–130; Bernheimer, *Figures of Ill Repute,* 8–33; and the introduction and notes to Corbin's edition of selections from the 1836 work, *La Prostitution à Paris au XIXe siècle* (Paris: Seuil, 1981).

195. Catherine Gallagher has argued that in *Our Mutual Friend* wet and dry signify improper and proper ways of producing wealth from waste ("Bio-Economics of *Our Mutual Friend*," 354). The distinction is characteristic of the London discourse; see also Handy, "Dust Piles."

196. Parent-Duchâtelet, *De la prostitution,* 1:6.

197. Ibid., 2:513.

198. Dr. Louis Fiaux, *La Police des moeurs en France et dans les principaux pays de l'Europe* (Paris: E. Dentu, 1888), 1:212; qtd. in Alain Corbin, *Women for Hire: Prostitution and Sexuality in France after 1850,* 1974, tr. Arthur Goldhammer (Cambridge: Harvard University Press, 1990), 53.

199. Parent-Duchâtelet, *De la prostitution . . . 3rd édition, complétée par des documents nouveaux et des notes par MM. A. Trebuchet . . . Poirat-Duval . . . suivie d'un précis hygiénique, statistique et administratif sur la prostitution dans les principales villes de l'Europe avec cartes et tableaux,* 2 vols. (Paris: J. B. Baillière et fils, 1857), 2:282–83.

200. Parent-Duchâtelet, *De la prostitution,* 1:23.

201. Lecour, *La Prostitution à Paris et à Londres,* 145.

202. Thomas Wallace Knox, *Underground; or, Life below the Surface* (London: Sampson, Low & Co., 1873), 407.

203. Ibid., 409, 415.

204. Ibid., 409.

205. Gustave Antoine Richelot, supplement to 3rd edition of Parent-Duchâtelet, *De la prostitution,* 2:395–879, at 629. The section on England and Scotland was published separately the same year in both French and in English, the latter entitled *The Greatest of our social evils, Prostitution . . . An enquiry into the cause and means of reformation. By a Physician* (London, 1857).

206. Ibid., 630.

207. For Lecour's numbers, see *La Prostitution à Paris et à Londres,* 119.

208. Bracebridge Hemyng, "Prostitution in London," in Mayhew, *London Labour,* 4:210–72.

209. Ibid., 224.

210. For a description of prostitution in eighteenth-century London with an emphasis on the sensational, see Lucy Moore, *The Thieves' Opera* (New York: Harcourt, Brace, 1998), 43–54.

211. Georg Lichtenberg, qtd. in Moore, 44. Lichtenberg visited London twice, in 1770–71 and 1774–75.

212. Parent-Duchâtelet, *De la prostitution,* 1:24.

213. Judith W. Walkowitz, *City of Dreadful Delight: Narratives of Sexual Danger in Late-Victorian London* (London: Virago, 1992), 21–22.

214. Orwell, *Road to Wigan Pier,* 21.

215. Stead, *Maiden Tribute*, 1:2.

216. Judith W. Walkowitz, *Prostitution and Victorian Society* (New York: Cambridge University Press, 1980), 146.

217. Glen Petrie, *A Singular Inquiry: The Campaigns of Josephine Butler* (New York: Viking, 1971), 139; Walkowitz, *Prostitution*, 138.

218. Flora Tristan, *The London Journal of Flora Tristan*, 1842, tr. Jean Hawkes (London: Virago, 1984), 81.

219. Ibid., 81.

220. Karl Marx and Friedrich Engels, *The Holy Family*, vol. 4 of *Collected Works* (London: Lawrence & Wishart, 1975), 5–211, at 55–77, 162–211. The chapters on Sue were credited to Marx.

221. Clark, *Painting of Modern Life*, 46.

222. Yves Guyot, *Prostitution under the Regulatory System French and English*, 1882, tr. Edgar Beckit Truman (London: George Redway, 1884), 7.

223. Ibid., xi.

224. Harsin, *Policing Prostitution*, 205–12.

225. Ibid., 205; Stead, *Maiden Tribute*, 2:2.

226. Harsin, *Policing Prostitution*, 116.

227. Guyot, *Prostitution*, 7.

Chapter 4. Urban Apocalypse

1. *Harper's Guide to Paris* (New York: Harper's, 1900), 180. For a sense of the care with which the planners of the mining exhibition considered the problem of representing mining as spectacle, see George Bousquet (reporter) and Edouard Gruner (introduction), *Musée rétrospectif de la classe 63: Exploitation des mines, minères et carrières à l'exposition universelle internationale de 1900, à Paris; Rapport du Comité d'installation* (Paris, 1900): "Where to find . . . an ensemble of documents and objects belonging to the history of the art of mining and presenting an intrinsic interest due to their artistic character or their symbolic meaning?" (11)

2. *Harper's Guide*, 180.

3. Ibid.

4. Vicomte de Kératry, *Paris Exhibition 1900. How to see Paris Alone. English Cicerone* (London: Simpkin, Marshall, Hamilton, Kent & Co., 1900), 36–39.

5. Walter Benjamin, *The Origin of German Tragic Drama* (1928), tr. John Osborne (London: Verso, 1985), 235.

6. Giovanni Macchia, *Paris en ruines*, tr. Paul Bédarida (Paris: Flammarion, 1988), 362–63; tr. of *Le Rovine di Parigi* (Milan: Mondadori, 1985).

7. Simon Lacordaire, *Histoire secrète de Paris souterrain* (Paris: Hachette, 1982), 86–87.

8. Walter Benjamin, *The Arcades Project*, tr. Howard Eiland and Kevin McLaughlin (Cambridge: Harvard University Press, 1999), 92 (Convolute C5,1); see also Macchia, *Paris*, 392.

9. See Benjamin, *Arcades*, Convolute C; Macchia, *Paris*, 392.

10. Edmond About, "Dans les ruines," in *Paris-Guide, par les principaux écrivains et artistes de la France*, 1867, intro. and ed. Corinne Verdet (Paris: Editions La Découverte/Maspéro, 1983), 32–39, at 38.

11. On the tradition of the New Zealander visiting London in ruins, see Lynda Nead, *Victorian Babylon: People, Streets, and Images in Nineteenth-Century London* (New Haven: Yale University Press, 2000), 212–15.

12. Richard Jefferies, *After London* (1885; London: Oxford University Press, 1980), 206.

13. Ford Madox Ford, *The Soul of London,* 1905, ed. Alan G. Hill (London: Everyman, 1995), 106–7.

14. Ibid., 106, 107–8.

15. Paul Fussell, *The Great War and Modern Memory* (New York: Oxford University Press, 1975), 123.

16. Marcel Proust, *Time Regained* (1927), in *Remembrance of Things Past,* 3 vol., tr. Andrea Mayor (New York: Vintage, 1982), 3.707–1107, at 864.

17. Macchia, *Paris,* 413.

18. Christopher Prendergast, *Paris and the Nineteenth Century* (Oxford: Blackwell, 1992), 100–101.

19. Max Beckmann, "Wartime Letters: Roeselare, Wervicq, Brussels," *Self-Portrait in Words: Collected Writings and Statements, 1903–1950,* ed. Barbara Copeland Buenger, tr. Buenger, Reinhold Heller, and David Britt (Chicago: University of Chicago Press, 1997), 151–77, at 163 (April 23, 1915).

20. Jay Winter, *Sites of Memory, Sites of Mourning: The Great War in European Cultural History* (Cambridge: Cambridge University Press, 1995).

21. Ibid., 68.

22. Ibid., 205–10.

23. Qtd. in Peter Hall, *Cities of Tomorrow* (London: Blackwell, 1988), 80.

24. Ibid., 7.

25. Le Corbusier, *Urbanisme* (1925), tr. Frederick Etchells, *The City of To-morrow and Its Planning* (1929; New York: Dover, 1987), 284.

26. For a comprehensive analysis of the spatial dynamics of *Metropolis,* see Pike, "*Kaliko-Welt*": The *Großstädte* of Lang's *Metropolis* and Brecht's *Dreigroschenoper,*" *MLN* 119, no. 3 (2004): 474–505.

27. The London-based *Architectural Review,* a staunch booster of modernist architecture, greeted the Franco-American design of Vincent Korda's sets as a leap forward in the area of "film functionalism," and included a still of Everytown in a spread on Le Corbusier (Christopher Frayling, *Things to Come* [London: British Film Institute, 1995], 68).

28. For a detailed discussion of the postwar dynamic of Céline's writings, see Pike, *Passage through Hell: Modernist Descents, Medieval Underworlds* (Ithaca: Cornell University Press, 1997), 35–61.

29. Jean Giraudoux, *La Folle de Chaillot* (1946; Paris: Livre de Poche, n.d.); Reid, *Paris Sewers,* 128.

30. Giraudoux, *La Folle,* 94.

31. Fanciful yet solemn allegory was a common mode for representing the war, a means of indirection during the occupation, as in the drama of the Devil's tormenting of a pair of lovers in a medieval castle in Marcel Carné and Jacques Prévert's *Les Visiteurs du soir* (1942), and of avoiding any direct confrontation with the facts thereafter, as in Jean Cocteau's retelling of the Orpheus myth in the Left Bank literary world of postwar Paris in *Orphée* (1949). It is not accidental that so many Parisians used an explicitly mythic structure to frame their underground metaphorics; what was at stake was a viable mythology for representing the war years that could somehow impart their moral gravity, psychic trauma, and general confusion within a discourse that permitted only the most polarized and formalistic ideologies and categories.

32. From 1940, the Resistance cell of the Musée de l'Homme (housed in the Palais de

Chaillot) held its meetings in the tunnels of the quarter, amid the remains of the 1900 exposition (Patrick Saletta, *A la découverte des souterrains de Paris* [Antony: SIDES, 1990], 138–40).

33. For an analysis of the use of descent journey in holocaust memoirs, see Rachel Falconer, *Hell in Contemporary Literature: Western Descent Narratives since 1945* (Edinburgh: Edinburgh University Press, 2005), 57–112.

34. George Steiner, *In Bluebeard's Castle: Some Notes towards the Redefinition of Culture* (New Haven: Yale University Press, 1971), 54.

35. Primo Levi, *If This Is a Man/Survival in Auschwitz* (1958), tr. Stuart Woolf (New York: Collier, 1961), 105. See also Falconer's more contextualized analysis of the same episode (*Hell in Contemporary Literature*, 80–84).

36. Ibid., 82.

37. Keiji Nakazawa, *Hadashi no Gen* (1972–73), *Barefoot Gen: A Cartoon Story of Hiroshima*, tr. Dadakai and Project Gen, 4 vols. (Philadelphia: New Society Publishers, 1987–94), 2:141–61.

38. Haruki Murakami, *Underground: The Tokyo Gas Attack and the Japanese Psyche* (1997–98), tr. Alfred Birnbaum and Philip Gabriel (London: Harvill, 2000), 203.

39. In a poetically fitting, if ultimately tragic twist to their infernal vision, the nine tableaux of *Hell* were destroyed by fire in an East London warehouse in May 2004. Various details of the work are reproduced in Jake and Dinos Chapman, *Hell* (London: Jonathan Cape/Saatchi Gallery, 2003), 46–66."

40. Walter Moers, *Adolf* (Frankfurt am Main: Eichborn Verlag, 2000), [5].

41. Jennifer Toth, *The Mole People: Life in the Tunnels beneath New York City* (Chicago: Chicago Review Press, 1993), 39. See also *Grand Central Winter: Stories from the Street* (New York: Washington Square Press, 1998), the memoir of a descent to and return from homelessness by a man who lived in, under, and around Grand Central Station.

42. For a detailed exposition of this argument, see Pike, "Urban Nightmares and Future Visions: Life beneath New York," *Wide Angle* 20, no. 4 (October 1998): 8–50.

43. Mayor Ali M., in Toth, *Mole People*, 196.

44. In addition to Toth, members of the Amtrak tunnel community have been sensitively portrayed in Margaret Morton's photo-essay, *The Tunnel: The Underground Homeless of New York City* (New Haven: Yale University Press, 1995), and Mark Singer's documentary, *Dark Days* (2000).

45. Toth, *Mole People*, 165–68.

46. See, for example, Edet Belzberg's documentary on a gang of children in a subway in Bucharest, Romania, *Children Underground* (2000), and Lawrence J. Taylor and Maeve Hickey's study, *Tunnel Kids* (Tucson: University of Arizona Press, 2001), of children living in the drainage tunnels under the U.S.-Mexico border, between the twin cities of Nogales, Sonora, and Nogales, Arizona.

47. Jaime Jaramillo, *Los Hijos de la oscuridad* (Bogotá: Norma, 1999), 21–33.

48. Ibid., 25–26.

49. See, for example, David Harvey's exemplary analysis of the development of Baltimore harbor in *The Spaces of Hope* (Berkeley: University of California Press, 2000).

50. Ze'ev Chafets, *Devil's Night and Other True Tales of Detroit* (New York: Vintage, 1991), 3–6.

51. Camilo José Vergara, *The New American Ghetto* (New Brunswick, N.J.: Rutgers University Press, 1995); *American Ruins* (New York: Monacelli Press, 1999).

52. Not to mention the full arsenal of synergistic publicity, as became clear when the Time-

Warner publicity machine declared 2003 "The Year of the Matrix," and saturated every aspect of popular culture with Matrix-branded products whirling around the two sequels to the first film, taking advantage of the enormous cult that had grown up around the universe of the Matrix.

53. One of the few truly intriguing aspects of *The Matrix Reloaded* and *The Matrix: Revolutions* (both 2003) was the possibility that the dour settings, ham-fisted acting, and overwrought plotting of the Zion scenes were an intentional commentary on the self-serious undergrounds of 1960s and '70s Hollywood urban dystopia science fiction, from *Beneath the Planet of the Apes* (1970) to *Soylent Green* (1973), with the wooden Keanu Reeves a worthy stand-in for the earnest vigilantism of previous figurehead Charlton Heston.

54. Naomi Klein, *No Logo* (London: HarperCollins, 2000), 202.

Index